THE COAT

THE ORIGIN AND TIMES OF
THOMAS DOGGETT'S IMMORTAL WAGER

THE STORY OF THE OLDEST ANNUAL
SPORTING CONTEST

By R. G. CROUCH
H. M. BARGEMASTER. EMERITUS

This book is dedicated to the unknown Thames Waterman, who by his skill and effort, impressed Thomas Doggett to such an extent, that he was unknowingly used in formulating an event to honour The King and to set the rules for Mr. Doggett's famous and immortal wager.

© Copyright 2005 Robert G. Crouch.
All rights reserved. No part of this publication may be reproduced, stored in a retrieval system, or transmitted, in any form or by any means, electronic, mechanical, photocopying, recording, or otherwise, without the written prior permission of the author.

Note for Librarians: a cataloguing record for this book that includes Dewey Decimal Classification and US Library of Congress numbers is available from the Library and Archives of Canada. The complete cataloguing record can be obtained from their online database at:
www.collectionscanada.ca/amicus/index-e.html
ISBN 1-4120-5528-8

Printed in Victoria, BC, Canada

 *Printed on paper with minimum 30% recycled fibre. Trafford's print shop runs on "green energy" from solar, wind and other environmentally-friendly power sources.*

TRAFFORD
Offices in Canada, USA, Ireland and UK

This book was published *on-demand* in cooperation with Trafford Publishing. On-demand publishing is a unique process and service of making a book available for retail sale to the public taking advantage of on-demand manufacturing and Internet marketing. On-demand publishing includes promotions, retail sales, manufacturing, order fulfilment, accounting and collecting royalties on behalf of the author.

Book sales for North America and international:
Trafford Publishing, 6E–2333 Government St.,
Victoria, BC v8t 4p4 CANADA
phone 250 383 6864 (toll-free 1 888 232 4444)
fax 250 383 6804; email to orders@trafford.com

Book sales in Europe:
Trafford Publishing (UK) Ltd., Enterprise House, Wistaston Road Business Centre,
Wistaston Road, Crewe, Cheshire cw2 7rp UNITED KINGDOM
phone 01270 251 396 (local rate 0845 230 9601)
facsimile 01270 254 983; orders.uk@trafford.com

Order online at:
trafford.com/05-0426

THE STORY CONTENTS

Chapter one	The Fickle Thames
Chapter two	The Perilous City
Chapter three	Origins and Apprenticeship
Chapter four	Choice and consequence
Chapter five	Kenneth and the bawdy Tavern
Chapter six	Ebenezer and the hapless lighterman
Chapter seven	The black face job
Chapter eight	The dreadful life of James
Chapter nine	Mr. Doggett's journey home
Chapter ten	For the love of Mary
Chapter eleven	Trapped at the tavern
Chapter twelve	Shipped to adventure
Chapter thirteen	The Queen is dead. Long live The King
Chapter fourteen	The Race

Copyright (C) Robert George Crouch 2006

PREFACE

For each of the years since 1715, a competition has taken place on London's River Thames, which is now unique among sporting events. This, the oldest of the continuously held annual sporting contests, has been competed for by qualifying young Thames Waterman since the very first race, as decreed by its instigator Thomas Doggett. Although well known among Londoners, the race for Mr. Doggett's Coat and Badge remains an enigma. It is the only Thames rowing wager from those early times to survive. It is still a major annual event among the Waterman of today, who simply call this race, 'The Coat'.

In the story handed down among the river fraternity, Doggett is said to have formulated the rules for his wager, from an experience he once had while travelling home by water, one stormy night. He travelled from the City near to the playhouse where he was working, to the inn where he was staying at Chelsea, a distance of nearly five miles. The experience of this rough-weather voyage, rowed by a newly licensed young Journeyman, is said to have impressed Doggett to such an extent, that when in 1715, in line with his political affiliation to the Whig party, he wanted to honour the anniversary of the accession of the new King George, the first of the Hanoverians, he used the experience he had gained on that night, to inaugurate the race and to set the rules for his now famous wager.

Doggett decided that the prize for his four mile, five furlong race, between young watermen who had just completed their apprenticeship, would be a coat of orange red livery, on the arm of which would be carried a silver badge, depicting 'Liberty', the white horse of Hanover. It is through the good offices of The Fishmongers City Livery Company, who took over the responsibility of the race soon after Doggett's death, that the prize remains today much the same as in Doggett's time. The coat is still being tailored in the style worn by the working wherrymen of the early eighteenth century and the silver badge is of the same design and dimensions as that designed by Doggett himself.

Thames Watermen of that time can be likened to the taxi drivers of today. They used the river, the natural highway of London, to carry fare-paying passengers in small licensed boats called wherries. Passengers would be rowed from points across and along the river, to destinations, which stretched as far to the east as Gravesend and westwards to the boundary stone at Windsor. Like taxi-drivers, watermen were examined by their Guild, on their knowledge of this vast stretch of water, and if proficient, were granted a licence to carry passengers for reward.

In this novel, the story is told through the eyes of Edwin, that unknown young waterman on whom Doggett supposedly based the rules of his wager. In truth, we do not know if the legend is any more than a myth. However, we do know that Doggett was a frequent user of the Thames and most probably was affected by the lack of wherries to take him home. He may not have known why the wherrymen shunned the Bankside stairs at night, or how they avoided taking fares they did not want, but he was obviously impressed by their ability and their fortitude. The truth therefore, may well be an amalgam of his experiences, which he used to set the rules and inaugurate his race. This story of the river in the early eighteenth century, has also given the opportunity through the imaginary characters involved, to describe something of the hard life-style of the working journeymen of the Thames and to portray something of their view of the world, gleaned from a study of their Guild's and the City's records.

The research for this book threw up many interesting facts, which have been built into the story. It has given a chance to tell of the pride these men had in their trade and of their close knit community. It tells of their fears of impressment, of the harsh governing power of their Guild, of their own deviousness, and their undemanding expectations of life. The difficulties and dangers of what we today would consider brutal, and hazardous times.

"When a man with gold rings and gay cloths may swear before the Justice or at the justice; may reel home through open streets and no man take any notice of him. But if a poor man gets drunk or swears an oath, he must to the stocks without remedy".

Daniel Defoe 1651-1731

PROLOGUE

London in the early eighteenth century lay comfortably in the rich soil of its fertile river valley, where in spite of the cold winters, it reaped the benefits of the temperate climate brought to this favoured island courtesy of the warm waters of the Gulf Stream. The City was also more favoured than most, by being situated near enough to the sea to become a great port, the activities of which, delivered vast quantities of merchandise from all over the world, while in return the bountiful home produced products were exported aboard the numerous trading ships, continuously leaving for the far-flung nations of the globe. The great wealth generated by this trade was a wondrous boon for the City, but could also be a curse to its citizenry, depending on a man's standing in society.

Snaking through the metropolis, like a giant, pewter coloured serpent, lay the River Thames, the liquid resource to which the City owed its growth, its wealth and its very existence. This omnipotent watercourse, embracing the conurbation in its gentle folds, acted as the city's artery, its natural highway. The ample waters of the Thames also provided London with a natural arena, an amphitheatre, a stage on which the boastful pride of the rich and powerful could be acted out, and on which the great pageants and sporting events, which Londoners so admired could be orchestrated.

Vessels of every size and shape navigated the river's length, especially through the section of water that ran through the capital. Here the concentration of differing craft was overwhelming. Great trading ships queued as far down river as Greenwich, waiting their turn for a berth in the Pool of London, anxiously wanting to discharge their valuable cargos. Small wherries rowed up down and across the river, taxiing passengers about their business or to their pleasures. Rich shallops sped along, delivering important patrons to their riverside mansions, and barges of all sizes and shapes continuasly progressed   along the liquid highway. This excited throng of boats and ships moved to and fro with the endless motions of the tide.

The tides of London's river were the breathing life-rhythm of the great water serpent, and therefore of the City itself. The tides of the river gave a pulse to the population. Londoners were very aware of the state of the tide, they knew by the activity of the birds, and the smells in the very air they breathed, if it was on the flood or ebb and when the turn was due.

The bustle and tempo of the boats passing to and fro, would rise and fall in tune to the slow pulsating dance of the water. Even the weather that they enjoyed, or sometimes endured, was affected by the tides, often altering as the 'currents direction changed.

For the working watermen of the Thames, the river was truly a vital living being. Its ebb and flow and its rise and fall, ruled their very lives. For these men, the river's moods affected them even more profoundly than it did their land-based cousins. Men of the river, without the need to read or write, could tell the time of day and especially the lunar months, by the state of tide. They understood by the measure of the water, when the high tide would be higher, the low lower, and how the weather conditions might change with the turn of the tide. They could read its speed and its power, by observing the flow passing the stones built into the wharf sides, and into the arches of the old bridge. They would exploit this information to plan when best to use a draw-dock for repairs, or when to drown their wherry in a creek to tighten her planking, or make arrangement for profitable business by locating themselves at the most convenient plying stairs in advance of a river celebration, and thereby reap the benefits of passengers wishing to attend the great water pageants, rowing wagers or river spectacles, which were always planned to make best use of the tidal conditions. They would think up novel ways of using their river when it was frozen into grotesque shapes, during the harsh winters of the period.

The watermen said the river was in their family blood, they felt close to its contrary waters unto their very death. But unlike these men who decay as time passes, the river is regenerated by the gravitational pull of the Moon, the Night Goddess of water, who brings life back to her watery servant, refreshing him with a magic lift, causing a flood of water which flows up-river to meet the fresh rainwater running off the hills. Her life giving force revitalises the river and starts the cycle anew, so continuing the eternal rhythm of water, the 'universal carrier'. Through her power to regenerate the river, the Night-Goddess will also revive and sustain the City, its Port and its population.

CHAPTER ONE
The Fickle Thames

The month was July, in the year of our Lord 1700, as by the grace of God the seventeenth century rolled discreetly on into the eighteenth. It was a fine, summer Sunday morning without a cloud in the sky, or any of the usual smoke from the City's chimneys to obscure the glorious sun.

Mr. Graystone the beadle, was squatting down among the riverside reeds, peering down intently at the river below him. He carefully parted the stems of the tall plants with his hands to gain a clearer view of the scene below; but in doing so he disturbed a small plague of flying insects, which angrily sought vengeance on this giant for invading their tiny world. Soothingly he waved his hands about his face, trying to pacify the horde with calming motions, willing the venomous creatures to call off their attack and return to their miniature parallel existence. He made the movements cautiously, not wanting to make any noise, which might give away his position. The insect assault gradually abated and his attention returned to the business in hand, the work of snaring his chosen pray. He stared down at the causeway protruding out into the river, concentrating intently on the ferryman sitting in his boat alongside the narrow timber planking of the landing stage.

Graystone was feeling hot in the heavy, blue serge uniform of a Watermen's Guild Inspector, he was uncomfortable in this cramped, crouching position. Warily he moved his body into a more comfortable position and carefully adjusted the heavy wooden truncheon, which hung from the brass fixing on his belt. He also changed the arrangement of his feet to allow more blood to flow into his aching legs. These adjustments made him feel a little better. The sun was getting hotter as the day advanced, but he was prepared to put up with all this discomfiture, for he was determined to catch out Henry Woodworth the ferryman, in some infringement of the Sabbath rules. The Guild's beadles had been instructed in no uncertain terms by the Rulers, to curb the growth of illegal working by the watermen on the Lord's Day, and he, Alan Graystone, Senior Beadle, was resolute in his determination to do just that. Plus of course there was the likelihood of a little gain of something for himself in the process. He strongly suspected that old Henry was doing very well from this ferry service across to Wapping. It was a popular and busy route, for it saved passengers the long walk up to the old bridge to cross the river and then down the other side, thereby cutting the journey-time by more than an hour. "Yes, to be sure, the old rascal is up to something" he mumbled to himself.

Earlier that morning, he had been down to confront old Henry, only to find to his disappointment that the man's permission to ply for hire on the Sabbath looked as if it was up to date and properly signed by the Company's

Clerk. Although his reading skill was poor, the beadle could recognise the Clerk's mark at the bottom of the page. The boat itself seemed to be in good order, although he had looked carefully for any damage, or some other cause to stop the ferry from operating, and as far as he could tell, there was no other waterman helping the old rascal with his rowing work. However, he was convinced that the ferryman was up to something. A waterman who did not offer a little something to an inspecting Beadle could not be trusted. After all it was expected that a waterman with a lucrative turn like this ferry service, would cross the palm of a Company Beadle for a little smoothing of the way, by perhaps being a little lenient with the inspection, or not checking the permission too precisely, or turning a blind eye to a cracked oar-lock.

"I'll wager he is making good business here, the greedy scoundrel," reflected Graystone, quietly to himself.

"Nevertheless, I will catch him out, no doubt of it. I just need to bide my time, he will show his hand, and I will teach him a sound lesson on how to deal with the Company's Beadles". A brilliant thought suddenly occurred to him.

"Or better yet, I'll have his permission transferred to my cousin. Now that would be the best outcome by far," he smiled to himself at this new idea. His heart leapt at the thought of the benefits that would accrue to the Graystone family from such a result.

The crunch of boots on gravel made the Beadle look up towards the higher ground to his left, a dozen yards or so along from his hiding place. "Ah! Now this could be what I have been waiting for" he mumbled quietly to himself," another river rogue come to assist with speeding up the crossing and thereby carrying more passengers to make more profit." The Beadle's hopes of an arrest were growing in his mind.

As he looked surreptitiously at the newcomer who was now standing and gazing out across the river towards the City, the Beadle could see that the man had a small boy with him.

"Teaching his pup the devious way of the river-trade no doubt," mused Graystone as he observed the pair standing silently looking out over the river's sparkling water.

"They start them at an early age as I know to my cost," he thought, recalling the problems he had so often encountered with the young apprentices of the river trade.

"I will have the lot of them before this day is out. They will rue this day for not allowing me my rightful share. I'll see them both with their licences suspended if I have my way of it."

The man and the boy stood on the high ground above the riverbank looking out across the water. The day was unusually bright, the strong morning sun glowing and sparkling on the roof tiles and spires of the old City. The man was breathing in the air, as if drawing the dazzling scene deep into his body. The Port lay spread out before him, with its maze of tall masted ships in the foreground, gently jostling each other at their moorings in the Pool of

London, a wide lagoon seemingly separated from the City by the presence of the old London Bridge.

"A fine sight" said the man proudly, half to himself and half to the boy. "A golden City with a silver river, rich with trade from the entire world". The boy did not answer; he knew that his father was only speaking his thoughts aloud. Instead he looked up into the man's face; he could see a shine in the grey-blue eyes and looked away confused, a little embarrassed by the rarity of the moment, this small show of emotion in the man was unusual and beyond the understanding of the nine year old.

"Come along lad, we will make our way down to Dog and Duck Landing Stairs and ask old Henry to take us over to Wapping, I must meet there with a man and truck with him for the dues he owes me". Again, the boy did not answer but followed unquestioningly as the man led the way along the gravel path, which dropped down to the river bank.

To any onlookers, the boy looked like a small version of his father, he had the same wide shouldered build, albeit in much smaller proportion; he wore the same old-style, knee length coat, with matching soft-brown breeches. The mother had carefully made these Sunday-best for them both, using material that had been pilfered by her husband from a ship in the Port, good stout, wool-cloth that had once been destined for a far distant land. The man wore his coat unbuttoned, to show off the mustered-yellow waistcoat with black horn buttons, which he proudly wore underneath the coat. His grey stockings matched the grey felt of the tri-cornered hat seated squarely on his head. The boy had a matching hat, also shaped with the back and the sides pinned up to form a peak at the front. They were dressed in the fashion that was prevalent among London's watermen.

The narrow gravel track, which led down to the water, gave access through its overgrown leafy sides to Dog and Duck stairs and causeway; the air was pungent with the smell of the white bindweed flowers and the myriad nettles and dock-weeds, which lined the path. The man and the boy climbed steadily down the stone stairs set into the end of the pathway and stepped out carefully onto the greasy timbers of the causeway. Alongside the far end of this wooden walkway, thrusting its way out into the tideway, was moored a high sided, timber-planked boat, aboard which the ferryman was seated at the rowing thwart with his back to the shore. The man was roughly dressed in a leather jerkin over a homespun shift with heavy cloth breaches, topped off with a white headscarf tied at the back of the neck. He was working intently at a spliced eye in the end of his catch-line.

"Henry!" said the man loudly, knowing that the man was a little hard of hearing. His sudden strident voice startled the ferryman somewhat.

"Well met this fine day," he continued, genuinely pleased to see his friend and sorry to have made him jump by his discordant greeting.

"I see that you still have the permission then?" he observed with a hint of concern in his voice.

"Good morrow Alfred", replied the ferryman, smiling back sheepishly, a little annoyed with himself for not having heard them approach.

"Yes, I still take the turn, but for how long is the great wonder. They threaten constantly to withdraw the permission for my ferry to run on the Sabbath, but I have my ways and contacts and I am still here for the time being. That devil Graystone was here again this morning trying to catch me out, he must have shit the bed to be about so early."

"What trickery was he up to this time? After a bribe no doubt", suggested Alfred.

"Graystone was here to check my permission and my boat and to see that I am working alone. He made the hint about me passing him some coin, but I know the secrets he hides, he only keeps his position because the Clerk can so easily manipulate his stupidity, he will get nothing from me, the piece of dog's dung. I know too much about him and his naughty family to be afeared by his threats." Henry spat into the water with vengeance at the mention of his perceived enemy.

The boy watched intrigued as the white froth of the ferryman's gob spread out upon the water's surface next to the boat. It grew into a larger and larger circle then began to break up as the tide played with it and moved it on. As the water divided and engulfed the gobbet and carried the spittle away with all the other impurities of the river, he wondered where the tide would take it. This question about the water's destination was something that occupied his young mind for some time of late. He cleared his small throat to see if he had enough phlegm for a good spit, but he could feel that it was insignificant, so he swallowed it back disappointedly. He wished he could call up a great gob just like the ferryman's and propel it into the river. In his young mind, it was a sign of true manhood.

The men were talking in dull tones in the background; the boy had missed some of what they were saying but tuned in his ear once more. "The men are becoming concerned, they have noticed that the squeeze is on again to try to stop our Sunday working even when it is a necessary service," his father was saying.

"Surely, sense and reason will prevail in the end. The Lord knows that the ships of the Port must be attended whatever the day of the week. The captains, crews and their agents must be able to get afloat to go about a ship's business on all the days of the week," Henry was saying. The boy was half listening to the conversation but it was of little interest to his young mind. Unexpectedly he heard a gay little laugh, a sound tinkling with enjoyment. Looking in the direction of the merry sound to the sandy beach next to the causeway, now uncovered by the tide, he saw a young boy a little younger than himself, with a girl about the same age and a small child of about four years.

All three were dressed in their Sunday-best clothes and were running about on the hard packed sand in full enjoyment of the pleasant day, playing a game of 'Catch me if you can'. The small child was strikingly beautiful; she had a bonny pink round face, with large bright blue eyes, and apple red cheeks now flushed by the exhilaration of the game, her rosebud mouth, and large, dazzlingly bright eyes were a delight to behold. All this babyish beauty was adorned with a head of the most arresting golden ringlets, which glowed like precious metal as they bobbed in the bright sunshine. The gay laughter was coming from her, indicating her pleasure at being chased by the two older children, they were running up and down the beach and along the water's edge towards the decaying timbers of an old boat-wreck, then back again towards the causeway. All three were laughing joyously and out of breath with the exertion of their game.

The boy looked away from the children playing on the beach, back to the liquid scene at his feet. His fascination with the water of the river was his obsession of late; it intrigued and worried his young mind as to where the countless floating objects being carried along on its surface were going. Did all drowned things float away; to eventually sink to the bottom, even wooden objects, and the large pieces of timber the river carried along? He was not convinced by such a theory. Perhaps there was a great island somewhere that was forever growing, as more and more flotsam arrived, it was truly a great riddle to his young mind. Suddenly, through these intriguing thoughts the boy heard his name mentioned.
"So this is your Edwin," the ferryman was saying.
"A fine lad to be sure, he will no doubt do you proud one day Alfred". The man smiled with pride, pleased with his friend's remarks.
"How goes it with your own son, young Harry? Is he still at sea?" asked Alfred with true concern.
"Yes, and that's the pity. It has been two years since he was taken, and only one message from him in all that time. You should know the sharp tongue I get from his mother on the subject. She still blames me for his capture, as if I could control a young man in his prime and protect him from the traps of those confounded impressment gangs." Henry the ferryman spat again into the water and shook his head at the impossibility of such a task.
"He is aboard the Queen's ship 'Association', that much we know. We heard that she has been in a great sea battle with the French. Now we wait for news and pray for his safe return."

Noises from the stairs made the two men look up. Two well dressed gentlemen with a young woman walking between them were approaching the causeway.
"I say there, ferryman", called out the taller man in the foppish, cultured tones of a superior, perhaps even a theatre player, judging by his manner of affected speech.
"Are you in service this day? We would make Wapping within the hour if you please."
"Yes Sir, to be sure, come aboard if you will your honour," invited Henry, indicating with a sweep of his hand the passenger seats of his boat.
"But be careful how you step good Sirs and your Ladyship, the tide is out and the causeway very slippery in spite of the grit I have laid down." The three gingerly walked along the greasy planking, giggling and laughing in the way of actors and people of the playhouses. On reaching the boat without mishap, they stepped into the waiting vessel. Once they were safely aboard and seated, Alfred and his son followed. Edwin was told to sit with

the passengers while his father went forward into the bow seat of the ferry to help balance the boat for the oarsman.

"Don't touch an oar or even a rope," warned Henry to his friend, knowing that Alfred was likely to try to help him with his rowing task.

"If that dog of a beadle is hiding in the reeds as I suspect, you and I will be in trouble for sure, you for working at your trade on the Sabbath and me for allowing you". Henry sat down at his oars then looking over towards the children playing on the beach he called out to them.

"Ahoy there you youngsters, be off with you, the tide is making and this place is dangerous on the flood, away home with you, play your game on higher ground." The children stopped their chase and stood quietly surveying the ferryman, but they did not move away. Edwin looked again at the beautiful little girl and noticed that she was wearing tiny red shoes, with little white ribbons at the instep, fashioned into the shape of pretty miniature flowers.

The boat slipped away from the causeway as smoothly as a hot iron on silk. Henry, pulling skilfully at his work turned the boat's head around to point across the water and the crossing over to Wapping began. Edwin immediately felt a thrill rise inside him. It was the feeling he always had when his father took him out in his boat. It was a sensation of pride and magic, a sense that this was his element, his river. He felt sure that the other passengers would recognize that he was the son of a waterman, part of the river family and would therefore know of his importance out here. The two male passengers were talking animatedly to each other in their foppish tones and seemed to be long time friends. The young woman who was somewhat left out of their conversation, tried to catch Edwin's eye, as if she wanted to engage the boy in conversation, but he looked away and did not speak to any of them, holding his young head high with unwarranted pride. The smells of the reeds and the summer flowers from the shoreline began to fade as they pulled out into the main stream. The aroma now changed to the usual tang of London's river, smells of tar, rope, of damp sail-cloth and old timber, plus the ever present faint odours of the City's effluent, all of this flooded their nostrils as they rowed across the tide towards their destination. The young woman produced a small white handkerchief, which she held to her nose in an attempt to obscure the unpleasant affront to her nostrils. Edwin however, still full of self-importance, breathed the aromas deep into his lungs and gazed around him at London's Port as if surveying his world. All about them seemed deserted, devoid of life, the ships and boats of London, which on any other day of the week would be full of activity were as if dead. The great vessels at anchor were like ghost ships, with not a sailor-man to be seen on the deck of any of them, not a saltwater seaman nor a sweetwater riverman were working on this the Lord's day.

The two actors were now deep in merry conversation, but it was an exchange that was dominated by the taller one whose name seemed to be Mr. Aston. This man was in full swing of a story and Edwin surreptitiously listened in, trying to interpret their flowery way of speech and to follow the anecdote.

"Doggett, I tell you it was a laugh altogether, you know me I am never out of my way; or if I meet with a Slightly House when I am Itinerant, I would soon find the Name, Title, and Circumstances of the Family, curry them over with my humorous Verse, and by that means get something to bear my Charges to my next Station. My Finances, like those of Kingdom's, are sometimes at the Tide of Flood and as often at low Ebb. In one, where my Stream had left the Channel dry, yet ready to launch out on a trading Voyage without a Cargo, or Provisions, I called up my Landlord, to whom there was something due, told him of my Losses in my present Voyage, and being sent for to go to another Place, desired that he would lend me a small Sum upon my Wardrobe (which I showed him in a large Box) worth ten times the Value of the Debt owing, or the Sum borrowed: The honest Landlord, seeing a proper Security, easily complied, gave me the Sum demanded, locked up the Trunk, put the Key in his Pocket, and retired. But as no Vessel can make a Voyage without Sails and other proper Materials, I had therefore contrived a false Bottom to this great Box; I took out the Stuffing, and by Degrees, sent off my Wardrobe by my Emissaries, all unperceived by the Landlord. And that the Weight should not detect him, I filled up the Void with Cabbage-stalks, Bricks and Stones clothed in Rags to prevent them moving about, when the Vehicle was to be taken the next morning into the Landlord's Custody. Every thing succeeded to his Wish, and away I went, but far wide of the Place I had mentioned to mine Host. A Week was the stated Time of Redemption, which the Landlord saw elapse with infinite Satisfaction (for he had a Bill of Sale of the Contents in the Trunk); he must have opened it with great Pleasure; but when he saw the fine Lining; he was I suppose motionless, like a Statue carved by a bungling Hand. He of course thought he had recourse to Revenge, knowing where I had gone. A Bailiff with proper Directions was sent to the Place mentioned by me; but if he had discovered the least Wit in his Anger, he might have thought that Tony would know better "

(*Extracted from Thomas Doggett Pictured by Water Leon)

"Tony, you are a rogue indeed and a clever dog into the bargain," said his smaller friend laughing at the tale.
"Thomas," said the taller man.
"I am on this earth but a short time and can not be held back from my travels by a small matter of debt, I vow that everyone benefited from the experience I put upon them, even the Landlord will be more suspicious in the future and by this probation be a more profitable house-keeper in future." The passengers laughed together at the story and continued chatting with much gesticulation. Edwin had understood the story in large part, but could not see why it was so funny. He felt sorry for the landlord who had been cheated. However, in truth he was more interested in the water of the river about him, than in the unfathomable affairs of the rich.

"Now Tony," the man called Doggett was saying. "Tell me, what think you of this short cut to Wapping? Is it not useful to know the workings of these rivermen? For a small payment we have saved ourselves a long walk, or an expensive, bone-shaking ride up to and over the bridge and then down the north bank to our destination, have we not saved time, soreness, pain and money?"
"Yes to be sure, I salute your knowledge of the workings of old Father Thames, your knowledge is prodigious and extends even to the Lord's Day," approved the taller of the two players.

<========>

Mr Graystone was now angry; he wondered if they knew that he was watching. That dog of a waterman and his young pup had not assisted the ferryman and now those passengers arriving had made it impossible for him to even lay any false accusation against either of them. The men and woman would most certainly support the ferryman in any argument, not wanting to lose their passage over to Wapping; they were obviously of superior class and could make trouble if he tried such a ruse. Damnation, this was proving to be a wasted day; no doubt more people would arrive as the day progressed, also ruining his plans for an arrest. The boat was now out of site, so rising from his cramped hiding place he stretched his aching bones and made his way down to the causeway; perhaps he might find some incriminating evidence, but somehow he doubted it.
Young children were running about on the sand, making far too much noise for the Sabbath. The smallest child, a young girl still almost a baby, skipped over towards him intrigued by his tall hat, dark uniform and the long truncheon swinging from his belt. However, before she could speak, he turned on her violently and let out a great roar of anger to frighten her away, a fearsome noise to which he added a twisted face of snarling evil. The child almost fell backwards in her terror of this great demon, but somehow keeping herself upright, she ran helter-skelter down the beach towards the river and along towards the old wreck by the water, wanting to hide away from this dreadful danger. The other children also frightened by the sound of the great fiend dressed in dark blue, panicked and ran for their lives in all directions, as fast as their young legs could carry them.
"That will scatter them all about and teach them to behave with more restraint on the Sabbath", smirked Mr Graystone to himself, pleased with this small demonstration of his power on this most unprofitable day. "When they arrive home in such alarm, perhaps the parents will also learn from the experience and keep better watch over their offspring in the future." He turned back to the causeway, looking around on the decking for some sign that the ferryman had been repairing to his boat or for some other infringement, but as he feared, nothing was to be found. Then in a foul temper, for which his long-suffering wife would need all her endurance to tolerate, Mr Graystone turned on his heel and headed off towards the City muttering angrily to himself.

<======>

After some fifteen minutes of hard rowing across the strangely deserted water, Henry brought the ferry gently alongside the Wapping causeway, the boat stopping with a light crunch as its keel slithered into the crushed chalk alongside the worn timbers of the walkway. Alfred and Edwin waited while the passengers paid Henry their fare and bid the ferryman goodbye. Once they had stepped ashore and with much laughter and merriment had wobbled their way along the causeway's slippery, uneven planks to the steps at the shore-end. Alfred turned to his comrade.
"Henry, my thanks" he said, smiling at his friend.
"Come up to the inn later and I will buy you a draft of ale for your trouble."
"Ah, a pleasant thought," laughed Henry, licking his lips with relish at the thought.
"But I hope for some good business on this tide and must grit this landing planking in preparation."
"If I am able to get away, I will come up later. If not, I will touch you for a flagon or two when we next meet." The boatman chuckled again at the pleasing thought of a future draft or so with his comrade. Alfred clapped his friend on the back and signalling to Edwin to follow, stepped out of the wherry onto the algae-infested planking. Then, with their boot-studs giving them a good grip on the slimy timber, the father and son made their way to the end of the landing and there climbed to the top of the steps, which led out onto the pathway above.

The tavern was only a short walk from the landing; it was an old wooden building, robust but not over-large. However, its magnetism to the eye was the startling sag in the middle of its low pitched roof. This unsettling looking dip had caused the building's chimney to lean over at an alarming angle, as if about to fall through onto the heads of the customers inside. The walls were also curious, for they were bowed outwards like the sides of a well cooked loaf, the whole effect looking like the bloated waist of a man, who seated contentedly on the river's bank, was enjoying the sunshine and showing that a good life of wine and food had left him with a full girth amidships.
"The drunken sailor! It is a good name for this place," said Alfred chuckling and looking up at the building as they approached the doorway. Then pointing to stairs at the side of the tavern nearest the river, Alfred instructed the boy.
"Lad, you can go up on to the terrace, find a comfortable seat, and wait for me while I truck my business inside. I will send you out some victuals and something for you to drink, I may be some time before I am finished my dealing, but do not wander from that balcony".

Edwin obediently climbed the rickety wooded stairs up onto the large timber staging, which hung precariously out over the riverbank and went over to the edge to look down at the water. The structure seemed to be supported on thin timber piles set deep into the river mud. He turned back and looked around this structure, which resembled the deck of a ship. There were several rough wooden tables with seating benches each side, set out in rows for those of the tavern's customers who wished to take the river air with their drinks and victuals. Such people however seemed to be scarce, not a soul was to be seen outside of the building. Even on this glorious sunny day it seemed they preferred the dark smoky atmosphere inside. Edwin decided to relax and enjoy the warm sun while he waited. He chose a suitable bench to one side of the decking and putting his feet up onto the table, lay back against the railings and pulled his hat down over his face. He had seen the boatmen doing this while waiting for a fare and it made him feel good copying their casual stance. Inside the darkness of his bonnet and the close thoughts of his young mind, he was now a full grown wherryman, taking a pot of well earned ale between fares, waiting to be called to row an important superior all the way upriver to the village of Chelsea, there to be paid in good coin for his efforts.

Suddenly his daydream was interrupted by the pleasant voice of a young woman.
"There you are young master," said the pretty voice.
"I have here your victuals and thinned wine for your thirst, by your leave" Edwin moved his hat back and looked up to see a lovely young serving maid standing before him. She was carrying a wooden tray and was smiling at him through perfect white teeth. He was suddenly extremely embarrassed and scrambled up into a sitting position. He kept his eyes down, saying nothing for fear that his voice was not manly enough to use on such mature beauty.
"Come now" said the maid, recognising the signs of shyness, an affectation which she had often seen in her own young brothers.
"Your father sends you good food and wine-water for your pleasure." She looked around as if seeing the tavern's outside for the first time. "It is pleasant indeed out here today." She paused and looked at him. "I have a few moments free from my duties, can I sit and talk with you?"
"No! No!" said Edwin in alarm, perplexed at the very thought.
"I am well enough alone if you please," he declared in panic, now going red at the thought of this vision of loveliness sitting with him for all to see.
"Well if you do not want the company of a handsome maid, I will take myself off," she said in mock affront, tossing her head with practised effect so that her blond locks flashed in the sunlight. She smiled at his increasing discomfort, then feeling a little sorry for causing his obvious embarrassment, she laughed prettily and walked back toward the tavern, but could not resist playfully swaying her hips, to add just a little more to the fluster she had caused in his immature mind. Once she was gone, Edwin felt relieved and fell upon the cheese and bread and quickly drained the weak wine. When finished he laid back, resuming the earlier position with his feet up and hat pulled down over his face.

Back under his hat, Edwin was once again daydreaming; this time he was at the helm of a great sailing ship, riding the huge green acres of the sea, the

sails were full to bursting with powerful wind, the ship was pitching and rolling, but his sturdy hands on the helm kept her straight and true to her course. Through the pleasant mists of his thoughts, he heard footsteps on the wooden decking; the sound was accompanied by a curious scraping noise. Although intrigued, he decided to remain in his comfortable position and not to look up, it might be customers from the tavern, or possibly that young woman again, perhaps she would think him asleep and leave him alone.
"What ave we ere then?" said a strange sounding voice. It was, decided Edwin, a young person straining to reach an octave lower than was his normal vocal pitch.
"Looks like a dead'en, all laid out for burial", said the voice. "Perhaps it's been washed up by the river," it went on. Edwin tried to ignore the words but to no avail.
"What's yeh name body?" the voice insisted, now accompanied by a prod from a bony finger. Edwin pushed back his hat and sat up. Before him was a boy of about his own age, dressed in tattered clothes, topped off with the most battered high-crown hat Edwin had ever seen, then looking down at the boy's feet, his eyes were confronted by an even more startling sight.

On the deck next to the newcomer's split and broken boots, was a younger boy of about six or seven. At first glimpse, he seemed to be just a head set upon a pile of dishevelled cloth. However, on closer inspection Edwin could see that this poor lad was seated on a square, flat board, which seemed to have small wheels or slides fitted underneath. His shoulders were drooped and at the ends of his arms were wooden blocks, which he gripped tightly in his thin white hands. It seemed that these pieces of wood were used to propel himself along the ground on board his small, flat, podium. The legs were absent, missing almost to the waist. In their place were two dirty rolled-up bags, which had once been breeches.
"That's me Cousin Martin," explained the older boy, following Edwin's gaze. "Lost his legs under a carriage when'e was a nipper, but'e can get about on his slide well enough. Say good-day Martin." the boy on the slide did not answer, but kept looking up at Edwin, his open mouth dribbling spittle from each corner onto his chin.
"Me, I'm known as Turk," continued the older boy, seemingly full of self confidence.
"To me friends that is". He eyed Edwin closely.
"You can call me so if you like, co's I likes the cut of ye jib". Then standing Full Square with hands on hips.
"Nar! What's ye name an' what's yer game." Edwin was at first taken aback by the forthright manner of this new acquaintance, but there was something disarmingly endearing about him.
"My name is Edwin. I'm the son of Alfred Crossback a good waterman of this City." Turk's eyes brightened.
"A Thames waterman eh. Is he a wager man? Has he won pulling races?" Edwin was delighted at this question, this was his favourite subject, and Turk had led straight into it.

"Yes to be sure, he is among the best at it" he exaggerated proudly. "Last year he pulled against eleven others for the Vauxhall Wager and beat them all. This year he won the Bankside wager and got a good purse for both races." Edwin was proud of his father's achievements in the wagers. He loved it when passengers asked about the wins listed on the backboard of Alfred's working wherry, the Anna,.

Alfred, although a reasonably good oarsman, had won but two of the several races he had managed to get himself enter into. It was difficult to be selected for any of the river wagers; there was always a great number of wherrymen wanting to compete at any of the events, all were looking for their chance of winning a purse or a prize. The betting fraternity of London knew the best oarsmen and would try to make sure that their fancied waterman was in every race. Newcomers therefore could only fill the last few available places, which were usually chosen by ballot. Alfred had two half-hearted sponsors who had taken an interest in his rowing ability. These were City men of middling standing who sometimes managed to get him into one or other of the less important wagers. Unfortunately Alfred had built up a reputation among the gamblers for being difficult; he could be awkward and independent, he would for instance, refuse to 'tickle' his boat. This method of lightening a vessel, by thinning away its planking, ribs, or even its seats was illegal, as it was likely to make a working wherry dangerous when used for its normal business of carrying fare paying passengers, but the practice was rife among the racing rowers.

The Watermen's Guild frowned upon the practice of 'tickling' they saw it as a risk to passengers and therefore ruled against this method of reducing of the weight of a wherry for racing. They instructed the company's Beadles to check for any boats altered in this way. However, there was much corruption in the sport and an oarsman's sponsors could easily buy off an inspecting Beadle if he threatened to report the wherryman to the Guild. Alfred thought the practice stupid as well as dangerous, and saw no reason to take such a risk.
"A wager-rower's prime is short lived, perhaps five years if he is lucky," he argued.
"It is a short time in which to gamble your livelihood", he warned Edwin while they were talking about the mater one day, while out working together.
"But you can row into old age with your licence clean, to make a good enough living" Alfred also knew that it was expected that gaming men would try to nobble a competitor's boat, preferably the night before the race. This could take the form of damaging the vessel so that she would take in water during the race and become heavy, or by weakening the oars or rowing locks, so that they might break under pressure. Alfred would have none of this and warned his sponsors that he would withdraw from the race if they tried to give him an unfair edge; he would take no chance of losing his licence and thereby his living.

Edwin was now in full flow, his pride in his father was shining in his words, and his small audience was listening intently to the story.

"It was only last year that my father raced in the Bankside wager and won the purse. I was there to see it with my mother; we had a grand view of the finish line from a good vantage point on the shore. It was altogether exciting, when he beat the best of both the Thames and the Tyne. The night after the race, Father told us the full story of the race from start to finish and how he had managed it. He had started the race, one of ten watermen, eight from the Thames and two from the river Tyne. The night before the race, the boat of one of the Tyne men had been nobbled, a hole was stabbed into her bottom-boards and she was drowned. This had forced the man to use a borrowed wherry in the wager on the following day, leaving him at a strong disadvantage in a boat he was unused to. Father said it was done by the supporters of John Graves, the Thames man who was the favourite to win the wager. They had nobbled the Tyne man's boat. Knowing that the man had won many wagers on his own river, they would take no chance on their man being beaten on the Thames, wanting to make sure that their bets on him should prove profitable".

Alfred had explained, to his family seated around the kitchen fire, their eyes bright with excitement, that the race had started from near to the old bridge. He had drawn a start position over to the south bank and sat his boat calmly, waiting for the command to go. However, an argument erupted between the two champions, the Tyne man was accusing Graves of drowning his boat, while Graves was shouting that the man was only looking for an excuse, because he knew he was the weaker oarsman and could not win in any event. The start was therefore delayed and when at last the starter dropped his flag in frustration. The start was an untidy affair, owing to the other competitors being distracted by Graves and the man from the Tyne haranguing each other with accusations and threats. Alfred however, had seized the opportunity and took off into a good lead, while the others were still trying to calm their tempers and concentrate on the race. He was the outsider in this wager, not many had risked coin on his winning. A shout went up from the crowd as Alfred took the initiative, Graves had belatedly seen Alfred's move and was soon in hot pursuit.

As they raced over the first half mile it became clear to those watching, that the outcome would be between Graves and Crossback, the others being too far back to make up the distance they had lost from the start. The Tyne man, struggling with an unfamiliar boat, was out of the race. At Vauxhall Gardens, Alfred was ahead by some three lengths and turned his bow towards mid-stream where there was a little more of the flood tide for him to make use of. Graves however, was curiously hugging the south shore, keeping very near to the multitudes who were watching from the shore and from the spectator boats, which were moored along this side of the river. It was as they came abreast of Vauxhall Gardens that Mr. Graves crafty plan unfolded, it was a scheme that involved him taking a great risk. He had decided to take the chance that the way would be clear for him to row inside the barge-roads at Johnson's boat-yard, to cut the corner of the river's bend and attempt to take the lead while out of sight of Crossback. Alfred said afterwards that Graves was very fortunate that no vessels were swung across the inshore stream, waiting their turn to go into the Drawdock, as was often the case. However, the way was clear for him on this day, and by putting in a great effort, Graves plan had worked well, he came out from behind the mooring roads ahead of Alfred by some three lengths. At first Alfred did not realise that Graves had taken the lead. He had lost sight of the man among the spectators, and thought himself still ahead. He was therefore pulling well within himself. It only became obvious that something was amiss, when he heard the crowd cheering with the excitement of the contest. Looking over his shoulder, Alfred suddenly realized what had happened. It was a shock to see that Graves had reversed their positions and was now substantially ahead of him. He felt the first pangs of panic, knowing that the man was a champion of many more races than he had even competed in. However, by strength of mind he controlled his raging thoughts and took stock of his situation.

"My father is a strong puller," Edwin was saying to his small but enthralled audience.
"He told us that he realized that Graves had made such a great effort to pull from three lengths down to three lengths ahead, that the man must have used up his reserves, whereas father still had much of his strength intact. He therefore decided that his best answer to this problem was to row long and strong at the champion, avoiding the temptation to look around to see if he was catching up.
"You see", said Edwin his eyes flicking from one boy to the other as if imparting a great secret,
"My father says that each man only has so much power in his body, and that he must decide how best to use it during a wager race. Graves was a great oarsman and had more power than most, but had used up a great deal of his reserves in pulling through those six lengths. He was relying on my father panicking when he witnessed his rowing prowess, and hoped he would waste his own power in a quick attempt to pull back the lead, Graves's plan was to sit on father's bow, match his efforts stroke by stroke, and thereby destroy his confidence in his own ability. However, father is no such fool, by rowing long and strong at the champion, with no let-up and no sign of weakening, father knew that Graves would have no chance to relax and recover from the efforts he made inside the barge roads, and thereby he would gradually be worn down." Edwin thrust his chin forward in pride, as he imparted this example of his father's shrewdness.
"Father said it was when they came level with the village of Pimlico, that from the corner of his eye he got his first glimpse of the stern of Graves's boat. Only for it to disappear again as the man made another great effort to keep ahead, but it then appeared again a few minutes later, and this time stayed in sight for longer. My father said it was then that he remembered something that an old waterman rower, one Jack Westerly, had once told him to perform in such circumstances, and summoning up all his reserves,

he played the artful trick on Graves. He slowly turned his head, looked across his left shoulder, straight into the champion's exhausted face, and smiled a large grin at him. The great oarsman was crestfallen at this show of confidence and gave up the contest at that point. Soon my father was past him and went on to win the wager by several lengths."

"What excitement to be sure," cried Turk, banging his fist on the table in his enthusiasm.
"Did ye 'ear that Martin, the boy's father is a rowing man indeed, wot finks ye of that". Edwin continued his storey to the very end, not wanting to give up his moment of importance as a storyteller.
"Mr Graves never spoke to father after the race, but let it be known that he felt he had been cheated, by 'the unfounded accusations from that fiend from the Tyne' and an 'unscrupulous common wherryman'. Father said that although he was sure Graves was the stronger puller, he lacked wisdom. He had let his animosity towards the man from the Tyne River rule his head, and as a result, had misjudged the use of his power during the race." He told us to remember that,
"A cool brain is the best partner to a strong body."

"Did ye 'ear that young Martin?" shouted Turk, thumping the table again in his excitement, the boy on the wooden slide looked up at his cousin with mouth wide open, the dribble still running down from the corners onto his chin.
"Shall I tell him of me Uncle Jack?" said Turk looking down again at the boy, who still made no reply. Then looking up at Edwin. "Well I fink we can trust ye. Ye seem to be a good en," he commented, eyeing Edwin closely.
"I fink it not in ye interest to spread abroad what I'm a gona tell ya" then settling back onto the bench he fiddled about in his bulging coat pocket, pulled out a short piece of broken, clay pipe and began to suck on the empty bowl. Then began his turn to tell his tale, trying his best to outdo Edwin's story.

"Me Uncle Jack is a 'Man of the road', he said almost in a whisper, then reassured that the secret was now out, he stated in a louder more confident tone.
"Yeh, a real live shooter, a fighting an a kicking Highwayman", claimed Turk, true pride tainting the tone of his curious voice.
"Looks after all of us in the family ye know. We go short for nofin do we, just ask Uncle Jack, an' we gets wot we wants." Edwin looked at the boys' tattered clothes doubtfully, but Turk continued as if not noticing the slur on his truthfulness.
"Carries two pistols in his belt, a sharp sword in its girdle and a cosh in his back pocket as well, and he knows how to use 'em all." Turk was warming to his story and like Edwin, was beginning embellishing it in the way that only children can, seemingly not caring if the listener believes them or not.

In truth, Turk's uncle was a footpad, no more than a common thief, making his living by robbery and intimidation. However, the boy's grandfather had in truth been a highwayman of some renown, preying on carriages travelling along the Highway of Wapping, which ran parallel with the river's north bank and led into the City. Like most of his profession, he had come to his untimely end on the gallows at Tyburn many years before. Highwaymen in their prime cut a glamorous figure among the poor of the City. They were said to rob the rich and give to the poor, a myth that they were eager to promote, for it brought them fame as well as fortune from their ruthless activities. Turk's family still lived off the reflected glory of their long dead relation, although to judge by the condition of the two boys, this glory had worn very thin over recent generations, and now brought little by way of victuals or textiles. Highwaymen In reality were ruthless robbers who lived the high life during the short years of their notoriety and usually died an early death at the end of a hangman's rope, or sometimes even worse.

Turk related the story of his uncle's imagined heroic deeds. As he did so, the exploits got more and more extreme, but as is the way of children, Edwin enjoyed every minute of it. The wonder and daring of leaping forward on horseback, to confront a carriage full of wealthy passengers travelling along the Wapping Highway and robbing them of their valuables, was a thrill to his ears.
"Sometimes," Turk explained, "When fings got too hot for 'im along the Highway, made so by the King's Men lying in wait. Me uncle crosses over the river to lighten travellers of their purses on their way through Kent". A particular hill over there, where the horses become weary from their efforts of pulling heavy coaches up to the top, was a favourite place for men of the road to stop carriages and make challenge with their pistols. It has become so notorious that it is known as Shooter's Hill.

Turk was at a particularly gory episode in his fantasy story, when he was interrupted in mid flow by the arrival of Edwin's father, who had appeared from within the tavern.
"Father, I have made new friends," said Edwin his face flushed with the excitement of the yarn. Turk stopped his story instantly and looked up admiringly at Alfred, his esteem for the man he had heard so much about from Edwin story was obvious from the shine in his eyes.
"What have we here then" said Alfred, looking down at the trio of boys, their eyes glowing with the exhilaration of the story telling. Alfred had caught the tail end of the saga on his approach.
"Tales of robbery and violence do I hear tell?" he said. Then looking down at the poor deformed body of Martin, he hunched down to peer more closely into the vacant eyes of the little cripple. He stood up, surveyed the tattered clothes of both boys, and noted the thin little bodies beneath, then he said with a friendly smile" How would you lads like some victuals to sustain your storytelling?" Turk looked a little embarrassed.
"Relating such a chronicle of dastardly deeds needs sustenance," said Alfred

persuasively.

"Well I dare say we could manage a mouthful or two Sir," said Turk, pulling himself up to his full height with touching self-importance.

"We 'ave a big meal awaiting us at 'ome this evening, but a morsel or so would tide us over till then".

"Service out here when you will," called Alfred back into the tavern. His call was quickly answered by the pretty young wench who came sweeping out onto the veranda, Alfred went over and spoke to her quietly, pressing some coin into her hand, she looked across at the boys, smiled a sad smile and went back into the tavern.

"It is done; food and drink are on their way. I am sorry that we cannot stay to join you, but it is now well past high water, the tide is ebbing strongly, so we must leave." Then putting his hand on Edwin's shoulder he said. "Come Edwin we must catch old Henry before he finishes up for the day." Turk thanked him again for the victuals, and clapping Edwin on the back, said in his pretend grown-up tones.

"Come again ta see us lad, an' I'll tell ye more of me Uncle Jack"

Edwin's head was full of the excitement of meeting his new friend, as he walked with his father back along the riverbank to the causeway. They found Henry just arriving with a boatload of passengers and waited while he took the fares saw them safely ashore. When all was clear, the pair boarded the ferry and sat down quietly, while Henry counted his coins, and secured them safely away in his money-belt. He turned to Alfred.

"You have been a long time, the tide has peaked and is now well away," he looked across the water.

"I've been too busy to join you for a bumper of ale, but I have made good business this fine day, so no loss, no loss".

"I have been longer than I meant, but I fell in discussion about the Lighteningmen leaving the Woodmongers Company and joining our Guild," commented Alfred.

" Ah! Now there's a difficult matter, I can't say as I favour the joining of our trades, but who am I to oppose it. There is great discussion within the Guild I am told, I am not surprised that you were delayed by such a subject."

"It is a question that will simmer for years to come, is my prediction" said Alfred, wondering if the joining of two trades would ever work to anyone's benefit.

There being no other passengers wishing to make it over to the south bank. Henry decided to take them on their own, and slipping the catch-line free of the mooring post, he sculled the boat out and away from the causeway. Again, Edwin felt the thrill of being afloat on the river. The sun was now low in the sky, creating dark shadows alongside the ships chained at their anchors. Each ship had a clutch of empty barges moored alongside, Once again the scene was as if in an oil painting, no life could be seen, not a sailor man nor riverman. Edwin looked away from the lifeless scene, peering over the side of the boat, enthralled yet again as it glided smoothly through the water. Pieces of flotsam, little islands of wood, old cloth bundles and little

rafts of unrecognisable debris were all around them, pulled out from their hiding places among the pilings by the high tide, and now on their way east with the flow of the ebbing water. Where did all this rubbish go to? Wondered the boy yet again. Was there really a great land full of refuse somewhere to the East that was forever growing as this floating waste landed on its shores? His father had told him that water was the 'universal carrier' the most wonderful of all the elements, He explained that it could carry great ships of the line and small boats alike, it could support a small piece of kindling or a drowned body, it could transport a speck of dust, or a great island of ice. It could carry food into a man's body or into a plant. However, he had said that it could also carry disease and had the strength to kill anything in its way, when it was angry. He explained that water could travel into the sky to clean itself through the rain and storms, but when Edwin asked more about these wonders his father just said he must wait, he would learn all of mysteries of water when he was apprenticed to the waterman's trade.
"Know for now my boy, that water is renewable and pure, life giving to fish and men in equal amount, to be called a waterman is special, it is a great honour to work with the universal carrier".

Edwin was suddenly startled from his thoughts by his father's concerned voice.
"What is happening over by Dog and Duck Henry?" Alfred was asking the ferryman, he was shielding his eyes to get a better view of their destination. Henry looked over his shoulder towards the causeway.
"There are people on the sand, it is to do with those children I'll be bound", said Henry.
"I thought they had gone away, I have not seen them for some time," the ferryman looked worried, as if a sudden dreadful thought had struck him. Edwin could see that a small crowd had gathered on the little beach alongside the causeway. The tide had been in while they had been away, and had now gone out again, leaving the stony sand to be slowly uncovered by the falling tide. As they came nearer, he could hear a woman wailing in great anguish. Something awful had happened, Edwin felt sure of it, he could also feel the tension growing in the two men. As the boat approached the causeway, an inexplicable fear and foreboding gripped his juvenile mind.

The ferry grounded its keel into the chalk bed next to the causeway, Alfred leapt ashore leaving Henry to moor the boat. Edwin nervously started to follow his father onto the sand, but stopped short of approaching the people. A strange knot was forming in his stomach, a feeling of pending doom was invading his mind at the thought of what they might discover. His father was now talking to a man in the group, he saw him put his hand reassuringly on the man's arm, then leaving the crowd, he returned to Edwin and Henry, who had now moored the boat and was waiting by the side of the causeway.
"The small maid is missing," said Alfred solemnly.

"She was playing with her brother and sister on the beach, when a man in a dark coat and tall hat frightened them all off. The little one has not been seen for some hours, her family have looked everywhere ashore, thinking that she had run home to hide, as had the other children, but they have found nothing. They have finally come to the conclusion that they must return here to search the beach where the children had been playing."
Edwin could read the anxiety in his father's face.
"I've said we will help search along the shoreline. Henry you look up river from here and I will take Edwin and investigate past the old wreck."

Closing their ears to the wailing of the women, Edwin and his father began looking along at the edge of the water for any sign of the child. They reached the broken timbers of the old wreck and rummaged around its decaying ribs, looking under each post and broken plank for any sign of the child, Alfred then moved further up the beach; he was now looking inside the gates of an old disused draw-dock. Edwin's mind was in a frenzy of apprehension, he did not want to be the one to find a small body, he was afraid that he might lose control of his emotions. He was therefore relieved when his father said,
"Given the time lapsed between the last of the flood and the first of the ebb, she could not be further down river than this; I think we will do better to retrace our steps higher up the beach. Keep a sharp look out lad, perhaps Henry has found something further up river." They began their return to the causeway.

Alfred and Edwin slowly made their way back and rejoined the group of people standing anxiously on the beach. Alfred went over to the man with whom he had spoken earlier, no doubt telling him that their search along the shoreline had been to no avail, Edwin felt sure it was the child's father. The man looked to be in shock and was visibly shaking, there were tears running down his face, Alfred was trying to comfort him, no doubt telling him that nothing being found was good news. Edwin looked away embarrassed, his own emotions were confused, the knot in his stomach had grown and was now joined by another great lump in his throat, he could feel tears burning behind his eyes. The mother of the child was inconsolable; other women had arrived and were restraining her from throwing herself into the water.

Edwin found that like the child's father, he was also shaking, his knees were trembling like sheet ropes in a strong wind, he knew that he was about to cry, he could feel the hot tears rising behind his eyes. He did not want anyone to see his lack of self-control and decided that he must get away from the people around him. Making his way quickly over to the deserted causeway, he climbed up onto the slippery planking and walked down to its end, where the timbers were being gently lapped by the water as they disappeared into the river's depths. He stood looking down at the water, trying to gain control of these terrifying feelings that were so new to him; he had never before felt such a mixture of fear, desperate sadness, and awkwardness. Looking up and out across the water, he breathed deeply, filling his trembling chest with the cool, calming air. Was this the same river that only this morning had seemed so beautiful? The same Thames that he had been so proud to be part of, as they had rowed over to Wapping? Had his wonderful river cruelly taken the life of that beautiful little child? He stood there silently, hoping against hope that suddenly they would hear that gay little voice, laughing and calling for the game of chase to begin again.

Half lost in his own world of confused, new sensations and self-conscious feelings, Edwin choked back the tears and began to slowly gain control of his emotions. Calming himself with the deeply inhaled breaths of fresh air. He let his eyes scan slowly from across the river, down to his feet where the water was lapping against the planks of the causeway. He was concentrating at the point where the wooden slats disappeared beneath the surface, there was some comfort to be had from focusing on the water and he began to feel a little better. Perhaps the little maid was even now safely with a relation or neighbour waiting for her family to come for her, knowing nothing of the worry and anxiety she had caused. Yes that was it, after all, they had found no sign of her, she had for sure run off to a place where she felt safe.

Suddenly his heart stopped, a great wave of dizziness swept over him, he staggered to keep his balance. For the first time in his short life, he felt the full impact of inexplicable dread. For there at his feet, floating just under the edge of the causeway's side-beam, bumping itself gently against the timber of the walkway, and looking like a fairy's wherry waiting for a miniature passenger, was a tiny red shoe with a diminutive flower, made of white ribbon sewn onto the instep.

CHAPTER TWO
The perilous City

It was now late September in the year 1712. The new century had rolled on by over a decade since the young maid had been lost to the river. Edwin had grown into a fine young man, apprenticed to his father to learn the trade of watermanship. His father, now in his late forties, did not remember much detail of that fateful event at the Dog and Duck causeway. The child's death had not affected him in the same dramatic way that it had his young son. Edwin still remembered the event in every aspect, and experienced the occasional bad dream about the incident. He had come to know the family of the maid, and had learnt from them what a wonderful little child she had been, always smiling and happy, with a joyful and contented nature. Her father had once told Edwin that God had given them a glimpse of an angel.

During his life, Alfred had seen many tragic drownings, some accidental, others more sinister in his view, probably wrought from devious purpose. He had pulled many lifeless bodies from the water, rowing them without much feeling, over to the north bank of the river, where on the City side he would be paid a better bounty for the recovery. Sometimes he would even receive a finder's reward from a grieving family, who were wretchedly mourning the loss of their loved one. Too many of the capital's citizens, caught up in life's dangers, found that the only escape from their ruinous circumstances, was to seek a final release by giving themselves up to the embracing waters of the Thames. Alfred, in his phlegmatic way considered those who took their own lives, to be no more or less than victims of the City's wickedness. Probably caught out by their own greed or faulty lifestyle, and had thereby fallen into a spiral of inevitable decline, that slippery slope that awaits all unwary men, a fate that, as it proceeds, is difficult to reverse. His view was not one of compassion, but of dispassionate inevitability. If a man did not keep to the straight and narrow course, if he was tempted into the traps set by the lies and devious claims of others, then it would usually end by death, in one of its many lurking, untimely forms   .
"Life is much like a mirror," he would observe   .
"What you put in is what comes out. If you show evil by doing the devil's work, evil will be returned to you. If you show compassion, you will be offered compassion in return." His way was to covet no man, but to find contentment with his lot in life, to steer a safe and middle course through the rough waters of temptation and inducement.

Alfred Crossback was known to most as a good person, a man of quiet character, thoughtful, although perhaps, as his wife would confirm, sometimes difficult, certainly stubborn and over cautious on occasion. He was physically tall and of burly build, sporting the wide shoulders, nipped waist and long powerful fingers, typical of his trade. His premature white-grey hair was abundant, and grew thick aboard his square shaped head, it was cut long enough at the back to be made into a short tail, this he tied tight with a thin black ribbon in the style of the old seamen, but without being tarred as was their fashion. Alfred was an intelligent man; clever and worldly wise with much experience in the ways of his fellow man. He was easily contented and not in any way ambitious. He did not require great riches, which he was convinced led to most of life's problems. His only desire in life was to be allowed to enjoy his family and his trade as a wherryman of the Thames, of which he was extremely proud. In his eyes he already possessed all that a man should reasonably want to make a contented life. "A man can only wear one suit of clothes, or live in one house, or smoke one pipe at a time", he would say to his sometimes-frustrated wife, when she wanted some small decoration for the house or for herself.

"Trivialities cost coin, and of what use are they? Can they be worn for warmth? Can they be eaten? No to be sure, but they can cause jealously and envy". Over the years of living with Alfred however, Nell had found her own ways of outwitting him, and achieving her little undemanding aims. "I will get it without his agreement and he will then soon find the means to pay, for he hates debt," she would say. It was like a little game that they played, Alfred never objected, he knew his wife would not be so extravagant as to put him in serious liability.

Alfred the quiet man was well known in the small circle of friends he frequented, he did not curry the favour of any, but had a good many acquaintances, few however were close to him. His wife Nell was his best friend and his confidant; he did not therefore feel the need, or as he would see it, take the risk, of having an intimate friend in whom he might trust his confidences. Such a person would in Alfred's eyes, always is a potential enemy. He thought it to be foolish indeed, to provide anybody with the weaponry of his secrets, such a risk was foolhardy and unnecessary in his eyes.

"How long will a friendship last compared to a good marriage?" he would ask.

"How easily you might fall out with a friend over something that offends you from his lifestyle, or something he opposes in yours? Then you have him against you, that one you have confided in, who now has you at a disadvantage by what you have told him". This was his belief.

"Keep all friends at an arm's length for your own good, as well as theirs," was his maxim.

"They will stay friends much longer if you do." This was Alfred's way, and it had served him well enough throughout his steadily navigated life.

His daughter Agnes was a happy and healthy maid and had inherited the same phlegmatic approach to life as her father. She was now walking out with a young apprentice cooper. Alfred thought him to be a suitable young man, who although he was younger by three years than Agnes, seemed to be sound and affectionate in the relationship. Alfred was pleased to see that she was quietly training him to be a good husband and the future father of her children. His son Edwin was more like his mother in character. The boy was more outgoing than his father or sister, and a little rash at times, but Alfred knew him to be a sound young man, even if his youth made him a little headstrong and unwary at times. The boy had followed his father into the river trade by apprenticeship and this pleased Alfred greatly. "A little straying off course occasionally, and a little listing from a level keel now and again, is only to be expected in a young man", he would reassure his wife, when she would worry about the boy being late abroad. Alfred was not over concerned about his son's attempts at finding liberty; he felt that an independent mind was a good sign in the lad. He knew that Edwin was sound at heart and not as rebellious as many others, the lad had been taught about the dangers that surrounded him, and knew the safe places to frequent, when abroad at night.

Alfred, as Edwin's apprenticeship master, was responsible for his training into the mysteries of the watermen's trade, but as his father, he also kept his other responsibilities to the fore of his mind. He had been steadily and carefully training the boy over the years along the same vigilant path, he trod himself. A route, which had served him well throughout his watchful, but contented 48 years. He wanted his only son to learn the ways he had developed in dealing with the world about him and how best to navigate a safe course through it, the people he must expect to encounter, the strong and the weak, the open hearted and the devious, the good and the bad. He wanted Edwin to be ready for those events in life that he would inevitably be faced with, foreseen or unforeseen, fair or unfair, the problems that he would encounter as he progressed through his allotted number of years in this dangerous world. Alfred was pleased that so far Edwin was holding a reasonably straight course.

Unlike most of the Watermen of the Thames, Alfred was only second generation; he had been apprenticed to his father, who was the first in the family to work on the river. This man, Edward Crossback had been part of a family of fifteen children, who at the ripe age of fourteen years, had been sent out into the world to find his fortune, taking with him the clothes he stood in, and a bundle containing a little food and the few coins his mother could spare. Edward left his home in Kent and made his way to the big City, which although he had never before seen, had heard much about. He had listened many times to the stories regarding the great Port of London, and was determined to visit the capital where he felt he might find work that he would enjoy. After many days of travelling and much disappointment from his attempts to be taken on as an apprentice, he finally arrived at Greenwich.

One day walking down to the riverbank, he stood looking at the great Thames in wonderment, watching the bustle of ships and boats passing to and fro. Near to where he stood, a man was loading bags into a small boat, which was pulled up onto the shore. After watching for some time Edward could see that the man was struggling to lift some heavy bags into the vessel, he approached the man and asked if he might help lift some of the bags. The man stood up from his labours and ran his eye over the small frail looking young boy.

"You think you could manage this weight unaided then?" he asked with a twinkle in his eye.

"I am willing to try sir, I am stronger than I look" and so saying Edward set about lifting the nearest bag, which he found contained coal. He struggled at the task, but no matter how he tried, he could only get one end of the bag off the ground at a time. Determined to succeed however, he wrestled on at the task until the man laughing loudly, intervened.

"Come lad, stand off, you have given it a good go; perhaps you have even learned a lesson for better use of your labour. Let us lift the weight together and see if our joint strength will prevail." They took hold of an end of the bag each and although it was still hard work, the bag climbed up into the boat and dropped with a thud onto the burden boards. Edward looked at the man grinning and the man smiled back.

"What's your name lad, what brings you here to old Greenwich?" Edward started to tell his story, but the man interrupted him.

"I can see this will be a lengthy story; let us sit aboard my wherry and drink a draft of beer to lubricate this tale along. Once seated, Edward continued his account, bubbling out the story of his short life. The man who said his name was Mr Riddle, was a good listener and soon he knew as much about Edward and his family in Kent as any other.

"So you seek an apprenticeship young man" Edward nodded in nervous anticipation.

"Well come work with me for a moon's round or two, and we will see if you have a waterman hidden away in that scrawny body of yours".

Edward had no idea of what this meant, or that he was being offered entry into a trade, closely guarded against outsiders. What he did not know was that Mr Riddle had a family of seven girls, with no son to bring into the trade. In truth he had liked Edward from the outset by the innocent way he had offered to help with the hard work, and his obvious lack of cunning or knowledge about London and its river.

"You were like a painter's blank canvas," he once told Edward later in their relationship.

"I always wanted a son to whom I could pass on my hard won knowledge, and you came out of the countryside just at the right time".

Edwin, as the grandson of this man, was therefore a third generation riverman on his father's side. However, from his mother's family came a richer source. She was from a family of watermen whose ancestry went back to before the Great Fire had destroyed all the records at Watermen's Hall. Her relatives although all long dead and buried, were remembered well by the river community. This stood the new Crossbacks in good stead by the family connection. The trait of continuous patronage of watermen's families was inherited from a time long before the formality of apprenticeships. It was a structure of continuance, that banded Watermen and their families together into a protective community, a close society, not always fully understood by those outside the trade. The river people could be likened to a village community ingrained into, but still somehow separate from the population of London itself. By means of intermarrying and father to son apprenticeships, Thames watermen generally kept close family and trade ties. Like many of the other trades of London, watermen tried to keep the secrets of their profession within their fraternity. The skills and mysteries of the river were jealously guarded, passed down from father to son or uncle to nephew; only occasionally did an outsider find his way into the Guild. It had been thus since anyone could recall. However, since 1555 this knowledge had been carried on by formal apprenticeship.

Alfred as his son's master, had passed the knowledge gained from his father on to Edwin, who had now completed the term of his apprenticeship. He had been examined, had passed, and was at last a freeman, unbound from his master. He was now licensed to work as a Wherryman on the waters of the Thames and its tributaries, from Windsor in the west, to the 'Watermen's Stone' at the river's estuary in the east. He could now earn his living as a wherryman in these changing and dangerous times of the reign of the vengeful Queen Anne.

It had been only five years earlier that the Queen had signed the Act of Union, when it had become increasing clear to both her and to Parliament that dual monarchy of England and Scotland was failing to work. Like many Englishmen, Alfred, and Edwin were confused and concerned by this change. Many like them were having difficulty in coming to terms with the new term 'British'. Could it really be, that by this simple act, Englishmen were to consider themselves brothers, with their old enemy the Scots? "A hard cross to bear, and a pretty penny for Englishmen to pay, no doubt of it" was Alfred's given opinion. The war with France, that other ancient enemy was still grinding on interminably, but like this new union with the Scots, seemed somehow remote from London's river. In the Parliament, the usual bitter battles between the Whigs and the Tories continued unabated, each vying to gain prominence over the other. Alfred had little time for what he called.
"Those gasbags, who liked to spend the hard-earned coin of others, albeit so politely done, with fake smiles, promises, and false pledges which never came to be."

In the City, the new Bank of England was now a financial power; Alfred had noticed that among his more affluent passengers, the advent of this new bank was providing an air of wealthy extravagance to those involved with the City's financial affairs.
"Those bankers are giving themselves airs and graces they have not earned, they are spending the money of others as if it were their own, look at the grand buildings they are constructing and the opulence inside", he would complain. He could see this extravagance daily, in the fashionable clothes,

they wore, and in the condescending, haughty attitude, they showed towards his class. For Alfred and his like, all this spurious prosperity only increased the concerns they had towards their own daily grind, as they tried to make a living on London's river. Life for the poor of London was as ever, the normal mixture of alarm, confusion, and resignation towards the antics of their superiors.

As Alfred went about his daily business, he had heard much about another strange happening that was exorcising the minds of many. It was called 'The south Sea Bubble' and it was apparently slowly inflating. This questionable investment phenomenon was giving vent to the frenzied expertise of both the clever and the foolish. Men who were able to arrange credit were taking every chance to invest in the seemingly inevitable wealth that was on offer through share speculation, financial opportunities supposedly available in far away places. Only the poor were forced to stand aside and watch this crazed extravagance unfold around them. They did this as they always had done, with the resigned air and resentful stares of those unable to take part, because of what they accepted as their unfortunate birthright. Like the runts of the dog pack, they were snarled away from the feast by the more powerful. The poor could only look on and hope that any disaster, which might befall those involved in this 'bubble', would not affect those who had not participated, but they had their doubts. "The whole City is inflating with madness, not opportunity" was Alfred's considered opinion; he was one of the few who would not have invested even if he would have had the means.

For Alfred and his son these were indeed difficult years to be living in London England, making a living from the 700 000 inhabitants of the City, by rowing a licensed Wherry and plying for hire on the Capital's perilous river. The great shipping port of London was dangerous indeed, not only because of the rough water and the hard winters, or the river's strong tidal eddies, which lurked malevolently around the bridge arches and the wharf pilings. It was also dangerous because of the activity around many ships moored at wharves and at buoys in the tideway, each one loading or unloading their cargoes at a speed and urgency, which baffled reason. The multitude of boxes, bags and bundles flow through the air on the worn, frayed, ropes, of the creaking, rickety, ship's derricks, then to be flung into warehouses, or into the dumb barges held alongside the ships by seemingly frail ropes. The port's activities were dangerous indeed and took a heavy toll on the lives of the river workers.

Life was also perilous to the watermen because of the throng of vessels busily working their way up and down the bustling water-highway of London, each seemingly missing the other by no more than the thickness of a wisp of hay. This of course was the normal and the accepted life of the rivermen and of the numerous river workers. They acknowledged these dangers as part and parcel of their working environment. Life however, was also hazardous because of the insidious intrigue, which permeated the City and its port, the trading trickery of the merchants, officials, ship owners,

Captains and Clerks, each of them caught up in the prevailing corruption and greed, which pervaded the very essence of society at this time. It was a period of imperative trading and frenzied investment. This core craziness was making life dangerous for each and every member of the population of London, rich and poor alike. There were plenty of individuals living in the capital, made wicked by the overcrowded, hazardous and menacing world of trade and politics, who were only too willing to do anything. For a payment they would maim a rival, or even kill an enemy; these willing hands were unashamedly used by the wealthy and ambitious to further their desire for more power and influence.

All such concerns were in constant reckoning in the mind of Alfred, Edwin, and their fellow watermen, and yet, even these were not their entire jeopardy. The most pernicious danger of all was something else, something that if you were able, you would steer clear of altogether. It was however, a menace that could not easily be avoided. The most creeping and slowly destructive danger of all was 'religion', a peril that had plagued the English, since the old King Henry had opened the floodgates to the new Protestant way of thinking. If a man was unlucky enough to get himself caught up in the religious intrigue and interdenominational disputes perpetrated by the spies of the Church, he could easily be made to pay severely for his mistake. If he should say the wrong thing, at the wrong time, to the wrong person, or in an unguarded moment take the wrong side of an argument, perhaps even be just going about his normal business, without keeping a wary eye about him, the consequences could be disastrous. The Queen Anne reigned over the land with a strong, religious, and vengeful hand.

It was rumoured that the Queen had been pregnant a total of eighteen times, thirteen of which had not carried to full term, the other five of her children who had survived birth, had died in early childhood. It was said that it was because of the many, mournful funerals held for the Queen's offspring, that Her Majesty took out her vengeance on those of her subjects who held to a faith different from her own. The rivermen did not much like the Queen Ann. She had a nickname among the river fraternity being secretly and irreverently known by the watermen, as 'Mistress Carriage', due to her many unhappy and unfulfilled pregnancies. Her misfortunes and difficulties in bearing children, which she was convinced, were due to her religious inadequacies, in not making her faith prevalent, had made her an extremely bitter woman. Her bitterness being aimed towards all forms of religion other than her own. For her, there was but one faith. She was a staunch Protestant.

Alfred had only ever seen The Queen from a distance, whenever she passed him in her Royal Shallop during one of her river journeys. He had heard it said, that in some ways, the Queen could be generous, even kindly to those close to her. Many of her subjects were pleased that she continued the custom of 'touching'. Like all Kings and Queens of England, she was considered by many to have the power of curing illness and disease by touch, but Alfred doubted if he or his would ever benefit from such magic, for he or they had no way of approaching the sovereign. He knew of one fellow waterman, who would need such a touch to cure his tormented body, but then on consideration, he doubted that the man in question believed such things were possible from a Christian Queen; his faith rested in an older, secret, enchantment. He felt sure that James believed in the ancient, almost forgotten spirit of the water deity in all her varied forms, liquid, solid, mist, and frost. His belief was in the old pagan deity of the river the Lunar Goddess.

What Alfred and many others did know however was that behind the Queen's occasional good nature, if it ever existed, she had the blinkered sight of the religious fanatic. It seemed that she was convinced that her miscarriages and difficulties in bringing her children even through childhood, was a consequence of her lack of achievement in freeing the land of all alien forms of religion. In atonement to her God, for these perceived defects, she had sunk ever deeper into fanaticism. Although obsessively religious herself, she was completely intolerant of the religious beliefs of others. Everyone knew that the Catholics were her main targets, but the Jews also felt her vengeance, Alfred had been told that it was the Queen's personal intervention that had been instrumental in these poor souls being forced out of the City of London, because of their insistence in observing Saturday as their Sabbath. Any faith other than her own was considered heretical and its practitioners were in mortal danger.

For the men of the river the Queen's vengeance was asserted in one particularly cruel way. Any unfortunate wherryman who found himself caught up in the Queen's fanaticism would know her wrath by the ruthless way she ordered not only the punishment of Catholics, but also of those who might help them. Some of these frustrated souls, deprived of access to their God and looking for a secret means of observing their devotions, had taken to using enclosed barges, moored afloat in mid-stream of the river, to hold their religious gatherings. Whenever these floating meetings were discovered, any watermen found to have been involved in ferrying the congregation off to the assembly, would be severely dealt with by the Queen's men. Alfred knew of several men who had been summoned before the Court of the Watermen's Guild, and accused of assisting Catholics in their religious practice. In spite of their pleadings, they had lost their working licence for periods from three months to three years depending on the depth of their involvement. Such a penalty and loss of income forced many to turn to crime. Some had even given themselves up for a voluntary turn of service in the Royal Navel ships, hoping for the remote possibility, but certain risk, of winning prize money from the capture of enemy ships. All this danger confronted the wherrymen for simply working at their trade. It was easy to make a small mistake and pay a heavy price. "Stand well off from religion. Give it a wide berth", was the watchword for prudent Watermen, in these threatening years of the Queen Anne.

Most Thames Watermen working as wherrymen were constantly on the lookout for extra employment. The business of the journeymen was subject to the strict rules of their Guild. They therefore sought out any extra income that would act as a foil against the inevitable turndown in their earnings caused by their vigorously controlled trade. Their business also suffered from the intervention of bad weather. The ice flows of the freezing winters and the flood-water of early spring were predictable. However, heavy rain, hail and storms, would also affect their business adversely, sending their customers hurrying for the protection afforded by Flanders carriages and Sedan Chairs, new forms of transport that were slowly gaining acceptance by the citizenry in spite of the uncomfortable ride over the cobblestones of the streets.

Fortunately for the watermen, wherrymen, and lightermen of London's port, there were occupations that sought them out. These men by their employment were among the fittest and strongest of London's workforce. Watermen were used to carry out the delivery of post and parcels to the ships of the port, and to the riparian buildings along the river frontage. They were employed in carrying the stores and victuals to the ships of the port. These activities, which provided extra income for many. Even holy books, rowed out to the ships at anchor, was work paid for by the church. Every form of additional work was potentially a good supplement to a riverman's earnings. Some watermen would seek a place in the crew of a Shallop Barge, owned by one of the wealthy families or a titled person. Most of the aristocracy had their own retinue of oarsmen to crew and row their shallops. Watermen called from among the ranks of the Guild manned these fast vessels. This employment was much sought after, as persons of superior station were able to protect their watermen from the dread of impressment into the Navy. Such work however, was carefully controlled by the Guild; a man needed good connections and a willingness to recompense his benefactor to gain a place in a Shallop crew. Alfred was unwilling to work for any of the nobility; to him it was like pinning his colours to one mast, like taking a side in life's battle. He preferred not to be beholden to any particular side; he favoured the middle course, always looking to steer away from potential trouble. However, like most of his trade he wished to protect himself, and thereby his family, from the likelihood of being taken for service in the Queen's navy. He had eventually found the answer to his dilemma quite by chance.

<=======>

Some years earlier, Alfred had been carrying a fare downriver from Westminster to a mansion near to 'All Hallows Stairs' in the City. At the end of the journey, as they approached the water-gate of the building, his elderly passenger had pointed to a plume of smoke and sparks rising above the corner of the bridge over on the south shore. "Boatman what do you make of that?" he said pointing at the black cloud. "Do we have yet another fire near the bridge to threaten our City?" The man was a little anxious, as the fire seemed to be coming from a direction near to

the house of a good friend of his who lived on the bridge.
"Looks to me Sir, that the fire is beyond the bridge near to Horseley-Down Stairs" said Alfred looking over his shoulder in the direction of the smoke. "Shall I take you though the bridge for a closer look to see for yourself?" He looked expectantly at the old gentleman.
"No thank you my man, I have no wish to shoot the arches this late on the tide" said the old man, with genuine trepidation, as he looked at the stern of a sailing barge tipping up high as she passed down through 'Nonesuch Lock' arch of the old bridge.
"I will hear soon enough if the inferno spreads to be sure, The Mayor will no doubt send men to break the fire's advance if it is not controllable by dousing." Alfred pulled his wherry near to the stairs and took the coin for his payment, then coming alongside the landing, he held the boat tight to a mooring-post and handed the old gentleman out onto the steps. He watched as the elderly man climbed unsteadily to the top of the white stone steps, on his rickety old legs.

It was approaching the time when watermen would not shoot the bridge even without a passenger aboard. Alfred weighed up his options, should he stay above the bridge or run down through. There did not seem to be any sign of business at All Hallows, so he resolved to save his tide down through the bridge and take a closer look at the fire over at Horseley-Down. Backing his wherry away from the stairs, he turned Anna's head downstream. He looked carefully at the run of water through the arches and at the traffic passing through. There seemed to be less activity over to the south, he decided to shoot through 'St Mary's Lock'. It was important at this state of tide, with such a deep drop through the bridge, to have equal water pressure on each side of the boat as she passed through; he therefore shaped up his approach to run through the precise centre of the span. It was always exciting to shoot the bridge at this time of the ebb, he felt the usual thrill as Anna's bow dropped, and her stern rose up as she fell through the turbulent water of the lock arch. The most hazardous moment, as Alfred knew well, was entering the disturbed millrace just below the bridge; he must keep his boat straight until he was well through and out into calmer water. As he came racing through, he felt the boat straining to turn to starboard, starting to come around beam-on to the water rush. Quickly he took a few strong strokes with his left-hand oar to pull her straight, then as suddenly as the rush had started, it was over, he was through and out into the tranquillity of the Pool of London.

Over on the south shore he could now make out clearly that a warehouse building on the riverfront was ablaze. He could also see that there was another wherry moored at the nearby causeway, which was sited a little down river and up-wind of the fire. The wherryman was standing at the top of the steps, up on the wharf's decking, watching the attempts being made to control the fire from the riverside with buckets of water. Alfred rowed over, moored his boat to the causeway's post, and climbed up onto the wharf to join other man.

"Ahoy Smithers", called Alfred stepping onto the frontage deck of the wharf. "Is it coming under control yet?" he asked approaching the man whom he knew, but did not particularly like.
"Ahoy yourself Crossback," said the man, showing by his expression that the feeling of dislike was mutual.
"Come to see if there is business to be had, caused by this blaze?"
"Not I" said Alfred," ignoring the insinuation and the man's ominous look. "I see that you are ahead of me anyway looking for 'misery money' from any unfortunate souls caught in this tragedy. You will no doubt offer to transport their goods away from the flames for a heavy price as always." He eyed the man with unabashed contempt. Then looking again at the fire.
"All this water about us in the river and little of it able to be used to fight this blaze," he said, half to himself. Smithers looked at the river but did not answer. Then ignoring the man, Alfred went further towards the fire, partly to gain a better view but also to get away from Smithers.

As he approached the burning warehouse, he turned down a narrow alleyway between the buildings and came out into the street beyond; he was now near enough to feel the heat from the flames. The sight before his eyes was a scene of disorder; Sacks, bags, and boxes of goods were littered about the street and were still being thrown out from the loading windows at the top of the building where the flames had not yet reached. Glowing debris and bright red embers from the burning timber were sprinkled about the cobbles, being beaten out by men with damp sacks. In the middle of all this chaos stood a lone water-engine, two men in large wide brimmed, leather hats, were working the pump, while two others were playing the water from the hose up onto the flames, seemingly to Alfred, having little effect. Suddenly there was a great crash as the building next in-line of the one on fire fell to the ground, pulled down to create a fire-break by a group of men with ropes and horses. The Mayor's men had sacrificed this building in an attempt to halt the fire. Another water-engine now arrived pulled by a crew of sweating men. The hose was quickly run out towards the fire and another dropped into the nearby well to join its compatriot from the first engine. Two of the crew started to pump furiously and soon a second jet of water attacked the blaze. Alfred watched fascinated as the water from the two pumps, gradually gained control of the flames.

"It was an exciting occasion altogether Nell." Alfred was telling his wife that evening over their meal.
"And who do you think should be part of the fire crew?" he paused for effect. Nell looked blank and did not answer, to her fires were a normal part of city life and of no particular interest unless near to her own home.
"Why! Matthew Ross, the man I was apprenticed with", Alfred smiled and shook his head with pleasure remembering the good times all those years ago.
"He has been a fireman for the Sun Insurance Company for some five years, and I knew nothing of it," He peered at his wife intently, for she was showing very little interest in his story.

"Nell, do you not understand how useful it is to have a friend in the insurance fire service? Firemen are exempt from impressment." He waited for his words to take effect.

"What!" exclaimed Nell now listening intently, suddenly realising what her husband meant.

"Alfred can you become a fighter of fires and never be taken by the press?" She was now very interested as she realised the significance of what he was telling her.

"The Chief of Matthew's crew is in need of a new man to replace one who is now decayed with age". Again, he paused for effect. Nell had her apron up to her mouth in anticipation.

"Matthew has promised to put in the word for me," he said grinning from ear to ear.

"He thinks I might well be accepted."

His friend had indeed recommended Alfred as a Fireman to the Sun Insurance Company and to his great relief had been appointed. He now had the great advantage in being one of the Firemen of London. The appointment to this band of men willing to risk themselves to save any property insured by one of the new insurance companies, and to perhaps even save a life or two in the process, but most of all it now gave him exemption from impressments into the Queen's Navy, a very valuable immunity to men of the river, who were constantly preyed upon by the press gangs. Since his own appointment as a fireman, Alfred had quietly endeavoured to get his son appointed, but so far, he had not been able to arrange it because of Edwin's youth.

The work as a 'Sun Fireman' was hard but interesting; Alfred was on call with one of the weekday crews. His duty area was south of the river to the east, his times were from midday to midnight, Monday to Friday, between these hours, he must be available and ready to muster at the water-engine when alerted by the alarm; Alfred's engine was housed in an old stable not far from the Crossback's home. It was also here that their special clothing was kept. Each man was issued with a tightly woven felt coat, with the 'Sun Insurance' metal emblem displayed on the left arm. They also wore a heavy leather helmet with a wide brim. Both these items gave protection from the sparks and flames when at close quarters to a fire. Firemen when needed, would be summoned by the ' Fire-bell', or by a message. They must rush to collect the engine-pump and run with it through the narrow streets of the City, ready to quench a fire at the house of any owner, who held a paid up Sun Insurance policy, and displayed the company's plaque on the outside of the premises.

Each of the other Insurance companies in the City had their own force of firemen. These crews consisted mainly of watermen, wherrymen, or lightermen, men who, due to the outdoor and physically exacting life they led, were preferred for this work as they were relatively fit and healthy, when compared with the normal citizenry of London, Alfred was proud of his "Fireman" status and enjoyed the work. He had seen many incidents during his years of duty, some very sad, involving death and or disfigurement, as well as the destruction of property. However, as an observer of life he found it very interesting to witness people's differing response to pending disaster. Some would fight with the power of ten men, as they watched their whole life's work go up in flames before their eyes, they would fight even if the fire had too much of a hold and would obviously prevail. Others would stand wringing their hands, waiting for the water-engine, when with quick action they could have controlled the flames themselves.

The lucky ones, who could afford to insure themselves against fire, had the possibility that the firemen might save some of their property from the blaze, but the insured were still few and far between, especially among the poor, who could only stand and look as all they had in the world was lost to the inferno. Fires often started in kitchens or in chimneys in the wooden houses of the poor, it could quickly take hold and spread to the whole house, from where it might race through the neighbourhood taking other property and life in its path. The water-pump engines of the insurance companies were not often seen in the poorer parts of the City. Sadly, the only response to a threatening fire in this area was for the Mayor's men to be sent in to pull down houses in the fire's path, in an attempt to create a fire-break. Such intervention might well prevent the fire spreading, but no compensation would be paid to the owners whose property was so sadly used. These unfortunates could only depend on the charity of others, for having given up their home for the protection of their fellow citizens.

<========>

Alfred and his crew were sometimes involved with humorous incidents, which occasionally arose out of the dramatic situations. One afternoon during Alfred's turn of duty, he arrived home to be greeted by his wife with an urgent message to muster for fire attendance. He hurried to where the engine was housed just in time to see it being rushed off along the road towards a plume of smoke rising into the sky in the near distance. Alfred quickly joined the crew, not bothering to grab any of the protective clothing that was kept at the engine-house. On arrival at the scene of the fire, half exhausted after the hard push, the crew found a house with black smoke and sparks billowing out from one of its chimney.
"It's only a soot fire" called out the crew captain to his men, and disappeared into the house to assess the situation from inside. The rest of the crew made ready the engine and ran out the canvas hose. While they were busy at this task, a cry of went up from the crowd of people that was now gathering.
"Look up there". Alfred looked up in the direction of the pointing fingers, to see a small man astride the apex of the roof tiles, with a bucket of what

seemed to be water, held in his teeth by the handle.
"It's the little tailor himself" called out someone in the gathering crowd, who obviously recognised the man.

The corners of Richard's mouth were stinging; his teeth were sending small lightning strikes of pain into his brain. The inside of his knees felt as if the flesh had torn away from the bone by the roughness of the roof. The muscles in his groin were burning with the pain of long under-usage and his soft Tailor's fingers were bleeding from the scratches caused by the coarseness of the tiles. Added to all this physical agony, he could hear the high pitched, screaming voice of his little fat wife billowing up from below, urging him on in his effort to reach the burning chimney.
"Get along quickly you lazy good-for-nothing, I have told you a thousand times to have that chimney swept, your meanness will be the death of us all." How could she blame him? He thought to himself. He who put the bread on the table for them all. He who worked as hard as any to provide for their needs. True he did not, nay could not, afford to waste good coin, he was careful, he admitted it, but a good provider never the less. Perhaps it was that cheap coal he had obtained from the port, yes it was that, it did not burn well in the grate, and it made a great deal of smoke, that must have been the cause of the fire.

Through the pains of his body Richard considered his predicament, perched high up on the roof of his house, how had he got himself into this ridiculous situation? The panic of the entire household had erupted when it was realised that they had a chimney fire. This had caused him, as it did the women of the house, to run about like a headless chicken, not knowing what to do. It had been his apprentice who had run off to call out the firemen. It had been his wife who had given him the bucket of water and sent him onto the roof to put out the fire, now that he was up there he sorely regretted doing her bidding. If he had stopped for a moment and thought the matter through, he would have realised that a Tailor was not equipped to climb onto roofs, to carry great buckets of water in his teeth. A moment of thought and he would have remembered, as his apprentice had, that he was insured against fire, he should have simply waited for the firemen to do their work. Now he felt embarrassed by the crowd that was gathering, too chagrined to go back down, he would look a fool and a coward if he did that, he might as well finish the job now that he was here. He moved his raw knees and painful fingers further along the rough ridge tiles towards the chimney, a black, smoking, monster that he now hated with all his being.

Alfred knew from his experience with this type of fire, that they would need to play water from the hose onto the outside of the chimney stack, to cool the heat away from the burning soot inside. He also knew that this had to be done carefully. If the fire had a good hold and had been burning for any length of time, too much water applied too quickly might crack the chimney and release more sparks onto other houses nearby. The first job, however, was to dismantle the fire in the grate inside the house. This was exactly what the fire captain was about to do.

Captain Jones knew his job well. His experienced eye had told him immediately on entering the kitchen what needed to be done. He knew his men would start pumping the engine and would carefully play cool water onto the roof and when he gave them the signal to do so, onto the chimney stack itself to bring down the temperature. It was a simple job, probably caused by not having the chimney swept often enough. An hour, perhaps two at the most and they would be on their way back to their base, they would put the engine away again and make it ready for its next call out. When he and his crew had arrived, he had quickly looked up on the wall of the house and seen that the Sun's insurance plaque was prominently displayed, indicating that they could fight this fire on behalf of the company. It would be an easy job and no person or property would be damaged. Then, with one of the crew who had followed him into the house helping him, they started to rake the fire out from the hearth, and to douse the burning coals with sand from the bucket, which all houses kept beside their hearths. Captain Jones could hear shouting and the sound of the crowd gathering outside, but this was quite usual and he did not take much notice.

Up on the roof, Richard was now in even greater pain and distress; he was now oblivious to the shouts from his wife and the crowd below. He was determined to complete his mission. He would show them that he was a hero. His wife down on the ground was now beside herself, for one of the fireman had told her that her husband must not put water near the hot flue. It would be most dangerous if he tried it. Richard, however, seemed to ignore her screams and pleading. A man dressed in black from head to toe and covered in soot, pushed through to the front of the crowd to confront the distraught woman.
"This is the result of your husband's meanness madam," he shouted at the hysterical wife.
"I was turned away not a month ago when I came to sweep your funnel. That mean tailor of a husband of yours looks to save every penny, and has now put you and your neighbours in jeopardy." The little fat wife could stand it no more and with her head buried into her apron, she ran back into the house sobbing.
Richard with a great effort of will had now reached the chimney. He could feel the heat from the fire through his legs and on his face. His ears were ringing with pride; he was the hero of the hour. To him the shouts from below were shouts of encouragement. He carefully took the bucket from between his teeth; the relief on his jaw was almost overwhelming. He could hear from below, that they recognised his heroism, he knew they were cheering him on, oh what fun and delight would await him when he got down. He would be the saviour of the neighbourhood; the Mayor would give him a medal for his bravery. He lifted the bucket in triumph, the noise from the crowd rose to a new crescendo, he was convinced they were

cheering his bravado, little knowing that all but he, were aware of the menace he was about to invoke. It took his last drain of strength to place the bucket on the rim of the chimney pot, and with a final effort, he pushed it over to spill its contents down into the depths, from where the acrid smoke was billowing. All went quiet, the crowd stooped shouting, Richard supported his aching body against the hot stack and steadied himself ready for the chorus of praise he expected to engulf him.

Down in the kitchen, the captain was close into the hearth, reaching inside the grate to rake the last embers from the far corner of the fireplace. The Tailor's wife came running into the room waving her arms and shouting in her high-pitched voice an unintelligible babble of words. Suddenly a sound like that of a large animal's cough came from the hearth, the captain looked up to see the source of the noise and was immediately engulfed in burning soot, and red-hot sparks. The whole kitchen was now a hot, black, dungeon of brimstone, flares, and flashes. The two firemen and the little fat wife were dancing about in panic as the hot soot and sparks found their painful way into every crack and crevice of skin and piece of cloth they were wearing. To make matters worse they could not see to find their way out of this hellfire, and kept bumping into each other in their efforts to breathe and to rid themselves of the burning sparks.

Up on the roof there was now an even more pitiful sight. The explosion had collapsed part of the chimney stack, causing Richard to fall forward across the gaping hole where the chimney has once stood and from which now poured, even more smoke and sparks curling around his body. The fire's heat now examined this new human obstruction and was delighted to find it a new source of fuel; it started to burn into his waistcoat. Throwing himself backward away from this latest attack on his person, Richard now lay for a moment on his back balanced along the ridge tiles of the roof. He was now able to deal with his smouldering waistcoat by patting the simmering cloth with his poor and grievously damaged hands, but the balance required of this new position was precarious.
First he found himself rolling a little to the right, then overcompensating he rolled violently to the left, then completely lost control of his body weight and slipped away down the back of the roof, out of sight of the onlookers. After his exploits on the roof, it was almost a pleasant sensation sliding down the tiles, but then came the edge of the roof and the sickening weightless fall to the yard below. With a thud accompanied by a cracking sound, Richard landed on the lid of the back yard's cesspit. For a fleeting moment he recalled his wife on many occasions trying to get him to pay a carpenter to have the rotten wood of the pit's lid replaced. No he had said, he was sure it was good for a few more years, given normal use. This however, was not normal use, how could he be held to blame? With a splintering sound, the lid gave way, and he was now falling again, it seemed somehow dreamlike, like slow motion as he passed down through the few feet of stinking air above the pit's disgusting contents, then with a splash he landed in the mire. As he went under, he had the presence of mind to shut

his mouth and eyes, even when he surfaced he did not dare open his mouth to call for help. He grabbed out for something to hold onto and found a small hand-hole in the greasy brickwork, he slowly pulled his aching, contaminated, body up the holes built into the wall of the pit, and finally flopped over the side to lay sprawled on the cobbles of the yard.

His body hurt everywhere, pain to such an extent that he could not tell which part hurt more, he opened one eye and tried to make an examination of his person by touching it in various places, but that only hurt even more. Richard looked around him, nobody had come to help him; did they not know of his misfortune? He rolled over and painfully got to his knees, then staggering like a drunken vintner, he clawed his way onto his feet, staggered to the back door of the house and entered. Still nobody was to be seen, he squelched his defiled body through into the parlour, but this room was also devoid of life. Still not daring to open his mouth for fear that some awful disease might enter his body, he stumbled on.

He could faintly hear laughter coming from outside. He cleared some of the debris from his ears, the laughter was now louder, and it was coming from the front of the house. He padded his wet, slimy way out through the front door into the evening's dimming light. The laughter now erupted into a crescendo of fresh delight, as the crowd recognised this pile of wet dung, as Richard the little tailor. He walked over to his blackened, dishevelled wife, whom he hardly recognized in her tattered, soot-stained clothing. His only wish was to be comforted in his misery. Still not daring to speak, he stood looking at his little singed spouse, beginning to wonder what had happened to her. She was crying uncontrollably into her scorched apron, while at the same time she was being harangued by two equally blackened and singed firemen. There was also an aggressive chimney sweep berating her. The sweep now recognising the tailor, diverted his vitriolic attack onto his person. The world about Richard gradually dimmed over, and partly from exhaustion, and partly from despair, the penny-pinching tailor fainted into the plump arms of his little, fat, shrew of a wife.

Alfred had told the tale of the tailor's chimney many times and still laughed at the thought of the incident. This and many other stories, some humorous, some tragic, were of intense interest to Alfred as an observer of life. However, the advantages of this extra employment as a fireman, was the thing that was most gratifying to him, apart from the extra income, it was the protection from the Press-gang it offered that satisfied him the most. However, the full range of human emotions to observe were meat and drink to his observing nature. He could think of no more enjoyable way of protecting his family than being a fireman, and he was determined to continue his efforts to get Edwin accepted into the service and thereby allow him to also enjoy the benefits.

CHAPTER THREE
Origins and Apprenticeship

A strong westerly breeze blew down the Thames that evening pushing the first fitful movements of the ebb tide into tiny white water-horses. Edwin peered out from under his bonnet; he needed to gauge the weather for the night ahead. Looking up into the dark, storm gathering sky, then down into the gloom of the river's water, he was carefully calculating the strength of the first stirrings of the turning tide. It seemed as if the ebb was gathering itself reluctantly for its long run to the sea. The water seemed distracted by the light rain, as if not yet ready to rush with full force down through the arches of the old Bridge on its way to join its mother the great ocean. There was something curious about this evening's cool rainy air; something restless about the approaching night. Was it to do with this delayed ebb? Was it just his imagination? Or was it perhaps connected with the unsettling feeling that had been with him all day? He shivered and again looked closely at the water, he knew from experience that these were not good signs; later on this ebb, the weather conditions could become worse, perhaps even stormy. It would not be a good tide for taking a fare westward, rowing up river against the wind, tide and the land-water run should be avoided. The rain over the last weeks had run off the hills upriver, and was now using the Thames as its natural conduit to find the open sea. He knew that he should make every effort to avoid taking a passenger up-river, he must find one wanting a local trip, or if early enough, to go down river through the bridge, and he was resolved to do so.

Edwin was one of six watermen waiting at Old Swan Stairs for a fare-paying passenger. Each man was sitting in his wherry, in a world of his own thoughts. Like the others, Edwin sat slumped on the passenger thwart of his boat, his broad young back resting against the vessel's brightly painted backboard. He was in that dream-world, half asleep and half awake, enjoying the ever interesting place of his private thoughts. He quietly reflected on the other five wherrymen about him, their characters and their personalities.
Edwin was now just into his twenties, he had grown into a tall, well-proportioned young man. The memories of his childhood carefully stored away in the back recesses of his mind, to be retrieved during times of quiet contemplation, when he would enjoy recalling the wonderment of his boyhood, and muse over the irrational fears, which had bothered him at that time.
Edwin had inherited his mother's black hair, and dark-eyed handsome features. However, there was also a great deal in him from his father's family. The long upper body with proportionally shorter legs were pure Crossback. As were his wide shoulders and narrow waist. His long, strong, fingers were exact duplicates of his father's. In fact, Edwin was blessed with

a build, developed over many generations, to meet the needs of a rowing man. The physical effort of so much pulling on an oar from an early age, combined with the healthy open-air lifestyle, aided by the good victuals provided by his mother, had given him all that was needed to succeed as a Thames Waterman in the dangerous and changing times of London in the early eighteenth century.

Edwin was comfortable enough, closely wrapped against the night's cold drizzle in a heavy, blue serge coat, fastened with wooden pegs and rope loops, tight up under his chin. The thick coat with its high collar, although old and worn, was shielding him well against the evening's chill wind. Under it he wore a wool shift, and heavy serge breeches pulled in at the waist by a stout leather belt, which was held fast by a strong brass buckle. His legs were encased in heavy woollen stockings, which showed by the many neatly darned repairs, that he was well cared for. His head was protected by a wax-coated bonnet, which he wore over a white headscarf. His feet, which were tucked back into the dry place under the passenger thwart, were thrust into hard leather boots, which although of unfashionable design and scuffed and worn by much use, had a good thick layer of wax to protect them.

Edwin was sitting in the typical, long practised posture of a wherryman waiting for hire. His whole person, like the other men waiting at the plying stairs, was covered against the evening's light rain by a tarred pull-on. A piece of canvas sailcloth prepared with coats of lamp-black, linseed oil and tar, each ingredient imparting good waterproofing qualities onto this commonly used, multi-purpose cover. The tarred pull-on was an item that all Wherrymen kept in their boat, which they used to protect themselves or their passengers from the vagaries of wind and rain. Watermen had old Capt. Vernon to thank for developing the waterproofing mixture for canvas, when he had invented his 'Grog Coat' for the navy. Since then, men working on water had eagerly taken up the recipe, and used it to great effect against the elements. The mixture was now widely used by the ships of the Navy and by the sailors of the merchant fleet; it had proved a great innovation in the protection of both men and equipment, from the costly effects of continual wetting and drying out.

Apart from the irritating feeling that had bothered him all day of some impending incident, Edwin was quite comfortable in his warm, mini climate of damp, clammy, cloth, his senses lulled by the gentle movement of the boat, the soft sounds of the water about him, and the all-pervading smell of the river, it was the odour of tarred rope, intermixed with the indefinable aroma of the London Thames. The tide was just past high water, as usual on the top of the flood; there was also a slight tang of brine in the pungent night air, salt brought up by the tide from the sea to this, its brackish inland limit. As he sat drowsily in his wherry, half mindedly watching the night's drizzle slowly forming itself into a water drip on the hard brim of his bonnet, the other half of his mind was drifting off elsewhere to more interesting thoughts. He distantly heard the bridge-watch call out the London time.

"The hour is ten by the grace of God, all is well, all is well See to your hearth and secure your locks, it's ten of the clock and all is well".
Edwin did not know the date of the month by the church calendar, his life being ruled more by the lunar cycle of tides, but he knew it was Friday.

There was only one more day of work before he could rest on the Lord's Day. This Sabbath was the day when watermen did not work at their pulling trade for fear of the wrath of the Church.

If caught by one of the Guild Beadles even cleaning your vessel on the Sabbath without special dispensation, the fines and penalties inflicted by the Watermen's Company for breaking the Sabbath rules would be severe. Anyway, Edwin enjoyed his day off, even if he lost income. It was a chance to spend time with Mary his sweetheart, his true love, the one whom he hoped to marry some day if she would have him. He had arranged to take her for a long walk on this coming Sunday, they were to visit an old friend in the village of Penge, a few miles south of the City. He hoped the outing might provide the opportunity for him to profess his feelings to her, and perhaps if luck was with him, even get a favourable response. He hoped it would prove so, for he knew that he loved her truly, and wanted her for his life's partner. He smiled to himself with pleasure at the thought of how his life with Mary would be. He would build a comfortable home for her, a small house in that grassy green place near the Greenwich marshes, which he had admired immediately when he first saw it. He had found the place during a walk along the high ground, which ran near to the old King's Deer Park. He was excited at the image in his mind of their modest home together. It would be just far enough away from the menacing bustle of the City, but comfortably near enough to the various plying stairs he used with his father. He would be content indeed if he could achieve it, but first he had to wait for the right opportunity to persuade the maid.

By the glow from the flickering torches high up on the bridge, and the light from the spluttering wands of the waiting wherrymen, Edwin gazed about him through half closed eyes. He fidgeted a little in his seat, he wanted his thoughts to wander back to consider his situation, and the plans he was making for his life ahead, but the strange uneasy feeling of expectancy that he had awoken with that morning, was still plaguing his mind. Had he forgotten something important? Was it something that he had promised to do that had slipped his mind? Was he supposed to meet with someone? Had he forgotten the arrangement? The feeling had played at the back of his mind all day. Annoyed at his inability to identify the feeling, he snuggled himself more comfortably on the hard wooden thwart of the boat's passenger seat, pulling his face down deeper into the warm inner collar of his thick coat. His eyes had now grown accustomed to the gloom and were now wandering contentedly over the boat, Anna his wherry, or to be accurate, only half his, the other half belonging to his father.

Anna was strictly built to the standard measurements set by the Watermen's Guild. A standard of length, breath and type, that had been agreed by the court many years before, as being the best to suit the trade of the Thames Wherrymen. He enjoyed looking along Anna's lines; he took an owner's pride in her equipment; her neatly coiled manila mooring ropes, the thinner catch lines, the carefully stowed copper candle lamp, the oak bailing pot, and the neatly tied bundle of cleaning gear. She was a sound boat, well built of sweet-cherry planking on an oak keel and ribs. Like her sisters in the trade, she had the wide middle section, typical of all Thames wherries. A design that had developed over centuries, well suited for carrying the citizens of London about their business. Her keel was slightly curved up at each end, a design modification that allowed watermen to bring their wherries gently alongside a causeway, there to lie evenly on the crushed chalk of the berth. As the passengers stood and moved forward to disembark, their weight would tip the vessel slightly down onto the front curve of the keel, there to hold steady as if part of the land itself. When embarking passengers, the opposite occurred, the boat would hold steady until the passengers had moved aft and were seated, their weight now pushing down the keel curve at the after end, thus allowing the vessel to tip down by the stern, and up in the bow, and to float free of the berth. This small adjustment in design enabled the Wherryman to paddle the boat gently backwards out into open water. It was a clever see-saw movement that made life much easier for the oarsman; who did not have to leave his rowing position, to push the vessel out into the river. Wherries were graceful boats to handle, their ancient Viking design, made them good carriers and fast through the water. The Crossback's Anna had all these qualities.

Edwin was particularly proud of the wagers his father had won in Anna, which were depicted on the brightly painted backboard of the passenger seat. Any prospective passengers faced with a choice of boats plying from a causeway, would see this information, and gain reassurance of a boat and the wherryman's prowess. Some watermen, having gained the support of a rich gaming-man from the City, made an extra living from competing in the many races organized by the betting fraternity of London. Prizes of coin, elaborate coats with badges of silver, even new wherries were offered as prizes for some of the races. Edwin remembered as a child, the excitement in the house when his father came home with winnings, they would eat high on the haunch for a month, and the house would be merry with pride. He hoped that now he was a licensed Freeman, he might find a supporter to enter him for wagers; someday he might win a race, and record it on Anna's backboard alongside his Father's achievements. As his eyes wandered along the Anna's gunwale, he noticed that a small crack had appeared in the timber of the starboard oarlock.

He must keep a watchful eye on that, this part of a pulling boat took a lot of punishment, it was often the first piece to give out, and before it got any worse, he should ask old Johnson the Shipwright to make up a new lock, just to be on the safe side. The Anna must not lose her wherry licence over such a small thing, or he would surely answer to his father.

Edwin's thoughts turned lazily to his father, the man among all men he most admired. The man who was his mentor and his guide, who had steered him through his apprenticeship and had helped him achieve his goal in life, to be a wherryman, his trade that for the most part he enjoyed. This achievement had meant attending the Guild's overseers, taking an oral examination before the Court of rulers before he could gain his freedom, and a licence to work as a wherryman.

He remembered well that day at Watermen's Hall, it had been a long wait with the other apprentices and their Masters, all of them standing nervously on the winding stone stairs leading up to the Court Room. At last Edwin and his father were summoned into the ornately decorated room, with its high ceiling and portrait encrusted walls. They entered with some trepidation when they were bidden, and as instructed by a beadle, stood before the large oak table, arranged a little off centre of the room. On the other side of this great oaken sea of a paper-strewn timber were seated nine old men. Some were in casual conversation; others were sucking on long clay pipes, while yet others were engrossed in the papers spread out before them. These were 'The Rulers' and 'Overseers' of the Company of Watermen and Lightermen of the River Thames. The Guild that had recently been enlarged from its watermen's origins, and now included the associated trade of Lightening-men, the ship-lighteners and carriers of goods. The grey haired, tallow skinned old men seated in front of Edwin made up the Examining Court of the Watermen's Guild.

The room had eventually fallen silent. Edwin could feel the cold, rheumy old eyes looking him over. The senior Ruler seated in the great chair at the centre, on the opposite side of the table, was a small, hungry looking man; he had thinning grey hair and bulging, watery, eyes. The Ruler cleared his throat loudly and sucked on his lower lip, which by its purple colour and plump size, looked as if it was often so used. Then looking up angrily from his papers, which had obviously not furnished the information he needed, he glared across the table at the Clerk to the Court, and in an alarmingly high-pitched, rattling voice, he snapped.
"Clerk! What is the family name of this apprentice?" There was an embarrassed silence while papers were rustled, and enquiring glances directed at the flustered Clerk. Edwin was suddenly startled to hear his father's voice from next to him say.
"Crossback Sir". The old man in the great chair was startled by the bold voice, and looked aggressively at Alfred. For a moment, Edwin thought that his father would be rebuked for daring to speak. The old man seemed about to say something, but then changed his mind; deciding that he was satisfied to gain the information from any source.
"Proceed then, proceed, " he ordered, writing the name on his papers and directing a penetrating look in the direction of the Clerk. Another of the examiners then asked Alfred as the boy's Master, if his apprentice was fully

prepared for examination. On answering in the affirmative, Alfred was told to stand off, and not to interrupt the proceedings.
The still abashed Clerk, motioned Alfred to stand at the back of the room. Alfred retreated, and stood under the painting of 'The justice of Salomon', hung no doubt in this position to give inspiration to the members of the Court, for it was also here, in the three sided dock, that fines and punishments were administered by the Company's Rulers.

Edwin was now completely alone, he felt like one of the river's numerous cormorants, standing on the top of an exposed timber pile at high water. It was as if he was perched on a small island, surrounded by a treacherous sea, but unlike the bird he could not fly away, he must face the ordeal and do his best to answer the questions about to be fired at him. He felt a strange light-headedness; his legs were trembling under him, he was aware of the smell of old men and tobacco. The room fell silent, then after a short pause, the questions began. They came slowly at first but as he answered in a strong clear voice, they began to be launched at him from all angles. It was a nerve-racking experience to be sure, he could feel his knees quivering, but he kept control of his emotions and held his voice steady. To his relief the questions seemed not as difficult as he had expected. He answered them all, even the ones of which he was not fully certain. He gave his answers with confidence just as his father had taught him.
"Don't show them your true feelings" Alfred had advised him. "Men with power will always attack the weak. Show them you are not afraid, and you will gain their respect".

The questions concerned in-depth, local knowledge, of all parts of the Thames from the Watermen's Stone near Gravesend in the East, to the Boundary Stone at Windsor to the West. He was asked about the tide regime and the moon's phases, about knots and ropes, about different types of, ships, boats, and barges and told to name their parts, and about the bridge and its dangers. He was asked about the vessels visiting the port, their differing sizes, their equipment, and its uses. He was told to describe an imaginary journey in a wherry, from Wapping to Hampton Court, describing the places he was passing and the condition of the tide and its effect on his vessel, about the landwater, the way it set into the river's bends, and about the dangers of the water's flow around fixed objects. He was stopped several times while speaking, and given an emergency or unforeseen occurrence, and asked how he would deal with it. He was questioned about respect of passengers, particularly about courtesy to superiors, and he was questioned about the fares that wherrymen were allowed to charge for various passages. Did he know how many wherries were working the Thames? Edwin thought he remembered being told that there were some 3000, but was not sure of the exact number, and said so. He was asked about the winter frosts, and how to protect his boat from being crushed or drowned by the ice, particularly when it was melting into the springtime ice-flows. Could he name the recently built plying place at

Chelsea and describe its exact position? Finally he was asked the name of the Lord Mayor, Edwin thought for a moment.
"Sir Richard Horse" said Edwin with confidence. The Court looked at each other; some of them were quietly smiling. Edwin could not tell if his answer was correct or not, from looking at these old, time-warn, faces, but he knew it was a name something like that. He stood still, head up with a straight back, silently daring them to ask him more.

Surprisingly, the examination had not been too difficult for Edwin, for he had been taught well by his father. They had spent many hours together, talking about the river and the City, discussing the wharves and creeks, considering the tides and their effects. Edwin liked it when his father told him about their trade and the history behind it all. It was a fascinating story to which he could listen for hours. The best times he could remember from his earliest memories, were those evenings, sitting with his mother and small sister in the warm, dark, kitchen of their home, while his father, holding a jug of ale cupped in one hand, his clay pipe smouldering in the other, with the flickering light from the hearth throwing shadows across his face, when he would tell them in a deep, nut-brown, voice, the story of his river, a story which started even before the time of the old Romans. It was a fascinating saga of water, the universal carrier. It was the story about man's inventiveness, of his discovery of how best to use this wonderful element, how boats were developed from the very first floating tree-trunks cut down by ancient man, how ways of propelling themselves along the rivers must have evolved. It was a story about man's fight to prevail against nature's unpredictability, her frosts, storms and hot suns   .

The story he told was also about the Crossback family and the Seymours on his wife's side, and about many famous rivermen. It was also the story of the growth of the City and its port. It told about the greed of some and the goodness of others, about jealousy, and destructive envy, about the unquenchable desire of a few to dominate others, it was also about good, and the kindness that could be found in people. However, it was mostly the story of London, and its wonderful river thoroughfare, about the City's neglect and abuse of this God given, water highway, a favourite topic of his father, and one that the family quickly moved him on from.

In the past the Watermen of the Thames had been unlicensed, free to trade within the unwritten rules of their fraternity. They had then used a verity of types of boat, with only a partial control exorcised over them by the City. The City fathers tried to set the fares, and to control the plying places, but this was difficult because of the great distances covered by the trade. Watermen could roam from Windsor in the West, to the river's estuary in the East. The vast majority of this area, through which the river flowed, was therefore outside of the City's control. In some parts, it passed through wild open, wind-swept lands, of little interest to the rich merchants of the City. The river however, flowed through them all without fear or favour, and so the Watermen followed, forming themselves into specialised groups by local knowledge and expertise. The only possible control of such a disparate trade could come from the Monarch, or Parliament itself, both of whom had little inclination to involve themselves in the menial service provided by the watermen of the river.

From the times of the infamous King Henry Tudor however, the extraordinary growth of the Port and the City, meant that ships must wait for long periods for a berth to unload their cargo. The seamen being put off pay on reaching port, tried to work the ship's boats as watermen, to make a living. This practice had made it necessary to introduce stricter rules and regulations, for the safe working of the river through the London area, and to exert a better control over the trade. This had eventually been accomplished by a series of Parliamentary Acts.

The King put up the first Bill of 1514. It was no more than a form of tax on the watermen for committing misdemeanours, the fines being treble the fare charged, which was then split between the King and the aggrieved citizens. However, the fines were easy to avoid by the offending watermen. They could not easily be identified or caught by the King's men, when dispersed into such a large area. It soon became more and more obvious that it was necessary to introduce proper controlling regulations, It was therefore deemed by subsequent Bills and Acts, that all Watermen working as Wherrymen must be licensed, and to show their competence, must carry a numbered Licence-Plate worn on the upper part of their left arm. It was also deemed necessary that an experienced Master Waterman would train a boy in the trade through an Apprenticeship system. All these regulations were to be controlled by a new City Company, a Guild of Watermen.

This organisation would have the power through its Court to inflict fines and punishments on any who did not observe the rules. Edwin of course had never known the old ways of working, but he often wondered if those times of freedom, were not better than the often corrupt and unfair circumstances of his time. He, as part of this apprenticeship system must answer to his master, also to the Guild and their Court.
Edwin and his father had spent many hours rowing together in the Anna, his father all the time teaching and explaining, with the young Edwin listening and learning. Sometimes for the young man, with the hot blood of youth racing through his veins, it would become tedious to go over the same things time and time again, he had often wanted to be out with his friends. He felt envious of the boastful stories they told of their conquests with the tavern maids, of their drinking bouts, and the fights, in which they of course always triumphed. He knew that it was mostly lies and youthful bravado; nevertheless, it made his heart leap to hear them talk, he wished that he could go out more often with his comrades, to have lively adventures, and interesting tales to tell.

Edwin's father was too wise to forbid his son absolutely to follow the boisterous crowd of his contemporaries. His way was more subtle, he sought a restrained control, he would sit and talk with his son, asking searching questions of him after each of Edwin's excursions out with his mates. Alfred always wanted to ask why, and discuss the reason Edwin had gone to a particular inn, and try to discover the reason behind Edwin's restlessness. For the young man these feelings could not be explained, which of course Alfred knew. He had himself, during his younger years, been through the same immature turmoil, and he had his own secret exploits stored away in his memories .

Now as a father, he knew his job was to act as a balance to Edwin's natural feelings, and the vigilant life he himself followed, but he also knew that he was no match for those youthful hormones raging within his young son's body. He would just make the jaunts a little more awkward, and try to explain the rational way of dealing with life's temptations. Edwin must anyway learn for himself, he had to discover, strive, and thereby gain maturity.

Edwin had not learned to read or write. It seemed to him unnecessary to spend time and effort in achieving the skill, an accomplishment for which he had no need. However, he was proud of the fact that his father had mastered the art, and fully expected that one day he might insist that Edwin put his mind to the task. One day he broached the subject. "Father should I learn the art of reading, will it be of use to me?" They were sitting in the Anna waiting for a fare, his father carefully considered his answer, he looked intently at his son .

"I have found it a useful ability on a few occasions, but I could have lived happily enough without the knowledge. My father thought it wise that I learn the skills, but he warned me that it was a spiky talent with two sharp edges. I have found to my cost that his words were true. I told you many times, Edwin, not to trust the words men use, but instead to observe their deeds and actions, as this would betray their true intention. I can tell you that there is as much falsehood in writing as there is in speech, words once written cannot easily be disputed, whereas talk can be argued over." Edwin was confused, his father seemed to be advising him that it would be a wasted effort. Alfred saw the confusion in the boy's face .

"I never want to put you in danger my son, and I fear that reading and writing can do just that to the unwary. Reading in particular is hazardous, because it can control a man's mind. It is true that it can lead to much useful knowledge, but when emanating from an evil source it can also be used to corrupt the reader, sending him to fight the battles of others. Writing also is dangerous, because you will be judged by what you set down in words, even if you no longer agree with what you first wrote. A scribe is always a target, and must be adept at defending his written views." Edwin nodded his understanding, relieved that he was not expected to make the great effort of learning his letters .

"However, son, when you feel you can deal with the responsibility that accompanies such learning, then I am willing to teach you."
"No father, I heed your warning and I think I am better without such dangerous knowledge."

<======>

On that day in the Courtroom, after some thirty minutes or so of the rough tongued questioning by the grey beards of the Watermen's Court, Edwin and his father were at last ordered to leave the room, and to wait outside. As they stood again at the top of the stairs, under the searching gazes of the other apprentices and their Masters, still anxiously waiting their turn, Edwin could feel the tension in his father, he knew it would look bad on him if his son did not pass for his freedom. After what seemed an eternity but was in fact only a few minutes the Clerk to the Court came out. "Crossback, you are called back before the Court." Edwin and his father re-entered the room and stood anxiously in front of the table, looking at the time worn faces of the Court members for some hint of their decision. There was much mumbling and shuffling of papers, then after an agonising pause, "Well, young Crossback" said the senior Ruler in his high voice, leaning back in his large uncomfortable looking chair   .
"You have passed this examination for watermanship, and I am pleased to tell you that your licence to work as a Wherryman will be issued this day," then looking closely into Edwin's face, now shining with elation. He announced in his screechy voice   .
"You are hereby granted freedom from your Master and are now your own man, but take note, your father has taught you your trade well, you are now freed from his instruction. However, you are still young and should maintain respect. Continue to listen to his advice, I can see that he has your best interests at heart, you understand me I think?"   .
"Aye, Sir" said Edwin, not sure if this was advice or a rebuke.
"You are both dismissed," said the Ruler, returning his red-rimed eyes to the papers in front of him.

Edwin's feelings were now an even stranger mixture than before. He was of course relieved and overjoyed, to have come through the ordeal with relative ease, but he felt somehow numb, the world about him seemed to have slowed down, it was as if he was walking in a dream as they left the room, all about him seemed to be moving at a snail's pace, his head was light, and strangely he could not properly feel his hands or feet. They descended the stairs to complete the necessary paperwork, which would take place in the senior Clerk's office downstairs. Once there, standing before the high wooden desk, they both began to relax, Edwin found that he had to choke back a giggle, a mood of gaiety was invading him, mentally he had to take better control of his feelings.

They now had to go through the usual checking procedure, a task that involved the Clerk matching the two halves of the original indentures, a paper which had been divided at their 'binding ceremony' those many years before. At this ritual the document had been torn into two halves, to be given half to the apprentice, and half to the Master, which they must keep as proof of their dual commitment. The one to teach and the other to learn by apprenticeship, Edwin could still remember the wording of the document, which his father had read to him on many occasions.

THIS INDENTURE.

Hereby witnessed, That Edwin George Crossback, Son of Alfred James Crossback, of the Parish of St. Alphage, Greenwich, in the County of Kent, doth put himself, Apprentice to Alfred James Crossback, of the Parish aforesaid. In the County aforesaid, as an apprentice to the trade of.

WATERMAN AND WHERRYMAN of THE RIVER THAMES.
To learn his art, and with him after the manner of an Apprentice, to dwell and serve upon the River Thames, from the day of the date here of until the full end and term of seven years from thence next following, to be fully complete and ended, during which term, the said apprentice his said Master faithfully shall serve. His secrets keep, his lawful commandments everywhere gladly do. He shall do no damage to his said Master, nor see it be done by others but he in his power, shall let or forthwith give warning to his said Master of the same; He shall not waste the goods of the said Master, nor lend them unlawfully to any. He shall not commit fornication, nor contract matrimony within the said term. He shall not play cards, dice, tables or any unlawful games, whereby his said Master may have any loss. With his own goods or others during the said term, without licence of his said Master, he shall not buy nor sell; He shall not haunt taverns or playhouses, nor absent himself from his Masters service day, or night, unlawfully, but in all things as a faithful Apprentice he shall behave himself towards his said master, during the said term. And the said Master in consideration of services of his said apprentice in the same art which he useth by the best means that he can, shall teach and instruct or cause to be taught and instructed finding unto the said apprentice meat, drink, apparel lodging and all other necessaries, according to the custom of the City of London.

In witness whereof, the parties above named to these indentures.*

(*Extracted from History of the Watermen's Company by Henry Humpherus)

"Make your marks here and here" said the Clerk, turning the great book of records around to face them, pointing his finger next to the two imprinted red wax seals. Edwin's father took the proffered quill and dipping it into the silver, dolphin shaped, inkstand, wrote his full name in a purposeful manner. He was one of only a few watermen who had mastered the art of writing. Mr. John Shooter, the Company Clerk, had once been a working Waterman himself. It had been his ability to read and write, acquired with such difficulty, which had propelled him into the high station of 'Clerk to the Watermen's Guild'. He gave Alfred a quizzical look wondering why this man with such an ability, had not progressed further up life's ladder. He shrugged at this unnecessary thought, and pushed the book across the desk to Edwin who made a cross where the Clerk had indicated.

The pair had eventually left the Hall building, declining several offers to join the other newly freed apprentices and their Masters for a celebration drink in the local inn, where they would be joined by others who wanted to drown their sorrows, who would try to explain why they had not passed. Edwin knew this would be a long night of fun and laughter for the newly licensed young men.

Once again he felt that pang of loss at not joining in with the others in their moment of triumph. His father had ignored the unfriendly looks, and had quickly led the way from the Hall, pausing only at the door to drop a coin into the bowl of the 'Door Widow' and take a draft of the ale she offered. Then passing the goblet to Edwin for him to take a drink, he inquired of the pale-faced woman
"Good day Marion, Are you well?"
"Yes Alfred, we are managing well enough by God's good grace", replied the woman, Alfred touched her on the shoulder with a friendly concerned pat, and the men passed out through the doorway into the bright, sunlit, cobbled street outside.

Looking back at the 'Door Widow' sitting with her jugs of ale on the Hall step, Edwin thought he recognised her, she was the wife of a Lightening man he had known quite well. These men of the cargo carrying trade, were now known as Lightermen, and had only latterly, after many years of petitioning, been allowed to join the Watermen's Guild. This woman's husband had been recently killed, when the cargo in his barge had collapsed on him. Edwin had heard the story of what happened from his friend Kenneth. It had occurred at a wharf in the Pool, while the man was down inside the hold of his lightening barge fastening the pull-on sheets, used to protect the bags from rain and spray. Edwin knew that his widow would only be allowed to occupy the steps of the Hall, to collect money in the Bachelors Bowl, until she was displaced by another riverman's wife, more recently widowed, and therefore decreed to be in more need. This new widow would be allowed to take her place at the Hall door, and collect the shillings of the men passing their freedom, or those attending the various courts of the Watermen's Company, in return for a draft of ale. He hoped that Marion would have the concession for long enough to build up much-needed funds, to support herself and her children. She and her family were anyway in for a hard and bitter life ahead thought Edwin.

Alfred had taken his son over the bridge to the little secluded, oak beamed, tavern called the Rose Garden, where he was well known and where he often arranged a meeting to discuss business with a fellow wherryman or others of the trade, or to settle up accounts. Alfred indicated a quiet table, and they sat down. He called for ale to be brought to them, and when the

jugs of the good, clean liquid were placed in front of them, Alfred raised his pot in a salute to his son .
"Well done lad, I flew my hopes high for you this day, and you did not disappoint, you sailed through with all colours flying." They were seated in a warm corner of the tavern, and Alfred was grinning from ear to ear with pride in his son. Edwin, a little embarrassed and self-conscious, did not know what to say, then looking his father straight in the eye, he remembered the Ruler's warning .
"Father now that I'm free from you as your apprentice, I want you to know that I remain your obedient son," said Edwin looking very serious.
"Well, I will hold you to that the next time I find you out in a mischief," laughed Alfred .
"Now son, enough of the formalities, I have important business to discuss, now that you have your working licence". Edwin looked into his father's face for some clue of what he was about to say .
"Son I offer you this day, a half-share in my Wherry the Anna," Edwin was shocked, and showed it on his open-mouthed face .
"What say you to that?" smiled Alfred. Edwin was elated, fumbling over the words to convey his gratitude. It would normally have taken a young Waterman many years to obtain even a small share of a licensed Wherry, yet here was his chance to build his future life .
"Father` you do me great honour. How can I ever repay you?"
"You will repay me well enough I am sure, with hard work and effort," said Alfred pleased with his son's response.

Alfred went on to tell him that he must pass over one third of all he earned when plying for hire, excluding any drink-geld he might be given, this he could keep and would be counted outside of the reckoning. That he would also be responsible for looking after the Anna and for all her repairs. Alfred continued, saying that he was planning to have a new wherry built soon, therefore Edwin could look forward to having full use of the Anna six days of each and every week in the near future, and that he would have the chance to buy out the other half of the boat if trade went well. Edwin was delighted, this opportunity would be so much better than having to work half day at the Wood Borers Wharf, or as a second hand rowing in Randan for small return.

It was a very good and fair deal, and a chance for Edwin to plan his future. With money saved he would be able to marry Mary, and start to raise a family, his blood surged at the very thought of his life ahead.
Edwin hurriedly blocked himself from thinking of such things, he knew it was tempting fate to plan too far ahead, as with rowing, a man must take each stroke one at a time, in life only one move before the next was a sound rule, just as his father had so often advised. He must be watchful for life's dangers, even more so now that he had a life-plan, and a course set for the way ahead. Until he could find exemption, he must at all costs avoid the Queen's Navy-men and their ruthless Press Gangs, that scurvy lot who preyed on Seamen and Thames Watermen alike, were now his sworn

enemy, he must certainly avoid being taken away for years of service at sea.

He did of course, know of a few watermen who had prospered in the Navy from the luck of winning prize money, and others who had volunteered, and claimed that they had enjoyed the life of adventure at sea. On the other hand, he knew of others who were lost, or had come back maimed. His friends had told him of men who had left home one morning, never to be seen again, a letter, if lucky, being sent to the man's family from a ship's Captain, informing them that he had been killed in some great sea battle. Sometimes the letter would say that the man had died from disease or from a flogging, or was lost overboard in a storm .
Even the new system being initiated by their Guild, aimed at organising the numbers of Watermen required for the Navy, with a promise of a small payment to be made to the men's family, was inadequate, agreed by all to be unacceptable to the licensed men of the river. The small sum, if ever paid, would be little compensation indeed to a wife and family for the loss of their breadwinner. Sensible watermen therefore, would go to any lengths to avoid the Press, and now Edwin's mind was made up, he would keep a good look-out for himself and Mary's future.

The two men sat in the corner of the tavern and drank the good clean ale. They called for victuals and were served cold pork, with green pickles, and fresh warm bread. Alfred looked across at his son as they ate. "Tastes good ah lad? Everything will taste and smell good over the next few weeks, it is a good feeling to be free of your apprenticeship."
"I feel as if I am outside of my body," said Edwin, trying to come to terms with the happenings of the day. This morning he had been a worried and anxious boy, by the afternoon he was a full Freeman with a licence, and a half share in his father's wherry .
"I must get back inside myself and take stock of my new situation, I can't yet appreciate these new feelings, I must also tell my friends of my good fortune this day." .
"Take it steady lad, reef in your topsails a touch, these are good trade winds blowing for you now, but you will need to keep a sharp watch for the next storm, set your rigging for a cautious passage".

Edwin and his father were deep in their cups by the time they returned home that evening. Nell had her own way of finding out the outcome of Edwin's examination, she and Agnes knew that all had gone well with the day. The girls had spent the time preparing a special meal for the occasion, they were excited and happy to see the men walking arm-in-arm down the street, doffing their bonnets to the neighbours as they passed.
"Like two little boys out for a lark," Nell commented smiling to herself. It was not often that her husband let down his hair in this manner, even a little.
"He will feel all the better for some laughter, and so will the lad", she said to her joyful daughter .
"Well done you great bag of bones" cried Agnes as she hugged her brother,

CHAPTER FOUR
Choice and Consequence

Edwin, sitting in the Anna at Old Swan stairs, was quietly recalling the pleasure of that day when he had passed for his freedom and had finally gained his wherryman's licence. He could remember the tangled feelings of pride and gratitude that he had felt, feelings he had been unable to articulate. He had wanted to embrace Mary, Agnes and his mother altogether, and hug them until they squealed with pleasure. He had wanted to throw an arm over his father's shoulder and thank him for all his help and forbearance. He had wanted to slap Tom on the back, and tell him what he felt inside, but like a silly young child, he had just stood there with a wide grin on his face, saying nothing for fear that his emotions would leak out through his eyes in unmanly tears .
He hoped his family had understood his inability to express those deep feelings welling up inside him, somehow he felt sure that they had. Women had a great advantage over men in this respect, they could cry and spill out the words to explain their feelings without any shame of their emotions, but a man must keep his to himself. What his father had said that day, even if spoken through a thick mist of ale and wine, had been true. All of them had shared in the happiness of his day, just as he had shared in their good fortune when one or other of them had managed to clear one of life's hurdles. He was indeed fortunate to have such a good and supportive family.

As Edwin sat in the boat, protected from the evening's rain by his waterproof cover, enjoying these cosy thoughts, he was suddenly aware again of the strange feeling that had bothered him all day. Was he meant to attend a meeting with someone later? It was a feeling that something out of the ordinary was to happen; still unable to identify it, he shrugged the feeling off. His train of thought now broken, Edwin looked about him at the other five men, all five were ahead of him waiting for businesses this night, so it could be a long wait. Had he made the right decision, should he change his mind? He still had enough time to shoot down through the bridge arch into the Pool, and wait below the bridge for a fare. No, somehow he felt that he was in the right place for this night's events, whatever they might be. He sat back and resigned himself to what might lie ahead.

Relaxed again, his thoughts wandered back to the start of this day He had woken at first light in the low-ceilinged sleeping room of his father's house. Climbing out from his cot, he stretched his back, his arms reaching up between the rafters of the roof. He had first relieved himself into the night-pot, then turning to the small chest of shelves next to his bed, he filled the pewter bowl from the water jug left out by his mother and had washed his face in the cold water, then using a soft cloth held tight over his finger, he carefully used it to clean his teeth. He was proud that he had only lost two of his pegs so far in his twenty-one years. Most men of his age had many

planting a wet kiss on his cheek
"What is all this fuss about"? Cried Nell, "anyone would think my son might have not succeeded, I knew better, now come the pair of you and eat, before you fall down in the street and shame me in front of my friends." Some of the neighbours were gathering about the two men, slapping Edwin on the back, and congratulating Alfred on his son's good fortune. Nell ushered her men inside, where the table was creaking under the weight of a great assortment of food and drink
"Edwin! Edwin well done, well done indeed, my heart is overflowing with the joy of it all." It was Mary; she had waited inside to give the family the first contact with Edwin, and to be out of sight of the neighbours. Edwin found himself hugged about the neck and almost fell over from the unexpected weight
" Come about Mary, stand off, let me sit before I fall" cried Edwin, laughing at his own unsteadiness
"Well done Edwin, you have indeed excelled this day." It was Tom, Agnes's young man, who had also been invited to share in the celebration with the family.

A loud bang from the table made them all turn to see the cause. It was Alfred, now seated at the table's head, and holding the pewter pot, which he had just used to strike the timber and gain their attention. "This day my son has come of age in his trade," he said in a serious but blurred voice
"He is now a freeman, and I do him honour in that. I speak for all here in congratulating him". Alfred's words were slurred but all were listening. He went on
"However, he should remember before his head grows too big for his bonnet, that there are those here that have nursed him through illness, have bandaged his cuts, and have cleaned up after him for many years. They have fed and clothed him, have witnessed his temper and his bad moods, have comforted him when he was down, and supported him when he was up", then looking sternly at his son
"Edwin, mark what I say. You are fortunate indeed, not because of your achievement this day but because you are loved", he paused for full effect.
"I tell you in truth young man, that love is the most precious thing in your life, remember these words my boy, always return the gift of love and you will not flounder."
Then looking at the serious faces around him, he decided to break the spell and brightening the moment, he said with a smile.
"Now come you all and enjoy this table the women have prepared for us, let us all think on Edwin's and our own good fortune". He raised his tankard inviting the others to do the same
"To Edwin, a new Thames Waterman".

more black gaps on show than he, when smiling their tombstone grins. Then, using a wooden scraper, he reached deep down to the back of his tongue, to thoroughly scrape away the white phlegm that had accumulated overnight. This was a trick he had learnt from Mary; it was a good way to stop his breath from smelling. He dried himself off on the woollen cloth hanging from the back of the door and checked the result of his ablutions in the polished pewter mirror-disk, nailed above the chest. It was as he had looked at his reflection that he first felt the uneasy sensation of expectancy, a feeling that had plagued him all day, had he pledged to do something or to meet with someone. It was a strange mood that he still could not identify.

It was Friday, only two more days of working and it would be the Sabbath, the day when he would go for his long walk with Mary, he planned to make it a special day out and his heart skipped at the thought of being with her. Quickly finishing dressing he came down from the attic room into the cosy, warm, damp-smelling kitchen, pushing his way through the moist newly washed clothes, hanging up to dry on cod-lines stretched across the room. He gave his mother a tickling hug from behind; she was in the process of stirring something delicious in the large pot, hanging over the kitchen hearth fire. He knew she liked to be squeezed in that affectionate way, even if she made a great fuss each time he did it .
"Be off with you and about your own business you great oaf," she yelped in mock annoyance, wriggling out of his grasp .
"Stop bothering your poor old mother on her busiest day of the week"; she chided him, taking a playful swipe at his head with the long handled spoon she was using, but deliberately missing .
"Oh you poor old woman", said Edwin sarcastically .
"You say that every day. It stands to reason that only one day can be the busiest of the week, now which day is it?" Nell did not answer, not following the logic of his question. He sat down at the heavily scrubbed table, with its exposed uneven grain. She brought him the food she had prepared to break his fast and he ate the good feast of oatmeal, cheese, and hot, spiced milk.
Nell was as full of life as ever and chatted to Edwin as he ate. She talked about the latest tale she had heard, concerning a local stonemason. This man had taken two friends of hers to the very top of the dome of the new St Paul's Cathedral, where he had been working on the construction of the building for many years. Her friends had told her that this man knew Mr. Wren the great architect of the building and the designer of many other churches in the City .

The stonemason had shown the two women the views across the City from the top of the dome, and the wonderful new structures being built for the wealthy to the West. They could see more clearly from this height, the huge Palaces and white stone buildings, with the great paved squares that shone bright in the sunshine. They had been able to see the Thames meandering away to the East, as far as the eye could manage .
"Oh! How much I wish to see that view, and to visit the gallery of whispers up inside that great dome," she said with feeling .

"I must go to look, even if many people do not like the building. They say it is too Papist for a Protestant church, but I would like to see it for myself". Then looking pleadingly at her son
"Edwin, do you not know someone who could take me up there? Your father won't go near the place." Then resolved in her determination, she argued. "God has allowed it to be built; therefore he must want people to visit."
"I will ask my friends for you and see if we can arrange something," promised Edwin, wondering whom he could possibly ask

Edwin's mother Nell was a tall, well-built woman, of two and forty years. Her raven black hair was now showing silver strands at her temples, where she kept it tied back from her square, good-looking face. She had dark brown, almost black eyes, roofed over by thick black eyebrows; she had a good strong nose and plump ever-smiling lips, complementing her handsome features. Nell was well liked by most, and friendly to all. A trait that her husband Alfred often warned her about, but her good nature and quick, natural wit, won over even his careful and sometimes sour disposition.

Nell was happy that Edwin, unlike most young men of his age, still lived at home and had not yet married. She knew he could be secretive and sometimes went off with undesirable friends, but she loved him, faults and all. She was in fact very pleased with her small family of only two children. "Others may have many more children, but mine are quality if not quantity," she would say with her merry laugh.
Edwin was the eldest at twenty-one and her daughter Agnes four years the younger, Agnes, like Edwin, was also still living at home, but likely to marry soon with Tom, a young Cooper she had been walking out with for the last two years.
Nell knew that she must encourage Agnes to marry; time was now passing for the girl. Although she hated the thought, she must let her go to start her own family. Nell was content with her life, her husband Alfred, and the two healthy children. Her family of four was tiny compared with the average of the times, but she knew that she had been very lucky. In spite of the fact that both births had been difficult, she had come through those ordeals to these happier times. She knew that she might easily have lost them both during the pregnancy, and that her life could have taken a very different course. She could have become a resentful childless old woman, like Wild Bridget who lived at the next house in the street.

Bridget was a bad lot in the opinion of most, a small, bent over, wizened old woman, with a little pinched, tight-lipped face. Her long, sharp, pointed nose seemed to Edwin the perfect warning of her interfering nature. She had thin, stooped, shoulders, which gave her the look of a bottle. She also had a high-pitched irritating voice. Bridget was always making trouble, usually by starting vicious rumours, this gossip mostly involved those about her, particularly the ones she did not like, which in truth included most people she knew. She interfered in the affairs of her neighbours and caused

planting a wet kiss on his cheek
"What is all this fuss about"? Cried Nell, "anyone would think my son might have not succeeded, I knew better, now come the pair of you and eat, before you fall down in the street and shame me in front of my friends." Some of the neighbours were gathering about the two men, slapping Edwin on the back, and congratulating Alfred on his son's good fortune. Nell ushered her men inside, where the table was creaking under the weight of a great assortment of food and drink
"Edwin! Edwin well done, well done indeed, my heart is overflowing with the joy of it all." It was Mary; she had waited inside to give the family the first contact with Edwin, and to be out of sight of the neighbours. Edwin found himself hugged about the neck and almost fell over from the unexpected weight
" Come about Mary, stand off, let me sit before I fall" cried Edwin, laughing at his own unsteadiness
"Well done Edwin, you have indeed excelled this day." It was Tom, Agnes's young man, who had also been invited to share in the celebration with the family.

A loud bang from the table made them all turn to see the cause. It was Alfred, now seated at the table's head, and holding the pewter pot, which he had just used to strike the timber and gain their attention.
"This day my son has come of age in his trade," he said in a serious but blurred voice
"He is now a freeman, and I do him honour in that. I speak for all here in congratulating him". Alfred's words were slurred but all were listening. He went on
"However, he should remember before his head grows too big for his bonnet, that there are those here that have nursed him through illness, have bandaged his cuts, and have cleaned up after him for many years. They have fed and clothed him, have witnessed his temper and his bad moods, have comforted him when he was down, and supported him when he was up", then looking sternly at his son
"Edwin, mark what I say. You are fortunate indeed, not because of your achievement this day but because you are loved", he paused for full effect.
"I tell you in truth young man, that love is the most precious thing in your life, remember these words my boy, always return the gift of love and you will not flounder."
Then looking at the serious faces around him, he decided to break the spell and brightening the moment, he said with a smile.
"Now come you all and enjoy this table the women have prepared for us, let us all think on Edwin's and our own good fortune". He raised his tankard inviting the others to do the same
"To Edwin, a new Thames Waterman".

CHAPTER FOUR
Choice and Consequence

Edwin, sitting in the Anna at Old Swan stairs, was quietly recalling the pleasure of that day when he had passed for his freedom and had finally gained his wherryman's licence. He could remember the tangled feelings of pride and gratitude that he had felt, feelings he had been unable to articulate. He had wanted to embrace Mary, Agnes and his mother altogether, and hug them until they squealed with pleasure. He had wanted to throw an arm over his father's shoulder and thank him for all his help and forbearance. He had wanted to slap Tom on the back, and tell him what he felt inside, but like a silly young child, he had just stood there with a wide grin on his face, saying nothing for fear that his emotions would leak out through his eyes in unmanly tears

He hoped his family had understood his inability to express those deep feelings welling up inside him, somehow he felt sure that they had. Women had a great advantage over men in this respect, they could cry and spill out the words to explain their feelings without any shame of their emotions, but a man must keep his to himself. What his father had said that day, even if spoken through a thick mist of ale and wine, had been true. All of them had shared in the happiness of his day, just as he had shared in their good fortune when one or other of them had managed to clear one of life's hurdles. He was indeed fortunate to have such a good and supportive family.

As Edwin sat in the boat, protected from the evening's rain by his waterproof cover, enjoying these cosy thoughts, he was suddenly aware again of the strange feeling that had bothered him all day. Was he meant to attend a meeting with someone later? It was a feeling that something out of the ordinary was to happen; still unable to identify it, he shrugged the feeling off. His train of thought now broken, Edwin looked about him at the other five men, all five were ahead of him waiting for businesses this night, so it could be a long wait. Had he made the right decision, should he change his mind? He still had enough time to shoot down through the bridge arch into the Pool, and wait below the bridge for a fare. No, somehow he felt that he was in the right place for this night's events, whatever they might be. He sat back and resigned himself to what might lie ahead.

Relaxed again, his thoughts wandered back to the start of this day He had woken at first light in the low-ceilinged sleeping room of his father's house. Climbing out from his cot, he stretched his back, his arms reaching up between the rafters of the roof. He had first relieved himself into the night-pot, then turning to the small chest of shelves next to his bed, he filled the pewter bowl from the water jug left out by his mother and had washed his face in the cold water, then using a soft cloth held tight over his finger, he carefully used it to clean his teeth. He was proud that he had only lost two of his pegs so far in his twenty-one years. Most men of his age had many more black gaps on show than he, when smiling their tombstone grins. Then, using a wooden scraper, he reached deep down to the back of his tongue, to thoroughly scrape away the white phlegm that had accumulated overnight. This was a trick he had learnt from Mary; it was a good way to stop his breath from smelling. He dried himself off on the woollen cloth hanging from the back of the door and checked the result of his ablutions in the polished pewter mirror-disk, nailed above the chest. It was as he had looked at his reflection that he first felt the uneasy sensation of expectancy, a feeling that had plagued him all day, had he pledged to do something or to meet with someone. It was a strange mood that he still could not identify.

It was Friday, only two more days of working and it would be the Sabbath, the day when he would go for his long walk with Mary, he planned to make it a special day out and his heart skipped at the thought of being with her. Quickly finishing dressing he came down from the attic room into the cosy, warm, damp-smelling kitchen, pushing his way through the moist newly washed clothes, hanging up to dry on cod-lines stretched across the room. He gave his mother a tickling hug from behind; she was in the process of stirring something delicious in the large pot, hanging over the kitchen hearth fire. He knew she liked to be squeezed in that affectionate way, even if she made a great fuss each time he did it .
"Be off with you and about your own business you great oaf," she yelped in mock annoyance, wriggling out of his grasp .
"Stop bothering your poor old mother on her busiest day of the week"; she chided him, taking a playful swipe at his head with the long handled spoon she was using, but deliberately missing .
"Oh you poor old woman", said Edwin sarcastically .
"You say that every day. It stands to reason that only one day can be the busiest of the week, now which day is it?" Nell did not answer, not following the logic of his question. He sat down at the heavily scrubbed table, with its exposed uneven grain. She brought him the food she had prepared to break his fast and he ate the good feast of oatmeal, cheese, and hot, spiced milk.
Nell was as full of life as ever and chatted to Edwin as he ate. She talked about the latest tale she had heard, concerning a local stonemason. This man had taken two friends of hers to the very top of the dome of the new St Paul's Cathedral, where he had been working on the construction of the building for many years. Her friends had told her that this man knew Mr. Wren the great architect of the building and the designer of many other churches in the City .

The stonemason had shown the two women the views across the City from the top of the dome, and the wonderful new structures being built for the wealthy to the West. They could see more clearly from this height, the huge Palaces and white stone buildings, with the great paved squares that shone bright in the sunshine. They had been able to see the Thames meandering away to the East, as far as the eye could manage .
"Oh! How much I wish to see that view, and to visit the gallery of whispers up inside that great dome," she said with feeling .

"I must go to look, even if many people do not like the building. They say it is too Papist for a Protestant church, but I would like to see it for myself".
Then looking pleadingly at her son
"Edwin, do you not know someone who could take me up there? Your father won't go near the place." Then resolved in her determination, she argued. "God has allowed it to be built; therefore he must want people to visit."
"I will ask my friends for you and see if we can arrange something," promised Edwin, wondering whom he could possibly ask

Edwin's mother Nell was a tall, well-built woman, of two and forty years. Her raven black hair was now showing silver strands at her temples, where she kept it tied back from her square, good-looking face. She had dark brown, almost black eyes, roofed over by thick black eyebrows; she had a good strong nose and plump ever-smiling lips, complementing her handsome features. Nell was well liked by most, and friendly to all. A trait that her husband Alfred often warned her about, but her good nature and quick, natural wit, won over even his careful and sometimes sour disposition.

Nell was happy that Edwin, unlike most young men of his age, still lived at home and had not yet married. She knew he could be secretive and sometimes went off with undesirable friends, but she loved him, faults and all. She was in fact very pleased with her small family of only two children. "Others may have many more children, but mine are quality if not quantity," she would say with her merry laugh.
Edwin was the eldest at twenty-one and her daughter Agnes four years the younger, Agnes, like Edwin, was also still living at home, but likely to marry soon with Tom, a young Cooper she had been walking out with for the last two years.
Nell knew that she must encourage Agnes to marry; time was now passing for the girl. Although she hated the thought, she must let her go to start her own family. Nell was content with her life, her husband Alfred, and the two healthy children. Her family of four was tiny compared with the average of the times, but she knew that she had been very lucky. In spite of the fact that both births had been difficult, she had come through those ordeals to these happier times. She knew that she might easily have lost them both during the pregnancy, and that her life could have taken a very different course. She could have become a resentful childless old woman, like Wild Bridget who lived at the next house in the street.

Bridget was a bad lot in the opinion of most, a small, bent over, wizened old woman, with a little pinched, tight-lipped face. Her long, sharp, pointed nose seemed to Edwin the perfect warning of her interfering nature. She had thin, stooped, shoulders, which gave her the look of a bottle. She also had a high-pitched irritating voice. Bridget was always making trouble, usually by starting vicious rumours, this gossip mostly involved those about her, particularly the ones she did not like, which in truth included most people she knew. She interfered in the affairs of her neighbours and caused

many a clash between a man and his wife. She would do this by telling falsehoods or by simple innuendo. All this unhappiness for the need of some children was the opinion of Nell. Fortunately for her, Nell Crossback was one of the few people that Bridget accepted, this rare predilection due mainly because Nell was a good listener. She seemed to have an understanding of this strange and wicked woman, being always ready to help or intervene in her good-humoured and happy way whenever one of Bridget's indiscretions caused an upheaval. She was even able to make Bridget laugh on occasion, if you could call that fighting-cock cackle, a laugh.
"Bridget is not all bad," she would say in defence of the old hag, only to be reminded by those about her of a dozen accounts of the woman's wickedness.
"Mind you are not tarred with her brush," Alfred would warn her. "When she gets her just rewards for her evilness," the 'Witch-catcher General' might think you to be her peculiar .
"They still burn witches in the countryside you know." He would say, frightening his wife with the very thought. This usually led to a time of quiet reflection by Nell; she hated the thought of Bridget perhaps being a Godless witch.

After the birth of Agnes, Nell and Alfred had hoped for more children as a foil against their old age, or the very probable loss of at least one child through illness or accident. There were also the many other dangers surrounding the population of London in the 18th Century, and a large family was a comfort against ill fortune. However, no other issue had emerged for Nell, but she was very content that both her offspring had survived and had grown strong. She was grateful that she had not had to face the trauma of loss in her small family, she was indeed pleased with her lot in life. Alfred, her husband, was a good man, sober, and a good provider. Although the passion of their early years of marriage had waned, they were still 'in love' in a gentle caring sort of way. Their relationship had developed into true friendship, with a deep understanding of each other's ways. They communicated their feelings for each other in these middle years of marriage, in the way that contented couples do, by a touch on the shoulder, or a squeeze of the hand .
The children were good and healthy, well taught by Alfred's example, although Edwin could be independently minded and Agnes a little secretive, they had both benefited from their father's ability to explain life's complexities. He had taught them how to exist in this treacherous City. Nell's only worry was that, in this hazardous world, even with Alfred's steady hand on the tiller, her happy little family vessel could change course in the blink of an eye .

Having bid his mother farewell, with a promise to give a message to his father, to bring some fresh fish from the market on his way home.
Edwin had made his way to the Pipe Borers Wharf, a little down river from the bridge, on the way to Southwark. It was here that he had a morning's

employment, before taking over the Anna from his father. The work involved helping to prepare lengths of fresh cut tree trunks for water-pipe making. It meant trimming off the bark and lifting the heavy trunks into the boring frames, in readiness for the trunk-borers to work their sorcery. These men would turn each length of fresh cut tree into a section of water pipe, shaped narrow at one end and opened up at the other, so that each length could fit closely into the other. These sections were to be joined and laid under the streets of the City, to bring water to the important buildings and houses of the rich. The pipe-boring men were truly specialists. From an early age as apprentices, they had learnt the secrets of using the long boring tools, designed to take out the soft centre core of the newly cut tree trunks. Their arms and shoulders were developed out of all proportion to the rest of their frame, by the continuous use of their upper body muscles. Tall or short in stature, they all looked as if from the same wide-shouldered mould. They were a burly brotherhood, a good and friendly lot, strong but gentle giants, with a ready humour and a continuous light-hearted banter. Their trade however, had the black cloud of change hanging over it; new ways of making water pipes were progressing, and now slowly taking over, making their trade redundant. Like many other trades of the City, their demise was near at hand. Edwin enjoyed his few hours working with these men each morning before his own work started. His pulling trade would only begin when he took over the Anna from his father.

After his morning with the pipe-borers, he had found his father waiting with the Anna as arranged, just before mid-day at Temple Stairs. It was past high water and the tide was falling. Alfred was in the process of cleaning out the boat. All of the seat benches, the burden boards and the backboard were laid out on the causeway, and he was scrubbing the boat's inner planks with river water and a stiff brush. Edwin helped to finish up the task and gave his father the message about the fish. They chatted a little about the day's work, and how much had been taken in fares. Edwin then bade his father farewell, and on his advice, pulled away to make his way up to the Lambeth Plying Stairs. He was often lucky there in getting short fares at this time of day, usually a clergyman or church official, wanting to go across to Westminster or down to the old City; these men were wealthy and would sometimes give the boatman drink-geld, if they got them to their destination quickly. Lambeth however, was an uncomfortable area for the Crossbacks to ply from, Edwin knew he would need to keep the usual sharp lookout for any of the Chambers family, while plying from the Lambeth stairs.

<=======>

The Chambers were a family of journeymen watermen, not much better than criminals in the opinion of the Crossbacks. They mainly worked out of Richmond and thankfully did not often trade down as far as the City. However, when they did, they liked to ply from Lambeth. This family perpetuated a strong animosity towards Edwin and his father, in response to an old and somewhat obscure occurrence. It was in fact a feud between the two families, fuelled by misplaced pride and damaged dignity on both sides.

The enmity between the families bordered on hatred. It was in fact due to a long-past quarrel between Edwin's grandfather Edward, and the then head of the Chambers family Joseph, both of whom were now long dead. The original cause of the feud was over the rescue of a Western Barge adrift on the tideway. This vessel was one of the many large craft, so named because they worked west of London Bridge, voyaging into the upper reaches of the river, some even finding their way as far as the town of Oxford to the West. This particular barge had been laden with a valuable cargo of coal. The event, which had happened those many years before, should have been long since forgotten by the later members of both families, but the assumed affront was still remembered passionately by both sides.

The barge had been spotted adrift in mid-river with no crew aboard, trading along with the tide towards the old bridge. Both watermen, having seen the dangers attending such a heavy craft adrift and unattended, had rowed out to rescue the vessel in their respective wherries, the idea being to board her for a salvage claim. Old man Chambers had been most aggrieved that Edward had reached the vessel at the same time as himself, for he had intended to perform this rescue alone. After the Western Barge was pulled to the shore, moored up and made secure, there appeared other members of the Chambers family, all very agitated and annoyed with Edward because of his intervention. Edwin's grandfather had slowly realised that it had been one of the Chambers family who, knowing that the crew were ashore, had set the barge adrift in the first place.

The whole event was obviously a planned trick, to obtain money from the owners of the barge under false pretences. The incident would also have certainly meant the master of the barge losing his livelihood, for not having moored the vessel safely, and for his perceived lack of diligence in leaving his barge unattended. Knowing this, Edward had considered the rouse grossly unfair on the barge's master, and had refused to claim salvage. He only wanted a small payment from the master for working the barge to the shore, mooring her up, and making her safe, which he considered to be fair in the circumstances. He was determined not to be involved in the Chambers fraudulent plot to claim salvage for the cargo from the owner. This decision had meant that old Joseph could not peruse his own claim, and so would have to forgo his own demand for salvage.

The two men had come to blows over the matter, a confrontation that had led to Edward being stabbed with Joseph's blade, and Josef being thrown into the river, as part of the brawl. In all the years since this happened the two families had been at a state of war with each other, even though the original participants were now both dead and buried. Over the years the war between the families had settled into preserving their own version of the event and adopting a simmering stand-off position. The successive watermen from each family had established an alert wariness of each other and now tried as much as possible to keep to their respective parts of the river.

<========>

That day at Lambeth stairs, Edwin had been lucky. There being no sign of any of the Chambers or any other wherrymen, he had plied alone from the landing. He noticed that most wherrymen seemed to be busy working between Westminster and the City. He wondered if this meant that something political was going on. There was a rumour that the House of Commons were to debate the withdrawal of Parliament's protection from the impressment of their own servants. He knew this would affect some of the journeymen working from the Westminster stairs and the household watermen of Parliament, who operated from Black-rod stairs. None of this affected Edwin, however. Neither he, nor his father, plied from Westminster.
"That den of gasbags and users" as his father called the Parliament. "Those wasters of money, hard earned by others." This was his strongly held view, but only ever confided to his son, as it was dangerous to say such things in the hearing of others. Edwin decided to stick to his plan to stay at Lambeth, It had proved profitable, he had picked up some lucrative work, short trips mostly, within the area, ferrying back and forth across the river.
Later on in the day, Simon the local Wherryman for Lambeth joined him; he was just returned from a long pull to Barnes village and back. Edwin liked Simon well; this young man worked a wherry for a wealthy Waterman, Mr. Foully, and was not bothered that Edwin was working the Lambeth stairs.
"I have already earned enough for the day to satisfy old Foully." He grinned his good-natured grin. As the pair talked and joked together, they heard a cry drifting over the river wall .
"Pies, fresh pies, good meat and fresh crusts, come buy my pies."
"Ho! Ho! The pie man," said Simon licking his lips ,
"Shall we have some?" he asked, looking expectantly at Edwin .
"To be sure, I could eat a crusty rat or two," replied Edwin .
"Go up while I watch the craft, you can catch us some victuals." Without another word, Simon leapt ashore and ran up the causeway before the pie man moved on his way .
"Ahoy there you seller of empty crusts, how much are you asking for your cat-meat pies today?" The pie man laughed, he knew Simon well and was used to his waterman's rude banter .
"It is not dog or cat today, young father Thames, it is best, plump, baby, fresh from the Church mortuary." .
"That will be an improvement then", said Simon with his usual cheeky grin. "I hope you removed the hair and fingernails, last time they got between my teeth." Simon took two of the plump pies from the man's tray, and with a few more words of gentle insult; he paid the pie-man and returned to the

wherries. The two young men had eaten together, sitting contentedly in Simon's boat, it was a good meal, the pies were fresh and meaty, adding to the contentment of shared company of good comrades. They washed the food down with ale from their flasks, the world about seemed full with gratification.

The rest of the late afternoon was quiet. Edwin sat and talked with Simon until his friend had been called away by a fare wanting to be taken over to a landing in the river Fleet. The two wherrymen exchanged some more light-hearted repartee with each other, before Simon pulled away across the water towards the mouth of the Thames tributary. Edwin, now alone again, decided to paddle over to the Old Church stairs of St. Paul's, listening out for a call for 'Oars', but the late afternoon, now overcast, had not proved profitable. Edwin took a turn at a mooring pile away from, and out of sight of the stairs, and spent this quiet time paring his fingernails with his knife. He looked down at his hands, he seemed to need to perform this chore more often than others, did his nails grow more quickly than other men's? He did not see them trimming their nails as often as he did. Then with still no sign of trade, he set about replacing some of the small metal pins he kept fixed under the edge of the Anna's passenger seat   .

These pins were Edwin's secret weapon against Roaring Boys and Runners, those passengers who would run off, when the boat came alongside the landing of their destination, thus avoiding paying for their trip. It was the Wherrymen's lot to have to accept this bitter practice and loss of earnings, for even if he chased and caught these naughty villains, a Wherryman was very likely to come off the worse, he might well have his licence number reported to one of the Guild Beadles for insolence or violent action, and be summoned to the Watermen's Hall. Being reported would usually lead to being brought before the Court, which rarely found in favour of the Wherryman. The Rulers mostly took the view that the word of a passenger was true and honest, and that of their own journeyman fickle, no matter that the boatman's hard work had not been rewarded; he would be fined, or worse, for his unhappy encounter. The Court usually took the part of the passenger, taking the view that they were of superior class to the roughly spoken Waterman, who would usually come off the poorer for his efforts at justice.

Edwin had developed what he thought a good strategy for dealing with 'Roaring Boys', a ruse that only his father knew about. He had positioned some small sharp pins, hammered halfway into the timber, just under the front edge of the passenger thwart. His trick was to distract his passenger with conversation and compliments as they were boarding his boat and settling themselves down onto the seat. While they were so diverted, he used the toe of his boot to ensnare the cloak, or some other part of the clothing onto these sharp prongs. He now did this as a matter of routine to all young men, for he had learnt that you could not tell which ones you could trust completely, and which ones might run. It was usually the men of

younger years who committed the tedious offence, particularly the drunken 'roaring boys' from Bankside .
"Runners and drunkards are the curse of the Wherrymen's employ", complained many in the trade.
With Edwin's trick, on reaching the requested destination and being paid, he would deftly use his foot to release the cloth, and all would be well. With so much practice he could now perform this manoeuvre in the blink of an eye. If however he was seen, he would make a great point of saving the cloth, by leaning forward to dramatically unhook the garment, saying he had noticed that it was caught on a splinter of wood. This was usually done to the great pleasure of the passenger, who saw a saving to himself of the cost of repairs to his garment. If Edwin did have a runner, or if there was a dispute over payment, then the damage to the man's apparel was a good revenge.
With this device, he had already acquired a good cloak, and on other occasions had been given drink-geld by passengers who praised him for his observance, and for freeing the clothing, seeing it as an act of attentive kindness on the part of their boatman. Edwin's father however, would not use this ruse. To him it seemed devious, bordering on dishonesty. He preferred to hold his boat off from the landing while being paid, even though this annoyed his passengers, by showing his distrust of them, He was prepared to upset the good with the bad alike, to be sure of payment, to him all passengers were the necessary evil of his trade; he neither liked nor disliked them, and he did not much care if they liked his method of working. This was his way of trading, and it served him well enough.

Earlier that evening in the gathering gloom, as the high tide wearily filled the corners and crevices of the river's banks. Edwin had been hailed for 'oars' from Blackfriars stairs. He rowed over and came alongside the causeway. It was two young men wanting to be taken across to Bankside. These young blades, fashionably dressed and with their purses no doubt full, were fidgety with excitement as they stepped aboard the Anna, settling themselves down on the passenger thwart and leaning nonchalantly back against the boat's backboard, talking agitatedly together, their eyes bright with anticipation of the night ahead .
"Boatman, take us to the Stews at Bankside, as quickly as you like," they ordered with expectant relish. Like all watermen, Edwin did not like being called 'boatman', it grated on his pride. Watermen working the licensed wherries of the Thames were 'wherrymen' and should be so called.

Edwin could see that he would probably have no trouble being paid for his efforts by these two proud young cockerels, at least for taking them over to the Stews. From their conversation, it would seem that they were out for the first time, without the escort of an older and wiser mentor to guide and protect them. However, he used his toe to snare the expensive looking cloak of one young man onto the teeth of his 'cloth trap', just in case. He hoped however, that he would not be unlucky enough to be called to bring them back in the early hours. By then, this naive pair would certainly have been picked clean. Their garments would be dishevelled and their purses considerably lightened, if not emptied, or stolen. They would have drunk their fill, glutted on food, shouted abuse at the players from the auditorium of some playhouse. Or if in a bloodthirsty mood, would have watched a dog or cock fight, in one of the several bloodstained fighting pits of the area. To finish their pleasures, they would probably have spent as much time as could be afforded with the 'Ladies of the Night' who with the help of their shadowy protectors would have taken all that could be squeezed from these two young innocents abroad.

By the time they wanted to go back to Blackfriars, these ungallant young blades in their dashing clothes, would have turned into drunken, peevish 'Roaring Boys' looking for free oars to take them back to safety across the water. Even if they had any money left over from the food, wine, pimps and prostitutes, they would suddenly feel the need to be frugal with their rests and to retain what little was left. The poor boatman wanting to be paid his fare would be the first to be financially punished for the night's overspending.

These two were the exact types who would most likely try to run off to avoid paying. If the Wherryman insisted too fearlessly on his fare, or perhaps remonstrated too strongly with these, his supposed superiors, then the next day he would probably be reported to a Beadle, or perhaps directly to The Hall. His licence number would be given by these two, by now forthright and sober citizens, now accompanied by a father or perhaps an uncle, insisting on the chastisement of the uncouth boatman who had insulted them.

"Avoid the Roaring Boys" was the secret rule among Watermen.

It was therefore sensible to avoid plying for hire at night, from the stairs and causeways of Bankside.

After disembarking the two young men at the Stews of Southwark, Edwin did not feel inclined to wait around at that time of the late evening, for any troublesome passengers. He therefore pulled his boat away from the landing, and stood off from the causeway. Backing his blades in the seemingly exhausted water of the high tide, he stopped his boat and thought of what best to do, to gain a profitable fare. He considered the consequences of the various options he had before him. As he pondered his best chance of gaining a good fare, he heard shouts of merriment and laughter drifting over the river wall; it seemed that the night's revelry in the Stews had started.

To stay here and wait for a fare was one option that he would not take, he would probably do better plying over on the City side, or perhaps further up river. Another choice was to shoot the bridge early, and wait for a fare at the stairs below in the Pool. He might get a ship's captain or officer wanting to return to their vessel further down river. This would take Edwin in the direction he would prefer to go. However, it would also mean he would miss the chance of a passenger from above the bridge for at least another hour or so. Those passengers would take boat from the nearest stairs, knowing that they could run through the bridge early, in safety. Such passengers would only walk down to stairs in the Pool, when the fall of water through the bridge made it hazardous to shoot through the arches. Anyway, ship's Captains and crew were a mean lot in general, always arguing about the fare and taking forever to open the strings of their purses.

Edwin knew that a meeting of the great Guilds had been held that day, and also that the Fishmonger's Court had been sitting. By going to Old Swan stairs therefore, he might be lucky and get one of the Livery Company officials wanting to go home downstream, anxious to take boat before the tide drop through the bridge became too dangerous. Those 'fat-bellies' would try to avoid walking down to the Pool stairs, reasoned Edwin. If he caught such a fare, it would also be a good result for Edwin. He could then moor up near to King stairs at Rotherhithe, where there was a place to lock away his gear, and go home for a late supper and some much needed sleep. He wondered what his mother would have left out for him. He began to imagine the smell of the food and his mouth started to water at the thought.

The tide had reached its zenith. It was now past high water, the flow was slowly turning from the full calm of high tide to the first movements of the ebb. Edwin could feel the movement through his feet as they rested on the boat's pulling stretcher. The vessel had seemed relaxed on the high water, as if taking a rest before the onset of the strong run of the ebb, started to push against her planking, now she seemed to be stiffening, making ready for six hours of ebb against her timber sides. Yes, he decided his best choice was to pull across to 'Old Swan' stairs and see if he could get a late working City Gentleman wishing to go down river, perhaps to Rotherhithe, where many of the City's Clerks lived.

Edwin also knew, as did most of the local wherrymen, of a little scandal that involved the Clerk to The Fishmongers' Company, whose Hall stood next to the bridge on the City side. This official had a regular liaison with a lady acquaintance, who kept a small Inn down-river at Rotherhithe. Although a quiet man who kept his own council, it had become obvious to the watermen plying from Swan Lane that this man had a secret. Intrigued by his many trips down river, and by his surreptitious manner when taking oars, also the way his speech faltered and sputtered when drawn into conversation about his destination .
Eventually he had been followed by one of the apprentices, and his furtive meetings uncovered. It was amusing to them all that he had no idea that his clandestine liaison was known to so many, this made it the more enjoyable when called upon to take this devotee to his lover. Perhaps thought Edwin, after a hard day's work attending to matters of the Court, the Fishmonger's Clerk might well decide to take boat and visit his lady, perhaps wishing to relive the tensions of the day, by playing among her under-linen for an hour or two. Yes, thought Edwin ,
"I will pull over to Old Swan Stairs and try my luck there".

Edwin knew the ebb would soon pick up speed. He was not yet near enough to the bridge to read the stones, through the gathering gloom, but he knew that the water level must be slowly falling, little by little, decreasing enough for him to be able to read the stones of the bridge arch. He rowed at a steady pace, knowing that he would soon be close enough to be able to see the building courses of the arched walls of the bridge locks. Even in the gloom of the night, he would be able to read the tide drop, and know the rate of fall of the water level, as the ebb tide uncovered more of the bridge cofferdams. This information would tell him the speed of the flow and how long before shooting the bridge would become dangerous .

There had been a great deal of rain over the past weeks and a lot of land water was running out to reinforce the ebb tide. At low water the difference between the height of the water up river of the bridge to that below, could be as much as five feet. The weight of the trapped water rushing down through the bridge arches, caused a strong weir effect, making it very dangerous for a boat of any size, but particularly a small wherry, to pass through.

It was a brave Waterman who would attempt this drop at the low water in his small boat, and an even braver passenger. Most fares wishing to travel further down river, would disembark at stairs above the bridge, walk down to the Pool, and there call for fresh 'oars' from a landing below the bridge rapids.

As he pulled across the river towards the City, Edwin pondered the consequences of his decision and the various choices he had considered for gaining a profitable fare. What if he had stayed at Bankside? He might have been lucky, had he decided to stay. He might perhaps have picked up a kind old gentleman who had prospered well at the tables, who with his purse full, might have been in such a good mood that he would reward his waterman well, for taking him home safely to his grand house in the west-end.

Edwin knew this was unlikely, but then stranger things had happened. What if he had chosen to shoot the bridge, maybe he would have found a good paying fare wishing to be taken from the Pool to Rotherhithe, giving him an early night into the bargain? What if he had rowed up-river to try for business at Westminster? It was a curious truth that he would never know what the outcome would have been of any of these choices, but Swan Stairs was the action he had decided on. He wondered as he rowed if the consequence of his decision had anything to do with the strange feeling that had plagued him all day. Edwin did not know of course that his decision that night to go to Swan Stairs, would be historically significant, or that his efforts would play a significant part in the night's drama ahead, or that he would remain anonymous and that his name would never be remembered

<========>

Edwin moved himself into a more comfortable position on the hard timber thwart of the Anna, as the tide played with her, making her nudge gently at the causeway of Old Swan. He looked about him in the gloom. For a few moments he watched the flickering shadows cast by the lighted torches of the wherrymen, their eerie shapes dancing on the river wall, and on the stonework of the first bridge arch. He looked up as the lights played on the great blades of the large water wheel, housed in this first opening of the London's old bridge, a great timber wheel, shinning with water, which was rotated by the strength of the tide flow, this movement in turn pumped water from the river into a huge storage tower.

The river water being of dubious quality was only used for supplying the poorer parts of the City. It had its uses, but most people did not trust the discoloured liquid for drinking, they preferred to drink ale or beer. Edwin's gaze wondered back to the men about him, all five were silently sitting in their wherries, covered against the drizzle, deep in their own thoughts. He knew them all, Kenneth his best friend, with whom he had just been talking, the ever active Ebenezer, the crafty Taylor brothers, and of course scary old James. Like these others waiting at Old Swan, he knew that all the recent ebb tides had been stronger than average. Like him, the others would try to avoid taking a fare, that would mean rowing upriver against the wind and the first hours of the strong ebb. They would all be looking for fares going down river. Such fares needed to be soon, it was now well after high water. The wherrymen would leave it as late as possible, but then, if they had no passengers going the way they wanted, they would probably decide to shoot the bridge and wait below the bridge for an outward bound fare.

The Rulers of their Guild frowned upon the practice of watermen working the tides to their advantage. Citizens often complained at the seeming lack of common sense among the watermen, for stupidly not putting boats in places where, and at the times when, they were needed. Leaving too many wherries plying for trade from the same place and none to be had going in the direction they required, wherrymen were often reported for refusing to take a passenger to his chosen destination, even though their license required them to take any fare to the landing place he desired, whatever the direction of the tide . But the watermen had good reason to work the way they did; they knew the easiest way to make their living, which was of course with the minimum amount of effort. Passengers, for all their professed knowledge of how the boatmen should organise their trade, did not understand the men's reasoning. When faced with these accusations from passengers, the watermen would wink to each other, or look blank and roll their eyes in mock incomprehension of the point being made, but out of ear-shot, they would say among themselves   .
"The passengers may claim to know a better way to organise our trade, but they do not have to do the pulling."

Chapter Five

Kenneth and the bawdy Tavern

Earlier that evening as Edwin had approached the landing at Old Swan Stairs, he had been able to see through the gloom of the approaching night that five other wherries were already there ahead of him. They were all loosely moored by their catch-lines to the causeway piling, waiting their turn to take on passengers. The five wherrymen were each seated in their boat, and at this distance looked like dark, glistening, pyramids, floating eerily on the surface of the water, each man covered against the miserable drizzling rain by his tarred pull-on. Edwin knew that they were all deep in their private thoughts. As he approached, Edwin gave a short intricate whistle and listened for the replies. This call was his recognition pipe. Like all Watermen he had his own distinctive call signal, by which he could be recognised at a considerable distance. Even in the dark Edwin's whistle although similar to his father's, could still be recognised as unique to him, but somehow it was also part of his family and recognised by his comrades as such. It was the same with his father's whistle, which in turn had been similar to his father's. The strong family bond among the river people even applied to the pipe-calls they used to contact each other .

In answer to Edwin's whistle, there came from out of the darkness a mixture of return calls. He recognised them all immediately, he knew then who was ahead of him waiting at the causeway, and began to evaluate the personality of each of them. While he digested this information and considered the men waiting ahead of him, and how they might affect his plans for an early finish this night, a gruff voice came echoing out from the causeway across the oily surface of the water .
"What brings the river to us now? Yet another river-rat come to take our fares and the bread from our children's mouths", accused the hard-edged voice emanating from the gloom by the river wall .
"It is the slimly tongued one," said another harsh voice .
"The newly freed apprentice, one of the nose-in-the-air Crossbacks". Edwin recognised both voices; the first belonged to Christopher and the other to Robin; they were the quarrelsome Taylor brothers.

The Taylor family normally plied from stairs in the mouth of the Fleet River, but were also known to trade occasionally from other plying stairs in the City. The Taylors usually had a lot to say for themselves always in their coarse, aggressive, tone, but Edwin knew well the reputation of this argumentative family, and that they were in fact quite harmless. "A pot without contents always makes the loudest noise", his father had once said of them .
"What's this?" called back Edwin in an equally unpleasant tone. "Do we have a flat calm tonight? That the timid Taylors have come out from

their stinking stream into the big dangerous river?" His father had trained him well; he had schooled him to react immediately with a cutting or aggressive quip, whenever he felt that he was being challenged or provoked. He had also taught him that the best way of doing this, was to have a riposte in mind, something prepared about each person that he knew, which would deter any further remarks from the attacker, for fear of further insult or mockery. The more hurtful the retort the less likely that a reply would come back from the attacker, and therefore an end to the matter.

Edwin had spent many hours thinking up these biting, offensive, oral arrows, which he kept in a mental quiver ready to be loaded and fired at a moment's notice; he had become quite well known for them. What his father had told him had proved to be very true. Everyone had an unfortunate characteristic, or some small deformity, perhaps a large nose, or the lack of hair, which although of no consequence to others, played at the back of their own mind throughout their life. This personal peculiarity, which could be physical, or part of the person's character, usually only needed be hinted at, or if the situation required, could be declared in venomous detail. The level of counter attack could thereby be increased or decreased as necessary .

The type of rough banter now taking place between the watermen at Old Swan, was typical of the rivermen's normal rude discourse with each other. To the outsider it sounded abusive, even dangerously antagonistic. The rough tongue of the rivermen against their fellows, was well known to Londoners using the wherries of the river as their means of travel. This repartee could be amusing, but sometimes could also be intimidating. For the working wherrymen it was a long used weapon, a well-proven method of control over their passengers .

Rivermen, albeit of lowly station and therefore not allowed to offend their passengers with insults or bad language, could spit out violent abuse at each other, they could shout things that they dare not say to their customers. Any passenger witnessing this show of verbal aggression between the men, would take careful note, after all, as a passenger, he would be alone with this man on the small island of his wooden boat, in what was very much the Waterman's environment, they were literally in the hands of these men, indeed in potentially 'dangerous waters'. On overhearing the rough talk of the wherryman, they would be aware that the man was capable of violent speech, and probably just as capable of violent behaviour, judged by the offensive language used on each other. They would certainly think twice before crossing him. In fact, 'rough talk' was very effective when used by Wherrymen in their watery profession.

As he had glided into the causeway, Edwin's boat had fetched gently alongside one of the waiting wherries. It was the boat of Kenneth, 'Merry Ken', as he was known to his friends. Edwin had been pleased to hear his friend's pipe-call as he had approached the stairs. This was a happy man and although some three years older than Edwin, he was a true mate, always prepared to help and ever ready with a new story, a joke, or perhaps just with an example of his humorous view on the world. To him life was full with curiosities and comedy, which he was extremely competent at mimicking and hilariously describing to any who would listen. Edwin liked Kenneth's way of seeing the world, his strange but quaint perspective on life made for some amusing adventures. To Edwin, his friend's happy attitude, was a balance to his own rather sombre and sometimes over-cautious manner.

Kenneth's happy approach toward his surroundings and his acceptance of his position in the world, came from his lack of ambition. He was not an overly intelligent man, he took what came his way with gaiety, not bothering to avoid any of the accompanying consequences, but cheerfully accepting whatever the outcome. He was always getting himself into scrapes, often with the wives or daughters of other men, but never with the womenfolk of men of the watermen's trade, these he considered sacrosanct. It must be said that many of his amorous encounters were not always his fault. He was a naturally generous man, tall and strong, his fair-haired boyish good looks, and happy personality made him attractive to most of the female sex. He did however, have his own strange sense of honour, even morality. Curiously, he would often choose the plainest Jane for his sexual affrays, and for this seeming lack of an appreciation of beauty his friends often chided him. He once told Edwin that he courted the comely looking maids, because he felt sorry for them and then with a wink." And they don't seem to be able to do enough to thank me for noticing them". His friends trusted him implicitly, they admired his highly developed sense of fair play and wonderful view of the absurdity of life, a trait that had on many occasions stopped an argument or a potential fight. He seemed never to lose his temper, and could always be relied upon to see the funny side of any situation.

Kenneth had leant across and deftly caught Edwin's catch line, then quickly making it fast around his own boat's thwart, he turned eagerly to his newly arrived mate .
"Did you hear the news about Great Bess?" he said in a low eager whisper. Edwin shook his head, as he carefully shipped his oars, keeping the wet spoons away from the passenger seat .
"No, what is happening?" he asked with eager interest.
"She is going to perform her candle trick again, this very Monday night at the Tavern, will you come with us to see the show again?" Edwin's heart leapt at the thought of a fun night at the 'Four Masted Ship'.
"Oh yes indeed, of course I will, are you sure that it's on? I will find a way to evade the old man's prying watch on me"; he said thinking excitedly of the last occasion.

This was news indeed; he was determined, to try to be there at the next performance of Bess's special show at the tavern, he must see it again. This time he would try to take keener observance of what happens. He knew that his father would be greatly disappointed, not to say angry, if he found out that his son had again ignored his warnings about the dangers of tavern-life, he was however determined to go. In truth his father would only be concerned for his son's safety, had he known of Edwin's plans. He had told Edwin many times of the dangers associated with Taverns, Alehouses, and Brothels, it was often in the shadowy walls outside these places, that footpads, thieves, and worst of all, the Navy's impressment gangs preyed on the seamen and rivermen. It was in these places that they set their wicked traps. But like all young men, Edwin and his friends thought themselves too clever to be caught. The excitement, the challenge of danger, and the overwhelming urge to be with his mates, would prove no match for a father's sober warnings.

Edwin remembered well the last time that he had gone with Kenneth and some of the others to 'The Four Master' the tavern owned by Great Bess. The building stood crouched in the shadows near to the Highway, which ran through Wapping. The other lads had been going there on and off for months, following up the numerous rumours, which were emanating cunningly from Bess herself. The gossip had been strong for months all over the Port, especially among the young watermen; an excitement had built up among them, all wanting to see Bess's famous, rare confrontation with the candle.

Bess was no innovator, all tavern owners tried to arrange events and entertainments to attract customers. Cock-fights, dogfights, bare-knuckle man fights, were among the many attractions at the Inns and Taverns of London, catering for the voyeur or the gaming man. The calibre of these diversions varied according to the geographical position of the venue. The nearer to the ships of the port, the rougher and more crude the spectacle would be. For men seeking more erotic entertainments, other taverns catered for their needs, employing voluptuous serving maids, whores, and harlots, to entice and satisfy these men and their desires. Other places specialised in good quality food and fine wines, catering for those of the population with a knowledgeable appetite and fresh coin in their purse.

A small group of tavern owners, of whom Bess was one, manipulated the minds of their customers by putting on extraordinary events. They would announce for months ahead that an astonishing event was planned to take place, finding excuse after excuse to delay or postpone the occasion, thereby keeping the expectation high. The more unusual, or more bizarre the event, the more it would attract patrons who were looking for a lift to the overwhelming tedium of their humdrum lives. The taverns of London were places of noise and merriment, places to sing bawdy songs, tell naughty jokes, and impart wonderfully exaggerated stories, embroidered to levels of pure fantasy. This was the background to Bess's tavern 'The four Master'.

<========>

For the twentieth time that evening, Fanny pulled back the threadbare curtain, which hung over the serving counter, and let her eyes search over the faces of the customers in the large smoky room. He was still not there; she snapped the curtain back into place with a quiet curse, and a little show of frustration. Where was he? she thought to herself, he had promised to come this evening, and it was now getting late with no sign of him. The tavern was filling up, she wondered if she could find a reason to reserve a table for Kenneth and his friends, but she knew from experience that such a thing would bring down the wrath of Bess on her. Fanny was worried, and her crooked little face showed it.

Fanny was a small thin girl, with straggly mouse-coloured hair, large, wide, rabbit like eyes, peering out over a small pointed nose, which roofed the thin tight lips of her slightly misshapen mouth. She knew that she was not beautiful, it was something she had always known. She also knew that her unfortunate gait compounded her unattractiveness. She could not help the fact, but she walked with her feet pointing outwards. When she was a young girl, her mother had tied her feet into the normal forward position for months on end, only releasing them when the pain caused Fanny to faint. It had all been to no avail. Do what she may, her walk always returned to that rolling crow-like saunter that made people laugh. The only man who had ever showed her kindness or any interest was her handsome, bold, Kenneth.

The other tavern girls, who were the antithesis of Fanny, could not believe it when he had first showed his preference for this runt of the pack. For them it was beyond understanding that such a handsome fellow should choose to offer his favours to the plainest among them. They would question her incessantly to try to gain her secret, deciding in the end, that her hold over this attractive young man must be witchcraft, they were convinced that she had passed a spell over him. All this talk and jealousy was above Fanny, she did not care what they said about her, she only knew that she was deeply in love, and that she would do anything for her handsome waterman. At first, she had thought that like all the others he was making fun of her, but then came that event, when he had proved to her his true feelings beyond any doubt in Fanny's mind.

She remembered the incident as if it were yesterday. The evening had started normally. Fanny had arrived at the tavern for her evening's work at the usual time, and Bess had put her to work emptying the night-soil pots, and spreading new straw over the damp patches of the flagstone floor. When she had completed this, she was sent to the galley behind the serving bar, to help clean and prepare the pewter plates and jugs for the night ahead. She was then sent to scrub down the tables in the tavern's main room. Kenneth had arrived early that evening. Fanny, being busy cleaning a corner table, had not noticed him arrive. Stealthily he crept over behind her, and gave her a playful slap on the bottom; in answer to which, , she turned with a whoop of pleasure and embraced him. After a few words of banter with his bright-eyed Fanny, Kenneth went to sit with friends at a table by the door. The group of young watermen showed all the signs of settling in for a long evening. Fanny was flushed with excitement and waddled about her duties distractedly, casting an occasional loving glance at his table.

On the other side of the room, seated on their own at a large table that could easily have accommodated more, were two sailors, both getting slowly deeper and deeper into their cups. These mariners were flushed with drink. The smaller of the two, was boasting about some exploit involving his skill with his knife, which he was waving about in a most threatening manner as his story unfolded, this animated, aggressive behaviour, being the reason that they had the table to themselves.

All seamen carried the wide bladed tool of their trade, usually in a sheath strapped to the side of their belt, together with a strong metal spike, which they used for splitting and splicing ship's ropes. Watermen also carried a similar tool of their trade, but because of the smaller sizes of the ropes and lines they worked with on the river's boats, their blades and spikes were much thinner and shorter than that of seamen. The watermen also preferred to keep their tools out of sight, tucked into the back of the belt. It was not profitable for them to display these frightening weapons, which might easily alarm their passengers. The second seaman was a giant of a man, tall and broad shouldered with arms the size of a normal man's legs. He had a cropped black beard and a flowing, tarred, pigtail. He seemed to be only half listening to the wiry little man, seemingly taking little interest in his story. The other customers in the tavern sensibly ignored them both.

A popular song started up at a table near to the serving bar, and other tables around the room picked up the refrain. It was a popular swinging ballad, and soon the whole place was alive with the happy song. Some of the serving girls joined in the merriment, dancing and turning between the tables in time to the melody. It was one of those happy moments that erupted from time to time in every tavern, when a song caught the atmosphere of the evening, and everyone joined in the gaiety. The serving girls, however, were sensibly keeping a wary eye on the two sailors, who were not joining in with the singing. The girls could tell that they were looking to grab one of them if they passed too close. Fanny, being more interested in Kenneth than in the dangers about her, was busy serving. She did not notice the potential trap and made the mistake of passing too close to the seamen's table. With a quick movement of his giant arm, the big man suddenly grabbed her by the folds of her full skirt, pulling her down onto his lap.

At first Fanny thought she could handle the situation, by using one of the many tricks that all tavern maids used to dissuade over-amorous customers. She laughed, turning and twisting her body to slip out of his grip, but his hold was too strong and the device did not work. She then decided on another well-practised rouse, she smiled and leaned towards the giant's face distracting his gaze, then with a quick flick of the wrist she spilt the content of one of the jugs she was holding over his hairy chest. Normally this action would have resulted in the man releasing his grip to clean away the mess, thus allowing her to be off, joining in with the communal laughter. This man however was not normal; he did not move or lessen his grip. Instead, his eyes narrowed, and he let out a great roar of anger.

From his point of view, he was doing this ugly wench a favour by even noticing her, he now felt insulted and humiliated, a great wrong had been done to him, the alcohol, his melancholia and his perception that the world was his enemy all welled up in an instant. In a flash he had unsheathed his wide bladed knife with the deadly intention of adding to this woman's ugliness. Fanny let out a scream of terror as she realised what was about to happen to her face, she starred transfixed into the bearded face of her assailant. Then just as all seemed lost, she saw Kenneth's face appear over the giant's shoulder from behind.

On hearing Fanny's scream, Kenneth had turned to see the attack on her, realising that there was no time for discussion, he was on his feet and across the room in two bounds drawing his own blade as he came, then gripping the great head by the pigtail with his left hand, he pulled it back and in one move passed his right hand, holding the knife, over the giant's shoulder and entered the point of the blade into the man's right nostril, then with a quick thrust, split the nose open up to the bridge. Blood spurted everywhere, as with another great roar of pain, the sailor threw Fanny to the floor and whirled onto his feet ready to face his attacker. His hand was now clutched over his nose, blood oozing through his fingers. Kenneth was an experienced fighter, and just like the seaman, knew from the work of his trade how to use his blade.

Kenneth knew he must press forward his attack while the sailor was still off balance, he lunged at the man's knife arm, and slit the arm from elbow to wrist with his razor sharp blade, the giant grimaced with pain, but this time made no sound, quickly he changed the knife to the other hand. Another danger now arose for Kenneth, in the form of the smaller sailor; this man had now leapt behind Kenneth, gripping his own blade with its point aimed towards the waterman's back. Kenneth was now trapped between the two furious seamen, both of whom had the experience of many sea battles, with much, close hand-to-hand fighting to call upon for help in this situation. They now had this young upstart trapped between them, and they were going to take full revenge for this evening's work. The big man was now shouting in a gruff voice .
"Stand off Jack, come about, this river-rat is mine, leave him to me I'll have his guts out on the deck here and now, for all to see" .

"Come on then salty, do your worst," cried Kenneth, who had now turned side-on to both men, his knees slightly bent, and his small blade was balanced comfortably in the palm of his right hand, waiting for the attack. If this was the end for him, he felt sure he would be able to take one of them with him.

Suddenly the big man's face contorted with more pain. He looked down to his thigh, at the handle of a thin marlin-spike sunk deep into his leg, there then followed a howl of pain, as the little seaman found a similar spike had pieced deep into his shoulder. Kenneth's friends were now standing around the tableau of the fight, with knives drawn and more spikes at the ready to throw.
The fight was over, the seamen knew it and dropped their blades. Two of the watermen walked forward and retrieved their metal spikes, taking pleasure at the pain they caused, as they twisted the metal free of the skin. The whole group now moved as one, manoeuvring the now terrified sailors towards the tavern door.
Fanny never asked what happened to the sailors outside, knowing it was best not to enquire, she was just relieved that she had escaped being maimed for life. Kenneth and his friends had soon returned however, sitting back at their table and talking quietly among themselves, in the now hushed and sober atmosphere of tavern. From that moment on, Fanny was overwhelmed with love for her brave Kenneth; she would do anything for him. It was Fanny who had tipped off Kenneth that Great Bess was in training and planning to perform her extinguishing trick.

<========>

Great Bess was proud of her trade, and enjoyed her responsibilities. She was a large heavy built woman, over six feet of dark eyed, good-looking womanhood, she had shining chestnut brown hair, crowning her strong, lantern jawed face, but her good looks were not her only attribute, she was also an extremely shrewd woman. By physique she was very large indeed, like her nickname, which came from the great four masted ship of the line 'The Great Bess'. Like the vessel she was also broad in the beam, high in the mast, deep drafted and armed with an array of formidable weaponry. Bess sailed the floors of her tavern domain with all the purpose of a Royal Navel ship on commission, she was always dressed to her 'Top Gallants' in brightly coloured clothes, which billowed like sails, as she glided about the place with her purposeful quick step. She was feared and respected by all her customers, although some pretended not to be intimidated, but this was only claimed when talking out of her earshot.

Bess was in fact some twenty stones or more in weight, and a match for the average sailor deep in his cups. In her business dealings she ran a tight ship, and ruled her tavern with a whip like tongue and a heavy hand when necessary. Like most tavern owners, Bess had a special relationship with many of her customers, they knew that they could truck a deal with her when they were going through times of hardship. They could barter for free board and logging while they looked for a ship to sign onto for a voyage, they could even borrow money from her. In return for this generosity, Bess would extract a harsh payment, which usually took the form of a share of the man's pay, or of any prize money that a Naval sailorman might be entitled to after a profitable commission. If they were in the merchant service, she would insist on a share of the seaman's will, sometimes even the whole amount, leaving the man's wife and children completely disenfranchised.

Bess could often be seen sitting with a seaman at a corner table of her premises, the table strewn with papers, brokering a deal on the man's chattels. She would argue that this was not exploitation, but that she was taking high risk, which of-course was true. It would be years before a man returned, or that word came that he was dead or drowned from some mishap. She often had to take her papers to the law-court, and there fight her case to get her rewards. It was pure speculation on her part as to whether she might be repaid for the room, rent, and vitals, or some other service she had provided.

Bess had a good crew of young girls working for her; these maids helped to create a cheerful atmosphere among the customers. Bess's tavern was a happy place for the average man to spend his evening, the company was good and with a few pots of ale inside, to take his mind away from his daytime trials and tribulations, the place was a good escape. The food was simple but fresh, served clean, and if not adventurous was of good value. Most evenings the place was awash with songs and laughter, it was frequented by at least fifty percent regular trade, with a continuous through-put of 'port-bound' seamen finding their way up to her premises from the ships waiting to discharge cargo in the pool of London.

Bess's crowning attraction, was her occasional performance of 'Dousing the candle', this show happened only when she felt that her tavern's trade needed a boost. She would begin the rumours herself slowly building up the anticipation over many weeks and months. Nobody knew exactly when she would perform her trick; therefore those men who did not want to miss the next performance would attend the tavern most evenings. The place would also be well used for months after a performance by customers gathering to discuss the event, and relate their version of what they had seen and how it had been achieved. Bess herself was aloof from all this speculation, sailing splendidly above all the chatter. She never discussed her infamous discharges, even with the girls who worked for her.

The Tavern was a long, low, misshapen building built of timber with a heavy thatched roof, and grey, uneven, flagstone floors. The straw-scattered rooms were equipped with crude timber tables and benches, which were scrubbed to an unevenness that sometimes made it difficult to stand a pot or plate in an vertical position. Each of the rooms led into the next through wide arches, giving the impression that the inside of the tavern was one large open area. The small windows were few and far between and like the walls and deck-heads were almost black, stained by the smoke of winter fires and the pipe smoke of its motley patrons. It was much like all the other taverns in the area, and like them competed for business by encouraging regular customers to spend their evenings in it's happy, comfortable, atmosphere, Bess's tavern created a congenial ambiance away from the miserable over-crowded housing, which was the lot of the poor majority of Londoners.

Tavern regulars could mix for a few hours with seamen and mariners from the world over, to hear tales of exotic far away places, they could live their dreams through the fabulously exaggerated stories told of those strange lands. They could join in the merry songs, and see the hilarious attempts of a drunken jester, perhaps trying to reproduce a new verse, he had heard at one of the many playhouses, or listen delightedly to the bawdy, and rudely altered, lines from a fashionable play. To his wife, a man would argue that taverns were places where information was to be gathered, and where something to his benefit might be heard. Although true, this was hardly the main reason for his attending. Taverns with their lusty serving maids were merry places, a home from home, that was inevitably better than home itself. Truth to tell many a man preferred to spend the evening at his favourite Tavern than with his family.

It had been Edwin's luck that on one of his rare visits to the tavern some six months earlier, a visit that was without his father's knowledge, that Great Bess had suddenly announced that she might perform her 'Extinguishing' as she preferred to call it. The warm smoky atmosphere of the tavern had immediately grown tense with anticipation, there was high expectation each time Great Bess appeared from behind the serving counter curtain, only to disappoint as she went about her normal chores with her quick flowing step, then to return to the dark mysteries behind the curtain. The tavern girls had been very busy adding to the mounting excitement by spreading rumours among their increasingly exhilarated customers. They mixed this information with their own opinions of Bess's intentions for that night. Yes, she was going to do it
"Once you have all had a good guzzle"
"No" she was not yet ready
"She is taking a few more pots of black ale and some of her special mixture," said one of the girls to a table of red-faced drinking men, in one corner of the main room. Drinks for Bess were being sent, offered non-stop by her fired up admirers. The excitement and anticipation slowly built up and up, as the evening turned into night. The girls were kept very busy bringing tankards of ale to their customers, with many pewter platters filled with coarse bread, and served with great slabs of hard yellow cheese, or heavy cuts of pork meat, covered with dense white fat

On their arrival at 'The Four Master' that evening, at about nine of the clock, Edwin and his young friends had heard of Bess's intention. To a man they elected to make a night of it. None of the customers knew exactly where Bess might perform her show, so the lads took their time on deciding what they thought would prove to be a good table. The young men eventually agreed on a position not too near to the serving counter but away from the entrance door. If they were wrong in their choice they might have to put up with a bad view, or if when the show started they were seated at the table to be used as the stage, they would have to move. Two old men who had been sitting at the table, sucking on their clay pipes and glaring their hoary loneliness into half empty pots, quickly moved away as the noisy gang of young Watermen moved in. It was still early and the lads knew it could be a long night, they also knew that Bess might well not perform, she was known to suddenly change her mind, and it would be a brave man who made complaint. However, the tavern was merry, and songs were starting up here and there, with most of the customers joining in with the chorus. Everyone in the room however, was keeping a weather eye on the threadbare curtain of the counter.

As the night wore on, the air of expectation in the tavern became almost stifling. The last time Great Bess had delighted her customers with her 'extinguishing', had been over a year earlier, therefore not many in attendance had actually seen her trick 'in the flesh' so to say. Many stories circulated, all of which contained much exaggeration, some even claiming feats that were physically impossible. In the end, it was obvious that the stories were mostly confused and that no one seemed to be sure of what they had actually seen; only that something exceptional had happened. The noise built up with more boisterous songs and noisy chatter. The deep-throated din of men who came from many occupations and different trades, vibrated the very timbers of the building. Some men had been coming almost every night for months, and resented those who were newly arrived, and who were seated in what might prove to be good positions. Tempers however, were being kept under close control; Bess had warned that a single fight or disturbance would mean that she would definitely not perform.

In one corner of the large smoke filled room, a deal porter whose regular heavy drinking had taken the little sense he had ever possessed, suddenly in a fit of temper, threw over his table in a total loss of self-control, infuriated over some perceived insult, from his drinking partner. This giant of a man then grabbed his friend, who was but half his size, and heaved him away, fortunately for all concerned, landing the man in the arms of men seated nearby. then with arms outstretched, the deal porter focused his red rimmed, menacing eyes on some other drinkers sitting at the next table, all of whom seeing the danger, rushed to get themselves out of the way of this madman. Molly, one of the Tavern girls who happened to be standing behind the enraged Porter, in an act of immense bravery, fetched her heavy metal tray down upon the man's head in one single mighty blow. The man did not move at first but then slowly he turned around to face his assailant, with a look of blurred murder in his eye, blood now trickling down through his hair onto his face. He opened his mouth as if about to let out a great roar, but before he could make any sound, six men jumped upon him from nearby and wrestled him onto the straw strewn floor. A rag was stuffed into his mouth, his arms were tied, and he was dragged outside. This had all been done hastily and hopefully before Great Bess could know of the trouble. The customers of the tavern were in no mood to be deprived of their night's entertainment by a drunken deal porter.

There was now a new tension in the room, had Bess heard anything? Was she going to claim that the commotion had put her off? Would they all have to go home disappointed yet again? Suddenly Bess appeared from behind the curtain, everyone in the room held their breath, but without even looking towards the corner where the confrontation had occurred, Bess sailed about her business as briskly as ever. It looked as if she had not seen or heard anything of the fight, they all hoped that perhaps it had been successfully nipped in the bud and that all was well; a silent sigh ran round the room. Many of the regulars raised their pots to each other, and knowing winks were directed towards Molly, who performed a pretty little curtsy in return of the salute as she went about her business. The tavern settled down to waiting again.

It was about midnight when Jane, one of the serving girls ran out from the back room looking flushed. She spoke at first to a table of her regulars who quickly passed on the word. It was definite; Bess was preparing herself for her show. Two of the other girls came out and quickly went to the table next to Edwin and his friends. They began to clear the pewter pots and platters away, and laid out a large thick brown cloth over the uneven timber surface. Those occupying the table were quickly moved to other nearby tables, where they pushed themselves in among its not too unwilling occupants, Edwin and his friends reluctantly made room for newcomers. The whole population of the tavern now centred its attention on the cloth-covered oaken platform. The young men had made a good choice, they were now situated at the table next to the proposed spectacle, and they had the best seats in the house. Edwin felt an unusual tightness in his stomach, which made him feel a little sick, and even light-headed with excitement, he began to wish he was a little further back from the action which was about to take place, he hoped he would be able to control his confused emotions.

After a short delay, there came from behind the counter curtain, the sound of a loud rough-music band, a great clash of metal trays to the beat of a drum, with a very fair accompanying flute. The flute was being played by Anne, one of the serving girls, who all now knew had hidden musical talents. The three maids entered to room, high steeping to the music and approaching the centre table, where they stopped and faced the counter, forming a guard of honour for the performer's entrance. To this fanfare, the serving counter curtain parted with a flourish, and to great applause from the assembled customers, Bess's great frame appeared.

All eyes were fixed upon her; her presence dominated the entire room. She was dressed in a multi-coloured creation of fine, flowing cloth, which revealed the great width of her porcelain white shoulders, and the bottomless cleavage between her enormous breasts. She was fat, indeed that was true, but at that moment every man in the room was completely under her erotic spell. With her hands placed on her undulating hips, she paused to let the power of her bulky beauty soak into each man's desires. She then sailed, as if on a calm sea, across the straw covered floor, towards the brown-clothed table prepared for her performance, then lifting the hem of her skirt with a surprisingly delicate movement of her unusually small hands, she placed a neatly shaped foot onto the low stool, which had been placed there by one the girls for the purpose, and stepped elegantly up onto the table's surface.

The whole tavern watched this dance-like movement, made so tantalizingly by this big but graceful woman, all were in complete wonder at the sight of this multi coloured Amazon. Bess seemed to be in her element; at heart she was a true performer, her face was flushed with the effects of the black ale, her normal haughty mannerisms now replaced by the sensual movements of this powerful vamp. She surveyed the room with a disdainful smile, and with the burning glow of confidence in her face, for a full two minutes she studied her open-mouthed audience as if daring anyone to speak. Then with a sound that made everybody jump, Bess threw back her head and let out a great peel of euphoric laughter. It broke the spell, the whole tavern erupted into merriment and cheering. Then through the uproar, with hands on hips, 'Great Bess' shouted her challenge .

"I am Bess of the candle," she cried .
"No man, woman, or beast can match my extinguishing. In my performance I reign supreme." .
She leaned forward displaying her heavy, white, breasts under the thin material of her dress; they heaved with the passion of her dialogue, the mountainous, soft, domes, jostled against each other like ships at anchor in a strong tide-run .
"I dare anyone here who thinks themselves capable, to challenge me in my endeavour this night". She looked around, but none responded to the goad.
"I have trained for this night, long and strict, it has cost me dear, in time and coin. It has meant eating great quantity of green cabbage, which I detested." She waited while everyone booed and hissed .
"It has meant drinking a great deal of black beer, which I enjoy." Now everyone cheered .
I trust you will appreciate my efforts, and will tell all your friends what you are about to see". She glared at them with menacing eyes .
"You will witness history in the making." With a long look around the room, Bess then quietened the mood of the tavern with a gentle wave of her hand,

she seemed to become calmer, to concentrate
"I now feel ready for my extinguishing," she said in a soft controlled voice. "I will however, need you all to help me in my efforts"
"When I give you the signal you must start a growling noise, like the wind in the sails of a great ship, a low note, deep down in your throats, it must slowly build into a crescendo of sound." To a man, they were now willing to do anything for this woman
"You will help me to summon up the necessary amount of power required to deal with the candle's flame", the audience was completely under her spell, and all shouted their readiness to assist; they were at this instant mesmerised to the last man by this enormously, powerful, woman, and were impressed at what she was about to attempt
She called for a practice 'sounding' as she called it, orchestrating the audience to give forth a low rumbling sound, then by agitatedly waving her arms, she got the noise a tone higher, and then again a tone higher still, she then stopped them and made them start again, and yet again, until she was finally satisfied with the result.

By now the crowd was eating out of her hand, she could have got them to do anything, even sign away their lives to the Navy had she asked it of them. Edwin thought to himself in wonderment at the power and control this woman had, at what could she have achieved over her fellow man, if she had been born to a higher station in life. As one of the superior class she could have controlled the land of England itself, he thought to himself. Turning towards the counter, Bess at last called for the candle to be brought forward. Jane appeared, and to the accompaniment of Anne's pipe and the drum, she stepped from behind the counter holding high a magnificent tallow candle. It was at least a foot in length, with a girth of some six inches. The flame itself was no mangy, small, insignificant flicker either; it rose up proud, at least four inches of white-hot flame. There was a gasp from the assembled company as they realised what was about to be attempted; this was to be no mean achievement.

Every man in the room was a good judge of the power of his own exhaust, but few if any would be willing to attempt to extinguish this scotching inferno. Jane, with some reverence, carefully placed the candle in the centre of the table, Bess eyed it with a mixture of contempt, cunning and expertise. She had no fear; she seemed to be willing her power and control over the flame. Then slowly she turned her back onto it, so that it was now directly line-a-stern of her great bulk. Several times she turned to look over her shoulder to check its position. Slowly she sank to her knees, keeping her body upright.

The tavern was now totally silent, not a hair stirred, all eyes were fixed in full concentration on the table tableau in front of them. Then very slowly Bess bent forward at the waist until she was on all fours, her head held up, her eyes staring over the heads of the bedazzled onlookers, straight at the wall ahead of her. This was now another person from the boasting woman of a few moments ago, Bess was quietly fading away before their eyes, only the bright colours of her dress seemed to stay in focus, the woman seemed to be disappearing.

Slowly putting both her hands back on each side of her enormous thighs, Bess grasped her full skirts, her fingers flickering slightly as she made sure of her grip, the tension in he room could be tasted. Then with a quick well-practised flick of her wrists, Bess's skirts were whipped up over her back and head, revealing to all, the shocked features of a great, white-faced giant. It seemed that everyone in the place took a sharp in-take of breath at the same time. It was truly a sight to remember, and Edwin like all those who saw it remembered it well, it was as if Bess no longer existed, she had disappeared and in that instant this aberration had taken her place. The giant had a personality of his own and he was very different to Bess. He had the pasty look of a well-fed prisoner, a man who had been locked in a dark place for many years, fed on uncooked dough and milk, and was now suddenly brought into the bright light of the world. His great chalk white checks, small painted eyes and a chestnut-brown, goatee beard, which gave him a shy and timid expression. With the help of the girls, Bess had painted the cadaver-like features of this enormous face onto her buttocks. It was a work of art, it was animate, and to those who saw, it was a real person.

It seemed a long elapse of time, while everybody studied this newcomer, but it was probably only a few minutes, before the unseen Bess began to move the giant's face closer towards the candle. Another pause, while the giant continued to stare at the candle with his dull red-rimmed eyes. Then from under the piled skirts Bess's voice called out, remote but authoritative as ever. As if from some great distance, she gave the signal for the sounding to begin, she had to give it again in a firmer voice, everyone was too fascinated by the giant face, to remember what she had told them they must do. However, with encouragement from the girls, the noise now started and everyone got into the spirit of the moment.
It was a low growl emanating from a hundred throats, at first orchestrated by the girls, but soon taken over with relish by the multitude. It grew slowly, as had been determined by Bess, until step by step it grew into a great upsurge of sound. Some men were red in the face from the effort they were putting into the strenuous cacophony of noise. For several minutes it seemed that nothing would happen, that she was unable to do it in spite of her audience willing her on.
The giant's face continued to glare at the candle's flame, with its lifeless painted eyes, but no exhaust came forth from those pursed lips. Everyone was leaning forward; Edwin had felt an elbow in his neck, as someone from behind tried to get a better view, he put up with it, for he felt no pain in the excitement of the moment, and craned even nearer himself. Then, when it seemed that the spell would break, it happened.

It all occurred so quickly, that to this day not many, Edwin included, could tell exactly what had really happened. He recalled that the giant's face moved slightly the cheeks seemed to draw in, he thought the eyes blinked, impossible as this was, he was almost sure of it, then all became confusion. A noise, a sheet of flame, an explosion, it all seemed to happen at the same time. Men leapt back in astonishment falling over each other in panic, those standing further back ducked or recoiled from the sudden detonation, and pandemonium of those who were nearest, tables and benches were knocked over in their panic. Half-full pots of ale, and platters of food, spilled their contents over the flagstone floor; all was chaos for several minutes.

When at last the upheaval settled down again, with peels of laughter at the relief, ringing around the tavern from a hundred excited mouths, it was realised that Bess was gone from the scene. The table now stood empty, with only the extinguished candle lying on its side, looking dejected, dead and forlorn. Now the inquest started with a vengeance, what had happened? Who had seen what? The description of the size of the flame and the noise caused by the explosion, grew quickly by exaggeration, the discussion passed from table to table. Some claimed to have been burnt by the heat, others said they had seen a yard long tongue of flame, others said it was a round ball of fire, like that emanating from a ship's canon, yet others said they had felt the tavern shaken by the blast. What everyone agreed however, was that Bess had honoured her pledge many times over, and had truly performed her extinguishing of the candle with great style.

Edwin had kept his own council concerning the show that he had witnessed, and did not mention the event to his father, or anything about that night, all-be-it that he would have sorely liked to tell him the story. He felt guilty, and a little ashamed, by this deceit, but as the days passed, and his father seemed not to have heard about the event, he assumed that he had not been told about it, or the fact that his son had been seen there. One day however, when they were working together on a long pull in the wherry, with Edwin rowing single oar randan in the bow of the boat. Alfred pointed to a house they were passing on the riverbank. It had two splayed chimneys, from between which, issuing from a crack in the roof, was a plume of dark smoke and glowing sparks. People were desperately trying to quench the fire with buckets of water, which were being passed up a rickety ladder. Alfred turned and looked at Edwin with a grin on his face. "Looks for all the world, like Great Bess doing her extinguishing, does it not son?" Edwin was shocked, did his father know something? Covered in confusion and now red in the face, he stammered "Er! Yes father" and fell to pulling on his oar with relish, to hide his embarrassment. He looked up at his father's back and thought he could detect a slight shaking of his shoulders. Could it be that he was laughing?

CHAPTER SIX
Ebenezer and the hapless Lighterman

Edwin sat back snugly in his wherry, mulling over the bizarre events of that night at Great Bess's tavern, trying to remember every little detail of the evening. His half awake, half asleep, state of mind, felt very comfortable. Edwin liked this dream-like feeling; it was like floating in the air. He could travel in his mind to any place he wanted, he could have adventures, and imagine wonderful experiences that he could never hope to experience in real life. Sometimes he felt quite annoyed when approaching a landing stairs, looking forward to a quiet period in which he could travel to one of the many special places he kept in his head, only to find that a fare was waiting. He would have to take the passenger aboard and begin the work, missing out on his anticipated mental escapade.

Suddenly Edwin was roused from his thoughts by the sound of a curse, and the rustle of sailcloth. He was a little irritated to be brought back to the dark, damp, world of reality. He looked up to see what had happened. It was Ebenezer Nasebury up from his seat and looking over the side of his boat. Ebenezer was by nature a very active man, fidgety, always full of movement. He was a good man at his trade, but very inquisitive. Nosy in his looks by the large hooked proboscis which dominated his face, as well as by character,
Ebenezer wanted, perhaps even needed, to know everyone's business. It was like an illness with him, he seemed to feed off knowing the most intimate concerns of others, he seemed able to garner the most secret information from them. He did this by seeming to confide in his victims with private tales and confidences of his own, when in reality he was only passing on the secrets of others. He had a phenomenal memory and knew the family history of all of his friends and acquaintances.

Ebenezer was a man in his late forties, with a pale, drawn, face, dropping down from a balding pate. He had surprisingly large, watery eyes, which somehow seemed at odds with his long nose. He was small man in build, but wiry and strong for his size. To Edwin, Ebenezer was an enigma, friendly and chatty but curiously secretive about his own family background, or his own personal affairs. Ebenezer was very clever at directing a conversation away from certain subjects, topics on which he could never be drawn. One of these Edwin had noticed, was religion, whenever beliefs or faith entered into a debate, he would introduce a snippet of news, which had seemingly just occurred to him, and would lead the conversation off in a new direction. Edwin's father was convinced that Ebenezer had Jewish blood running through his family. If it was the case that he was Jewish, it would explain a great deal about his secrecy, for any convictions of faith other than the Queen's own, must be kept strictly private at all costs.

<========>

The curse, which Edwin and the others had heard emanating from Ebenezer at the causeway, was in disgust at finding the bloated body of a dead dog bumping against the side of his Wherry, brought down from upriver by the early ebb tide. Quick thinking and active as ever, he threw off his tarred pull-on, ready to deal with this distasteful distraction to his private thoughts.

Ebenezer was now fully alert, ready and keen to avoid the potential affront the decayed dog's body might cause to the nostrils of them all. Edwin and the other wherrymen were now watching Ebenezer with concerned interest. They knew that this was a job for one man alone, as any more would get in each other's way, and thereby cause a nasal disaster. This work was best left to Ebenezer's adept use of his oar, if this sack of stinking flesh should tear open in the water, not only Ebenezer, but all within a twenty-yard radius would suffer the pungent consequences. The pollution from this dead animal would soak into every crack and crevice of their boats; the smell would penetrate even into their cloths. They each knew that they were relying on him to deal with this alarming situation carefully and expertly.

Ebenezer was up to the job; he skilfully manoeuvred the corpse along the side of his wherry towards the stern, using the spoon of his oar with gentle caressing movements. Then, carefully holding the offending carcass off into clear water, he warily stepped out of his boat onto the slippery wet timbers of the causeway, the studs of his boots giving him a good grip on the slimy planks. By steering the offending body ahead of him, he walked the stark white, blue-veined bundle, to the end of the greasy timbers, navigating the evil package past the other wherries.
After what seemed an age, he pushed it out into the tide, there to be taken away down river by the ebb, to become the problem of some other poor soul further along, perhaps thought Edwin this would be some unhappy seaman on watch at one of the ships moored in the Pool. Edwin smiled to himself at the thought of this unfortunate sailor, if he should be the one to split the skin in his efforts to send the bag of corruption further on its way, he would be the most unpopular man aboard for many days.

Each of the watermen waiting at Old Swan Stairs had watched Ebenezer's efforts anxiously, very interested in the outcome of this small event, judging his skill in ridding them of the potential stink. They collectively breathed a sigh of relief as the white, blotted, body of the dog was gently accepted by the watery fingers of the tide, and sailed slowly away toward the arch of the old bridge, to be taken up in the eddy, then away into the dark night. Ebenezer returned to his seat, and after some rummaging and rustling, he settled down once again, to join the others in quiet contemplation's of their own private thoughts. Edwin began to wonder half-mindedly where the body of the dog had come from and how it had become lost to the river.

<=======>

The night was very overcast at the camp of the tow-rags; no moon or stars lit up the untidy encampment situated outside the small riverside village of Barnes. Peter, his face a picture of concentration, was listening intently to the small rustling sounds emanating from the black shadows next to the camp's communal hearth. Judging by the sounds, something was after their meagre store of food. Peter reckoned it was too big for a rat, or a cat, he thought that it might be a dog. Perhaps it was a local animal, chased out from the village, and driven by hunger into raiding their camp. Maybe it was from a local farm. It could not be from the camp, no dogs were kept here; none could afford the extra food needed to feed an animal.

Peter crept out from his primitive, canvas shelter, and moved stealthily towards the food store. This little stone built larder consisted of a mound of bricks built into a simple pyramid, with a large, flat, removable stone at the front. In the gloom he could just make out some movement. He was now apprehensive, he did not wish to become involved in a fight with a large dog. Supposing this intruder turned out to be a vicious hound, or conceivably a man from the camp stealing the little food they had to share.

Peter was in no condition for a confrontation, his strength was now minimal, he was but a fraction of his former weight, the ravages of unremitting hunger and overwork had taken its toll on his body. However, he felt sure it was only a small dog; a man or a large animal would make much more substantial noises than this. As he drew nearer, through the darkness he could make out the shape of a small, white, dog, sniffing at the bricks and scraping at the large stone with its front paws. As silently as he could, Peter bent down and picked up a stout stick from the woodpile near the burnt-out camp-fire, reassured that the dog had not heard him, he continued to pad quietly towards the little beast. He felt sure the animal with its keen sense of hearing would soon hear him coming, and would run off before he got near enough to strike, but the dog did not seem to either hear or smell him. Peter's heart leapt at a sudden thought, if he could kill the dog, it would provide much needed meat for the camp's cook-pot on the morrow; they might eat well on the day ahead. He tightened his grip on the stick.

The dog was engrossed in the smells emanating from under the stones, there were odours of edible things coming from this place, there was something to eat in here for sure, but how to get it out from this little cave. A sharp prickling pain from the skin on his back, made him stop for a moment and turn to lick the offending place. He could taste blood; another place on his side now began to irritate him, he bent his body around into another position, trying to get his tongue and teeth within reach to deal with this added irritation. Why was his body itching so and why was there blood on his skin? Of late he only needed to nibble at the itchy flesh of his body and it would start bleeding, it was a puzzle.

Of late, the hair of his once thick white coat was also coming out in great lumps, his friends in the village had avoided him; even his master whom he had faithfully protected and defended since he was a puppy, seemed to have turned against him.

The man had chased him away each time they met. But the dog knew that his master did not mean him harm, it was just one of those strange moods humans have from time to time for no understandable reason. As soon as he got some food in his belly he would feel better, he would return to his master's house and take up his duties again and all would be back to normal. Another unbearable prickle interrupted his thoughts; this time it was attacking his chest just below his chin, a place that he could not reach. He sat back on his hunches and craned his neck in an attempt to deal with this latest discomfort. Suddenly, he felt a blinding pain on top of his head and the warm taste of blood in his mouth; his eyes were looking along a dark red tunnel towards a distant light, a bright light that was racing away from him into oblivion.

Peter was surprised at how easy it had been to kill the dog; the animal had been just sitting in the dark scratching itself. With one blow Peter had rid the camp of a thief and at the same time provided much needed meat for the pot. He pulled the dog's carcass back to his dark shelter and wrapped it in an old piece of sailcloth. He was pleased with himself, even more importantly he knew the whole camp would praise him when they heard about this night's adventure and the extra meat it would add to their food pot. The flesh would be very welcome and would provide for them all on the next day. Peter settled down again snuggling into the damp, musty smelling, bedding, he was happy with himself and was soon be back into the blissful oblivion of much needed sleep.

The morning presented itself wet and overcast, with a light but persistent rain. Peter looked out from his shelter. The men in the camp were mostly sitting under cover as best they could, waiting and watching. Two of them were trying to get the fire going, others, in an effort to quell the hunger pains that churned at their insides, were surreptitiously eating a little of their personal store of victuals, but mostly the men just sat and waited with the resigned look of inevitability on their haggard faces. The whole camp was waiting for the man who would bring them work, for this was the day the flash lock would be opened further up stream. It would bring work, hard work of course, but they would at least be paid something, and the coin would provide food and some clean ale to drink. They could for once avoid drinking the bad water from the river that carried many unknown diseases.

Peter looked across at the bundled up body of the dog lying by the entrance of his rough shelter. He shivered, what had become of him? Once he had been a happy man with friends and family. He was skilled in river work, having once been a licensed Lighterman, a part of the Watermen's Guild. He had liked a drink or two it was true, but he had provided a good home and a plentiful table for his family. However, his greed and stupidity had led him astray, he had been tempted and had found himself unable to resist. For the thousandth time he felt his heart sting with pain, as he remembered the night that had started the chain of events that had led to his downfall and caused him all this misery.

<========>

It had started five years ago, when a man dressed in simple, but good quality clothes, had approached him one evening in the alehouse. The man was friendly and open, and had seemed honest and true enough, they had talked quietly and comfortably together. The man was interested in the fact that Peter was a Lighterman. Over a few pots of ale, the man who said his name was Nathan, had suggested that Peter might be able to help him and his friends in a useful service, and that he would be well rewarded for his trouble. They were looking for a covered barge, which they wanted to be moored offshore in the river. It should be kept permanently afloat not too far from the Lambeth area but not too close to the Palace. The vessel was to be used for private meetings of their community. The man had added that any arrangement must be kept strictly confidential.

Nathan said that Peter need not be involved with their meetings, or even know of their purpose, he assured him that they were a peaceful group and wished no harm to any man. He said that he had been told that Peter could be trusted to be discreet, and that he might know how to acquire a suitable vessel for their needs. Perhaps he might even be willing to consider their ongoing needs; maybe he could also help them with the getting off to the vessel and back to the shore again after the meetings. If so it could be on a regular basis, in return for which he would be paid well for his trust and reliance.

To Peter this seemed a chance of a lifetime. He did indeed know of a barge, which he could truck for, and between the purchase price and the sale price, he might even turn an extra profit from these people. Further more he would be employed to attend their needs, and look after them continuously. Peter was no innocent, he knew that these were devout people, probably followers of a forbidden faith, he knew that what he was agreeing to do was illegal, and dangerous, but if he did not ask for details he could argue that he did not know their purpose. Others he knew had done so and had profited. If he was careful and kept his trap shut, here was a good chance for him and his to prosper. He agreed to make discreet inquiries about the barge, and they arranged to meet again at the alehouse in two days time to discuss the matter further.

In fact, Peter knew of two barges, which were both available and would suit the needs of Nathan and his group. One belonged to a shipwright, a man that Peter would have no truck with; he was a distrustful fellow and would double cross a friend as easily as he would an enemy. The other barge although smaller would do the job well enough, and Peter knew that the owner needed to sell it to settle some debts. Peter met with the owner and easily made the deal, including an understanding that there would be an extra payment left within the reckoning for his trouble. This meant that he would be paid by both sides for the transaction. Peter was a happy man, he only needed to conclude the deal and convince Nathan that the vessel was suitable for his group, and he would have plenty of coin in his purse.

Nathan was a little later than the time as arranged. Apologising, he explained that he had been watching from a distance to check that Peter was alone, then to Peter's delight he had quickly settled the financial part of the matter from a fat purse, which he produced from under his cloak. Peter was pleased that no awkward questions were asked, Nathan did not wish to meet with the owner or even see the proposed barge. He said he trusted Peter's judgement and happily signed the papers transferring ownership. They arranged a method of contacting each other through messages left with the owner of the Alehouse, and then Nathan took his leave and left.

Peter was overjoyed. He ordered a large pot of rum, and a dish of roasted mutton with green beans. He looked around the room, he wanted to tell someone of his good fortune, but sense prevailed and he kept his own council. The following day Peter rowed the barge, using its long sweeps, down river on the ebb tide to its new mooring, near the little used buoy-chains on the south side of the river, sited down-stream from the Lambeth Palace water-gate. He spent the rest of the day cleaning out the hold, and making some small repairs to the timber ceiling of the vessel. By the end of the day all was ready for the first meeting of Nathan's group.

It was a mistake; he knew it from the start, he should have involved a local waterman, but the lightermen and the watermen were still at an uneasy stage of acceptance of each other since the lightermen had left the Woodmongers Guild to join the Watermen's Company, a change that had happened only twelve years before. The jurneymen watermen in particular were unhappy with the inclusion of what they considered to be an inferior trade into their guild. Peter knew however, that his mistake had also been caused by his greed, and his wish to keep all of the profits of this business to himself, a greed that had led him to make the fatal blunder.

The first meeting of Nathan's group was to be held late in the evening of a prearranged day. Nathan had left a message to tell Peter the time that his group were to arrive at the little disused causeway; downstream from Lambeth Stairs, where they had agreed it would be quiet, and well away from prying eyes. Most importantly, Peter knew where the local waterman moored his wherry at night, at a place a little further downstream from the causeway. Peter had looked the boat over and felt sure his plan would work. Like most wherrymen, the owner had taken the oars away with him, to prevent unauthorized use. What Peter planned to do was to borrow some oars, use the boat to row Nathan's group off to the barge, bring them back after the meeting, and when they were finished, replace the wherry, carefully mooring it in exactly the same position. The wherryman would not be any the wiser and Peter could keep all the profits of the enterprise.

Nathan's little group arrived at the appointed time; there were only five of them, the others being afraid to come until the braver among their brethren had tried out this new venue. There was one woman in the group, a rather rotund lady, who was not happy with the movement of the small boat. She staggered and slipped as she came aboard the wherry, and when finally seated on the passenger thwart, gripped the gunwale with tight fingers and white knuckles. Peter could see that they would have some difficulty getting her out of the boat when they got off to the moored barge. Sure enough, she dropped her bag and her hat twice, while trying to disembark, each time Peter had to retrieve them from under the thwart. Finally, after much pushing and pulling of this plump lady, the little flock were at last safely aboard the barge and to Peter's relief were stowed away down inside the hold of the vessel. All was apparently well and Nathan's group seemed very pleased with the barge.

Peter, having rowed them off, waited alongside the barge while the group set up their paraphernalia and held a short service; he then helped them re-embark the boat and rowed them back to the shore. This time the woman was a little more at ease with being on water and although again dropping the bag that she was carrying, and spilling out some of its contents, she made less fuss. On gaining dry land, the lady thanked Peter profusely for helping her and stumbled off with the others into the darkness. Nathan arranged with Peter that they would meet again in three nights time, promising that there would be more of them attending their next meeting.

Peter returned the wherry to the mooring from where he had taken it, carefully checking that it was moored in exactly the same position as its owner had left it. With one final meticulous look around, he pulled the vessel over to the riverbank by its spring mooring line, and clambered ashore. He watched as the wherry slowly floated back with the gentle run of the water, to her normal position. Peter observed the boat for a few minutes to be sure that all was well, and then with a pleasant feeling of prosperity about him, he walked home, his step that night had the lightness of a happy and contented fellow.

John Foully looked down at the burden boards of his wherry suspiciously; he carefully examined the tallow on the oarlocks, and picked up the line lying under the forward thwart and looked closely at the way it was coiled. Someone had used her, he knew it immediately. Like all watermen he had his special ways of doing things, and he could tell that the boat had been moved. He looked carefully again at the oar-looks, the tallow was undoubtedly different, he used a light tallow to grease his oar leathers, there were now traces of a hard wax on the upright pins.

"Someone else's oars" he said to himself quietly. He was now filled with a cold anger, no waterman would take another's boat without asking, or if in an emergency, would at least tell the owner immediately after the event, he looked around the vessel for other clues. Taking up the burden boards, he bailed out the water from the bilge. At first he saw nothing, but then as the water receded between the boat's ribs, a glint from something shiny caught his eye. He leaned forward stretching under the thwart and he picked up the small, round, shining, object   .
"You black devils. I know you now", he said aloud and spat into the river in disgust.

<========>

"What name?" Asked the Clerk
"John Foully sir."
"And what do you want with the Ruler?"
"I want to report that my boat is being used by someone for illegal purposes," said John.
"A serious charge Mr. Foully, are you in any way involved?"
"No sir, and I would not be, it is against my religion to assist those fiends."
"Wait here" said the Clerk, and walked off quickly to disappear into the parlour. After a few minutes he returned and ushered John into the small but ornate room.

Three of the overseers of the Watermen's Guild, were seated at an oval table looking through papers spread out before them. All looked up as the wherryman entered. They could smell the river on him; his face seemed to have the consistency of leather, his clothes were stiff and weathered. The Ruler, who was seated at the head of the table, looked John up and down with the expression of a man who did not take kindly to being disturbed by a smelly rough handed wherryman.
"What makes you think your wherry is being used illegally?" asked the Ruler in an unfriendly tone. John starting at the beginning, relaying the story of his discovery detail by detail. He told them how he had bailed out the wherry and had discovered the evidence. Then with a theatrical flourish he held his hand out, and opened his palm for them all to see the object he had found in the bilge of his boat. Each man recognized the article immediately.
"You have done well Mr. Foully," said the Ruler with a sudden change of attitude.
"Will you help us to catch them?"
"I will gladly sir, and help to find the rogue who used my wherry to assist them in their evilness".

<========>

It was cold and damp on the bank of the river. Alan Graystone stamped his feet and swung his arms back and forth across his chest to warm his body,

his top hat tilting over to a jaunty angle with the effort. John Foully sucked his teeth in annoyance; if this fool of a beadle kept making such a noise they would have another wasted night.
"Keep the sound down Alan," whispered Victor the second beadle,
"You will give away our position". The beadle did as he was bid, settling down once again into the cramped squatting position he had adopted for the last two hours. Sudenly there was a noise, a small crack, they all heard it at the same time; it was the snap of a twig. John had laid twigs at the top of the path leading to the riverbank; one had been stepped on, and it had snapped. They each froze into statues of immobility, listening for more identifying sounds.

Peter stopped in his tracks as he stepped on the twig; he moved the heavy oars quietly onto the other shoulder. Was there another sound, had he heard something else? A thumping noise just before the twig snapped. Should he abandon this night's work? He waited listening to the sounds of the night. No, it must have been the boat nudging at her moorings; he was being stupid, no one would be here at this time, there was nothing but reeds and bushes along this stretch of the river's bank. Perhaps it was a rat, out from its nest looking for a meal. Anyway, he did not want to lose a night's payment from Nathan. He changed the heavy oars back again onto his best shoulder, and moved on his way along the dirt track in the direction of the wherry mooring.

Leaving the oars close by, where he could easily reach them, Peter swung himself over the edge of the bank, then holding onto a wooden pile, he pulled on the spring mooring line, to bring the boat over to him, lowering himself carefully into the wherry, he reached back onto the land, grabbing for the oars in the dark, but they were not there. With a silent curse he felt about in the grass for the absent blades, leaning further out of the boat onto the bank in his search for the errant paddles
"Are you looking for these, you thieving rogue?" said a voice from the dark. Peter jumped with fright at the unexpected harsh, words. He could just make out the shape of a man crouching in the reeds, then he saw two more shapes dressed in top hats, with the glint of metal badges on their arms. Peter's heart leapt into his mouth, they were the Company's Beadles here to arrest him. The crouching man stood up holding the oars, which he had quietly slipped away from the boat out of Peter's reach.
"So you think to take my boat from me do you? You dirty tow rag, come ashore this instant, I will know who you are?"
The voice was shaking with rage; Peter's heart sank as he realized that it belonged to the owner of the wherry. Before he could answer or make a move, Peter was unceremoniously dragged ashore by the Beadles. John now had his knife out, and wanted the do the thief irreparable damage. Alan restrained him, keeping himself and Victor between the two rivermen. Then as John's temper cooled, he forced the man to tell his story. It was Peter's only hope of redemption to now tell the truth, and throw himself on the mercy of these people. On discovering that Peter was a lighterman John

Foully went beside himself with rage. Twice more he had drawn his blade, and would have cut into Peter's throat if the beadles had not prevented him from doing so.

"These are the dung collectors we have allowed into our Guild," he stormed. "Are we now all to be tarred with the same brush as these villainous, shit hauling, lightermen, these carriers of goods and muck? Must we now share our boats with them as well as the good name of our Company?"

At last the Beadles calmed John down enough for him to see the sense of trying to catch the others involved with this night's work, but it would need the assistance of this man, help which he must give freely if he wanted to limit the punishment for his crime. They could catch a pretty net of smelly fish, and might all prosper this night. Peter, seeing his only chance, could not do enough to help, and with his assistance a trap was set. A plan of action was hatched, Victor was sent off to bring the Queen's men, Peter was to take the wherry to the causeway and the others were to settle down to wait and watch as their plan unfolded.

It was not long before the first of Nathan's group arrived. Peter stepped forward to meet them while John and Alan hid in the reeds. More men and some women arrived, bringing the number waiting on the bank to over fifteen. Peter then started rowing them off to the barge in small groups, using the wherry under the ever-watchful eye of John from the reeds. More people arrived, until in all some twenty were afloat, all contained in the hold of the barge, attending their meeting. Peter then returned to the shore to pick up John and Alan. Pushing Peter out of the rowing position unceremoniously, John took charge of his beloved wherry. They waited near the riverbank in the dark shadows, until out of the darkness came the splash of oars; it was the Queen's men's in their fast cutter. It appeared out of the gloom with Victor standing in the bow directing them to the place. The lookout posted on the barge's deck, did his best to warn the congregation below, but with little chance of escape for any of them, they bowed themselves to the inevitable. The cutter came alongside and the soldiers jumped aboard the barge. All those below were arrested and carried off, in spite of their pleading and protestations.

<=======>

Peter was nervous as he stood in the dock of the Watermen's Court; The courtroom was smaller than most City Guild courtrooms. It had a high, ornately decorated ceiling, its tobacco smoke stained walls covered with paintings of stern, pompous looking men, who had served the company over the centuries. The room smelled of men and smoke, overlaid with a strong whiff of fish and spices, wafting in from the nearby wharves and markets. Peter desperately hoped that for his part in the capture of Nathan and his band, he would be dealt with leniently. John Foully however, had other ideas. He did not forgive easily, no scurvy lighterman was going to use his boat and get away with it. Like many watermen, he had been against the inclusion of the lightermen's trade into the Guild, an inclusion that after many years of unsuccessful attempts had finally been forced through in 1700. Here thought John entrapment, was a good opportunity to show the Court what a mistake had been made.

The Court took their time in listening to the case, as reported by the Beadle, who carefully coloured the story to put himself in a brave light. They then heard the assistant beadle's version, followed by John Foully's vitriolic rendering of the night's events. Then with the greybeards of the Court leaning back from the table, sucking on their long clay pips, they dispassionately listened to the plea put forward by Peter, during which he emphasized the part he had played in the capture. The Overseers of the Court was made up entirely of watermen save for one man who was a Master Lighterman and barge owner. This man had decided from the onset of the hearing, that he would side with the majority of the Court, whatever his own opinion. The Company was still touchy about lightermen and he was not about to cross the watermen on the Court, and alienate his interests.

The Court having heard all the evidence, adjourned to the parlour to discuss their findings. They deliberated over the case, helped by a good meal of codfish, delivered fresh from the market, washed down with an equally good claret, finally and unanimously reaching their decision halfway through a rather good suet pudding topped with preserves.
"Guilty as charged", they decided. For corruption and greed. For the dishonour he had brought on The Company. For the disrepute he had caused them all, especially so on the new Lighterage members. Justice had to be done, and must be seen to have been done. At the end of the meal, sentence was agreed over large glasses of deep red port. A heavy fine, plus the removal of his licence for a period of not less than three years.

On returning to the Court Room, with much belching and farting, the greybeards took their seats at the table. The senior Ruler cleared his throat and in a short speech during which he slurred his words, and needed to refer to his papers for the details of the decision, he pronounced the verdict and the sentence. Peter was crest-fallen; he had not expected such a severe judgement. John was overjoyed, no man could return to the trade after such a length of time, even with help from friends. Peter was finished. Mr. John Foully felt very proud of himself; he had defended his Church and his trade all in one magnificent move, his vengeful nature had been appeased.

At first Peter had tried his hardest to overcome the effects of the sentence, he went to seek work within the other river trades, but the word was out against him. John Foully had seen to that. He even tried other trades, but as with his own Guild, outsiders were kept out as a protection of their knowledge. His wife and children had finally left him after six months of misery, and went to live with relations in Kent, on the strict understanding that Peter was not to follow. He was now becoming destitute, he begged and stole a little food, he even tried the various Churches in the City, but all seemed to know his story and were at the very least wary of this man, seeing in him a traitor against each of them.

At last he drifted out of the City, trying to find a place where his story was unknown. Eventually, now at his lowest ebb, he found his way to the camp of the outsiders the 'Tow-rags'. These were men who were outcasts from society; they lived in camps outside most of the small villages along the banks of the river's upper reaches. These beaten and forgotten dregs of humanity were employed for menial tasks, and mainly to pull on the towropes of the Western Barges, as these great, heavy, craft made their way upstream against the flow of the land-water running down river. Tow-Rags were cheaper to hire than horses, they were not as strong as the animals but in sufficient numbers could do the job. Sometimes these men were mixed in with the beasts, when horses were in short supply. The crews of the Western Barges considered and treated them not as human beings, but as an inferior source of power for their tow ropes, using them only as and when necessary, avoiding them socially as untouchable, undeserving, wrong-doers.

<========>

It was wet and uncomfortable as James made his way along the towpath to the camp of the outcasts. By keeping himself covered against the rain under a piece of canvas, he was protected from the drizzle, but was getting very hot inside this wrapping; he could smell himself within the canvas cover. He thought to himself in distaste that the odours were a mild version of the permanent smell of the outcasts camp. James was in a foul mood, he was damp, hot and irritable, he detested this job. It seemed that it was always him to be chosen by the skipper, to be sent ahead to arrange for the towing men or the horses to power their barge after the opening of the flash lock. He much preferred organizing the horses, but they were in short supply at this time of year, being used on the farms and for moving goods between the villages. He would need at least five ragmen to give the same strength as one horse; he spat on the ground in his annoyance. The thing he most hated was the smell of decay in the camp, it pervaded the place; it got into his nose and made him feel sick. The horses on the other hand, smelled nice, they smelled of warm hay and sweet oats, even their interminable expulsions of wind from their stern ends were not as offensive as the smells of the tow rags. Even from a distance the camp emitted its usual musty odour of death, it reeked of disease, there was always that pungent air of stale sweat and rotting feet, it felt dangerous to even breathe the air while in there, he always avoided touching anything while he was choosing the men, he had the feeling that if he did, he might catch something dreadful.

At last James entered the camp, he knew that there was no leader for him to truck with, he would just call out how many men he needed, and they would come out from their holes in the ground, ready to follow him back to the barge. They would line up as always and he would choose the best of the bunch by touching them with his stick. These chosen wretches would accompany him back to the barge where the backbreaking work of pulling on the heavy towing rope would begin. James knew he must hurry, the flash-lock would open soon and the skipper would want to be ready to start the long pull upstream, as soon as he could see the flow of the river increase.

James stood by the pathetic fire and called out to the men scrambling out from their canvas shelters, scattered untidily about the encampment.
"I will need twenty of you for two days" he said in a firm dispassionate voice.
"I will only take the healthy and the fit, you others need not waste my time". The men quickly formed a line, he noticed that some had shuffled forward on weakened legs, and mentally noted where they stood, they would not be hired. James strode along the line using his stick to touch the shoulder of those that he wanted, he came to Peter who was standing near the centre of the line. James looked at the thin round shoulders and the sunken eyes, he was about to pass on when Peter realizing that he would not be chosen spoke out.
"I was a lighterman sir, I have knowledge of barges and large craft".
"A lighterman? Why are you here then?" asked James looking the man over once again, and seeing no reason to change his mind. Peter started to tell his story but James cut him short, he did not want to hear this outcast's sad story, he wanted only to be out of this place as soon as possible.
"All right then, I do not wish to know of your troubles" and tapping Peter on the shoulder with the stick he moved on along the line of rags and smells.

Peter went quickly back to his shelter, pleased that he had the chance of work. As he collected the few things he might need, he suddenly remembered the dog's corpse lying near the entrance, he must give it to the other men of the camp for preparation in the cook-pot, he bent down and unwrapped the body. The dog's hair was white, but Peter could now see in the light of day, that its body was covered with hairless patches, with scratches and dark red eruptions on the pink skin, he turned the body over and was immediately aware of the sweet smell of corruption, it was an unnatural odour, it was the smell of danger. He knew immediately that they could not eat this meat, he must get rid of the carcass before the others knew of its existence. Far from heralding him for finding them extra food, the others would curse him to damnation, if he brought more disease into the camp. He carefully picked up the corners of the canvas sheet and carried the offending body out of the camp and over to the riverside, where he slipped the horrible contents gently into the water, to be carried away from the camp with the land-water run, down river towards the City that Peter hated so much. He then made his way along the towpath as fast as he was able, to catch up with the others who had been hired, this group were now well along the towpath, on their way with James to the Western Barge.

Peter did not catch up with the others until they had almost reached the vessel; James was pushing them along quickly in his anxiety to reach the barge. As the band of scarecrows, dressed in an array of torn, ill-fitting rags, came near to the barge, Christopher Bland the Master called out from the vessel's deck.
"James, how many did you get?"
"Eighteen Master," replied James.
"Get them onto the towing rope as quickly as you can, I wish to be ahead of the other barges and further up river before the flash lock is opened," he shouted with some urgency in his voice.

James ushered the men along the towpath to the forward end of the barge, where they took up the heavy towrope, walking it away well ahead of the vessel. When the rope was in a straight line, he arranged the men along it at about one fathom intervals, then at his command, the men picked up the rope and pulled it taut. It snaked out, making a graceful curved line from the towing men to its fixed point half way up the main mast. Peter knew that the next move would be the hardest part, but once they could get some movement on the barge, the going would become easier, the men strained at their work, each pretending to pull harder than was really the case, they all knew that to overwork their frail bodies at this early stage could prove fatal later, for it would surely bring them illness through fatigue, and leave their body open to attack from disease. James however knew this trick, and shouted threats at the men to make them work harder.

The rain had now stopped and the sun was beginning to come out, it would be a warm day, the sun's heat making the work even harder for the tow-rags. Peter was doing his best to look as if he was pulling hard, but James for some reason, seemed to be keeping a special eye on him, shouting and commenting about his spurious claim to have had a past life as a Thames Lighterman. Peter bit his tongue; he knew it would be the worse for him if he answered back.

The crew aboard the barge were pushing from the deck of the vessel thrusting hard against the riverbed, using long wooden barge-poles, with cross-section shoulder pieces at one end, and a forked shape at the other. Slowly at first, but then more quickly as she gained momentum, the Western Barge slipped out from her mooring into the deeper water. The towrope was attached to the mast rope, which was used to change the height of the towing point to a higher or lower position, to give the best lead. Christopher checked to make sure the towrope would pass over any reed-beds or fish traps that they would pass. Yes, he thought she was about right, provided that James kept the tow-rags to the towpath, the rope would not cause any damage to the various business interests sited along the river bank. He made his way back to the tiller and levered it over to Port, this moved the great rudder of the barge to steer the vessel further away from the bank. Now that he had steerage he felt a lot happier, she was answering the tiller well, he was now in charge of his vessel,

Peter was feeling dizzy, a little light headed; he knew it was the sun and the hard work affecting him. He eased back a little more on the rope, pretending to put his full weight behind his efforts, thankfully James was up at the head of the tow rope, berating a man who was almost on his knees with exhaustion. Now that the barge was moving work for the towing men should became easier. Peter knew that if the master was a good skipper and steered a true course keeping away from any shallows, the rest of the day might prove uneventful and worthwhile for the men of the camp. They would be paid in coin, and could return to the camp with food to eat and clean ale to drink, which would help repair and strengthen their emaciated bodies,

Having got the barge out into the deeper water, Christopher steered a good course a little away from the shore. All had gone well for about two hours, and they were making good headway. James was onshore directing the tow-rags. Christopher called out to another of the crew to take the tiller while he checked for water in the bilge; he liked to do this himself and wanted to be sure that she as dry. He had a cargo of bagged goods in the hold, which would be ruined if wetted. Robert, the young man Christopher had put on the tiller, was new to the crew, he had been with the barge for only two trips. Robert's father was a friend of Christopher and he had employed the lad partly as a favour. The boy had seemed to take to the work, he was quick and eager to learn and anxious to please, he was an able lad and seemed particularly good on the helm.

For Peter and the towing men it all happened very suddenly, the inanimate towrope suddenly seemed to take on a life of its own, it pulled back abruptly against the weight of the men pulling, many of them falling over with the unexpected resistance, then it suddenly went slack, those still standing and holding onto the rope hawser, now found no weight to pull against and fell forward to join the others on the rough stones of the towpath. The towrope now free, fell crushing onto the reed-bed that they were passing. Then another violent movement, this time caused by the swinging whiplash of the barge's mast, dragged the rope back violently through the crop of reeds, breaking them off at the root and ruining a great swath of the riverside planting. The towers looked up in astonishment to see what had happened, only to see that all their efforts had come to nothing. The vessel was aground.

<========>

Robert had felt very proud and confident to be left in charge while the Master went below. He eased the tiller, and the barge had come slowly round a gentle bend in the river, He could now see ahead of him that he had a choice of courses to consider, dead ahead of him was a small, half submerged, bank of land, he could steer the vessel further out to go around the object, but this would put them further out from the bank and into the stronger flow of the land-water and would add time to their journey, also putting extra strain on the towers. The alternative was to steer between the shore and the land bank, there seemed to be plenty of room with a enough depth of water for this plan of action. At first he thought to call Christopher and let him decide the best course, but he did not want the Master to think he was incapable of making decisions while navigating the vessel; Christopher might give his father a bad report. He decided to go between the half submerged mud bank and the shore.

After a few minutes and when it was too late to change his mind, Robert realized his mistake, he was too near to the island, he could see the river bottom when he looked over the starboard side. He felt a sudden rush of blood race to his head, his mind was in confusion, he was shaking all over and felt sick to his stomach, the overwhelming responsibility of the barge, the crew and the men on the shore suddenly hit his senses all at the same time. In short he panicked, he pushed the tiller to starboard as hard as he could in an attempt to avoid hitting the river's bottom, but in his excited state, he over compensated. The water flow coming through the narrow channel, now took hold of the barge's bow on its starboard quarter, swinging the vessel hard onto the shore. The momentum of the barge forced the shallow keel of the vessel to cut a deep furrow into the soft, shelving muddy ground of the riverbank, the barge now stopped in this new gully. She liked what she found, and listed contentedly over to port, then like an old lady making herself comfortable in a soft chair, rolled over to starboard and righted herself, to sit happily in her new and most agreeable position, firmly stuck in the mud.

Christopher, who was below dipping the bilge water level when the barge grounded, was knocked over by the impact. Getting quickly to his feet, he raced up onto the open deck. Robert was standing rooted to the spot, shocked into inactivity by his error of judgement. Christopher's eyes swept the scene, taking in at a glance what had happened. Brusquely, he pushed Robert to one side, and surveyed the situation in more detail, his mind leaping from one conclusion to another, as he sought an answer to the problem facing him. The water was flowing past the stern of the vessel, the bow was hard on the ground, and the towrope was collapsed down among the reeds. James was busy getting the towing men back onto their feet, the crew were already pushing against the ground with their barge-poles.
"James!" he called.
"Get those men quickly back along the path, we will give the towrope a new lead back from the bow to pull us out, and use some of those men to lever under the bow". He knew that the flash lock was being opened and that water level would soon be falling, he must act quickly. He decided to move some of his cargo further aft to lift the bow, and so set all his spare hands to the task, however, this would take time, a commodity of which he was scarce.

Peter now found himself up to his chest in water standing alongside James. They were both using sturdy poles, passed down from the barge's deck, and were levering under the vessel's bow trying to get air into the mud, to free the bow from the suction of the sticky sludge. The tow-rags were now pulling down-river on the towrope, which had been refastened to the bit-heads in the barge's bow, but nothing was happening; no movement of the vessel could be felt in spite of the effort being made by all concerned. Without realizing what he was saying, Peter commented half to himself and half to James,

"She will not come off this way, we will have to rig a breast kedge and shear her free".

What do you mean?" said James.

"Well," said Peter spitting river water out of his mouth.

"This is like the falling ebb tide we have down river twice each day, we can use its force to re-float the vessel". James looked at him with renewed interest; this man seemed to know what he was talking about.

"Wait here," said James and climbed up a rope ladder now hanging over the bow, to board the barge, he wanted to speak to Christopher.

"Master," said James a little out of breath from his exertions.

" I have a man down there who claims that he was once a lighterman, he says he knows how to get us back afloat quickly".

"Bring him here to me," said Christopher. Leaning over the side, James signalled to Peter to come aboard, Peter did so, climbing the ladder onto the bow and making his way aft to stand with James before the barge's Master. They were both dripping wet, their soaked appearance equalling out their differing social status.

"I am told you were once a lighterman in London" said Christopher.

"Yes sir, I was".

"Whom did you work for?" Peter named some of the Master Lightermen who had employed him over the years. Christopher recognized some of the names.

"What do you suggest we do to re-float?"

"I would use the running force of the water sir", said Peter.

"Tell me how," said Christopher.

"First I would remove that great rudder and put it ashore for now, it is catching too much of the weight of the land-water. I would then run out the forward anchor as a kedge, over onto the other side of that mud-bank," he said pointing to the half submerged island.

"It must have hard stones below to have survived over the years. I would take the lead from the anchor around the base of the mast and back onto the forward winch. If we then took up the weight slowly on the winch, she would stop twisting herself into the mud and will shear out like a pendulum. She will trade astern away from the shore. We must also have another rope ready to transfer the anchor lead onto the forward Samson-post, and the vessel will come around, back onto her course".

Christopher looked into the man's haggard face, at the sunken eyes, and at the thin emaciated body, could he trust this man's skill, He obviously knew his trade, and was used to working with the strong running tides of the London river.

"We will try it," said Christopher, and ordered some of the crew to unship the rudder from its pins. There was suddenly an atmosphere of positive activity aboard the vessel, James was sent ashore to arrange the towing men to pull the great rudder over to the shore, to be beached ready to be picked up later.

"Come with me," said Christopher to Peter "I want you with me on the winch"

Three of the crew were sent to bring up the small boat that all Western-barges towed behind them, the anchor was freed from the barge's bow, and rigged over the side of the little boat. A stout rope was run out as the boat was rowed around to the outside of the flat island. Peter watched intently to judge the best position, and at his signal the anchor was dropped. He and Christopher were now working a handle on each side of the waist high winch, which was making its familiar click, click, noise as the metal pall dropped between the teeth of the cogwheel. As they took up the slack on the anchor rope, the rope dragged slowly across the surface of the island, until the anchor bit good and firm into the hard stony ground of the little island. Peter then ordered a second rope to be tied off halfway along the anchor rope, with its other end fastened to the Samson Post of the barge. He told the men to leave this new lead slack, hanging in the water for the time being. Peter and Christopher then began to turn the winch handles, slowly winding in the now taut rope which snaked away toward the kedge anchor.

The barge was heavy, they could feel the strain on the winch, but at last Peter felt what he wanted," She moved," he said. Christopher had also felt it, he started to pull on his lever again.

"No sir, not yet. Let her find her own way out". Peter was now in his element, forgotten were the trials of the recent years, he was in charge of this vessel, and she recognised him as her master. Then he felt another little movement through the barge's deck,

"Now sir, just a little more to let her know what we want". They levered together a few more turns of the winch.

"Stop now, here she goes," whispered Peter, as the barge like a fat, old, woman rising from her couch, started to slip astern out of her comfortable, muddy resting place, shearing slowly away from the shore on the keg anchor rope. As she reached the point of the shear when the momentum stopped, and she would have started to turn on the opposite run, Peter ordered the second rope to be taken in and made fast to the Samson Post. As this rope took up the strain, the barge seemed to give a little curtsy and very slowly danced into her new position in the deeper water, with her head now pointing upstream. Christopher smiled with relief.

It took half hour to re-hang the rudder back onto its pins, to recover the anchor and get the tow-rags started in the upstream direction again. While this work was going on, Christopher went ashore to truck with the owner of the reed-bed. This man had arrived sometime earlier to watch the fun. He was delighted to see the damage to his crop, for he knew that he would be well compensated by the barge's Master for the loss of his reeds. In fact, this was not the first time a misjudgement of navigation in this spot had brought him reward.

The Western Barge, now safely back on its way, was travelling slowly upriver. Peter had not been ordered back to the tow, he had stayed aboard awaiting further instructions. Christopher stood at the tiller, happy now that he was back on course; he would still clear the flash lock in time. Surveying his crew, he first called young Robert to him and although out of Peter's earshot, it was obvious by the boy's stooped shoulders, that the lad was being left in no doubt as to the Master's analysis of his ability, and as to what the consequences would be of his action. The boy was sent forward in tears, dreading what his father would say when he heard of this day's doings.

Christopher now called Peter to the helm.
"You must have done something seriously wrong to be living among the tow rags at that camp". Peter opened his mouth to tell his story, but Christopher put up his hand to stop him.
"I do not want to know your story," he said.
"Just tell me truthfully. Did you kill?"
"No sir".
"Did you injure a fellow man?"
"No sir".
"Did you steal coin?"
"No sir".
"Then it must be religious," said Christopher.
"I certainly do not want to know any details of that, I hold my own beliefs, and consider all men should be allowed to treaty with their God in their own way, provided that they harm no others. He smiled at Peter. I am now short of one crewman, and would take you into my crew, if you will promise to serve me well and true".
"I will, I will sir," said Peter, his heart leaping with joy at the thought of employment.
" When did you last eat?" asked Christopher looking into the thin face.
"The camp is very short of provisions," said Peter, avoiding a direct answer because he could not remember his last meal.
"Go into the tilt, and find yourself some vitals", said Christopher, pointing to the hopped shelter over the after deck. Peter entered the canvas cover and found what for him was an abundance of food. There was cold meat in the form of a half eaten capon, fresh bread and hard pork fat in a large barrel, and he found clean ale in a china pot. He started to eat, quenching his thirst with the delicious ale between bites. Curiously, he could not eat as much as he wanted, his stomach had contracted over time, and his throat had narrowed during the long period of semi starvation. He took another

long draft of ale and returned the deck. Christopher smiled at the change in this man. He gave Peter the tiller and went forward to organize the crew, who were moving the cargo back to its original position. Peter watched as Christopher spent some time instructing and warning them to keep their eyes about them, and to call him if they noticed anything unusual.

Peter had not felt so happy in his life before, suddenly he could hear the birds singing along the banks, he could feel the barge moving under his feet, he could smell the grass, the trees and the water, at last his trials were over. He would never, ever, put a foot wrong again, he promised himself. He took one hand from the tiller and felt in his pocket. His fingers clutched the small round bead, which had been the cause of all of his troubles. He brought out the object of his woes, and looked down at it glinting dully in the sunlight. Had this small glass bead, drooped by a lady in the bilge of that horrible waterman's wherry, at last come to his aid, had it brought him the change of luck he had so desperately hopped for? The Clerk of the Watermen's Company had given the bead to Peter after the trial, to remind him, he said, of his greed and foolishness. Had this holy, blessed, Papist object, delivered him out of darkness onto a course out of his torment. Peter looked closely at the bead in the bright sunlight, he noticed for the first time that it was not black, as he had thought; it was in-fact a very, very, dark red. Peter kissed the glass Rosary Bead reverently, and carefully put it back into his pocket.

Chapter Seven
The 'Black Face' job

Edwin looked across at the other boats waiting alongside the causeway, sniffing at the harsh smell of the smoke from their flickering torches burning near the river wall. It was very gloomy at the point where the slatted timber causeway joined the dark granite stone of the steps of 'Old Swan Stairs'. The stairs were cut deeply into the wall and led directly up to the lane above; this narrow path in turn gave access to the northern approach of the old London Bridge. The burning wands, made of heavily tarred rag, were the wherrymen's way of indicating their availability to prospective passengers. From a distance it was a sign that oars were available for hire, and that wherries were waiting at the landing stairs for passengers.

Two of these burning wands belonged to the Taylor brothers. Edwin could see their dark silhouettes in the glimmering light. They had given up their quiet contemplation and were now in a huddle of conversation; this was quite usual for the brothers; they never stayed silent for long. To Edwin, the Taylors always seemed always to be talking quietly in corners; he had even seen them with their boats tied together in midstream, drifting along with the tide flow and talking animatedly. As he watched them now he could see that as usual they were gesturing with their hands. They were holding their boats tightly alongside each other, tied by their catch lines, while they chatted energetically in their usual conspiratorial whispers. They were obviously discussing something very private, probably some family business thought Edwin, or perhaps they were arguing over the split of the day's earnings.

Just as with the other men waiting at the stairs that night, Edwin knew the brothers very well, he also knew much about their family. He ran his mind over what he had discovered about this pair and their bizarre relatives. At forty, Christopher was the eldest over his younger brother Robin by about four years. They were at first glance obviously brothers, facially they looked alike although Christopher was a little taller and more heavily built than his younger sibling, they were both rather short in stature, with a stocky physique, both had a bald pate with a cluster of hair grown in a thick ring around the sides and backs of their heads. Without their hats, they reminded Edwin of saintly monks. However, the roughness of their language when angry and the coarseness of their behaviour belied their religious appearance.
Christopher was the senior of the pair, he was not only older and slightly bigger, but he was dominant, the craftier of the two. It was always Christopher who lay behind the many moneymaking exploits the Taylors

were noted for. He was also the slightly better looking of the two, with rather boyish features that belied his ruthless nature. Robin, who had more fully inherited the family's round, moon-face, and bad eyesight, had always lived in his brother's shadow. This younger brother was not 'the brightest penny' in the Taylors' purse, or very quick to react to any changing situation, but he was methodical, naturally wary and fiercely protective of the family name. He had a deep admiration of his brother's cleverness, which bordered on hero worship, seemingly oblivious to the fact that it was usually he who came off worse when one of their cunningly hatched plans misfired.

Robin's misplaced loyalty in Christopher mystified Edwin; the younger man would often find himself in trouble by defending something which had been instigated by his elder brother. For both men however, their overall loyalty was to their kin, a family which was large and many faceted, dating back in its origins to a time when records were not kept and only word of mouth stories could give an inkling of the links to those bygone times. They were particularly proud of one ancestor, John Taylor, known as the 'water-poet', who had been born in the time of The Queen Elizabeth. Robin in particular liked to bathe in the glow of the fame created by this celebrated ancestor. Although Robin could not read or write himself, he would at any opportunity tell one of the many of stories that he had learnt by heart, concerning his ancestor. John Taylor had written many tales about his travels and Robin would repeat them, never embroidering the account, but sticking to the truth as he had learnt it.

<========>

John Taylor was born at Gloucester on the twenty fourth of August in 1580 and lived during the traumatic period, which spanned the reigns of Queen Elizabeth, King James $1^{st.}$, King Charles $1^{st.}$ and the dictator Cromwell. He was taken by impressment for service in the Royal Navy no less than seven times; he served under nine Captains, in twelve ships of the line. He had sailed to many countries of the world and fought in several sea battles. Edwin's father once commented that he was suspicious of the man's motives, for to be caught so many times by the press, he must have been either very careless, or perhaps liked the opportunity to get away from an irksome wife. Taylor died in 1654, having served under a Queen, two Kings, one of whom was beheaded, and a dictator.

His earliest writing was about the battle of Cadiz, in which he fought as part of the English fleet, as a sixteen-year-old impressed apprentice waterman. He wrote about his fellow watermen who were there with him, of whom there were many. Taylor had many adventures during his long life, which he set down in his own style of writing, prose, verse and doggerel. In later life Taylor was appointed a Royal Waterman and was used in the crew of the Royal Barge.

The watermen and wherrymen of John Taylor's era, owed him a great debt, for it was he who to a great extent used his connections within the high places of society, to better the lot of the rivermen, particularly the wherrymen. He had done so by using his influence and writings, to help stop or delay anything that might adversely affect the income or importance of his trade. Sedan-chairs, bridges, and the most hated of all forms of transport by the watermen, the coaches and carriages, which were increasingly taking business away from the river onto the roads. The Watermen's Company Guild was of course also interested in the outcome of the same encroachment into the trade which concerned Taylor, but looking for compensation to swell their coffers, rather than alleviating the effect on the working men. On their side, John Taylor and the journeymen were trying to preserve the use of the river as London's highway, something which involved their very existence, Robin would often quote from one of his forebear's verses with great relish. It said.

> "Carroches, coaches, jades, and Flanders mares,
> Do rob us of our shares, our wares, our fares;
> Against the ground we stand and knock our heels
> Whilst all our profit runs away on wheels.
> And whosoever but observes and notes
> The great increase of coaches and of boats,
> Shall find their number more than ever they were
> By half and more, within these thirty years;
> Then watermen at sea had service still,
> And they that stay at home had work at will:
> A man could scarce see twenty in a week;
> But now I think a man may daily see
> More that the wherries on the Thames can be."

Robin knew all of John Taylor stories and poems by heart, from the many tellings of these tales within the family.

By all accounts, John Taylor had the wanderlust in his soul; he was a great traveller and travelled to many Cities in England and also on the continent. One story that Edwin liked to hear Robin tell was of John Taylor's visit to the City of Hamburg in Prussia. It was in the year 1612 when Taylor was 32, and during his long trip through Europe.
He arrived one day on the outskirts of the walled city of the seaport of Hamburg. As he approached the outskirts, he could smell the City's odours, which became stronger as he proceeded, a stench which gradually overpowered the fresh, gentle, fragrance of the countryside. It was the usual smell that all large Cities exuded, a mixture of urine and dung, with undertones of rotten vegetables and damp cloth. He looked up at the high wall, which was intact as far as he could see. Some cities, London among them, had let their walls deteriorate, which John thought to be very foolish,

after all it was a City's main defence and had served most of them very well over the centres.

There seemed to be some commotion going on outside the north wall, much more activity than one would expect for a place like this at this time of day. People were everywhere, standing about in small groups talking excitedly; others were making their way towards a small mound outside the city walls. This hillock was obviously man made; it seemed to have been constructed for some special purpose and had a shallow, dry moat around it. People were gathering, settling down in groups along its edge. John could see that the places nearest to the hillock were filling up quickly; he made his way over towards this centre attraction to get a better view of what was happening.

On top of the hillock John could make out a man working hard at hammering what seemed to be iron pegs into the hard ground using a heavy wooden mallet. Nearby to this man, laid out on the ground, were two large cartwheels. John spoke to the people around him as best he could in the language of the Prussian people, enquiring with words and expressions of his hands, asking what was happening. Realising by his way of talking that he was an Englander, an old woman, who could speak a little English, took it upon herself to explain the events about to be acted out before them.

He soon realised by her few words of guttural English and her gestures, that there was to be an execution on this site, and that the whole City had come out to witness the enactment of Prussian justice. To John's surprise the crowd seemed to be in a happy, festive mood; they were not the over excited, bloodthirsty horde which always attended an English execution. Taylor could not detect any drunkenness in the crowd, as would have been prominent at an English slaying. There was none of the ribald comments and crude banter, which accompanied such occasions at home. The crowd here seemed to be in a holiday mood. Some were spreading out clean white cloths and laying out food for their families; young children were running about playing games on the grass.

The area was soon crowded with people meeting and greeting each other, as if it were a market day. The old woman pointed towards the City gate, indicating the approach of a small group of men with a two-wheeled cart pulled by a single donkey. John realised that the woman was now telling him something serious. He concentrated on her words and understood that the man in the cart had slain a young child. He looked on with interest as the group made its way towards the mound. On arrival at the dry moat, the man, dressed only in a loincloth, was pulled from the back of the cart and forced to cross a removable, planked bridge over the moat, then to climb to the top of the mound. He was struggling and making strange gurgling sounds, he dropped to his knees several times, only to be roughly lifted up again and pushed forward, inexorably he was dragged to the top of the small hill. John could now see that a stick was forced into the man's mouth between his teeth and tied tight at the back of his head with cord. The loincloth he was wearing was soaked with urine; he obviously knew that his fate would be terrible.

The two men in charge of the execution threw the man to the ground and spread-eagled him out between the four peg-hoops, which had been hammered and half buried into the ground. They then tied an arm or a leg to each hoop, leaving the writhing body to dance about in fear and dreaded anticipation of what was to come. The two men then each took up a cartwheel and raised them up high in the air to show the assembled crowd. A great cheer went up and the men repeated the salute several times, circling the terrified prisoner as they did so. Then taking up position on each side of the writhing body, they raised the heavy wheels, and in one fearful movement brought them crashing down on the man's forearms. The crowd cheered as the body arched its back from the excruciating pain. The men now repositioned themselves at the man's feet and again raised the heavy ironclad wheels in the air. Again, the crowd cheered as the great wheels came down, crushing the ankles of the prisoner.

John could now see the full extent of this punishment and watched as the men methodically crushed the bones of the arms, the legs, the pelvis, the chest and finally the head of their victim. Taylor later commented on the execution in his writings as being particularly barbaric. He said that by comparison, the English method of hanging, then drawing and quartering the victim, was to be preferred.

Edwin knew that since the time of their ancestor, parts of the Taylor family had prospered. He also knew that the family name was everything to the Taylors, spreading as they now did over many of the City's trades. Large parts of the Taylor family were now shopkeepers, put into these relatively lucrative businesses by the fortune of prize money, earned at great personal cost by the family's watermen when taken by the press gangs in earlier times. This wealth had been hard won in sea battles over many generations serving in royal ships destined for fortune. This good luck seemed to be a fortunate, if dangerous, attribute at which the Taylor family were seemingly adept.

The many faceted trading activities of the family, seemed to outsiders at odds with the normal way of life in the City. Most families kept to one trade and accepted their place in London's social order rankings. The Taylors however, were different. Some parts of the family were very religious, others were relatively wealthy, some lived in good housing, while others lived in the poorest parts of the capital. Somehow, in spite of this inequality, the family kept its links, albeit that this contact was sometimes accompanied by seething disagreement, reluctance and much internal quarrelling.

Edwin remembered that one member of the family was now a third generation patten maker by trade. This diversity had come about over generations of Taylor watermen, who had acquired enough money to buy into the trade. Pattens were still good business in London, even though some of the streets to the west of the capital were slowly being paved over and thereby becoming cleaner, thus avoiding the need for pattens, the wooden overshoes, which were still a necessary accessory for the Gentry when using the uneven and dirty streets of the capital's pathways, thoroughfares that still formed much of the eastern part of London. Pattens gave a good protection, fitting over the delicate court shoes, or the other more sensitive shoes worn by superiors, footwear that could otherwise easily be damaged on the rough, uneven, surface of many of the streets and lanes. In the 'square mile', pattens were vital when navigating the muddy mess that followed even the slightest rainfall.

Edwin looked down at his own footwear. Like most of his class, he only ever wore the heavy, leather shoe, or the short boot, which was the staple footwear of all watermen. These sturdy types of footwear were reinforced with metal hob-nails punched into the sole, and a horse-shoe shaped bar nailed onto the toe and heel, devices that gave longer wear, They made an awful racket when walking on cobbles, but good care and continuous coats of thick wax, could make this footwear last for many years. Pattens were only for the superiors, designed to protect their delicate shoes. Watermen's footwear however had other uses, the heavy boots had a more sinister employment; they were a very useful weapon in a fight.

Some of the Taylor family were still watermen, working mostly as wherrymen up into the River Fleet, where they seemed to find enough business to keep them comfortably supplied with victuals and clean ale, plying as they did between the Fleet, which served deep into the West-End of London, and the old City to the east. There was a great deal of new building taking place in the western part of London. Grand new sweet-smelling squares, displaying the latest fashionable designs for housing, built it seemed, up into the very sky itself. All this work to the west of the City formed a new district of opulence with its beautiful white buildings.

This new district was striking indeed when compared to the eastern parts of the capital, the famous square mile itself showed an especially stark difference. The old original walled City was slow to change or develop, even after the ravages of the Great Fire. Many generations of ownership and the vicissitudes of family fortunes entangled the rights of most of the properties within the area. The new money therefore, was being spent to the west, where claim to land was clean and unencumbered, even when after the fire, the chance for change had afforded itself to the City planners. They had not been able to sort out much of the complicated ownership of land and buildings of the original older London, and so many places had simply been rebuilt in their original position, in the same or similar style.

The old bridge was a case in point. It had stood for centuries and now looked of very ancient design when compared to the new modern structures rising from the ground further up river to the west. This new architecture with its wonderful palaces of gleaming white stone, sited in large open, paved, squares with wide flattened streets and piazzas in the foreign

European style, was amazing to see, particularly for the poor in the east, who could only compare them contemptuously with their own outdated buildings. Much of the new design was the work of the architect Mr. Wren, who, with the support of the Church, had produced many new churches. However, even his genius could not amend the property rights of the old City, therefore much of the old housing had not changed, leaving it looking rather out of place when seen against his beautiful new churches now dotted throughout the square mile. The East-West difference was especially noticeable down by the river and in the area around the old bridge.

The river Fleet was another anomaly; the ramshackle old buildings along its banks looked forgotten, they seemed to have stood still in time, while all around and behind them, away from the water looked new and foreign, as if recently arrived from some far away place. Edwin did not like the Fleet very much. His father called it a filthy ditch. True it was narrow and dirty compared to the Thames, but what Edwin hated the most were the acrid smells emanating from the water itself. The Fleet was still used by its waterside dwellers as an open sewer, the inhabitants of the houses and the businesses along the shore were seemingly oblivious to the stench they created. Smells that came from the many tanneries sited near to where the Fleet's corrupted waters spilled out into the Thames. Apart from this misuse of a fine tributary of the noble Thames, there was also the floating detritus emanating from the activities of the butchers and the dyers of cloth, all of whom used the Fleet as their personal sewer. Many small businesses were situated on each side of the Fleet's entry into the Thames, giving them a convenient means of disposing of their unwanted by-products. At certain times and states of tide, the surface of the water slipping into the Thames was a great slimy, multi coloured, slippery patch. Wherrymen would be forced to row further towards the centre of the river, to avoid this mess sticking to their boats, and to avoid the offending smell.

The tanners were the biggest offenders, they had settled here many centuries before and were now well established within the City's hierarchy, they had many powerful friends and investors, many of whom held high and powerful positions. The methods used by the tanning craft created a great deal of evil smelling waste, which for the most part was thrown into the Fleet, from where it found its way into the Thames itself. Many attempts had been made by the 'City Fathers' to stop this pollution, but always without success. City laws for deepening and improving the Fleet in 1666, and even acts of parliament, seemed to have had no lasting effect. The tanners, butchers and dyers all had their high-born connections and were protected by their rich friends, many of whom had financial interests themselves in the trades, and relied on the business to make their profits. Although the tanners and the butchers produced the worst pollution, the dyers' trade added colour to the problem. Their waste products being chemical rather than animal based, were more offensive to the eye than to the nose.

The buildings along the Fleet's banks were built down to the river and overhung the water's edge. They were mostly two or three story timbered-framed structures. Their muddy footings had sunk over the years into the silt foundations, and over time they had taken on an assortment of weird and alarming shapes when seen from the river. It was as if these houses had spent a night out on the town and were reeling home in drunken disarray, holding each other up like a row of roaring-boys on their way home from an evening of debauched entertainment.

The dirty dull windows and crooked doors were the twisted faces of pure overindulgence, and the smell of the area like that of an innkeeper's breath. Inside these buildings the stench was even more intense. Until your nostrils got used to it, finding enough breath when you first entered was almost impossible. It was a stringent, throat catching sharpness, which hung in the atmosphere and pinched the lungs together, leaving those unused to it panting for air. The City Fathers had tried many times to curtail these smells, but all to no avail, the stink continued. This was the home of the watermen Taylor's.

All the members of the family were well known for their argumentative nature, their noisy public quarrels however, never seemed to come to blows, or much else of a serious nature. Edwin's friend Kenneth had once commented,
"They are like a keg of fighting ferrets, all spitting and hissing but no stomach for blood". It was true; Edwin had found that the Taylor watermen that he knew did not like his infamous, hurtful witticisms, quips that he had perfected over the years. He only had to refer to their moon faces, or lack of hair, or their filthy little Fleet River, to find them backing off from a potential confrontation. They were to a man, sensitive of any form of criticism. One thing above all however, was guaranteed to rile them into furious discourse, was any mention of the Royal Navy, or the exploits of the ruthless press gangs, which had plagued their family over many decades. In this they were somewhat justified, their family had suffered more than most, by their men-folk being taken for service as seamen in the monarch's fighting ships. The Taylor family claimed to have lost twenty men while serving in ships of the line. Six others had been crippled or maimed and another twenty-five had together spent a total of sixty prime years of their lives in the service. However, a few had done well by accepting the Queen's shilling, and had gained a share of prize money, from which they and the family had prospered. The Taylors were now spread wide and far throughout the City, and had their fingers in the pies of many disparate trades.

A new system for filling the demands of the navy was now being developed by the Watermen's Guild, but it was still in its infancy. The Company proposed organizing a roster of men to be called forward as required by the Admiralty for Naval service. They were to be called the 'River Fencibles'. The Guild would deal directly with the Admiralty and fulfil the requirements demanded for replacing the hordes of sailors lost in battles, or through accidents at sea. The journeymen watermen themselves, who now included the Lightermen within their ranks, were opposed to this new idea, which would give them even less chance to avoid service in the fleet. At least under the existing system a man could avoid being caught if he was careful and clever. The new Fencibles, however, would have no choice but to serve in their turn.

Edwin had mixed views about all this; in a way he admired the idea of going to sea and sailing to distant shores. He was excited by the idea of getting away from the choking fogs, the hard winter frosts, and the grinding worries of living in London. He liked to visit the wharves and docks of Wapping, and to see the variation of foreign seamen in the taverns and inns of the area. He was intrigued by the differing sizes, shapes, skin colour and looks of these men. He liked to listen to the old sailors in the alehouses, telling stories about their exploits in distant lands. All this fired the blood of a young man; he was tempted by the idea of visiting these strange places to see them for himself. Whenever he voiced this opinion however, his father would reminded him of the hardships the saltwater-men faced and the strict punishments meted out by the Navy, sometimes for very trivial misdemeanours. He told Edwin of the many wives and families he knew who had lost their men-folk in the service. One woman lost her husband and all three sons in the same sea battle. Now destitute, she lived by begging for food at the roadway.

It was the practice of the Navy, when the press brought a newly captured man on board a ship, for the Captain to offer him the chance to volunteer rather than to be forced to serve. If the man took the Queen's shilling and signed on as a volunteer, he would then be entitled to a share in any prize money that could be raised by selling captured ships, cargo, or goods, which had been taken in battle. This share-out was very unevenly distributed between the Admiralty, the captain, officers and crew, but sometimes the prize was so great, that even a small share amounted to a fortune for a poor man. It could be a sum substantial enough, that if a man survived to the end of the ship's commission, he could be discharged with enough prize money to set himself up in trade. Many such men could be found in and around the City. However, any man who stuck to his principles by not volunteering to serve when caught, would still have to serve the length of the ship's commission, carry out the same duties and would be liable to the same punishments. He would also have to fight in the same battles, but he would not be included to share in any prize money earned by the rest of the crew. He was considered to have been pressed, a forced man. Most men therefore swallowed their principles when captured, and signed the ship's log as a volunteer.

Edwin, with his eyes half closed, listened to the two Taylor brothers arguing by Old Swan Stairs, he noticed that their voices had risen an octave or two and that he could now make out some of their words. He looked up and could also see that their torches were waving erratically in the air as they argued. He strained to hear what they were saying and could see that the other wherrymen were doing the same.

"You are a foolish devil Rob." The words were now becoming clear as the argument heated up. It was Christopher's domineering voice.

"Why can you not do just as I ask, without all this fuss?" Robin made some answer, which Edwin could not make out. Whatever it was, it made Christopher even angrier.

"I am cursed with a brother who is not only a fool but a coward into the bargain. If I had the time I would do it myself and leave you out of the reckoning. I should leave you to your Tavern whores where you can hide away from any danger". Robin was now angry and raised his voice to an audible level

"It is you, not I, who is in the wrong and shames our name with your animal needs in the whore-house. I will no longer do your dirty work for you". It was the angry voice of Robin shaking with rage. Edwin wondered what this could be all about.

<========>

Some weeks earlier, the two brothers had been seated at the corner table of a noisy tavern, trying to hold a conspiratorial conversation interspersed with furtive glances around the room.

"Can you not get some other to do it this time?" Robin Taylor was saying to his brother

"Robin" said Christopher, having to raise his voice above the clamour.

"There is no danger," he said reassuringly to the younger man.

"I know this lighterman well, and the night-watchman. I have dealt with them both before. They can be trusted". He looked intently into his brother's eyes, looking to gain control of the younger man.

"I only wanted to say that I do not like doing this 'black face' work." Said Robin, feeling uncomfortable at disagreeing with his elder brother.

"Come about, Rob, you can trust me, I know what I am doing, I know what is good for us both". Robin shuffled his feet; he knew that as always he must give in.

"Well just one more time, if you say it is safe," said Robin, speaking loudly to be heard above the din.

"It could not be more so. It will take you only an hour or so and you will be back in your warm cot." Christopher smiled, he knew that he was again back in control of his downtrodden brother.

"Now Rob, listen carefully. Tomorrow night the water will be low at about midnight, am I right?" Robin nodded his head.

"You will drop down on the last of the ebb and put your boat under the trots at Downing's Barge chains in the lower Pool. Keep yourself well hidden". Robin unenthusiastically stared into his brother's face. Christopher could see the lack of enthusiasm, but carried on.

"Later you will hear a man whistling the tune 'Drunken Cobbler'. When you hear this you will know that the coast is clear, for it will be the night watchman himself giving you the signal." He looked closely at Robin to see that he had understood.

"Next Rob, you must row over to Reed's Wharf, near Mill Stairs. You know the place" Robin nodded.

"There is a ship moored there called the 'Black Rose', she is laying third bottom from the wharf, outside of her is the lightening barge we are after. I have arranged with the lighterman to only sham-lock her hatches on the starboard side aft". He again checked to see that his words were being heeded. Satisfied that they were, he continued, having to raise his voice to be heard above the clamour of a bawdy refrain which had just started up, with which everyone in the tavern seemed to want to join in with.

"Open up her corner sheet and slide back the first hatch. She is carrying a mixed cargo, but under that hatch you will find bolts of fine cloth. I have agreed that we will take only six, put them in your wherry and sham lock the lighter again, then quietly row back off to the trots. Once the tide turns you can bring the goodies up to our moorings at the Fleet and stow them down below in our floater". Robin wanted to say something, but seeing that Christopher would be angry if he questioned anything, he decided to keep his trap shu.t

"Now," said Christopher.

"The good news is that I already have a buyer, a tailor who will take all six bolts for a good price, and I have agreed to a lucrative split, half to us, and the other half shared between the lighterman and the night watchman. It is a good deal and we will show a tidy profit."

Sitting near to the two brothers, partly hidden by a curtain, pretending to be deep in his cups, and seemingly halfway asleep, was a small man dressed in a long heavy coat with its collar turned up and obscuring his face. He wore a wide brimmed hat which was pulled down over his eyes. However, Edward Bishop was most certainly not sleeping, nor was he drunk; in fact he was straining to hear the conversation between the two brothers. He knew of these watermen and of their sometimes dubious night-work. He could only catch parts of their conversation above the noise of the tavern, but he had heard enough for his purpose. Finishing his pot he got to his feet.

"Hallo my dear, buy a maid a drink an' see what ye gets in return?" It was a dishevelled, gin-pickled woman, about to throw her arms about him. Pushing away this unwanted tavern hag who obviously wanted to become friendly with him, Edward played the part of a staggering drunk, about to leave the place to stumble home as best he could.

"Women," he spat out the word at the wench.

"I have one of you at home who makes my life hell enough, I do not need a tavern harlot having her hand in my purse as well" then almost over-balancing the woman in her hurry, Edward Bishop quickly left the tavern. The tavern wench poked out her tongue at the back of Mr Bishop's head and turning her back on him she flicked her skirts in a little show of temper and disappointment, then swaying violently from side to side, went off in search of a more willing victim. The brothers continued making plans, none the wiser that a spy had overheard their strategy.

The following morning found Mr Bishop at the Guild Hall, where he was a regular visitor, and was nodded in by the doorman, who knew him to be an agent of the Town Clerk, Edward went straight to the Clerk's office, where he knocked stealthily, and on receiving the command to enter, he went in.
"Good morrow Mr Bishop, you are about early this day."
"I have some information for you, but it is urgent and will need quick action," said the spy rudely, without any of the normal preliminaries.
"Give me the news, and if I judge it worthy we can act quickly enough." The Clerk knew this man was good at his work and that his information was usually reliable.
"First sir I would discuss my commission". Said Edward. The Clerk bristled; he hated dealing with these greedy informers, but it was a necessary chore in such a corrupt City.
"If your information leads to a capture you will be paid the usual fee, and 5% of the value of any goods recovered," confirmed the Clerk. Mr Bishop seemed satisfied.
"I know of two Watermen rogues who will this very night steal valuable bolts of cloth from a lightening barge moored in the Pool." He then told the story of what he had overheard, giving all the details as he knew them.
"Thank you for this information I think I have heard this family name before," said the Clerk, mentally licking his lips at the thought of the profit for himself.
"It is perhaps time to give them a little scare, plus most likely others who will also be involved into the bargain. You may leave the matter with me, I will let you know the outcome". Mr Bishop looked pensive; he was not pleased to be left aside in the matter.
"I will be nearby tonight to see the outcome for myself," he said, annoying the Clerk by this show of interference.
"You would do better to keep out of the matter, your meddling may cause a mishap," suggested the Clerk.
"I will protect my investment, but none shall see me and I will not impede the work of your men." The Clerk knew that he had no way to stop the spy and shrugging his shoulders, capitulated on the point

<========>

Robin sat in his wherry, concealed by the deep shadow of a deserted wharf; he took out the small jar of the special mixture used by his family when wishing to hide their features when undertaking clandestine night-work. Pulling the cork, he reached inside with his finger and scraped up a good amount of the contents, it was a blend of chimney soot, linseed oil and goose fat. He began to spread the mixture over the skin of his face and on the backs of his hands, making sure that all parts of skin showing to the night would be covered. He then wrapped some strips of sacking around his oars where they held in the oarlocks, and spread extra tallow onto the

sacking, turning the oars in their locks to spread the grease evenly. "That will stop you thumping while I row," he said to his boat as if it would understand the reason for his action.
"We will work well together this night," he whispered to his boat. "If all goes well, I will have your stem-band repaired, as I have promised you for some time now." He patted the gunwale of the boat as if it were an old friend.

The tide was now almost at its lowest point. Robin judged that it was time to make his way down to the trots in the Pool and conceal himself in the shadows there. As he rowed he showed no light; his candle in its copper lantern was stowed away beneath the passenger seat. He kept to the shadows mostly, but seeing a chance to save himself some work, he sculled out into open water and caught a turn on the stern of a spritsail barge as she glided past in the dark, dragging him down river in the direction that he wanted to go. On reaching Downing's chains, he slipped his line off from the barge's sternpost, and using his oars, he pulled gently over to the trots and eased his boat snugly under the swim-head of a large flatboat. Then making sure that she was well hidden, he settled down to wait for the signal. After about half an hour of waiting, he at last heard the well-known refrain drifting out over the night air, a good sign he thought, all is well and to time.

He waited a few more minutes, and then rowed smoothly over to the barge his brother had described. The night was hushed; even the night watchman's whistling had now stopped. Robin pulled himself aboard the barge and looked around. He could hear the dull sounds of voices coming from the ship, but all was clear. He checked the starboard locks; each was in the sham position as arranged. He slipped the locks out and rested them carefully on the gunwale, then sliding the long batten bar back out of the way, he released the sheet that covered the corner of the barge's hold, then he carefully opened the first hatch, just enough to reach inside. Yes, the cargo was right up to the top of the barge's hold, well within his reach. He could feel the soft bales of cloth; they were wrapped in a strong sacking material. He soon had the six out and into his boat as ordered, then reaching back inside he pulled out another. This one seemed somehow different, he stowed this bale away from the others under the passenger thwart. This would be his sweetener for the night's work.

Having replaced the hatch with its cover-sheet, and again sham-locked the barge. Robin climbed silently into his boat and carefully covered the bales of cloth with his pull-on, then he gently rowed back to the hiding place at the barge chains, he now must wait for the tide to flood. It was not long before he felt the movement of the new tide pushing up river, he waited a little longer until he judged the flood to be flowing well enough for him to leave. He cast off and started to make his way up river towards the Fleet. He would however deviate slightly, he intended to make a short stop on-route. There was now more activity starting up on the river as the flood tide made its presence known. He noticed that other boats and barges were on the move. One in particular he noticed, like him she was not showing a light, he glimpsed her now and then as she passed from shadow to shadow, he could see that the crew had not blacked up, so why were they not showing a light? The vessel was an open cutter with four men at the oars and two passengers, which also made him wonder why, with such oar-power she was not making up on him more quickly. He did not like the feeling that he was getting about this vessel. He rowed over to the other side of the river only to find that she followed keeping her distance. When he returned to the Southside she followed him again.

Robin decided to take no chance and decided on a plan of action. On pulling through the bridge he waited until he was abreast of Red Lion Wharf then he quickly rounded hard behind a sailing barge, which was moored near the bridge arch, under her protection and hidden from view, he pulled down once again through the bridge. He caught a glimpse of the cutter turning to follow him, but he now had the edge. As he passed through the bridge he turned yet again, this time hard to starboard and hid behind another moored spritsail barge. Thinking that he was heading straight on, the cutter came through the arch at a rate of knots, now racing to catch up with their illusive prey, whom they thought to be now down-stream and well ahead of them. Once they had passed, Robin let go and quickly pulled over to the shore, turning hard into the bank inside the Clink barge-roads, where several of the Western Barges were moored.

On reaching St Olave's stairs, he came alongside the deserted causeway with some relief, then pulling out the extra bale of cloth from under the passenger seat, he quickly carried it up the causeway to the Horseshoe Inn, which stood in the shadows at the top by the river wall. Robin knew the Innkeeper well, and had arranged to leave the bale of cloth with him, to be sold and the money shared out later between the two of them. The Innkeeper was an observant man and had seen Robin arrive, he came out to meet him.
"Matthew," said Robin." I am on the work for my brother that I told you about, but I may have been followed. There is a dark cutter dogging my heels, I have here the bale for us, but can I also leave the rest of the cloth with you and pick it up later?"
"To be sure you can, I owe you many a favour, come I will help you bring them up". The heavy bales were soon up and into the store-cellar of Matthew's Inn.
"This is the one as an additional, which you and I can share," said Robin indicating the extra bale.
"Keep it to one side and we will deal with it when we have time." Matthew nodded; he could see that Robin was anxious to leave.

On returning to his wherry, Robin cleaned his face and hands from the black mixture with his kerchief and removed the sacking from the oars then cast off from the lonely causeway. Matthew watched as the waterman pulled away into the night, then returning to the cellar he pulled the extra bale over to one corner, and carefully tearing the paper covering, looked at the cloth inside, all seemed well so he put this bale into his special lock-up cupboard.

As Robin rowed out into the tideway and gained the centre of the river once more, he could again see the dark outline of the cutter, she was now ahead of him. Her crew had realised that he had not gone down river and had returned to come upriver again through the bridge. He was now astern of the vessel, which was hugging the south shore looking for him among the darkened wharves and drawdocks. Robin pulled across to the north shore and stopped to light the candle in his lantern, then he continued on his journey towards the Fleet. As soon as the men in the cutter saw him, they quickly crossed the river and fell in astern of his boat once again. Robin rowed on until; reaching the mouth of the Fleet River he turned in and came alongside the family chains and their mooring pontoon.

"Ahoy there boatman". It was the cutter coming alongside him.
"Yes Your Highness, what can I do for you?" asked Robin, relieved to know that he had got rid of the illicit cargo.
"We are the Mayor's men, sent by the Town Clerk to check your wherry. Stand hard I am coming aboard you" said the gruff voice from the dark. A burly man dressed in dark blue climbed over from the cutter into Robin's boat.
" We are seeking a boatman who is about this night and up to mischief ," said the man. Robin could not clearly make out his face, but he could smell that the man had been at the rum bottle.
"Then why are you boarding an innocent Wherryman going about his business? You should be out there chasing your prey, or back into your rum bottle and the tavern trollops". The man hated the rude remarks of these Wherrymen; they always seemed to have something unpleasant to say. Robin could see that the man was obviously looking around the boat but there was nothing to be seen, he even searched with his hand under the thwarts but to no avail. The Mayor's man knew he would have to accept the rough tongue of this Waterman on this occasion and withdraw.
"I will leave you this time boatman. He knew these men hated to be called 'boatmen'.
"You have outwitted us, but we will catch you in the end and have our way with you and yours, to be sure"
"Yes I know your way of it," accused Robin.
"You would want the Lion's share of anything that you might find in my poor wherry, anything that might be returned to its rightful owner, would be much depleted after your work was done, we of the river know full well who are the villains in this City". The big man wanted to be away from these accusations; he quickly got back into the cutter and without reply to Robin ordered the vessel to pull away into the night.
Robin was mightily relieved, he knew that if he had been caught, he might have been able to pay off the Mayor's men, but sometimes there were others

behind the scene who wanted to be rewarded, it could have been a very expensive affair altogether.

The next morning Robin met Christopher at their moorings and told him the story. He knew that Christopher would want him to be the one to fetch the cloth from Matthew and so would not find out about the extra bale. He could therefore hold to his secret.
"You are a fool Rob; you must have been followed to the lighter, how else would they have known? Now I will have to include Matthew into the reckoning, God I am cursed with an idiot for a brother"
"But Chris, I saved us from the Mayor's men getting their hands on the cloth, you know they would have taken everything and probably wanted much more if they had found the goods." He was annoyed that his brother did not praise him for his quick thinking in avoiding a disaster.
"No! No, you were followed all right; with your bad eyesight, I suppose you could not see the boat following you down. I should have done the job myself, I can not trust you to do the most simple things." Robin was hurt by the reference to his eyesight, but he kept quiet, smouldering to himself.
"Well, you will have to pick up the cloth from your friend Matthew and deliver it to the tailor directly. I do not have the time to do it myself and this time; try not to make any mistakes."

The following day saw Robin at Matthew's inn, talking with his friend over a jug of ale.
"So there have been no spies or suspicious enquiries?" ask Robin.
"No, not one," said the Inn keeper.
"Not a sign, and believe me I have been keeping a keen lookout"
"Good" said Robin.
"I have borrowed a cart," It is out at the back, come help me load the stuff, I want an end to this matter, it still has a bad taste for me". The men retrieved the six bales of cloth from where Matthew had stowed them, leaving the extra one in the cupboard to be dealt with later. Matthew said he knew of an old seamstress who might take it for a fair price. Robin bad farewell to his friend and pushing the cart ahead of him, moved off through the streets to find the house of Christopher's tailor. He did not notice the little man in the shadows of a doorway watching him. However, Matthew the Innkeeper did, ever cautious, he had observed the stranger from the window of his inn.
"I must get that cloth out of here and to the seamstress as quick as possible; there is more going on here than is plain to the eye."

Robin arrived at the address of the tailor without much trouble, although he was hot and sweating. Even crossing the bridge had been unusually easy, as he had pushed the cart ahead of him, mingling with the pedestrian traffic and the many other wheeled vehicles on the roadway, he then headed through the City, his cart's metal shod wheels chattered over the cobbles, sending vibrations up his arms and through his whole body. He had blended with the others going about their business and no one had

challenged him. Robin disliked the smells of the City, there was horse shit and straw everywhere, with the accompanying pungent stench of animal urine to assail his nostrils. The tailor was pleased at the arrival of the cloth, he was a greedy man by nature and planned to make a good profit when the cloth was made up into garments. He could not wait to work out how many he could make by skimping on the seems, and by careful cutting. Perhaps he should concentrate on children's outfits he thought to himself with satisfaction.
"With all this I will turn a pretty penny," he persuaded himself as he helped Robin to bring the bales into his workshop.
"You look as if you are in need of a drink, would you like some water?" inquired the tailor, looking at Robin's sweating, red face.
"Water!" spat Robin in disgust.
"Has the water become clean then here in this part of town?"
"No thank you, I would prefer ale if it please you". The tailor was a mean man and did not give good ale away lightly, but he called to his wife who fetched a small pot of ale for the thirsty waterman. Unwilling to wait any longer to see his newly acquired wealth, the tailor began to cut open the covering around the bales of cloth.
"What's this?" he shouted, opening up the first of the bales to see its content.
"This is but common sacking, what is afoot here."

Robin knew at once that they had all been duped, someone had exchanged the bales of quality cloth for cheap sackcloth. He had been uneasy from the very first about this adventure, and now he was the one to be caught. The tailor was ripping open the other bales only to find that they were all full of the neatly rolled sackcloth. Robin ran to the window and peered outside, there were men out there hiding in the shadows of doorways he was sure of it. Without saying another word to the tailor, he ran through to the back alley, he looked about him, it was deserted, the Mayor's men had not yet had time to close off all the escape routes. Robin knew the tailor was in trouble, but he also knew his brother would not have given any unnecessary information when making the deal, therefore, if he could escape capture and get away, he could deny everything. With luck the family would come out of this safe, if a little out of pocket, but it all depended on a clean escape. By running through alleyways, then walking through others, and by hiding in doorways until he was sure the coast was clear, he at last made it away from the tailor's house clear and safe. He breathed a great sigh of relief, leaning against a wall to recover his composure, the cart was abandoned, left for the tailor to explain away. Robin made his way carefully back to the Fleet and the family moorings, he would feel safe once back on the river, he did not feel at home in the dangerous streets of the City.

Christopher was beside himself with rage, when Robin told him of his narrow escape, not because of the danger his brother had narrowly missed, but because he could see that someone had played a dirty trick on him. "Who could have done this?" he shouted, and on being urged to keep his

voice down by Robin.
"Could it have been that friend of yours the innkeeper?" accused Christopher, his voice now a loud whisper.
"No I would stake my life," said Robin emphatically, he would not do such a thing to me, with his own skin at risk, I know too much of his past.
"No" mused Christopher, now thinking more clearly.
"That would be too obvious altogether, for he would be also under suspicion".
"No, there is some other hand behind this." He looked at his brother.
"I have found out that the lighterman and the watchman have both been taken." Robin was shocked.
"There you see? " Said Robin.
"The fault is on your side of this business".
"Shut up you fool," snapped Christopher.
"I must think about this some more, and discover the rogue behind it all. I will have his ears off for my revenge, you see if I don't."

<========>

The Town Clerk sat back in his high backed chair, looking dispassionately across the desk at his spy Mr Bishop.
"So it seems you helped us to get them all except for the Watermen involved?"
"Yes Sir, but I know who they are; the shame is I cannot yet prove it, but I believe it to be a good catch of smelly fish, a lighterman, a watchman and a tailor, you should I think be able to truck well for their freedom will you not?" He looked closely at the Clerk.
"The cloth of course will not be returned I suppose."

The Town Clerk changed the subject. He did not like the fact that this man knew, or guessed, too much of his private business. On his instructions, his men had changed the bales of fine cloth in the lightening barge for inexpensive sacking, he now had the originals looked away down in his own cellar. The owner of the cargo need never know what happened to his cloth, and after a suitable amount of time he would dispose of them at a full profit. In the meantime he would find out more about his captives. If they were not wanted by anybody of importance, then he would arrange with their families for a suitable payment for their release. Yes it would all turn out very well, he might soon be able to increase his investment in those overseas shares which were doing so well.

"Here is your fee Mr Bishop", said the Clerk sliding a fat purse across the desk, which the spy pounced upon, he wondered for a moment if this man knew what had happened to the missing bale of cloth, one bale however, was small fry, perhaps the spy had frittered away, or the men who made the arrest. It was best not to delve too deeply, therefore he would not pursue the matter, it might queer the pitch for his other plans if he pressed the point.

"Thank you Sir," said the self appointed spy, standing and making ready to leave.
"I hope to see you again soon with more gainful business".

<=======>

Edwin, sitting and watching the altercation between the two brothers at Old Swan causeway, thought he might know what this argument between the brothers was about. Everyone knew that Christopher had arrangements with some of the lightermen and light-horsemen who worked the ships down in the Pool. Like all the trades working with the vast amounts of cargo going through the port, these men had many tricks, and clever ways to pilfer and steal from the barges and flatboats. The vessels of the Port were often left unattended for long periods of time, while moored around the ships, waiting their turn to be unloaded. Although locked and supervised, all night watchmen could be bribed to turn a blind eye at the most opportune moment, while a black-faced job was in progress. Lightermen could be paid to leave their lighteners unlocked, making it easy to remove some of the goods from the hold. The crew and even the Captains of ships were, to a greater or lesser degree also corrupt, and the Queen's men, who inspected and counted the cargo, were the most adept of all in the ways of acquiring cargo for themselves. In their case it was not just pilfering, but substantial amounts could find its way to quiet wharves. Most surprising of all was that much of the shipment was stolen to the orders of the owner. This form of corruption involved insuring the goods at an inflated price from its true worth, then claiming this exaggerated amount after the cargo had been removed by arrangement. For all those involved with the handling of cargo within the port, these activities were seen as the normal perks of the capital's business. Most watermen, lightermen and most port workers, fed and supported their families, particularly through the bitter winters, with food and goods stolen from the ship of London's port.

Edwin knew that Christopher was one of the worst offenders; he would bribe the lightermen to leave their lighters moored on the outermost rank of the ship, or at a quiet barge-roads. The vessel would be only sham-locked, then Robin would be sent in his wherry to unofficially lighten the craft. This of course put the younger brother at the greatest risk, while Christopher would be supposedly working out the next robbery, by trucking with another Port-worker. Christopher was unusual in taking the risk of dealing with a person outside the safety of his own trade. Watermen tended to deal only with other watermen, and lightermen with lightermen. The lightermen were still seen by the watermen, as not fully trustworthy, and not truly part of their older profession. Edwin felt sure that some dirty deal had gone wrong, and the two brothers were arguing about whose fault it was.

The argument was now raging between the brothers, with much swearing, cursing, and brandishing of their hot torches in each other's faces. Finally, when it seemed that they would come to blows, Christopher with a great show of bad temper, drove his torch into the water to quench the flame, then throwing the now dead wand into the bottom of his boat. With grand sweeps of his arms, and irritable gestures of his hands, he angrily slipped his mooring line from his brother's vessel, and violently pulled his wherry back along the causeway, re-mooring it behind Edwin's boat, where he then sat sullenly, probably planning how he would again coax his brother into joining with him in his next illicit venture. Robin sat seething quietly in his own wherry, his emotions torn. At first he was going to tell Christopher about the extra bale of cloth, which he and the Inn keeper had rescued from this unfortunate affair, and offer to share his part of the proceeds he had made from the sale, but on being blamed for everything, he had decided to keep the secret to himself, his loyalty to his brother however, made it a difficult secret to keep; there was no pleasure in any of it for Robin.

A typical Taylor argument thought Edwin. Looking at the two sullen shapes sitting in their respective boats, all wind and puff, but no blows, it will all be forgotten by the next high water. The family bond was strong as ever.

Chapter Eight

The dreadful life of James

Edwin's mind was now sailing on a sea of many interesting and comforting thoughts, as he sat quietly in his wherry. This calm however, was abruptly disturbed by an unpleasant, rasping, noise, he could hear the unmistakable of sound of James Deveral's deep hacking cough. Edwin waited for the next sound, which he knew always followed the coughing fit. In his mind he could imagine the blood streaked phlegm forming in James's throat, being moved forward over the tongue and into his mouth. He waited for the soft explosion of sound as James expelled the frightening mess into the water next to his boat. It would form a great spreading gob, Edwin had seen it many times before, he looked over the side of his own boat down into the water and watched the fearsome mess float by him on the early movement of the new ebb tide, its hideous colours glinting in the flickering glow of the burning torches. He wondered as he always did how a man could live with lungs in such a state of disrepair as James's.

James was the sixth wherryman waiting at Old Swan Stairs that night whose story was now floating through Edwin's mind. In fact James was the first in line for a fare. If any prospective passenger would take him and his boat, he was nearest to the stairs and would be viewed by anyone coming down to take oars from the causeway, James's torch was smoking badly. The thick black smoke catching in his throat, had starting this latest coughing attack. Poor James suffered from an assortment of illnesses; apart from the alarming state of his lungs, he had a serious skin disease, which had plagued him all his life, parts of his body were covered in small erupting pustules, which after discharging their painful yellow content, would heal over into a red scar. In an effort to hide this affliction, and to keep the wounds clean, he wore thin, linen, fingerless bandage gloves, and a linen scarf, which were provided clean each day by his seemingly devoted sister. She, like her brother, was unmarried and of a similar age, she did not speak much and would hurry away when her business with her brother was concluded.
James always wore black, except for his white linen gloves and scarf; these stark white objects when added to the black clothes only supplemented his sombre, forbidding, appearance.
From James's point of view as a wherryman, he needed the gloves and scarf to hide his disfigurement, he must avoid putting off prospective passengers, and for the same reason he also preferred to work at night, he found that the people of the late hours, having had their fill of food, wine, or other pleasures of the body, were less alarmed by the look of their wherryman than those of the daylight, wishing only to get home to their beds. James however, had yet another problem, as a young man, his left leg had not developed properly, it was a good three inches shorter that the right one. This affliction gave him a strange lopsided, rolling walk, with a little skip at

the end of each second step. To meet this man on a dark night in a lonely alley, coming towards you out of the gloom, with his limping gate, could be quite a shock.

To Edwin it seemed incredible that a man with so many afflictions could live so long, for James was certainly well into his fifties. However, the man also had many strengths, he was a good oarsman despite his deformed leg, he could row as far as any of the others of his age, he was a wily intelligent man, usually a jump or two ahead of the rest, but most impressive of all to the young Edwin was the fact that James was the best man with a blade he had ever witnessed. He could throw accurately with either hand, and used his knife with a dexterity that Edwin would have given much to achieve. James carried two blades, both concealed in the back of his belt. Sometimes, when waiting at plying stairs, he could often be seen surreptitiously sharpening the edges to a razor like keenness.

The City of London, beneath its seemingly healthy exterior, nurtured a dark secret of illness and disease, apart from the pox, which was to some extent self inflicted. There was always the fear of another Black Death' epidemic; each year pockets of the plague would spring up in different parts of the capital, the people living within the square mile were not only frightened of suffering the dreadful consequences of the illness, but also the probable loss of their house and belongings, which were usualy burnt down by order of the Mayor as a precaution against the pest spreading to nearby families, while those showing any symptoms of the dreaded 'black death' including their close family members, were put into 'Pest Houses' for the duration. A person would either come out from these places as a copse, or as a pauper.

Disease of his lungs, his skin, and a serious limp, were all physical burdens to be born by the ailing James. However, he was a resourceful fellow, and seemed to have coin aplenty for his wants, his cloth was good, and was always in good repair, his wherry, which he owned outright, was kept in top condition. Both Edwin and his father wondered how James did so well for a night wherryman. The men working the dark hours usually had something to hide, or hide from; night work showed the least profit for watermen, but under its cover other business could be contracted of a more illicit nature. Edwin's father Alfred was the only person James seemed willing to converse with for any length of time; they could occasionally be seen sitting together talking quietly while waiting for passengers. Edwin tried to draw out his father's opinion about James, and to find out what he had told him, but he would only say that he was an intelligent man in many ways, but a very dangerous man, with many strange beliefs. He warned Edwin that he should steer well clear of James, but should be careful to do so without causing the man any offence.

Edwin remembered well his first encounter with Mr. Deveral. It was in the winter of a great frost in the year 1698 when Edwin was thirteen years of age. His father had then for some time allowed Edwin to help him with the cleaning of the boats, or with some of the other tasks that all vessels require and duly benefit from. That winter the wherries were all pulled up onto the shore, well clear of the icy water, for weeks on end the river was completely frozen over, from above the bridge to as far up-stream as the boats worked. During that winter, the weather varied between extreme cold and relatively warmer patches. The waters upriver from the bridge would therefore thaw out a little, only to freeze over again as the frost returned, trapping great ice blocks, which had been freed during the warmer periods, and turning them onto their sides, or even upright, then refreezing around them again, creating crazy shapes, which resembled drunken gravestones. So much so that the frozen river above the bridge looked like an old churchyard after a hurricane. In the mornings when the frost was thick and white, the view from the shore resembled a frozen hell. It seemed no place for man or beast. However, this was the only place where the watermen had a right to earn their coin.

In that bitter winter, the watermen were soon in dire straits, imploring their Guild to help them survive the hard weather, but what little help there was went to the most needy and the Crossback family did not qualify. It is said that "adversity brings invention" and for the Thames watermen this was true, they found ways of using their frozen river to bring them some reward and thereby respite from their desperate situation. The first thing they did was to pass the word about the City describing the wonders of the frozen river, the magic of the ice, the thrill of walking on solid water. The citizens of London, always looking for distractions from their mostly dreary lives, could easily be persuaded to investigate this strange and novel experience; they flocked to experience this world of ice. The watermen, with devious intent, would then man the plying stairs, keeping the ice clear from the causeways with salt and sharp sticks. By this means they could supply short plank-walks for helping people across onto the ice, on their way to enjoy the unique feeling of walking on 'old father'. For this provision of a crossing onto the ice, the wherrymen would make a charge.

Other watermen mounted their boats onto wheels and took paying passengers for trips in and out of the humps and bumps of the uneven ice flows, pulled by a gang of men, who were only too pleased to earn a few pennies for their efforts. Others rigged up tents on the ice, for trading in all manner of curios connected with the ice. These ranged form small ice-carvings, to ice-balls containing nuts or other curios. They sold food, drinks, and hot mulled wine to the merry makers. It was in their interest to portray this disaster of solid water, as an entertainment and a distraction for the citizenry of London, and also to the many visitors who came from wider afield.

One day James Deveral put a proposition to Edwin's father. After careful consideration of what seemed to be a good plan, Alfred had agreed to go into temporary business with the man. The idea was to show a gruesome tableau inside a tent erected on the ice. The plan was to borrow a newly departed female corpse from the church mortuary. He wanted a young woman who had recently died in childbirth, of whom unfortunately there were many at this time; he also wanted the dead baby to be shown with her. They paid the priest for temporarily looking the other way, and agreeing to pay a percentage of their profits to the family of the deceased. During the cover of night, a coffin shape was chiselled out of the ice inside the tent, into which the bodies were laid, the dead child being positioned in its mother's arms. This pitiful tableau was then covered with clean fresh water and allowed to freeze solid and transparent, forming an eerie and pitiful scene.

The next day found the young Edwin stationed outside the tent, calling to the ice revellers to come and see the 'Ice-mother and child'. Alfred stood at the tent doorway taking the entrance fees and bidding those who entered to consider the fate of the poor woman inside, and that of the numerous others in their blighted City, to remember the many that could not be shown to them in this dramatic way. As the viewers entered, now nervous of what they were about to see, they found themselves confronted with a most dreadful sight. James in black cape and tall hat, sat at the head of the ice-mother tableau, his dark cloth contrasting with his pale countenance of the bodies, in the flickering candle light, his deformed body exaggerated for good effect, seated in an altitude of deep mourning for the poor woman. The ice-mother's body in its thin white dress and the naked child at her breast looked so pitiful that many of the women burst into tears at the very sight.

For the two watermen it was an even greater success than they had hoped for, but Edwin had never forgotten Mr. Deveral's part in the event, as it played out to its unseemly end, especially his inhumane arrangements for closing down the show, when the river began to thaw and liquify. The men knew that the ice would start its melt from underneath, and that they must cut the body free from the ice before the river's flow took the bodies away from under the ice. Necessity, or was it greed made them leave it too late to accomplish this last unpleasant task? One morning on opening up the tent for a final day's business, they found the ice coffin empty. Alfred was distraught, he knew that Nell had been against the whole project from the instigation, and would surely blame him for loosing the body of the poor woman and her baby. The priest would be incensed when told, he would certainly report them to his Bishop, and of course to the Watermen's Guild for due punishment. The family of the corpse might well take even stronger revenge.

James was strangely unruffled at the loss, and began to steadily chip away at the ice while Alfred ran off with the young Edwin down to the bridge arch, to see if at least one of the bodies had fetched up there, perhaps caught up in the pilings of the bridge. With no success, they sadly returned to the tent, only to find James pulling the body of the baby out of the ice hole, by a little fat foot and dropping it onto the ice next to the opening, as one would a newly caught fish. He then started pulling on another cod-line, which had also been hidden under his seat, slowly pulling until one of the dead woman's feet came into view. Alfred, sickened by the sight, but relieved that the bodies were not lost forever, helped pull the woman's corpse out from the cold water, placing it next to the baby. He looked at James who was calmly coiling the lines neatly together. Alfred was now white with anger and stress, he turned to the young Edwin, sending him outside of the tent, but the boy stayed near enough to hear his father's angry, but measured, tones talking at great length to the silent James.

After what seemed like a long time to the boy, his father came out from the tent, saying that they were now going home, and that Mr. Deveral would finish up on his own. On the way to the house he told Edwin that although a fully-grown man, who was supposedly wise to the ways of this world, he had learned a cruel lesson that day, what they had done was wicked, and must never to be repeated. The dead deserved respect, to treat them as if they were no more that pieces of floating river debris was an affront to God himself. Edwin could tell his father was furious inside. That night from his attic room he could hear him talking quietly to Nell, no doubt telling her his views of the callous attitude of Mr. James Deveral.

<========>

Edwin's best friend Kenneth also had good reason to know the callous nature of Mr. Deveral. He once had an encounter with James, which had affected him deeply. It had started when a group of young friends were discussing the strangeness of the ailing wherryman, of whom little or nothing was known. As usual Kenneth had made a joke of their inquisitiveness, saying that James was but a sick man and not one to be feared. However, he was then challenged to discover the truth of James's private life, to find out where James lived and where he went, when not working his wherry. They also wanted to know from where he got his means and seeming wealth. Kenneth being brave to a level of foolishness ignored Edwin's advice to leave the man alone, and decided that he would follow James one night, so that he might discover some secretes about this strange and ailing man.

They all knew that James was an acknowledged expert with his blade. He was the only person that Edwin knew who was truly dual-handed with a knife. He could use or throw his knife with either hand, and with deadly accuracy and effect, he would often be seen perfecting his skill, by throwing his knives at a timber board marked out with small symbols and signs. He would balance this board on the passenger seat of his wherry leaning it against the backboard, while sitting in the bow seat of the boat; he could even turn his back, throwing the knives over his shoulder, invariably hitting the mark of his aim. All this was as nothing to young Kenneth; he had the confidence of youth on his side. In his immature innocence, he considered himself equally as good as James. Anyway, he did not intend that James should even know that he was following him, or be aware that he was looking to discover the mysteries of his private life.

<========>

Kenneth had arrived well before midnight at the jetty in Wapping, where he knew James moored his boat when not in use, thinking that he would be nicely early; with time enough for a pot or two in the local Inn before the man arrived. He was therefore surprised to see James already mooring up his wherry for the night. This seemed to be a strange time to be finishing, when the night's work had hardly started. There would still be many fares to be had, revellers wanting to return home after a night out at Southwark or Bankside.

Kenneth watched from behind a pile of logs, as James finished adjusting the ropes to allow for the rise and fall of the tide . He then pulled himself in the boat over to the jetty ladder and started the climb up to the top. Kenneth could hear James coughing with the effort needed to ascend the steep ladder. Once ashore, the man, dressed in his usual black cloth, watched from the top of the jetty, to check that the boat traded her way back to her safe moored position. Then taking a long slow look around, and seemingly satisfied that he was alone, he stood up to his full height, looking straight out over the river's moon drenched water. To Kenneth's surprise he then raised his arms straight out in front of him. It was as if he was praying, his hands were held palms up, as if catching the moonlight. After about a minute in this position, he made a slow short bow from the waist, then turned and shambled off, with his curious limping gait, towards the pathway that led inland. He stopped only to look through the window of the Moonbeam Inn, which was built attached to the jetty near to the landing pier. After a few moments of eyeing the inside of the Inn, he shuffled off along the road away from the river, with his normal hobbling, rolling, gait,

Carefully following behind, Kenneth moved from shadow to shadow, he had pulled some sacking over his boots to muffle the sound of his hob-nails striking on the stones. He was very good at tracking through the City; he had had much practice when a young apprentice, when at the behest of his Master, he would be sent to track people who owed money. However, in spite of this hard earned practice, and after only a few minuets, he suddenly realised that he had lost his prey. He stopped and stood quietly in a deep shadow; listening for the scraping sound of James's boots, or the raking cough he knew must soon betray his whereabouts. Although he strained his ears for several minutes, he did not hear that distinctive sound. After a little more time, Kenneth realized that he had lost his man, and must give up for the night. He was annoyed; this had been a waste of his time, how could the man have disappeared so completely? Was it possible that James had known that he was being followed? Kenneth thought not, he was too good a tracker for that.

Kenneth was about to head back to his lodgings, when he had an idea; a plan, which might mean this night's work would not be a complete loss. He decided to return to the Moonbeam Inn, to see what the place was like. Provided the tavern was not frequented by chalkies or long-ferrymen, it might perhaps prove to be a place that he could recommend to his friends for a night out. On reaching the morbid looking building and looking through the window. He decided to go inside for a pot of ale; perhaps they might even know something of their strange waterman neighbour.

On entering the gloom of the Inn, Kenneth was struck by its cleanliness; in fact, it was too clean to be comfortable. It had a strong, sharp smell of lime and soft-soap, which he found unpleasant, the windows were sparkling, and the floor was spread with freshly cut hay. He had a wide choice for an empty table and sat down at one near the door. The place was more than two thirds empty. A few older seamen from the nearby ships, were eating from pewter plates, but seemed only interested in their food, another table of elderly ship's porters sat over in one corner, they were all sadly concentrating on their pots of drink. No one was talking; it was like a church meeting. The place was not the sort of tavern that Kenneth or his friends usually frequented. It was lifeless and morbid; it had the air of a mortuary with customers like corpses awaiting burial. However, one attraction soon caught Kenneth's roving eye. A young buxom serving maid had emerged from behind the counter curtain. She was dressed in a clean white blouse, a bright red skirt, with a French blue apron tied about her waist. She was very shapely indeed and was looking his way.

Laura had seen Kenneth enter the Inn from behind the curtain which shielded the serving counter. It was rare for an attractive young man to come into the Moonbeam Inn. She quickly went into the back kitchen and through into the small changing room that she was allowed to use. There she tidied her hair, pinched her cheeks to bring up the blood and slipped the neck of her pleated blouse from her shoulders, revealing her cream white neck and the tops of her ample bosoms. Entering the main room again, she approached Kenneth with a disarming smile, and asked in her most attractive Irish tones.
"What is the young master's pleasure?" Kenneth, as ever with a bright twinkle in his eye, gave her a knowing look.
"A question that will need careful considering" he replied with a wink. "I will start the evening with a pot of ale, some vitals, and I would like to offer something for yourself to drink, if you will join me at my table". Laura smiled, then in her lilting Irish accent said.
"I will be delighted altogether kind sir" and gave a pretty little curtsy.

As Laura moved off to bring the order, Kenneth looked her over from astern as she walked across the room. She was of medium height, but stood well, which made her seem taller. She was slim, with he was sure, a very good figure under that billowing skirt. Her lovely long, chestnut coloured, hair was loosely tied back away from her face. He had noticed however, that her face stopped her from being a perfect beauty. When she smiled, he noticed that her top teeth were curiously gaped in the front. In fact, when a young girl in Ireland, Laura had lost a front tooth in a fight with he brother. Over the early years of her life as a young girl, the other teeth, having no support from their missing neighbour, had moved apart from each other to fill the space, which they had never quite managed. Now her widely gapped teeth gave an odd appearance to her otherwise ready smile. Another small disfigurement to her face was a small, stark white, scar on her forehead, which travelled through and misaligned her left eyebrow, giving her face a slightly quizzical look. It was a shame thought Kenneth because otherwise she would have been a rare beauty indeed.

On returning from the kitchen with the drinks, accompanied by a plate of fresh bread, a large chunk of hard, yellow, cheese and a bowl of pickles. Laura placed them on the table; she leaned unnecessarily low across the table to serve him. In doing so, she gave Kenneth a most pleasant view down the front of her loose blouse, where he caught a glimpse of two beautifully rounded pink-white spheres.
"Now there is a sight to heal a man's poor eyes," said Kenneth still admiring the view.
"I see you are admiring my two best friends?" said Laura playfully.
"Pretty friends to be sure" said Kenneth, pleased at the girl's forthright way of talking.
"They have indeed proved to be good friends to me", said Laura. "They have found me entrance into places I could not otherwise have ever hoped to enter".
"I have no doubt of that," said Kenneth still looking at her breasts.
"I would like to be properly introduced to your friends, perhaps a little later this evening?"
" I think they might well enjoy such a meeting young Sir," said Laura with a smile.
"It will be all my pleasure, and will make my young heart sing. What is your name that I may address you properly?" said Kenneth, increasingly liking this maid.
"My name is Laura, I am from far away Ireland, the land of the little green fairies and the fierce red giants". Smiled the girl.
"Well met Laura of the fairies, my name is Kenneth of the river," he said telling her all she needed to know in those four words.
"You must be the first gentleman of less than fifty years, to come into this inn since I arrived here". Replied Laura. Then moving around the table to sit with Kenneth, she said.
"My friends and I will be altogether pleased to meet with you, but away from this place".
"Do you not like it here?" Kenneth asked.
"Not at all, at all, I started here but three months ago", the girl replied.
"They pay me well enough, but the place is always dead, never any singing or gaiety. I am fed up and bored with the place, with the sad customers and with the light work. I am looking to find a position in a more lively place

altogether".

"Do you know the 'Four Masted Ship'? The tavern of Great Bess?" asked Kenneth". At the mention of Bess's place, Laura's eyes lit up.

"Oh yes, I have heard that the place is a most happy hostelry, full of life altogether. I have also heard of the strange shows that take place there on occasions".

"I have a friend who works there", said Kenneth.

"I will find out how the land lies, and let you know if there is employment to be had. I can put in a good word for you". Laura beamed with pleasure. Now on a good course, Kenneth changed tack.

"Tell me Laura," said Kenneth, "what know you of the lame waterman who moors his boat at the jetty outside?" Laura's happy face suddenly drooped into a concerned frown.

"I know nothing of him," she said as if to head off any further mention of James. Kenneth could clearly see that she did know something.

"Well you see Laura. It is like this. My friends and I work with this man, but we know very little about him, he is a close mouthed person, private in the extreem and very proud, we think that he might need help, but know not what we can do to assist him". Laura listened fixedly.

"I have promised my mates I would follow him," went on Kenneth. "To find where he lives, who looks after him, who his friends might be, and if they fully assist him in his needs". Kenneth could see that his story was convincing the girl.

"We mean the man no harm; it is just normal curiosity with a wish to help". Laura thought for a second or two, and then she said

"I am not supposed to talk about it, on pain of losing my position here, but as I am going to leave anyway, and as you seem to wish only to help the man. I will tell you what little I know, If you promise that you will do the man no mischief,". Kenneth assured her of his good intentions.

"First of all then, you should Know that he has coin enough. That man is the owner of this place, and of the jetty, plus some other property nearby. He never comes into the Inn, nor seems to worry if the trade is slack. His sister is the only one that Jack, the Innkeeper, trucks with". Kenneth was astounded at what he was hearing. Laura went on.

"She comes but once each week to settle the business. Jack said she is easy to deal with; they leave him to run the place, provided it is run the way she likes. It must be kept clean and run in a quiet way, without music." Laura seemed to relax again now that she had told Kenneth what she knew.

"That is all I know, and I would be most pleased to talk with you about something else".

"You are right to be sure" said Kenneth, assured that the maid knew no more.

"What time do you finish here?" Laura's eyes sparkled, the smile returning to her face as quickly as it had left.

"Jack might let me go early if I were to ask him nicely," she said with an impish grin.
"Go then and ask," urged Kenneth.
"If you can get away, I know a place with as much life as you can handle, are you game for a night of fun".
"I am that, altogether" she said, and ran over to talk to the innkeeper.

Kenneth could see that the innkeeper was looking in his direction, seeming to nod his head in an indifferent way. Sure enough Laura came dancing back, looking flushed and pleased with herself.
"Yes I can leave now" she said, her cheeks flushed. For Laura, this was a rare opportunity to walk out with a good-looking young fellow, with coin in his purse, and a willingness to spend it. They left the inn arm-in-arm chatting happily as they walked along the darkened roadway back towards the City.
Kenneth took Laura to a tavern he knew near Whitechapel, where he ordered a table in one of the alcoves. The place was awash with song, laughter and joking. Ballads would frequently break out in one part, to be picked up by others in another part of the room, until the whole place swung to the tune. They ate a good meal of roast capon, with swede-mash, washed down with a good strong ale. As the night wore on, Kenneth called for rum for them both. Leaning across the table, he whispered in Laura's ear.
"I hear that the rooms above are nearer to heaven." Laura smiled and nodded saying.
"That's a place I hope to frequent some day. Perhaps I should have a preview." Kenneth called the landlord over and asked if he had a spare room upstairs. The man said he did and the merry couple were soon alone in a heavily curtained chamber, furnished with a small table, two chairs, and a large four-posted bed. The bed was fitted with green linen curtains, feathered quilts, and great soft pillows.

The fire in the grate gave the room a warm soporific atmosphere. Kenneth started to stow his outdoor garments on one of the chairs. As he finished taking off his coat, he turned to find to his delight, that Laura had hung up her cloak and was already undoing the ribbons that held together the front of her blouse. As he watched, she let the garment fall to her waist and seductively, started to undo the laces of her under-bodice, this she also let fall away, then placing her hands on her hips she slowly came towards him saying.
"It is time to introduce you to my good friends, this is 'Puppy' and this is 'Kitten'" she said this without any embarrassment. Kenneth approached the new acquaintances, desire swelling up inside him at the sight of Laura's wonderful bosoms. Then, carefully taking a breast in each hand he gently felt the weight of the perfectly shaped, spheres; he lowered his head and courteously kissed each in turn.

"Ladies, I am delighted beyond words to meet you both" he said with exaggerated courtly reverence, then waving his hand to indicate the four-poster.
"Can I invite you both to join Laura and myself aboard this wonderful pleasure-vessel, to float away with us on a sea of feathers, to the island of love?"
"Master Kenneth" said Laura, her tone changing to a more a serious inflection.
"A moment please if you will, let us set our course for this night's voyage." Kenneth looked into her eyes slightly alarmed at what she might mean.
"I am willing to bed with you, and to enjoy a night of frolic, but I have a rule".
"Name it", said Kenneth his mind now raging with desire.
"We three are pleased to sail with you to the land of fondle and caress. We can climb the heights of delight and give each other much pleasure, but you can not have carnal knowledge of me this night", She looked into his bright shining face. She went on.
"When the time comes for you to expel your essence, I will keep you out. I have no wish to be with child for many years yet". She eyed him sternly, judging his reaction.
"Do you agree to the terms of your crew?"
"I agree, of course I will certainly concur with your terms", Kenneth declared, perhaps a little too anxiously. After all, he knew that this was the normal way of things with experienced tavern girls, he did not want any complications in his own life, and was quite used to these conditions being set. Then sweeping Laura up in his arms, he tumbled her onto the bed, where, with much laughter, they began to pull passionately at each other's clothes. When at last they were both naked and warm under the feathers of the thick quilt, the happy young couple settled into a blissful embrace, to enjoy each other's bodies without shame or inhibition late into the night.

<========>

The next day found Kenneth rowing furiously, his head was hurting from the night's extravagances, and his body felt slow and unnatural. He knew he was arriving late at Queenhithe stairs, for his usual rendezvous with Mr. Mann, the owner of the wherry that Kenneth worked. Mr Mann was standing on the causeway next to four, large, heavy looking chests. With him were two liveried footmen.
"You are late you lazy dog" said Mann, in his usual rough tongued way."
"Don't give me any of your usual excuses, I know of your whoring ways". Kenneth was embarrassed.
"Now hurry and get these boxes aboard. They are to go to Syon House with these footmen, and I mean quickly", commanded Mr Mann. Kenneth groaned under his breath, he did not fancy such a long row after the exertions of the night before. He had been hoping for a nice quiet day, with perhaps a few local fares, and lots of time between to reflect on the details

of the previous night's revellries, but there was nothing he could do for it, Mr. Mann was here to see him away, and he must make the best of it.

The footmen were of no help at all. Kenneth had to carry the boxes and stow them aboard behind the passenger thwart on his own. When the awkwardly shaped cargo was safely stowed, the footmen stepped gingerly aboard, settling themselves onto the passenger seat, giggling and laying their arms along the top of the backboard, with little playful pushes at each other. It was then that Kenneth realised that at least one, if not both, of these footmen were "warm boys". The smaller of the two was chattering away excitedly about being sure to make themselves very comfortable for such a long trip.
Then, looking at Kenneth with his cow eyes he said,
"We are lucky indeed to have found such a fine, strong waterman to take us all the way" and with a nudge to his friend he continued.
"Perhaps he will take off his coat later when he warms up, to show us his wonderful physique".
Kenneth ignored these jibes, he did not like 'warm boys', he thought their buggery and feminine behaviour was an affront to God himself.
"The fare is paid", rasped Mr. Mann.
"Now get away, or you will not make it by the time I have promised. If you pull my boat in the way I have just observed, you will not even make it before the tide turn". Kenneth was embarrassed at this slight against his skills; the footmen were smiling at him.
"By the way," said Mann". Put more tallow on that oarlock before it wears through to the timber, you cost me enough coin for repairs as it is".

Kenneth bristled at these remarks by Mann. He was now angry.
"No one can beat me on a piddling pull from here to Syon House. I'll cut the nose from any wherryman who says different" he said this, knowingly putting fear into his passengers at this mention of violence.
Kenneth was now in a bad mood, and he was also smarting still from the quip made earlier by the smaller of the two footman. Using the starboard oar, he gently pushed the boat astern away from the causeway, until she was out into the stream. With a few powerful strokes, he pulled the boat onto an upriver heading, then gripping the port oar by the loom, he used his knee, positioned under the shank, to flip the oar up and over and into the port oarlock. This was a normal trick of the trade that most wherrymen used to quickly position their oars with the least effort. Normally they were careful not to alarm their passengers with this movement, but this trip was already paid for, so with an exaggerated thrust of his knee, he let the oar sail high in the air, not to land in the oarlock, but for the spoon to fall hard onto the water. He knew exactly, the angle to hold the blade, so that it would hit the water sending a sheet of cold liquid over the little chattering footman, with some of the splash also wetting his thin, taller, friend. The man took in a shocked, breath and watched in dismay when his light blue livery turned a dark blue hue, as the water soaked into the cloth.
"Sorry your honour" said Kenneth, to the now thoroughly wet footman

"The joys of boating, you might say. There is a piece of sailcloth under the thwart if you would like to put it over you. You might well feel the cold now that you are damp, we must keep you warm must we not?"

The man did not answer, but giving Kenneth a most hateful stare, took out the smelly cover and nestled up to his friend, pulling it over them both. The men were now looking daggers at Kenneth, but decided that keeping their council was the most prudent thing to do while they were in this boat and at this man's mercy. This Waterman might well have other unpleasant tricks he could play on them.

The row was uneventful; gradually the physical exertion slowly revived Kenneth from his hangover. On arrival at their destination, the gardens of the great rambling house of Syon, he soon had the boat alongside the landing stage and moored it to a post. The smaller of the two footmen scrambled ashore and ran off to get help with the heavy chests. Kenneth quickly heaved the boxes out of his wherry onto the landing stage. He did not want to hang about at the landing unnecessarily, if the little chatterbox returned with servants from the house, who might well be his friends, the man might seek revenge for his wetting; Kenneth was in no mood for a confrontation, much preferring not to be here. Once all the boxes were ashore and under the guard of the remaining footman, he pulled away, heading his boat down river towards the City, leaving the boxes on the causway to be collected by others. He was sure there would be no drink geld for him from this trip. He did not bother to even look for a fare from Syon House, knowing that the house had their own fleet of shallops, which they used for river transport; they were unlikely to require the services of a journeyman.

Over the next few hours, he picked up only two short fares during his leisurely row back down river, and so had plenty of time to consider more fully the events of the previous night. He was more than ever convinced that James had a big secret, which he was keeping well hidden. Why would a man who owned a valuable inn like the Moonbeam, plus other good property, choose to work the hard conditions that a night-wherrymen had to endure, particularly a man plagued by as many ailments as James had to cope with. Perhaps Laura was mistaken, or had she misunderstood what the Innkeeper had told her about the ownership of the Inn. He decided not to tell anyone what he had found out so far, he would only look a fool if it was all wrong, He resolved that he would track the man again that very night, this time he would follow his prey more closely. Perhaps to his home, from where he might make more enquires of Mr Deveral's private life.

<========>

Kenneth arrived even earlier at the jetty than he had the last time. He wanted to prepare himself properly for tracking James, thinking also to have a quick word with Laura before the night's adventure; perhaps he could keep watch for James, from a window of the inn. However, as soon as he arrived at the jetty, he could see James already rowing down river, he was rounding his boat, coming in to tie-up for the night. So this was another early finish thought Kenneth, yet again surprised by James's actions. He looked for a place to hide himself and found the pile of stacked logs, from where he could see both the jetty ladder, and a view of the street leading off past the inn. Kenneth had made sure that he was wearing dark clothes this time, with a black scarf around his neck, and a black, wide brimmed, hat which kept his face in shadow. He pulled from his pocket some strips of thick cloth and carefully tied them over his heavy boots; this would muffle the sound of the metal shod soles, should he need to cross any cobbled surface during his stalking of the old man.

It was not long before James's head appeared over the top of the ladder. He was wheezing and coughing even more so than usual, he was having a bad time of it this evening. Perhaps that was the reason for finishing early, thought Kenneth, as he watched the man climb up onto the jetty. With a last look back at his boat, to make sure she was comfortable, James slowly turned looking around, thinking that he was alone, he once again did the little ceremony as if acknowledging the river, or the moon, in some way, then limping off towards the City, he stopped only, as he had done before, to glance through the window of the Moonbeam, before continuing on his way.
He would be easy to follow thought Kenneth, with all that wheezing and spitting. This time he kept nearer to his prey, it would be no problem at all with the shuffling, scraping sound James made as he walked. Kenneth followed more carefully than he had on the previous occasion, keeping his eyes peeled for any sudden change of direction. But James continued in the same direction at his slow haunting pace, only stopping for an occasional cough and gob into the gully which ran down the centre of the road, seemingly unaware that he was being followed.

After about a mile, James suddenly turned right into a narrow alleyway. Kenneth would have missed this shift of direction on the part of James, if he had not been closely watching his every move. Quickly stepping up to the alley, Kenneth looked along its length as best he could in the gloom. He could see that it was very narrow and dark, and that it was mostly filled with small workshops, their many differing trading signs hanging above the shop doorways giving the impression of the overhanging branches of trees in a dark forest. The smell of dampness and dung indicated that the sun did not penetrate this place very much, if at all. The floor level above the shops was the living quarters of the tradesmen. The fact that one or two had candles burning, gave the little light that filtered down into the alleyway below, allowing Kenneth to see the modest amount that he could. He could just make out the figure of James half way along the alley. He was peering into the darkened window of what looked like a hatter's shop. As he watched, the dark shape of James suddenly disappeared. Kenneth presumed the man had gone inside. Perhaps he lived above the shop. Kenneth felt he was about to find out something significant and so approached carefully to see where his man had entered. The shop was completely dark when Kenneth reached the doorway; it seemed deserted. He peered through the window, but in spite of straining his eyes, he could see nothing. He tried rubbing some of the dirt from the glass for a better view, but to no avail. Perhaps, he thought, his eyes would become accustomed to the dark if he gazed long enough into the dark interior of the shops.

Suddenly, Kenneth's legs were swept from under him, unable to stop himself; he fell heavily, scraping his hands and head against the wall as he dropped to the ground. He landed awkwardly on the hard surface of the alleyway, wedged in the angle of the hard packed earth and the shop's wall, his right arm was trapped under his body. All in the same instant, he felt his left arm forced up his back, pinned there into an excruciatingly painful position by what felt like the same bony knee that was also being jammed agonizingly into his spine. The strong fingers of a large hand had gripped his throat, a hand that was part covered in some sort of damp cloth. He could also feel the unmistakable point of a sharp knife, just penetrating the skin of his back below his rib cage.

The next thing to happen made Kenneth's skin go cold; it was the unmistakable sound of James's cough. He felt the warm pungent breath on his neck; he also caught a whiff of the sharp smell of lime, a smell that always accompanied James.

"So you think to follow me do you young Kenneth? Persuaded no doubt by those so-called friends of yours, I'll be bound". Kenneth dared not move; he could feel that the knife had force behind it and could easily enter his body.

"Are you so stupid as not to realise that those young accomplices of yours are using you?" whispered James eerily.

"You are a fool indeed to let yourself be so easily led ".

Kenneth tried to move a little, but he was in the grip of an expert and could not move a muscle.

"I could slit your throat here and now and nobody would be wise as to the killer," whispered James. Kenneth felt his blood run cold as these sour, smelling words came creeping unemotionally into his ear.

"That however, might not suit my own best interest", whispered James. "If you were to be found dead, it would only increase this annoying interest in my affairs. So, your luck is with you this night, young champion of fools. I will let you go, so that you can inform those cowardly tormentors this", he paused for effect.

"You will tell them that I am an ordinary man, of no interest to them or any others, that I live the quiet life of an ailing man, and should best be left alone with my misery." James paused to allow a bout of coughing to subside.

"I know you to be a brave young fellow, even to the point of stupidity, so I need to give you a sign, to convince you of the seriousness of my warning; I want that you will know my strength of meaning in this matter". Kenneth listened intently.

"If you do not stop the others in their persecution of me, you must be convinced that I mean what I have said by this counsel". Still unable to move or speak, Kenneth felt the knife prick withdrawn,
"This therefore is my sign for you to remember the serious meaning of my words." Kenneth braced himself for a blow to the head, but there was no blow, instead there followed a sharp piercing pain in his right buttock, then as James turned the knife blade deep inside the flesh, he felt another blinding flash of pain careering down his right leg.

Kenneth's mind was spinning away with the dizziness caused by the pain, he did not at first realise that the fingers had gone from around his throat, or that the knee was withdrawn from his back. He rolled over to his left, towards the centre of the alley, clutching at his throat and at his right leg. He was now lying in the smelly filth of the centre gully, the stench of the discarded debris soaking into his coat. Slowly he tried to sit up, only to find that the pain increased with vengeance, if he put weight anywhere near his wound. He knew that he must to pull himself together, he was shaking all over. This was a new experience for Kenneth, he suddenly realised that it was fear that made him tremble, he also realised that he was severely injured.

Kenneth lay sideways on the earth, anxiously looking around. James was nowhere to be seen. He could feel warm blood running across his thigh and into his groin. With great effort he shakily got to his feet, his right leg felt numb, he put a little weight on the offending leg, but pain shot up from the foot to the wound. He staggered and grabbed at the wall for support, leaning against the timbers of the shop front. It took a great effort of will to calm his tattered nerves, but at last the shaking subsided, and by taking a tight grip on the wound, to hold the opening together, he found that he was able to walk, albeit very slowly. Kenneth's feelings now turned to anger, he had never been beaten in a fight and here was a half-dead man twice his age, who had made a mockery of his courage. Thank goodness none of his friends had seen this dishonourable misadventure. He knew he must take revenge as soon as he was able, he could not allow himself to endure such shame.

Slowly Kenneth calmed his anger into a cold, seething, realism of his situation. He knew he had to get help. He could not go to his lodgings; his landlady could not be trusted to keep her trap closed for more than a few minutes. He thought he might go to Kate, or to one of the other girls he knew, but again he did not want to risk the story of his encounter with James getting out. Perhaps he could go to the Moonbeam Inn, to get assistance from Laura, he felt sure she would help, but he might be seen there and questions asked. He was also suspicious of how James had known that he was being followed. Could it be that Laura had told the innkeeper, who had passed on the information? He decided he could take the risk of going to the Inn.

The only person Kenneth could trust completely with his embarrassing situation and shameful story, the one person who would help him in full confidence, was his best friend, Edwin Crossback. Kenneth also knew that Edwin's family were people that would help and would not betray a confidence. He decided that he would go to Edwin's house. The problem was that Edwin lived on the other side of the river. Still gripping the cheek of his buttock, to keep the mouth of the wound closed, Kenneth worked out how he could make the journey to Edwin's home. There was a ferry at Wapping Stairs, which would take him across to Dog and Dock stairs and causeway. From there, it was a relatively short distance to the Crossback's house. He tried walking a few more steps and found that the pain had mostly receded from his leg, but was now concentrated agonisingly in his right buttock.
"Damn the man, he could not have cut me in a more awkward place" Kenneth said, in a whisper to himself through clenched teeth.
The hobbling walk to Wapping Stairs was slow and painful, Kenneth found it necessary to stop many times to steady himself.

As at last he approached the Wapping stairs, Kenneth made a special effort to look normal. The waterman in charge of the ferry, who knew Kenneth a little, noticed his strange gait.
"What have you done to yourself? You look as if you have shit your breeches".
"I have taken a fall and cut myself", lied Kenneth.
"I am going over to Crossback's mother to see if she can put a patch on me". This seemed to satisfy the man and he helped Kenneth settle aboard the wherry, he then turned to help two other passengers into their seats, who had just arrived.

Pushing off from the landing, the ferryman concentrated on the crossing. There was lots of activity on the river, it was high water and ships were arriving and leaving their berths on the top of the tide, their lights reflecting off the surface of the water. Many lightermen were underway driving the dumb cargo barges along the river. Under normal circumstances Kenneth would had enjoyed the trip, it was a pretty sight, with their candle lanterns flickering like little stars.
"Oh look, look at the lights dancing on the river," said the woman passenger to her friend. Some of the barges were piled high with bags or boxes; others were empty and stood high out of the water. He could hear the men calling to each other in the curt language they used, which few outside the trade could understand. All this activity seemed chaotic; the vessels seemed to be missing each other by a matter of inches as they passed back and forth.

The ferryman skilfully navigated his boat through all this confusion; he rowed in and out, around and past these many obstacles to arrive safely at King Stairs. Kenneth waited until the other passengers had disembarked onto the causeway; he then warily stood up and stepped cautiously out of the boat helped by the wherryman. Kenneth offered to pay for the trip, but the man refused to take coin from a fellow Freeman of the Guild. Kenneth reached the top of the causeway with much difficulty, climbing the few steps, which led on to dry land. He was now feeling decided giddy from the loss of blood, but pulling himself together, he made his way the short distance to the Crossbacks. He was forced to stop several times to gather his deepest reserves to make it to the house. He suddenly remembered that Edwin's father, who was also a fellow fireman and worked for the same insurance company as Kenneth, but sa part of the opposite engine team, was on fire-watch duty this night. The thought pleased him, he did not dislike the man, knowing him to be trustworthy and very clever, but Alfred was one of those men who was always right whatever the matter under discussion. Kenneth found this annoying.

At last he reached the door and knocking loudly, leaned heavily against the doorpost. It was getting late and the family might well be abed. After a short time however, a light flickered at the window and Kenneth heard the bolt being drawn. The door opened to reveal Edwin's sister Agnes in her nightgown, holding a candle in a small pewter holder.
"Kenneth!" she exclaimed, what brings you here so late.
"I am in some trouble Agnes, is your mother at home?"
"No" said Agnes
"She is staying with a neighbour who is very ill. What is wrong?"
"I am injured Agnes" confessed Kenneth.
"Is Edwin here"? There was no need for Agnes to answer, as the sound of Edwin's house-clogs clattered down the stairs leading from the room above echoed through the room.
"Kenneth! What is wrong?"
Edwin was alarmed at his friend's obvious discomfort, in all the years he had known him, Kenneth had always been the one who was never ill, or down in spirit in any way. Before he could answer, Kenneth felt himself going faint, the room was spinning and he grabbed at the table for support, then with a crash he fell to the floor. Agnes and Edwin quickly cleared the table and lifted the bulky frame up onto the table top, laying it out along its length.
"What is the matter with him?" said Edwin, looking anxiously into his friend's wax white face.
"He seemed to be favouring his right leg," said Agnes.
"I think he is injured there. Look there is blood on his boot". Edwin raked up the fire in the hearth and Agnes fetched more candle. They pulled the heavy leather boots off and peeled away the thick woollen stockings. The right one was soaked with thick, sticky, blood. Agnes ran off to bring fresh water and cloth to clean the foot. When this was done, they could still see no sign of a wound. Edwin tried again to question his friend, but Kenneth was out cold. Agnes was now unlacing the waist of Kenneth's breeches and with Edwin's help, they pulled the heavy buckskin away.

The sight before them was alarming. Kenneth's linen under shorts were congealed with blood and stuck fast to his skin. Edwin and his sister could

still not see a wound. With copious amounts of water administered by Agnes, they were able to release the linen and pull it away from the skin, then using his blade to cut the material, Edwin was able to remove the under shorts piece by piece. Without embarrassment, Edwin and his sister continued to clean and to search for the wound on Kenneth's now naked lower body. As the water being applied by Agnes diluted the mess and the thick congealed blood came away from Kenneth's private parts, she realised that there was fresh blood pooling on the table under his right side.
"It's in his back," she said straining to turn the heavy body onto its side.
"No here it is in his stern parts" she exclaimed as the body rolled enough, for her to look underneath. Agnes sighed with relief at having found the source of the blood flow. Together they carefully turned Kenneth fully onto his front; he made a little moaning sound and started to come round.
"Keep still mate" said Edwin.
"We will soon have you to rights".

The cut seemed surprisingly small for so much blood, but as Agnes pressed together the lips of the wound, they could see that it was very deep, bright red blood was still oozing out from the depths of the hole.
"I will have to sew it together" said Agnes, and dashed off to get her sewing basket. Edwin cleaned the table and prepared his friend, who was now dipping in and out of consciousness. Agnes returned and was soon neatly sewing the mouth of the wound together. Edwin used some of his father's brandy to clean around the cut, which because of Agnes's neat stitch-work, had now stopped bleeding. He forced a little of the fiery liquid between Kenneth's teeth, which caused him to cough and splutter. Edwin then fetched some of his own, clean, under drawers, for his friend, plus a pair of loose cloth breeches. Agnes had now re-heated some of the thick broth they had eaten early, and was feeding it to Kenneth with a large wooden spoon.

Soon they had succeeded in bringing their friend back to something like his normal self, although his white face was still a testament to his ordeal.
"How feel you now, you great ruffian", asked Agnes with a smile.
"Much better for your kind administrations," said Kenneth looking a little sheepish. Then looking down at his new clean apparel.
"I hope you will not relay this embarrassing incident to others".
"Well, I will not I am sure, but I must say to you, that I have heard many stories about your exploits with the maids of this town master Kenneth, and much of your amorous attributes, but having now seen for myself, at first hand, as might be said. I conclude that the tales have been much exaggerated". Then with a wicked little grin on her pretty face, she picked up her basket and left the room, knowing that the men wanted to talk together alone. She departed leaving a little giggle in the air behind her.

After an hour or so of warming by the now raging fire. Edwin helped his friend slowly up the steps to his the attic room above the kitchen, then into his own sleeping cot. Kenneth was still a little giddy from the loss of blood, but once settled on the soft hay-stuffed pallet, and covered over with a feather filled quilt, he dropped off into a deep sleep. Edwin meanwhile had rigged up a spare hammock for himself, tying it off between two of the house posts, as he had done many times before, when a friend had stayed overnight.

The next morning the boys woke to the warm smell of cooking, filtering up from the kitchen below. There was also however another smell; it was the wonderful sharp odour of mulled herb wine. Kenneth was feeling a lot better, but still looked very pale. They dressed as quickly as they could. Edwin providing Kenneth with some of his own spare clothes, after which they came down for the morning meal. Edwin's mother, who was now fully informed by her daughter, of the excitement of the night before, immediately fussed over Kenneth, enquiring as to his pains and overall feeling. He assured her that he was truly on the mend and that with a good breakfast would soon be on his way back to his lodgings. She however would not hear of it.
"You are not leaving my house to return to that woman's hovel, until you are fully recovered and able to stand up to that old hag's food, which in my opinion is not fit for young men" Nell had crossed swords with Kenneth's landlady on many occasions and could not stand the sight of the woman. It did not occur to Nell to ask what Kenneth had been up to, or what had been the cause of his wounds, she was only intent on bring him back to full health. The reasons for men getting themselves into trouble, was a mystery, and after a lifetime of consideration with no conclusion, it was of no interest to her at all.

Alfred was seated at the kitchen table, just home after his night's fire-watching duties.
"Good morrow Mr. Crossback" said Kenneth.
"My thanks to you and your family for such good assistance to my disability, I am in debt to you all, to be sure."
"Good morrow Kenneth" said Alfred with a reassuring smile.
"You are most welcome, come sit by me and have some victuals." Kenneth sat as best he could at the table. He found that by lifting his right buttock, and putting his weight on the left, he could take the pressure off the wound, but this gave his body a strange list to port, which Alfred noticed with some silent amusement.

Alfred was curious about the night's affairs, but waited his opportunity until the time was right so that he could determine what had happened to his son's young friend. He knew Kenneth, and knew of his reputation, he also knew of his philandering. However, he was a good judge of character and knew the lad's good points as well as the bad. After a good filling of cooked oatmeal flavoured with honey and herbs, followed by two mugs of the hot, thick, herb-laced, red wine, Kenneth was feeling more like his old self. He knew himself to be very lucky to have such a friend as Edwin, with such a fine and trustworthy family.

After a little banter from Agnes, hinting at what she had had to do the previous night, which caused Kenneth not a little embarrassment, Nell interrupted her daughter.
"Leave the poor man be, you have had your fun at his expense, it is enough now, so let him heal in peace". Nell could see that Alfred wanted to talk to the lads on his own. She and Agnes had much work to do in the back yard. It was washing day, and the large copper cauldron was boiling away merrily, steaming off its soapy vapours, and waiting for its fill of the family's dirty linen, the two women left the room to the men. Agnes could not resist an impish grin at Kenneth on her way out.

At first Kenneth was reluctant to say too much in front of Edwin's father, but soon realised that he needed to be open with them, in spite of his shame, and hurt pride. He soon found himself relaying the story of his unfortunate evening's employment. Although he usually felt awkward in Alfred's company, he decided to confide fully in Edwin's and his father's trustworthy natures and held nothing back. As Kenneth unfolded the story of the night's events, Alfred could see the anger rising in the lad. A cripple had damaged his pride in his ability as a fighting man, what was more; it was a man who was more than twice his age, and ailing into the bargain. He wanted revenge to annul his shame.

When the tale was finished, Edwin reluctantly had to take his leave; he was already late for his morning's work at the pipe-borers.
After his son had gone, Alfred indicated a seat by the fire, bidding Kenneth make himself as comfortable as was possible. In the soft lulling heat from the hearth, he gave Kenneth a pipe of his best tobacco, plus another jug of the mulled wine. He then started to talk gently to the lad, in the special, disarming way he had with people. It was not the voice of the father Kenneth had never known, it was not the voice of an older friend, of a compatriot. It was the voice of reason, it was as if he was able to pluck at the strings inside Kenneth's mind, stimulating a thought or feeling which was already there but had somehow been swamped by the anger and confusion of the many other, more dominant feelings flowing through this young man's head.

When he judged that the moment was right, Alfred thought for a minute or two; his next words would be important, he therefore chose them carefully.
"You should be grateful to Mr. Deveral for this night's work; he has done you a great courtesy". Alfred said the words deliberately shocking the young man. Kenneth's mouth dropped open at the unexpected words.
"Yes" said Alfred", he has brought you to a crossroad in your life. How you react after this encounter will determine much of your future life, perhaps even its length". Kenneth was still looking agog.
"What I am about to tell you is very dangerous for you to know, and for me to tell. It is for your ears alone, even Edwin is as yet too young to know of it". Alfred could see he had Kenneth's full attention.

"I will tell you of this man you know as James Deveral, and with the knowledge I pass on to you, you must judge your reaction to what he did to you, and the reason for his action. You must do this as a man, not as a boy, for this night was the change over for you, from one to the other. It is something that all young men must come to, at some time in their lives, yours is now upon you".

Kenneth was listening intently, his respect for Alfred growing by the second.

"Something you told me in your story, confirms my worst fears of the secret life of Mr Deveral. You said that you found out that he is the owner of the "Moonbeam Inn". That name is very significant. You also said you saw him paying homage to the river, or perhaps to the moon, that is also important. You see I believe him to be a follower of an old religion, a pagan devotee of the ancient rivermen's belief, in the deity of the Moon Goddess". Kenneth was astounded as he heard this.

"If this was the total sum of James's indiscretions I would not care," said Alfred.

"For I believe man should think freely in all things, including his choice of God. However I believe James to have no humanity towards others. I am sure that his beliefs allow him to commit atrocious acts against his fellow man without concern". Kenneth's face showed his astonishment at what he was hearing.

"I have made it my business to know James Deveral as well as any can", said Alfred.

"He is a sorry prisoner in his twisted body, the constant pain of which, coupled with the unkindness of others, have I believe turned his mind. I think him to be a killer for hire, an assassin". Kenneth started with even more shock at this, finding no words of his own to utter.

"Just look at the facts", said Alfred.

"Consider his secretive ways, his skill with his blade, his offhanded attitude to others, his wealth without any pride in it, but above all his bitterness at his lot in life. What you have told me fits well into the pieces of information I have discovered from his own mouth. I have spent as much time as he will allow, talking with him. I think him to be capable of any wickedness to his fellow man. I am sure his blade can be hired, and as you know there are many who would employ him for the use of it".

Kenneth was digesting what Alfred was telling him.

"Then it is even more important that I revenge myself, and at the same time perhaps rid society of this dangerous killer".

"Think carefully", said the older man.

"This is your first great cross-roads in life, what you do, will set your own future course".

"Do you not agree with me?" said Kenneth trying to understand what Alfred was suggesting.

"I will be a laughing stock if I do not revenge myself. If what you say is true, then all the more reason for taking revenge, if you find my reasoning

wrong, what do you advise?" Alfred knew that what he said next was of great importance.
"If I were in your shoes young man, I would first weigh the facts very carefully". Then before Kenneth could answer.
"I will do it for you, to save your blushes. You are a proud young man with many gifts. You have a strong and healthy body; you are brave and fearless. You are always willing to help your friends, ready to right the wrongs of the world. You have a kindness in you that is attractive to all you meet. You are generous to a fault.
But you also have a dark side. You play at life, you do not consider the effect you have on others, you hurt feelings without noticing. However, your saving grace is that you have your own strongly felt morality". Alfred paused for effect.
"The world would not be a better place without you." Kenneth fidgeted with embarrassment.
"On the other hand" continued Alfred.
"You are childish, easily led, rash and cluttered in the way you think. In short Kenneth, you are young and very inexperienced". The young man was a little angry at the truth of these words, he did not realise that anyone had such a close understanding of his character.
"Now let us consider your opponent. He also has gifts which serve his corrupted view of life very well", continued Alfred.
"He has no conceit, no pride to cloud his thoughts, he is expert in the devious ways of intrigue and pitiless killing, he has no fear of God, for he believes in another older religion. Life is unimportant to him, even his own. He is quick witted and a clear thinker. You are not dealing with a normal person, my young friend ".

Kenneth considered this new point of view, sucking on his now dead pipe. Alfred took a spill from the fire and re-lit the clay bowl.
"Alfred, I know you to be a clever man, your summary has the ring of truth about it. Tell me how to proceed on these facts that you have laid out". Alfred was pleased at the lad's reaction.
"You must decide for yourself Kenneth", said the man looking into the bright blue eyes.
"However, I would advise you to consider James's words very carefully, for I believe they contain the answer to your question. Alfred could see that his words were finding their mark.
"He accused you of being led by others, who pull the strings of your pride and honour for their own ends. I agree with him in that". Kenneth flinched.
"He warned you that you are no match for him. I agree with him again. To kill your fellow man by pre-arrangement, no matter how well deserved, is a gift thankfully not given to many.
"I believe you do not have it, but I am certain that James does." Kenneth was now nodding in agreement.
"He said he only wishes to be left alone without interference; he does not wish to harm a fellow Waterman. I believe him in that also. The old religion would not condone it; river people are in no danger from this man, if he is

left alone. The awful deeds he is paid to commit, I think are best left out of our reckoning". Kenneth was becoming convinced.

"In my view" said Alfred,"your best course is to keep your own counsel on this night's happenings. Six people know what happened. You can trust Edwin and myself and our women. James will not mention it; I can assure you of that". Again, he paused for effect.

"The weakest link in this chain is yourself." He could see that he had hurt the lad, but he pressed home the point.

"Of the six, you are the one that takes drink sometimes to excess. It would be easy one evening, when deep in your cups, to tell your story, or perhaps a part of it, you will then, when sober, be confronted with trying to save face, you will feel that you must do so by attacking your tormentor". Kenneth knew only too well his love of drink and merrymaking.

"However," continued Alfred.

"As long as you can keep your hatch closed on this subject, your problem will I think, gradually disperse." He paused, and then pressed home his point.

"Kenneth, it is time for you to become a man".

The young man felt greatly relieved, he could see the sense in Alfred's words, the way ahead was now clear to him. It would not be easy to tighten his self-control. He would tell the others that he had followed James to his home and that there was nothing sinister to report. He would tell them that the man was simply a poor cripple, and best be let in peace. More importantly he was determined that he would not allow himself to be used again by his so called friends. Alfred meanwhile had filled Kenneth's jug with the last of Nell's delicious mulled wine, suggesting that he drink it down, and return to bed, saying that he needed much sleep to heal his wounds. He also must also visit the land of dreams, after his night of fire watching.

"Sleep is the best of all medicine, for both young dolphins and old whales". He said smiling. They both laughed, and Kenneth, now feeling much relieved, and looking more like his old self, downed the wine and returned to the comfort of Edwin's cot.

Nell would not release Kenneth for three whole days, a time during which he was able to hone the story he would tell about his accident. He would say that he had taken a fall. Alfred promised to let the lad's employer know of his mishapand offer tempery replacement, leaving Kenneth to tell the many concerned visitors who came to see him, that he had slipped on a greasy causeway, and had fallen onto a metal piling spike, which had pieced him in a most awkward place for a rowing man.

At last, the woman of Edwin's family let Kenneth return to his lodgings, from where he returned to his work with Mr Mann's wherry, and also to his fire engine crew. He remained however; very anxious about the first inevitable meeting he would have with James Deveral. In spite of Alfred's assurances that the matter would be closed in James's mind, unless

Kenneth opened up the subject himself. Kenneth however, continued to worry about their first meeting, wishing it to be over.

Inevitably, the moment arrived. It came one evening when Kenneth, rowing into Irongate Stairs at the top of the tide, could see that a wherry was waiting ahead of him at the stairs, he whistled his recognition pipe call, and heard the reply he was dreading. It was James, he was the only wherryman waiting at the causeway, they would be alone. Kenneth could not turn back, even if he had wanted to, his passengers required this place at which to disembark. He brought his boat gracefully alongside the causeway, his wherry grounding gently on the chalky foreshore. He settled the payment with his passengers and disembarked them safely.

His first reaction was to row away again quickly, heading up river and ignoring James, but he considered the fact that James was alone, and that this was as good an opportunity as he would get, to determine the man's reactions. He decided to stay, waiting here for a fare, and to see what James would say or do. Kenneth was now fully alert, ready for anything, be it an attack or a verbal confrontation. James however was quiet as usual, Kenneth passed the time of day, asking what business was like at these stairs this evening. James replied in his usual quiet tones, that he thought they could expect passengers from this place shortly that it was worth waiting here. After a short pause, he then asked if Kenneth had seen Alfred Crossback in his travels. Kenneth's whole being was alert at the mention of the name. Was this some provocative trick? He answered that he had not seen the man all day.
"If you happen to see him", said James in his soft tones, "tell him I have some fish given to me by a market porter to pass on to him". James leaned over, looking into Kenneth's eyes searching the young man's face.

Kenneth knew that this was some sort of test, but he kept control of his feelings.
"If you would consider giving the package to me", he said,
"I am sure to see Edwin later; I will pass it over to him". The package was passed across from boat to boat; in the process, Kenneth felt the damp cloth of the man's bound hands, the feeling made him shiver inside.
"You are a kind lad, I know you to mean well, and thank you" said James. Kenneth knew exactly what was meant by the remark, pleased now that he had taken Alfred's advice, for he could see that James also wanted an end to the matter. From that moment on, the young man had an understanding, a guarded respect for the tormented older man, he felt sure that somewhere within that tortured body; a drop of humanity did still exist.

Chapter Nine

Mr Doggett's journey home

Thomas Doggett, actor, comedian and political sympathiser of the Whig party, stepped out into the cold night air of Southwark. He entered the narrow cobbled alley from the side door of the Playhouse where he had been performing, and looked about the deserted passageway. He was more than a little disappointed to find the place empty, not one person was there to bid him goodnight, or say that they had enjoyed his performance. In spite of this lack of admirers, Doggett felt sure that it had been a successful evening's work on stage. Perhaps this dearth of his followers was simply due to the bad weather, or because he was a little late in emerging from the theatre. He should be more careful with his timing in future, it was never good to upset one's public. They were not to know that he had stayed on late to discuss the evening's performance of 'Love Of Money' with Mr. Durfey the writer, the purpose of the meeting being for Thomas to mention some minor amendments, changes that he would like Durfey to make to his part in the next presentation.

Doggett was as always dressed in style, he felt that it was important to display his wares, as it were, so that his audience would easily recognise him when abroad in town.

A contemporary description*.
He wore an enormous wig with long lappets of hair hanging over his shoulders, which enveloped his head, and on the top of it was stuck a small cocked hat, which it would have been a great effort of balance to retain in place without the aid of pins: his orange red coat was very broad in the tails, reaching down below his knees, his waistcoat with flap pockets of large size extend half way down his thighs, his small clothes are tight and buckled at the knees, where they are met by coloured stockings, which rise out of square toed, red healed , silver buckled shoes: under his left arm he carries a clouded-amber coloured cane, while his right hand is continually titillating his olfactory nerve with snuff from out of a box set with precious stones, while his indispensable rapier hangs at his side. His shiny black Court shoes were made from the finest leather, with the most fashionable buckles ,and were protected by wooden Pattens.

(*Extracted form Thomas Doggett Pictured by Walter Leon)

Thomas was rather pleased with himself, his now quite famous dance 'The Cheshire Round' which he had offered as an encore earlier that evening, had been received well by the audience; once again it had been applauded with great delight. Likewise his new soliloquy "The Tory and the Whig" had also gone down well, although he thought he might make one or two small changes to perfect it to an even more topical intensity, perhaps reflecting more the ascendancy of the Whig Party, and the decline of the Tories. He felt that it was important for him to use his position on the stage, to draw full attention to the most recent changes to the current political situation. On the whole, he was indeed very pleased with himself; his suggestions had been accepted by Mr. Durfey, who agreed to write them in before the next performance. Doggett felt sure that the changes he had proposed were going to add considerably to his overall repertoire.

Doggett looked up into the dark sky and shivered a little at the drizzling rain.
"A dirty night is brewing, to be sure, weather to be avoided as it develops later on this night", he said out loud, gesturing with a flick of his kerchief, projecting the words as if he were still on stage. The wind was blowing from the west he noted, and the tide was probably away by now. It would be a cold and wet journey home to Chelsea this night, no doubt of it, no doubt. "Yes, I should have kept a better eye on the hour, now I will have to endure an uncomfortable trip, to be sure." As he spoke the words, he looked around hoping that someone might be listening to his intonations, but alas, the alley remained deserted, the glistening walls and cobbles were his only audience. His annoyance was growing, and he was now losing his good humour. Pulling his cloak more tightly around his body with a dramatic swirl, he walked down towards the riverbank, and along towards the water stairs at Bankside. There he would call for oars, and would presently be underway, keeping ahead of the brewing storm; hopefully, he would soon be on his way to his warm and well-deserved bed. However, on reaching the river wall and looking over, he found to his increasing irritation that no wherries were waiting at the causeway.
"Damnation" he said in a loud voice, forgetting for a moment to project over his tongue.
"Those damned boatmen are all gone again." This was not the first time that Thomas had found difficulty in finding oars from Bankside; his bad humour was now growing by the minute.

Further along from the causeway, some young men were sitting perched up on the low riverside wall, this group looked as if they were also waiting with the intention of taking a boat. Doggett looked them over, they seemed to be decently dressed, if rather dishevelled, but were acting too loud by far, with rather uncouth shouting and calling out to each other, Thomas realised that they were making merry in an altogether disagreeable manner. As he watched them, he could see that they seemed to be having great fun with a game, which involved pulling at each other's coats, and pushing one another from the wall. It sounded by the boisterous shouting, that they were exaggerating to each other the outcome of their night's exploits, he could hear much boasting and bravado and extravagant claims of sexual accomplishment. Thomas decided that they were too drunk, and best to be avoided; he therefore turned away from them, walking along to the river wall towards the old bridge, screwing up his eyes as he went against the drizzle and gloom to see better across the water. He peered over towards the City, across the rippling, wind blown, surface of the Thames. He could faintly see in the corner near to the bridge, that there were some lighted torches flickering in the wind. Putting his fingers into his mouth he blew hard, trying to make a loud whistle, but alas this was a skill that he had never properly mastered, he could not give the piercing whistle that others so easily managed, so cupping his hands around his mouth, he called out across the water in his loudest voice.

"Oars, I say. Oars. A wherry over here if you please". He waited for a replying call or an answering shout, but none came. The wind was getting up by the minute, whisking his words away as soon as they left his mouth; he stamped his foot in annoyance, letting out a curse.

The young men had now noticed him, and were beginning to take more of an interest in the fancily dressed actor; they were mimicking his call for a boat.

"Oars if you please, oars for whores don't you know." Doggett decided not to take up this verbal challenge, he could tell that they were inebriated enough to make trouble, they might well have no respect for his position or status and perhaps attack his person. It would be prudent to melt away into the shadows, where they could not see him. Having decided on this course of action, he did so with some haste, nestling back into the shadows of the wall of the nearby building.

"What to do for the best, what to do?" he asked quietly of himself, standing back in the darkness of a building. If he went back to the riverbank to call again for a boat, those young men would surely approach him; he was in no mood for a sour discourse with inebriates. He knew from experience that things could quickly turn nasty. People who would come to see him in one of his performances, might well cheer, and applaud him, but the same people, seeing him in his street, in his gay clothes, could soon to become aggressive and insulting.

It was Thomas's opinion that there was a sad lack of control over the riff-raff of society; he was convinced that the country needed a new leader, one with enough moral courage to drive out the coarseness and ugliness, which pervaded the land, especially the City of London. It was an unpleasantness that particularly plagued the lower classes. After all, he only wanted to get home for a little cold supper, which he knew Mrs. Pratt would have left out for him, and the warm bed she would have made up to soothe his tired body, then to sleep, perchance to dream.

There seemed nothing else for it, but to walk over the bridge and take oars from the City side on one of the wherries waiting at 'Old Swan', where he could see that watermen were plying their trade.

"Confounded boatmen," he thought to himself, as he began what he knew would be an unpleasant walk. Did they not have enough sense between them, to know that there was good business to be had over on this side of the river? Why did they always congregate together in swarms over there, while none were to be had at Southwark? His anger was mounting; he thought he might well complain to their Guild about the matter. As he began his long walk along the riverbank and up the steps to the approach to the old bridge, he mused over this problem; it was a difficulty that he had often encountered when the hour was late. Was there no way of getting a wherry to take him home from the stews at night, after his performances? Yes, he would make it his business to report the matter to the Watermen's Guild, he resolved that he would go to their Hall on the morrow, and make a strong complaint. He began to think about what he would say, the words he would use to impress them. He decided that it would be a performance worthy of his status as an actor, a presentation that would uphold the importance of the theatre, his chosen profession. Perhaps he might win some dispensation, they might arrange to order one of their journeymen to attend on his particular needs. Yes, to have his own boatman waiting on him, would be a most suitable outcome to this night's disappointment, but the cost of it, thought Doggett, he shuddered at the thought of such extravagance.

Thomas disliked walking over the bridge. During daylight hours it was always so busy, so bustling with the foul smelling dregs of humanity. Even this late at night, there were still some people about, mostly servants going about their master's business, although he could see that the weather was keeping even these poor souls mostly at home. The bridge smelt of dung and animal urine, did no one have the job of cleaning it? He was wearing pattens to protect his good shoes, but even so, he watched his step carefully. Now that the rain was strengthening, he knew he would inevitably slip and slide in the wet conditions. Another thing concerned him, he knew that footpads were known to frequent the shadows of the houses built along the roadway of the bridge. He must be aware of all about him; his very safety could depend on it.

Thomas kept his hand on the hilt of the blade, which he always carried under his cloak.

"This bridge is a disgrace to our fair City," he thought to himself, as he looked about him. It was old, tired, and just as in the song it seemed to be falling down. The houses were badly maintained, toppling lopsidedly towards each other, and leaning out over the river; they were not properly kept up as befitted an important city like London, some even had pieces of timber hanging precariously from their walls, ready to fall on an unsuspecting pedestrian. He knew of course that the song referred to the visual effect caused by the water rushing through the arches at a dropping angle, which on the ebb tide, which gave the illusion, that the whole thing was leaning up river to the west, and that on flood tide, it looked as if it was leaning the other way towards the east. He also knew that this old bridge had stood for some 500 years. However, he thought it was about time it was pulled down, to make way for a grand new modern bridge, perhaps built of beautiful white stone that would match in with the wonderful buildings beingg constructed further upstream.

Doggett much admired the changes taking place up river at Westminster to the west. The City of London was falling behind the City of Westminster to be sure. A thought struck him, perhaps this was something he could build into one of his soliloquies. Yes, he would give more thought to that idea, as he thought more about it, he began to play with the words that could best be used.

As he made his way over the bridge, passing from one pool of gleaming torch light to the next, stepping over puddles, avoiding the mounds of unmentionable, stinking dung. He kept a sharp look about him, vetting the few people passing, who were crossing with or against him. They were an assortment of individuals, each with their head down, seemingly only using the bridge reluctantly to complete an urgent errand to judge by their furtive glances and hurried steps. Even on this damp and windy evening, some people were forced to cross the river by its only bridge. One person in particular caught Thomas's attention, this man seemed to be taking undue interest in him.

He had first noticed the man coming towards him from the direction of the City, but on approaching Thomas, and before they would pass each other, the man had turned on his heel, heading back toward the City, travelling in the same direction as Thomas's. The man had since kept just ahead of the actor, now and then furtively looking back over his shoulder; it seemed as if he was checking that the player was still coming along behind him. Possibly, thought Thomas in alarm, the man might be waiting for a dark, quiet, patch, with fewer people passing, aiming to do him harm as soon as the opportunity showed itself. Doggett knew he had to be very careful, especially at this time of night. He knew that his bright fashionable clothes made him stand out as a likely target for any villain who might be on the lookout for a wealthy victim. Thomas had the strong feeling that he was being targeted, he tightened his grip on the handle of his blade.

As he approached the centre of the bridge, Thomas Doggett was now a very worried man. The footpad, for he was sure that this was what the man was, seemed to be waiting for his chance to turn and make a play to rob the actor. Should he turn and run back in the direction he had come? But if he did where would he go? Even if he could outrun the villain, which Thomas doubted in his awkward pattens, the playhouse would be closed and locked for the night. Even armed with his blade, Thomas knew that in truth, he was no match for a ruthless villain. A man, who lived by robbing others, was sure to be armed, and was certain to know how to use his weapon more proficiently than himself. In reality Thomas knew very little of the workings of his sword; for him it was but a theatre prop, he could wave it about with the best of them on the stage, but in a real fight he would be at a loss. He knew enough to realise that it took years to become a proficient swordsman, a noble art in which he was not well versed. "What to do, what to do?" thought Doggett; this was the downfall of being an actor. By the very nature of your profession, you had to travel to your home late at night, your public expected to see you dressed well, both of which, necessarily put one at the mercy of the naughty villains of this City. "What to do, what to do?" he thought to himself, beginning to feel the first pangs of panic.

Looking just ahead of him, Thomas had an idea. He had seen a chance to confuse, and possible to avoid the man. If it worked, and this scoundrel did not respond, then no matter, Thomas was simply wrong about the man's intentions, but if he were correct, then Doggett would not be alone, he would have a sound witness, he might also have the chance to give the man the slip. Thomas watched the man's back intently, noticing the time between the glances over his shoulder. Then as he drew level with the centre of the bridge and immediately after the rogue's next glance backwards, he quickly crossed the roadway and stepped inside the open door of the bridge's Chapel of St. Thomas A Becket.

As Doggett entered the gloom of the old Chapel, he could see that the priest was seated just inside the doorway, the man looked up, a little startled by Thomas's quick entrance. The cleric was holding a pewter collection plate, which he proffered towards the actor.
"A donation for the poor and decayed of this City", he said looking up into Doggett's face. Doggett, feeling into his purse for a coin, decided that he must tell this priest of his concern regarding the man he thought to be a footpad; he quickly placed a coin into the plate, making sure that the priest had seen its value. The cleric smiled his gratitude.
"Thank you my son, God's blessing on you for your generosity."
"I am pleased to help my fellow man," said Doggett.
"But I fear that my need may be the more urgent this evening".
"What is your dilemma my son?" said the Priest looking a little alarmed. Doggett explained that he was sure that he was being pursued by the rogue out to steal from him. A rough fellow who he surely felt was a robber of some kind, and that he was in some fear of his person. Without reply, the priest put his finger to his lips, pointing to a heavy curtain, which hung next to the Chapel entrance. Thomas quickly slipped behind the thick, brown, folds of the cloth. Well hidden, and feeling much safer now, he watched the open door of the Chapel through a small tear in the fabric. After a few moments, Thomas was much relieved to see his potential assailant pass by the door without even looking into the Chapel. His relief was short lived however, for the man returned and this time peered into the gloom of the entrance, and then came inside.
"Good evening kind Sir" said the clergyman to the villain. "A donation for the poor and decayed of this City", pleaded the priest. "At last a good citizen is come to make a donation for the needy of our parish". The man looked at the priest through squinted eyes but said nothing. He was dressed in a shabby dark cloak with a high standing collar. On his head he wore an old worn-out bonnet, which Thomas could see was badly battered and tattered. He carried a gnarled stick with a large knobbly head to it; Thomas's heart jumped at the sight of the weapon, he took in a sharp breath. He now knew for certain that this man was indeed a

dangerous villain, for the stick he recognised as a shalaly, an Irish fighting stick, Thomas knew these weapons well, from the old days back home in Ireland. He was certain that any scoundrel who carried a stick like this, would have no qualms abut using it. Such a man would stalk his pray, waiting for any chance to make an attack on his victim in some dark doorway, where with a quick knock to the head, to put his quarry out of action, he would cut the man's purse strings, and be away before those around even knew what was happening. Such a villain had no fear of the public; they would simply lash out at anyone who got in their way, without any thought to the consequences.
The footpad looked carefully around the gloomy, empty, chapel, ignoring the priest's outstretched plate. Then with a quick step he turned and sprang back out through the open door, to seek his elusive prey outside. Thomas was greatly relieved to have outsmarted his adversary. However, his relief was again short lived, just as Thomas was about to step out from his hiding place, the man re-entered the chapel. The priest looked up at the strange man once again.
"Can I be of help my son?" he said in a quiet reverent tone.
"Did a man in a red cloak come into this place?" demanded the stranger, but before the priest could make reply he put the head of his stick under his chin, lifting his head violently backwards.
"Answer me you sad old dog". The priest gulped in alarm.
"A man as you describe did enter a few minutes ago," he stuttered in a frightened high-pitched voice. Thomas froze to the ground, his bladder felt as if it was about to empty there and then, all was lost, the priest was going to give him away. Then to his relief he heard him say.
"That man seemed very agitated; he left immediately, and ran back towards Southwark, as if in great fear." Without a word, the footpad left the building, turning toward the south side of the bridge.
Thomas, now trembling in the dark, waited a few more minutes, then thinking that the coast must be clear he emerged from behind the curtain.

Doggett thanked the priest profusely and they exchanged a few more words of mutual comfort, agreeing that it had been a near thing. Like Thomas the cleric now realised what the scoundrel's intentions had been. Putting his head out through the Chapel door, Thomas carefully looked in both directions, he was relieved to see no sign of his potential assailant, thanks to God the man was nowhere to be seen. He decided it was safe to continue his crossing of the bridge. Briefly re-entering the chapel he expressed his heart felt thanks to the priest. Putting more good coin into the pewter plate, and bidding the man a heartfelt farewell and went out into the cold night air. Having left the safety of the chapel, Thomas went cautiously on his way, still keeping a firm grip on the hilt of his blade, promising himself that in future he would be careful where he wore this orange-red coat with its silver buttons. For sure it was his favourite, but it was also an invitation for such trouble as he had just endured, to attend him.

Having passed from the Chapel back onto the muddy roadway outside, he looked carefully about him at the few people passing. He could still see no sign of his potential assailant, but he knew that his good fortune probably meant that some other poor soul would suffer an attack and robbery this evening. That desperado was determined to gain his needs from someone. Doggett decided to cross the roadway again; he somehow felt safer on the down riverside of the bridge. As he looked between the houses down onto the river, he could see the lights cavorting in the mastheads of the many ships moored in the Pool below the bridge parapet, all were moving, dancing to the wind's mournful song as it hummed through the ropes and rigging. The forest of masts and spars were bobbing about as if in a Dervish whirl, now that the wind was beginning to flex its strength. The whole port seemed to be making rough music, the special sounds that ships make when closely moored together in port. It was as if the whole of the Pool of London was singing a sad and woeful song, the song of stretching ropes, and groaning timbers, intermixed with the faint voices of sailors, lightening men, loaders, and the assortment of other trades involved with the unloading and reloading of the cargo trade of London.

With a great inward sigh of relief, Thomas at last reached the City side of the Bridge. He hurriedly crossed the roadway again, leaving the bridge approach and turning left into Swan Lane. Looking over the river wall he could now clearly make out that there were six wherries waiting at Old Swan stairs; four of them had torches burning, indicating that they were for hire. He was annoyed to see that there were so many boats here, yet none across the river where the trade was to be had. He had been forced to endure that nightmare of a walk over the bridge; he had nearly been attacked, all for the sake of some of these brainless fellows trading over on the Southwark side. He would certainly make a strong complaint at the Watermen's Hall about this stupidity, not one boat over at Bankside to serve the needs of the entertainers, yet here were six altogether. "I was well near robbed, I could perhaps have been injured or even worse, those rulers of the Company will certainly hear from me in full vitriolic cry on the morrow," mumbled Doggett to himself.

As he passed the Swan Tavern he could hear music and laughter coming from the saloon inside. He was tempted to go in and take a pot of hot wine to revive his good humour, but it was already late enough on the tide, and the weather was getting worse by the minute. No, he wanted his supper and his warm bed so he would forgo the pleasure, he walked over to the river wall stairs and down to where the boats were moored alongside, calling out to the men waiting below as he approached, carefully, he picked his way down the few slippery steps, which led onto the causeway.
" Oars if you please. Oars to Chelsea and quickly"
The first man, the one nearest to the wall did not answer, but by the light of his torch, started unwrapping a dirty bandage from around what looked like a disfigured hand. Thomas wrinkled his nose; he did not like the look of this, it might be a slow pull, with a man in such a poor condition as this one.

He looked more closely at the gaunt face, and was immediately decided on not taking such a sombre fellow. Walking along the causeway he approached the next wherry.
"Where to your highness?" asked Ebenezer in his usual gruff, disrespectful tone.
"The Swan Inn Chelsea as quick as you can get me there" said Doggett, making ready to board the vessel.
"I will make it worth your while if you are quick", he continued, but as he made to step into the wherry. Ebenezer snorted. This was the last sort of fare he wanted on a night like this. It would be a long pull against the wind and flow, and he was sure to come back empty.
"Can't be done Sir", claimed Ebenezer, indicating his extinguished torch with a wave of his hand.
"I have a regular titled gentleman arriving at the eleventh hour, I would not be back in time for him if I were to take you".
"One of these other poor souls can earn your coin this evening".
Thomas looked over at the next two boats, it was the Taylors who were now back alongside each other, holding their boats close together. The brothers had heard the conversation with both James and Ebenezer and the man's required destination. Chelsea was nearly five miles upstream from here, they looked at each other, and before Doggett could speak, they both doused their touches into the river's water, indicating that they were not available.
"We both have damage to our vessels Sir", said Christopher, "We are waiting for a shipwright, we can do only short pulls till our boats are put to rights, the next man will take you".
Doggett was now becoming furious he looked across the narrow wooden causeway at Kenneth's boat. This was more like it, a big fellow was sitting in her with his brand burning, this one might be a better bet altogether for a quick trip home.
"You" he said, flicking his kerchief at Kenneth.
"The Swan Inn at Chelsea and be quick about your work".
Edwin sitting in the last boat, knew well Kenneth's situation. He worked a wherry which belonged to a wealthy waterman, one Frederic Mann. Mr. Mann was not a kind person to work for, and what was worse for his employees was that he paid by the timed system, only paying for the time agreed to be worked, this meant that Kenneth would be off pay at midnight wherever he might be at that time. On a pull to Chelsea he might arrive after midnight, and would spend much unpaid effort coming back in his own time. Edwin also knew that Kenneth was meeting one of his tavern wenches this evening, and was planning to finish well before midnight.

All the usual excuses for refusing a passenger having been used up by the others ahead of him, Kenneth felt that he would have to take the fare, for the consequences of not doing so would be fateful for him, Mr. Mann would be angry indeed, if he found that Kenneth had refused a profitable fare in his time, he would surely be dismissed from employment and Mann would take on another waterman to work his vessel. Kenneth knew that there were

many, only too willing to take on the work, no, he could not take the risk of refusing the fare.
"Damnation" he thought.
"I am trapped here in an awkward situation altogether".
Mr. Mann's system of payment was extremely unfair to those who worked for him. It meant that all money taken for fares before the finishing hour was for the wherryman to take a share in, but all money taken in Mr. Munn's time, after the finishing hour, was for him alone. All knew this to be bad, and unfair system of employment, a man could work hard all day, only to be paid by a passenger at the end of the journey in the owner's time, to the owner's profit. The wherryman would then be bound to hand the whole fare over without taking any share of it.
Kenneth knew that if he took this 'Cock-Robin' to Chelsea landing, he might be off pay before he ever reached the Swan Inn, he would therefore lose his share of that fare, and then have the long row back for nothing. Even if he could find a return passenger, he would have to pass everything over to Mr. Mann as it was outside Kenneth's time. Into the bargain he would miss his arrangement for a night of enjoyment with his pretty tavern maid.

There was however, another problem for Kenneth in working for Mr. Mann, his employer was also an 'Overseer' of the Guild, and sat on the Court of the Watermen's Company. The nine Overseers of the Watermen's Court were the rulers of the Guild. No working Waterman would ever consider cheating on one of these powerful men by not declaring all his earnings. It would not be sensible to antagonise a member of the Court, the consequences of doing so would be severe indeed. The Taylor brothers were listening to the exchange between Kenneth and the gaily-dressed actor, to protect themselves they would surely report Kenneth if he refused this fare. Kenneth's mind was in turmoil, but stoically he decided that he had no option other than to take this man to Chelsea, and put up with the consequences. He opened his mouth to bid the man to come aboard, but before he could say anything, Edwin stood up.

"Here Sir, over here if you please, do not think of risking yourself in that leaking boat, or with that argumentative and drunken fool of an oarsman. I will take you to Chelsea before any of these could get you as far a Westminster", persuaded Edward with a bright smile on his face.
Thomas Doggett was pleased and also very relieved to here this; he looked at the speaker. The young man was dressed in a shabby coat, which although repaired with many patches, had received maintenance that he could see had been well executed. He had a shining new licence on his left arm showing Doggett that he was a new Freeman of his trade. His shoes were protected with wax and the boat seemed clean and sound. In all it looked as if the lad was well looked after by someone who cared for him. Thomas immediately liked the look of this young man, much better and safer he thought to himself, than the bigger man, whose boat apparently might be unsafe. This last one was tallish, and as far as Thomas could tell from the outline of his covered form, and he seemed built well enough to-

boot. The other man, although bigger and stronger, was perhaps a little frightening to be out alone with on the river on such a night, particularly, if as this young man had intimated, he was a drinker. This one he decided, would do well enough, he would much rather go with a man who wanted the fare, than one who was reluctant. Thomas however, still felt a little uneasy he felt he was missing something here; he was not sure what was happening among these wherrymen, there was obviously something afoot, he felt as if he was being manipulated. It seemed obvious that apart from this young man the others were not willing for the long pull to Chelsea, even if it resulted in a good payment. Anyway, he now had a boat to take him home, and that was his primary concern. Thomas took Edwin's proffered hand and stepped aboard.
"Here Sir", invited Edwin.
"Make yourself comfortable on the passenger bench."
"I have kept the thwart dry for you, wrap yourself around with this pull-on to keep the dampness out of your bones, and before you know it, we will be to Chelsea's Swan Inn, in time for supper, and a hot toddy for the body into the bargain". Edwin leaned over the side of the boat to free his catch line from the causeway's bollard, looking over with a wily grin at Kenneth sitting in his boat.

Kenneth was overjoyed with this unexpected turn of event. Leaping out of his wherry, he made to help his friend untie his line, leaning forward to give Edwin a wink and a heavy but friendly punch on the shoulder. "You rogue, you tow rag" he shouted at Edwin, mostly for the benefit of the Taylors than anyone else.
"You would steal my fare from me, and take the very bread from my poor dying mother's mouth". He was now warming to the part of the cheated wherryman, and in his enjoyment and relief at not having to do the long pull, decided that he would make a scene, as if he really wanted this fare. "I will have at you next time we meet alone, to be sure, you dog's turd". Edwin knew that Kenneth was apt to overplay his hand, therefore he did not continue this farcical exchange by offering any answer, but gave Kenneth a knowing look, which doused his friend's enthusiasm for any more repartee.

Edwin skilfully backed his wherry away from the causeway, pulling on his left blade until he had the boat headed up stream, then with a growing resignation, that knew this would be a long and uncomfortable pull. He leant on his oars, and so to the task ahead, leaving the other watermen to settle back into their private thoughts, dreaming of a more suitable fare going down river. In spite of his flowery way of talking and his effeminate way of dressing, which being the way of actors, Doggett had adopted, he was not a stupid man. He realised that something had taken place at the stairs, which he did not quite understand, he could tell that the big boatman had been trying to play a part, and had played it uncommonly badly. He wondered if he had been manipulated into taking this boat rather than any another and if so, for what reason? Was this all part of a conspiracy?

Perhaps he was once again in danger this night? He looked the boat over, it seemed well looked after, the timber seemed sound, there was a little water in the bilge, but it was raining after all, so that was to be expected. Perhaps those men were villains and had tricked him into taking this particular boat for some underhand purpose, was it some sort of trap he mused, was he in grave danger for the second time this night. He looked closely at the wherryman who was now pulling hard at the oars, then turning his head surreptitiously, he tried to make out the license number on his badge, but the night was too dark to read it from this angle. He looked again at the wherryman; he seemed to be a young man in his early twenties, fare of face and fit of body, he was working hard at his task, he seemed to be strong enough for the work ahead.

Thomas studied Edwin as closely as was possible through the gloom. He felt sure that this young man could make short work of him in a fight; his hand moved over to take a firmer hold on his blade's handle. "No that will not do," he suddenly thought to himself. If the man should see him reach for his blade he might attack anyway, claiming to have been defending himself, on the other hand, he somehow felt safe with this young man; he knew that these watermen, although very aggressive and rough tongued to each other, could usually be trusted by their passengers. They were after all, heavily controlled by their City Guild. Thomas decided that he liked the cut of this one, who was now working stoically and steadily at his labour. Doggett determined that he was safe enough in this man's hands and pulling his neck deeper into the collar of his cloak, he drew his feet in to make a neat waterproof bundle of himself under the cover, settling back to think more about the night's disturbing events.

Edwin was working hard, concentrating intently on the row against the wind and the water flow. They had now almost reached Westminster. He was pulling steadily at his labour and was now sweating profusely. The weather conditions had deteriorated even more than at the start of this row. A lively wind was now blowing little spurts of spray over the bow of the boat onto Edwin's back, the water had soaked through his coat and shift onto to the skin beneath, he knew that this would not be a problem provided he kept at his task; if he kept himself warm by the effort of rowing, he need not be concerned to catch a chill.
The wind seemed to be playing with the oarsman, making fun of his skill by interfering with his rhythm. It did this by getting under the blade of the oar, obliging Edwin to counter the force with an upward pressure of his arms, and then the wind would ease, forcing him to adjust again quickly, by moving his grip further along the loom handle. It was a very tiring way to have to row, and he could already feel the effect affecting the muscles in his forearms. Edwin was however up to the challenge, for him, it had now become a competition between him and the elements.
"Long and strong, long and strong" He repeated to himself in his mind; he could hear his father's voice, reminding him of what he had taught him in weather conditions like this. He leaned back longer into his work, taking a

little more time when the spoons were out of the water to rest his arms. He looked again at his passenger, checking to see that he was not too uncomfortable in this filthy weather, but the man was well wrapped in the waterproof pull-on sheet, and seemed to be lost in his own thoughts, Edwin had noticed earlier that he had been trying to look closely at his badge number, he hoped he was not going to make trouble for him or Kenneth or any of the others.

"No, I think not, he seems contented enough," thought Edwin, switching his concentration back to the rhythm of his oars.

Thomas noticed the man peering at him between the oar strokes, as if to see that he was comfortable; he looked back at the boatman, pleased at the man's solicitude. His thoughts now broken from the adventure of earlier that evening, Doggett again studied the fellow he was travelling with in more detail. This young man was working hard, without any slackening, he had kept up this pace and rhythm since they had left Old Swan. Doggett was impressed, this was a difficult task, he was pulling their combined weights and also that of the vessel; the lad was doing extremely well.
"You have chosen a hard trade young man," said Doggett raising his voice against the wind.
"Yes Sir, that is surely true on a night such as this" replied Edwin, panting a little with the effort.
" Tell me" said Doggett, still annoyed at having had to walk over the bridge to find a boat.
"Why were there so many of you at Old Swan, and not a one to be had at Bankside?" Edwin considered carefully before he answered. It was dangerous to trust any outsider with reasons or information on how the watermen worked their plying trade.
"Were there no boats to be had there tonight Sir?" said Edwin innocently, trying to sound as if he was unaware of the situation.
"Not a one to be had, yet plenty of trade waiting for oars," replied Doggett with suspicion, he could tell that the wherryman did not like this subject.
"Perhaps there had been a rush of business earlier, and all boats had been taken before you arrived Sir," suggested Edwin, trying to concentrate on his pulling.
"We are doing well Sir, I'll soon have you home," suggested Edwin hoping to steer the conversation in a new direction. Doggett did not answer, but continued studying the lad.
"We are past Westminster now", Edwin commented still wanting to change the subject, he was concerned that it might lead to a problem, if this man found out why they all avoided Bankside at this time of night. This actor looked like a man who could make trouble if he was so inclined, he might report any information he acquired on the matter to the Hall, so he decided to take a different tack.
"I hope that you are keeping dry Sir, this weather is in for the night, and we will be a little time yet. I have another cover under the seat if you would like to have it."

"No thank you" said Doggett, recognising the attempt to divert him. "I am comfortable enough, I thank you for your solicitude." That was a crafty distraction thought Doggett, he is trying to change the subject, this lad is no dunderhead, I must deal with him carefully if I am to get any answers to my queries. The lad knows more of this matter than he is willing to share. Thomas decided to go along with a change of subject and to tell the wherryman of his adventure with the footpad on the bridge, he might perhaps win him over to a more open response to his enquiries. "I will tell you of the consequences of having to cross the damned bridge to find a boat for home," said Doggett, and proceeded to tell the story of his unpleasant crossing, which he considered was directly caused by the lack of a wherryman at Bankside. Being an actor, he embellished the story to good effect, playing up his ability with his blade, saying that the rogue was perhaps lucky that the fracas had not turned into a full confrontation.

He soon realised that he was holding Edwin's full attention, he could see that his small audience had some obvious admiration for his passenger. He went on to impress the lad even more, by telling him about his own life in Ireland, and after arriving in England on the London stage. He told him of his interest in the politics of the day. When his tale was finished, he said to Edwin,
"Now come young man, I have told you openly of my business, and my exploits this evening". He looked into Edwin's eyes.
"I sense however, that I am not fully informed of your purpose in this night's affair." Edwin kept his face composed and did not answer, Thomas went on.
"To start with, tell me the true reason for the lack of wherries at Southwark, I would, at the very least, like to know the answer to that mystery. It is irritating my mind to not be able to work out the reason." Doggett thought he could detect a softening of the lad's determination to preserve the secret. He went on, pressing forward with his enquiry.
"Next I would like you to explain, while you are about it, what was going on with that little performance you were acting out with the other wherryman at the stairs before we left, pray also enlighten me about that, for I am a good judge of a bad actor, and your friend fell into that category without doubt". Doggett detected a slight smile on the boatman's face, but he could see that the lad was hiding some information; he was now certain that he was on to something; he felt that the lad's resistance was melting, but he could still read some distrust in Edwin's eyes.
"If you doubt my sincerity and discretion, you have my word as a gentleman that this conversation stays within this boat; I would simply like to know for my benefit, I do not wish to make trouble for you."

The wind was now on his starboard side and they were shielded by the trees along the bank, making the going a little easier for Edwin, he looked closely into the disarming face, feeling that perhaps he could trust this man; this old actor who seemed to want to befriend him. Edwin decided that as there were no witnesses to what he might say, it would be difficult for the man to go back on his word, and report the ruse used by wherrymen to the Hall. The Company knew anyway that the journeymen had many tricks to avoid the difficult journeys that they preferred not to make, or difficult passengers that they wished to avoid. Perhaps a little understanding of a wherryman's lot in life, by an influential man like this, might not go amiss. However, he would not be direct, he would hint rather than proclaim. He would suggest rather than accuse, just to be safe.

Edwin started by explaining that with the conditions of weather and tide set as they were this night. To go to Chelsea would not only be hard wark, but also unprofitable on the return journey. Trade from Swan Stairs would soon be aboundant going down river with the tide, or perhapps to Westminster, which was but a short pull over the ebb. He then told of the difficulties a person had to endure as a young wherryman, and about the deviousness of some employers, the way many boat-owners like Mr Mann used young men with a good nature to their own profit. He told Doggett about what it would have meant to Kenneth if he had taken the actor, that Mr. Mann would have received all the fare even though Kenneth would have done all the work, and how into the bargain he would have missed his evening at home with his loving family. Edwin decided to leave out any mention of the tavern maid.

"Why then did you stand in for him?" asked Doggett.
"Will the others at the stairs not report the matter to Mr. Mann?"
"I am sure they will not" said Edwin, and described the background of the others who were waiting at the stairs.
"James the one who is ailing, the first man you approached, he keeps himself strictly to his own council, he is safe enough and will keep quiet because he does not care", explained Edwin.
"Ebenezer, the inquisitive one, will not tell, for he refused your fare on a lie. He did not have another passenger, I am sure of it, and to have to prove the point would be difficult for him. Overall he is safe, he likes to keep clear of the Guild's officials.
The Taylor brothers are too afraid of Kenneth's skill with his blade to cause him mischief; they will therefore hold their tongues without doubt. Mr Mann will only ever be told that I took the fare from him, not that Kenneth was unwilling."
"I can understand that, and I can see the reason for your comfort of any injurious outcome in the matter. However, it does not explain why you stepped in, taking on this odious trip with all the hard work it entailed."
Edwin looked surprised to be asked such a question.
"I am his friend Sir, he said amazed that the actor should ask.
"He would do the same for me if the circumstances were reversed."
"You all know each other so very well," mused Doggett, considering with respect such a strong friendship.
"We do indeed Sir, the good parts and the bad it must be said. We are all part of a river village community, a fellowship that dates back to the dark times before memories began. We might argue and fight among ourselves, but we defend each other against any attack from outside, we love and hate

each other with a will, but always keep together." Edwin stopped talking, wondering if he had said too much.

Doggett was impressed, he had never considered these people more than menials, he respected their fitness and skill with their boats, but never thought them capable of such deep feelings, and loyalties. "Why did you put on that little performance at the stairs? Asked Doggett, becoming more and more intrigued with the machinations of this group. "You could have been open with me." He argued persuasively. "We do not know you Sir, we thought to put you off the scent, not wanting you to know that we were manipulating your wishes." Edwin could tell that for all his fancy clothes and foppish speech, this man was very intelligent. He had got more information out of him in the last ten minutes, than Edwin had meant to give, he was a clever one to be sure, he could delve deep into a man's mind with his witty, gentle and disarming words. "Now" said Doggett."
"I am beginning to understand something of your reasoning, I find it commendable that your friendship is so sound, good comrades are hard to find, and should be helped when in adversity". Thomas sucked in a thoughtful breath before continuing.
"But you have not told me the reason for the lack of boats at Bankside." He paused for he could see the lad was uncomfortable with this question, and reluctant to confide any information in him.
"I might be in a position to help, if I could know the reason." He argued persuasively.
"A friend in a high places can be a good friend indeed," said Doggett, seeing that his words were having the desired effect.

Edwin was again struggling with the weather conditions, having to concentrate on his rowing to pull the boat across the river to work the slack water and make the exertion more bearable. He also used the time to gather his thoughts on how to answer the question so directly put by Doggett. Fortunately the sudden squall had made it necessary for his passenger to pull his head down inside his collar of his coat in an effort to avoid the sudden blow of the rain soaked wind, thereby suspending the conversation. As Edwin reached the calmer water under the trees on the opposite bank, he eased his stroke, relaxing his tortured back and arm muscles, then after some further consideration, he decided to throw abandon to the wind, and confide in this charming and disarming gentleman player.

He first told Doggett about the Roaring Boys, and the reasons for some of the Watermen's working practices, he told him about the runners and the non-payers, the Beadles and the harsh Company rules, he told him of the corruption of the Overseers of the Guild, and that of many others working in the Port, about the minimal, never changing, low fares, wherrymen were restricted to charge, and about the ever-present worry over the activities of the Press Gangs. By the time Edwin had finished his discourse, which was achieved with more than a little prompting from Doggett who wanted to know more and more as the story unfolded, they had almost reached Chelsea Steps. Thomas was astounded at what he had heard, this little understood group of men, vital to the transport of Londoners, who were working extremely hard under the very eyes of London's society. Yet the citizens were unaware of the effect that the brutal system these men were forced to endure, was having on the service that they provided. A structure which could have such a troublesome consequence upon themselves, and on how they might travel about their City. He thought that such working practices were scandalous, and said so, promising to look into what could be done to improve matters.

Edwin looked over his shoulder and made ready to line the boat up for the run into the landing stair causeway. He was wet through and exhausted by the effort of the long row, a pull that he must now repeat on the return. However, he was pleased with the achievement, it had been a challenge, and it felt good to have dominated the elements. As he pulled the wherry alongside the worn timber of the causeway at the Swan Inn landing, he wondered if he had told this old actor too much of the watermen's affairs, perhaps however, if he was as well connected as he had claimed, he might do something for the men of Edwin's trade, but he had his misgivings about that. A good meal, a hot toddy and a warm bed, and the information gained during the journey, would become just a fading memory, a distraction to help pass the time of an unpleasant trip home on a bad night.

Doggett looked at the lad who had rowed non stop from the City in this appalling weather. He could see that he was shaking slightly from the effort, and soaked through from the rain and spray. He wondered if he should offer him to come ashore for a hot drink, but decided against it. They both needed to get to bed, and to put this night's work behind them. Any delay, however pleasant for the lad, would mean that the return row ahead of him would be that much more difficult when he returned to the task. Thomas Doggett opened his purse, giving Edwin the fare he asked. Edwin thanked him, and leaning forward, slipped the edge of the beautiful orange-red cloak off from the nails under the passenger thwart seat, which he had ensnared earlier with the much practised movement of the toe of his shoe. Thomas noticed the movement, he was pleased to see that the lad was still concerned enough to protect his cloth from catching up on something sharp under that seat. He fished again into his purse, producing another large value extra coin, giving it to Edwin as drink geld.
"This is for your attention to my welfare, your effort in tonight's long pull, and for the information you have divulged to me".
"I will give much thought to what you have told me regarding the austerities practised upon your trade, and will consider what I might do". Thomas stood up and steeped forward, he felt the boat firm steadily onto the ground by his weight, settling itself into the crushed chalk of the shore.

He stepped carefully out over the port side of the wherry, out on to the wet causeway, he looked down at the wherryman sitting in his wet, worn, coat,

thinking how he might improve the lot of these men of the river, he must give the matter more thought, then turning towards the land, and with a long practised, theatrical wave of his hand, he made his way cautiously up the slippery causeway to the roadway above, which led directly to the door of the nearby Swan Inn. He was home; he had made it safely after all. His supper and his bed were calling him. Then with a sudden thought, he stopped, turning to look back at the wherryman. The lad was now preparing the boat, and himself, for the long pull back to the City. Doggett shivered at the thought of having to repeat the journey he had just made. "What a strange life," he thought to himself, so much hidden pride, yet true gratification in a trade, employment that others would avoid at all costs, what was it the lad had said? Ah yes he had said.
"The river gets into your blood ." How strange to say that, how very strange, yet it was true in a way. Their business is much like the stage in that respect, which can also get into one's very being, however, these people's origins go back even further than players do. Intrigued by this thought he went on his way. Was there something he could do to help these people of the river, he had liked the young man, and admired his attitude to life, he was intelligent despite his lack of breeding or education, a good Englishman, proud to defend his country to be sure, He had the makings of a 'Whig', thought Doggett.

Edwin looked about him at the causeway; there was not a person to be seen, he was wet through with rain and sweat, and was already feeling the chill of the night on his skin under his shift, he must continue to work, or he might catch a fever. He decided to make the most of the ebb and the wind by immediately pulling his way back to London. He draped the pull-on over his shoulders and backed the boat out into the stream's flow, then with a steady stroke to keep himself warm, but without effort to cause sweating, he should build up enough warmth during the pull back to dry out a little before the walk to his house. As he rowed he considered what he had said to the old actor, had he confided too much information? Well it was too late to concern himself with that now, what would be, will be. He put the concern out of his mind and set about his work. In spite of the slightly uncomfortable wetness and the aches and pains from the long pull, Edwin's found that his spirits were high. He did not know why he should feel so happy, but he felt contented, somehow relieved. In spite of the awful conditions of the night, he was comforted that he had completed the task. It was a nice feeling; he had enjoyed meeting the old gentleman, and hearing his story of the playhouses, and of the land of his birth, he had also enjoyed telling him something of the waterman's trade. Smiling to himself as he pulled along, Edwin suddenly realised that the nagging feeling that had been with him all day, had lifted, that feeling of a pending event was gone completely, he was at last free of it. Whatever it was, that he should have done, was now over, perhaps the great effort he had put into the row, had been the cure. He felt somehow that he would never know.

Chapter Ten
The love of Mary

It was Sunday morning and Edwin was up with the lark. He looked out of the small attic window, at the beautiful morning, giving all the promise of a lovely day. Strong sunshine played on the rooftops and around the chimneys of the neighbouring houses, sunshine that was much deserved after all the bad weather of late. Edwin was very pleased with the potential that this good start to the day offered, for this was to be a very special one. Excited at what he hoped lay ahead; he washed himself down, and dressed quickly in his Sunday best. He had promised Mary to take her to a little village called Penge. A good friend of the Crossbacks owned a small inn in the village and Edwin planned to visit the innkeeper Robin and his wife Jane. He wanted to show off his Mary, to enjoy the fuss he knew that they would make of her.

After a light breakfast of oatmeal bread smeared with pork fat, saved from last week's roast, which had been allowed to harden. He washed it down with a bumper of warm milk. The hard pork fat was his favourite; he dug his knife down deep into the pot, to get at the brown jelly always to be found at the bottom. A barrage of questions and much unnecessary advice accompanied his meal, all emanating from his mother. Finally, with many promises, which he had no intention of keeping, he managed to get away, leaving his home to make his way over to Mary's house.

As he approached, he could see that she was already waiting for him in front of the squat little building. She was sitting on a low wall swinging he legs, smiling as she saw him approaching. She looked beautiful in her best blue and white dress, her chestnut hair shone with the oil she had massaged into it after a sound washing the night before. Mary had a very good figure, which matched perfectly with her charming face, her large dark eyes and rose-coloured cheeks, complementing the white porcelain texture of her skin; she was indeed a beauty. Edwin wondered again what she saw in him. She could have had the pick of any, if she had so wanted, but she had shown her affections towards him alone, and he felt proud of such flattery.

They exchanged greetings shyly, with a little awkwardness, but after a little teasing banter, and some friendly compliments on her appearance, any ice between them melted away into the sunlight of the day. At Mary's bidding, Edwin entered the house; there to help her pack the small basket of victuals she intended them to take on their walk. Mary's mother fussed about, trying to persuade her daughter to take more provisions than were necessary. Edwin explained that they would be eating at his friend Robin's inn, but she persisted, saying that they would need sustenance during such a long walk.

At last they were allowed to take just a little drink and fruit, with a small loaf of bread to sustain them. When everything was finally packed ready for the journey, and after exchanging a few more pleasantries with Mary's parents, the two set off for their lengthy walk to Penge.

The day was even more beautiful than Edwin had hoped, there was not a cloud in the sky, with not the slightest breath of wind to stir the heavens. Their hearts sang, as they walked, chatting their way along the country roads, heading out to the south away from the smells of the City. Edwin was very proud and pleased with his lovely maiden, he thrust out his chest with pride as they proceeded, he was sure that he was the envy of every man they passed. He felt that everyone was looking at them, each person seemed to be smiling, was it just this lovely weather putting everyone in such a good mood? Or was it his Mary's beauty? He felt sure it was the latter. Edwin was filled to bursting point with happiness and pleasure, as they continued on their way deeper into the countryside exchanging greetings with the local people they passed.

After about an hour's walk, they came across a field in which several brightly painted, covered wagons were parked in a semi-circle. Lots of young children were running and dancing about, seemingly having great fun. Mary insisted they stop and watch the fun, but as the children saw the strangers approach, they stopped their game, suspiciously watching the newcomers, Edwin tried to reassure the children, urging them to continue their play, but they remained still, sullenly rooted to the ground where they stood. The sudden lack of merry making caused some of the doors of the wagons to be flung open, men and women appeared at the steps leading up to the doors. Three swarthy looking men, with a strangely dressed old woman came forward to face the intruders. They leaned on the fence of the field, making it obvious that they would watch the intruders until they passed. Edwin felt uncomfortable under their disrespectful gaze. "Egyptians" he said under his breath to Marry.
"Leave the talking to me; these people can become aggressive for no reason whatsoever".
"Good morrow" said Edwin doffing his bonnet at the group of men. "Good passing to you both on your journey this day," said the old woman with a thick foreign intonation. Then staring intently at Edwin she said. "Young Sir! Would you like your lady to know of the future, before you pass?" Edwin looked at the men who were still looking forbiddingly at the couple, he was about to decline the offer, when he suddenly changed his mind. It might be good to know Mary's future, and perhaps amusing to have her outlook foretold; he had heard that some of these people had a gift of foretelling events.
"What would it cost me to know such information?" asked Edwin, looking intently at the old woman. Mary gave him a dig in the ribs; she wanted to be on their way, not wanting to tarry any longer with these foreign people. She had also heard of the Egyptians, and knew that they had an ominous reputation.

"Cross my palm with a coin, and I will tell you all I can see" said the old woman persuasively. Edwin suddenly felt very confident, and deciding to put his trust in providence said.
"Come, Mary, these are not bad people, I believe they mean us no harm, let us find out our future".

The atmosphere seemed to change immediately; the sour look on the men's faces lifted, and they removed the bars from the fence, helping the young couple through into the field of the encampment. The children were now chattering brightly again, circling around the newcomers with much interest. The old woman led them over to what was to prove her own wagon, where she indicated that they were to climb the steps and go inside. As they entered through the ornately carved, and brightly painted doorway, they were surprised to be faced with a magnificently decorated interior, it was immaculately clean and tidy and seemed somehow bigger on the inside that it looked from the outside. There were elaborately carved and painted cupboards with well fitted doors, there was an area to the back which was curtained off, but as the drape was not quite pulled together, Edwin could see through the gap to a sleeping cot with a bright coloured quilt, and more little cupboards, all painted in the rainbow arrangement of colours which seemed so attractive to these people. In spite of the bright sunshine outside, the inside of the wagon was dark, the little windows on each side being closed off with pretty wooden shutters. An oil lamp was burning dully, hanging over a small table, giving a soft glow to everything that its light fell upon.

The old woman gestured to the bench-seat at the furthest side of a small table, then as Mary and Edwin sat down, she sat herself in the seat opposite. Once seated she looked into Edwin's eyes, holding out her hand invitingly. Edwin felt into his purse and fished out a coin, then pressed it into the woman's outstretched palm. She looked disappointedly at the coin then looked back at him again. Realising that she required a coin for each of them, Edwin handed over another, she seemed satisfied, and spitting on the money, opened a small drawer to the side of the table, and dropped the coins inside. Then reaching further into the drawer, she produced from its depths a bright object. It was a glass ball the size of two fists held together, which she placed it on a ring of rope, also taken from the draw. The old woman was now looking intently at Mary. Leaning forward, she took hold of the maid's hand. She did not speak for some minutes, but at last she said quietly in her thick foreign accent.
"You are a healthy young maid, you will have a fine family in the future, three boys and two pretty maids. Two other children will be lost to you." Mary did not answer, the woman continued to stare into Mary's face, then looking down at the glass ball on the table, as if for conformation, she said. "You will have happiness in your life, but first you will know sorrow, fear, and deep anxiety." She patted Mary's hand.
"This darkness you will know only in the first years, and you will need all your health and strength to prevail, but triumph you will, you must never

give up hope during those dark times, for happiness awaits you at the end".
Edwin was a little angry that this old hag was ruining his day; he did not
want Mary upset with this nonsense of bad fortune, he was about to voice
his opinion. When, as if reading his thoughts, and before he could speak his
mind to the woman, she turned her gaze on him. Her eyes seemed to bore
into his very essence.
"It matters not if you are a believer in the old ways or not. What I speak is
the truth, but it was for your ears alone, the maid will only hear the good
things I have said." She reached over and took Edwin's hand, looking down
into her globe.
"I see water, and much knowledge of the ways of that element. You will
have a hard life young man, but an exciting one." She paused, then again
consulted the glass.
"You will be maimed, you will know true fear, but your knowledge and
skills will help you through your ordeals. There is a benign influence in you
life that leads you straight, you have learnt your lessons well, and will
remember them." The old woman put her head on one side as if trying to
read an upside-down book, after a time she looked again into Edwin's eyes
as if searching for something.
"You have in some way touched the future, or influenced another who will
be remembered. I can not see clearly through the mists of consequence, it
seems that you are not named, but still there, as if behind a curtain. It is a
strange sign, one that I have not met before." Suddenly she grabbed up the
glass ball, and quickly returned it to the draw. Standing up, she opened the
door, indicating that they should leave.

Once outside in the glorious sunshine, the spell was broken and once more
their good humour was restored. A dark haired woman took Mary's hand
and led them to a large table in the centre of which stood a steaming pot.
All the Egyptians of the camp stood about this table; they were taking cups
full of the hot liquid and drinking with relish. The dark haired woman filled
two cups, offering them to the couple. It was a mulled wine as far as Edwin
could tell, but with something else added which he could not define.
"This is delicious," said Mary drinking deeply from her cup.
"What kind people they are. Quite the opposite from what I have been told
of them".
"We speak your language maid," warned a man standing near to them, who
had overheard her words.
"I take no offence at your words however, we know what is said about us,
we are foreign to your land, even though we have lived here since before
any can recall." He said this with a disarming smile. Edwin looked at the
smiling man.
"I have heard it said that you never visit the City, or stay long in any one
place." He asked, genuinely interested in these people, of which he had only
heard strange stories.
"We like to travel, it is our way to live, we prefer to live out in the open, to
move to new pastures when the mood takes us, or if the signs dictate." He
glanced at Mary.

"What did Meg tell you of your future young maid?"
"All wonderful things, I am pleased to say, I am to have a happy life with many children"
"Did she not tell of anything bad or difficult?" said Edwin.
"No not a thing, but I am not so dull as to think that such total happiness is possible. However, she has made my day even happier than it already was." She smiled contentedly. Edwin could not believe his ears, had Mary not heard all that the old woman had said?
"What think you of what she told me?" he asked.
"She kept your mood happy too, saying that you are strong and skilled, and will live a long and joyful life." Edwin was astonished that Mary had understood such a different version of their fortunes.

After being pressed to take a second cup of the fiery drink, they took their leave and left the camp returning the waves of farewell. Time passed quickly, and soon they were approaching the village of Penge. To call it a village was perhaps elevating it to a higher status than it deserved. It was a small hamlet of a place, very pretty, with its few black and white cottages, standing alone each side of the narrow road. The inn was at the far side of the settlement. As they made their way towards it, they passed an old man tending the garden of his cottage, Edwin doffed his bonnet as they passed, the man nodded a greeting in return.

As they approached the building; Edwin explained to Mary that the owner, Robin Ridley, had once been a Thames waterman. He had been taken by the press, and had served for several years in the Queen's Navy. He had lost an eye to a cutlass thrust, and now wore a patch over the damaged socket, on which his merry wife Jane had painted a winking eye.
"So Mary do not be feared by the first sight of him," warned Edwin.
"During the same battle, which cost him his eye, Robin's ship took as a prize, a Spanish ship much larger than their frigate. It happened to be a most profitable catch, for on board was a French ambassador, with rich gifts for the King of Spain". Mary's eyes were open wide with wonder as she listened to the story.
"When the prize money was shared out, after the decommissioning of their ship," continued Edwin.
"Robin's share was enough to buy him this small Inn here at Penge, where he is now settled very well indeed" Edwin looked at the old building, overgrown with climbing flowers and ivy.
"He is a good man, who has accepted life's difficulties with fortitude and good grace, with his ever happy wife Jane at his side; they live a most contented existence away from the bustle of life in the City."

As the two approached the inn, Edwin gave his watermen's whistle call. There was an immediate answering pipe from within the inn, and through the open door appeared a large broad shouldered man with a shock of white hair and a broad smile.
"Jane, come Jane" he called back into the inn.

"It is beauty and the beast come to visit us". The two men clasped each other around the shoulders, giving each other playful punches to the body, as they teasingly insulted each other in the way of rivermen. Mary looked on in amusement at this show of male affection.

Jane emerged from the dark doorway, blinking in the strong sunlight. She was wiping her hands on her white apron, trying to see who had come to visit.
"Edwin", she shouted with genuine affection and pleasure.
"What a pleasant surprise to add to this already beautiful day," then looking at Mary.
"Who is this beauty you bring to our poor home?". Edwin glowed with pride; he was pleased to receive so positive a response in front of his maiden.
"This is Mary," stammered Edwin not quite knowing what to say.
"Come in, come inside Mary, away from that dreadful sight of a husband of mine. He is like to frighten the ducks from the pond, let alone such a delicate young person. Come inside do, please to excuse our little home."
They were ushered inside, and invited to sit at one of the tables, which was soon covered over by Jane, with a snow-white cloth.
"You have walked a good piece this morning; you must be starving, to say nothing of thirst." She fussed with true concern.
"Robin, where are your manners? Give our guests a draft, to quench their thirst, while I make ready some victuals." Grinning from ear to ear, Robin brought a brimming pot of fresh cider for each of them, and they set about the drink with relish.

A meal was soon set out on the table in front of them, and they ate heartily on a delicious meal of locally produced pork and vegetables, washed down with more large tankards of the strong cider. The conversation was relaxed and happy, Mary soon found herself joining in with the repartee, relating little stories of her first meetings with Edwin. At the end of the meal, Edwin said that he wanted to show Mary around the area, and asked if they might be excused, as they wanted to walk off the effects of the meal and perhaps explore a little. At this request Robin gave Jane a knowing wink, for which he got a quick slap on the shoulder in return.
"You leave these young people to their own company, or are you now too old to remember our first love." she chided him. Robin smiled his good-natured smile.
"I suggest that you walk up through the old orchard at the back of the Inn, and go up onto the heights," he said, then with a knowing smile. "I think that there, you will find a place to suit your needs", then looking conspiratorially at Edwin.
"I am sure that at least two of our children were begun up there," Robin roared with laughter at his own words, his painted eye seeming to beam with merriment. The young couple were both embarrassed by Robin's openness, but with a warm feeling in their bellies from the food and the

strong cider, they made their way up the hill at the rear of the Inn as directed.

On reaching the heights, they looked around them at the wondrous scenery, they could see the smoke haze in the sky to the north, which indicated the direction of the great City of London, but from here the dirty air was only an interesting addition to the view. They found an open area of heath land covered with heather, with lush islands of lavender growing thick, dotted about the field. For Mary this was the final good luck sign, lavender was her favourite herb. She had not allowed Edwin's advances to go too far since they had first met at that Maypole dance two years ago. She had been but sixteen then and Edwin just nineteen. They had kissed and fondled a little since then, but she had kept his approaches under control, waiting until she was sure that he was the man for her.

Mary remembered her growing up years very well. She had developed slowly, and remembered turning from a girl into a woman more slowly than most. At first the swelling of her breasts had caused her embarrassment, but she soon found that they gave her a sense of confidence and power. Men began to look at her in a different way. She soon learnt to use her new found figure and natural good looks to her advantage. She began to understand men, their simple desires, and their sometimes childlike ways. Her mother had once told her that men were like horses, strong but gentle, and obedient for the most part if handled carefully. She liked and enjoyed being a woman. She had delayed Edwin's suggestion of this walk to Penge; because her cycle dictated that this Sunday was the safest for love making. She now considered the heather, the lavender, the lovely day, the new friends, and Edwin's attentive behaviour as perfect signs. Even the Egyptian woman's words seemed to have given a good portent. She would not resist this time.

Edwin noticed her looking at the purple heather, and deep blue lavender, and said as if he had thought of the idea himself. "Mary lets sit ourselves in the middle of the field, among the lavender fragrance". She let go of his hand, immediately running to the centre of a patch of soft heather, surrounded by tall stands of lavender, and there looking back at him with a bewitching smile, she slowly sank out of sight among plants. Edwin quickly followed; he liked it when she made fun. He reached her and sank down beside her, overwhelmed by the heady aroma all around them. They lay alongside each other on the yielding heather not talking, the effects of the meal, the cider and the strong scent from the lavender, were working a magic spell over them both.

Edwin turned onto his elbow, looking down into Mary's lovely face. Without even thinking that he might be rejected, he bent forward and kissed her full on the lips. She did not move away as she usually did, but returned his kiss with relish. A thrill ran through his young body, he moved his hand to her shoulder, on the way deliberately brushing against her left breast. She did not protest, but sighed a deep sigh, and with a half smile on her full lips, she looked him full in the face, her bright eyes radiating love. Encouraged by her reaction, he brought his hand purposely back resting it fully onto her breast, again she sighed, she was obviously enjoying the feeling as much as Edwin. He slowly massaged the firm round mound, feeling the wonderful softness through the thin cloth of her summer bodice. She reached up, pulling his face down to her own, she kissed him again passionately on the lips, letting her tongue play sensuously just inside his slightly parted lips. Edwin slipped his hand inside the top of Mary's bodice, her response was to put her shoulders back, pushing her breast further into his hand, he felt the nipple, it was hard and protruding. A little moan escaped from Mary's throat.

Edwin was now carefully unfastening the ribbon of her bodice. The garment fell away, freeing Mary's breasts from their captivity, only the thin cloth of her chemise now stood between his hands and their erotic goal. He rose to his knees, gently pulling the top of the loose chemise down to reveal the full wonder of Mary's milk white, full rounded wonders, to the full glare of the sunlight. Overcome with love for this marvellous creature, his breath came in a quick gasp, for he had forgotten to breathe. Mary heard the gasp and opened her eyes, the look on Edwin's face told her all she wanted to know. She took his face in her hands, pulling it down, to sink into the luscious flesh of her bosom, his mouth cupped her right nipple, his tongue running around its hard erect shape. She once again felt the power of her womanhood, as she cradled him to her heaving breast. She now allowed him to pull the chemise down to her waist, freeing her arms in the process. He was now gently licking her breasts, then kissing the soft flesh of her belly alternately, like a child in a wonderland of treasures, as if not knowing which he wanted to enjoy most before the other. He was lying half across her, his elbow had pushed her skirts between her legs. She again took his head in both hands, gently moving it to the terrain below her waist. This was all new territory for Edwin. He had of course been with other women during his nights out with his comrades; but Mary had never allowed him to go this far before. It must mean that she really loved him; he was overjoyed at this realisation. He nuzzled his face deep into Mary's groin, he felt her move her legs at little, accepting him into her most private part, only the thickens of her skirts dulled the feeling.

Mary was now at a high state of desire, the wonderful feeling of Edwin's face and hot breath pushing between her legs was extreme. She slipped her hands down her sides, slowly pulling at the fabric of her skirt, the material slipped easily up over her silk stockings. As soon as Edwin realised what she was doing, he brought his own hands down to follow the hem of her skirt on its sensual rise. He felt the silk of her stocking pass under his rough hands, and then the delight of yielding skin as his hands passed over the stocking tops onto the soft flesh of her thighs. The couple were now beyond retreat from this ecstasy of love, they both felt as if the body of the other was their own, they coupled as only a man and woman can, when truly in love. The heavens spun about them, they were floating on a wave of bliss and desire, all the suppressed feeling of the past years bursting out in a crescendo of adoration. They were now as one.

<=======>

Back at the Inn, Robin was at the rear window of his kitchen, with his telescope raised to his good eye, looking up towards the hill where Edwin and Mary had gone. Suddenly a sharp pain erupted on the back of his head; he spun around to find Jane standing astern of him, one hand on her ample hip, the other holding a large wooden spoon, with which she had dealt him the painful blow.
"That will teach you to spy on those youngsters you 'Jack at the window'; have you no shame about you? Would you like to be watched during your amorous advances? Now get about your duties before I withdraw your own ardent rights for a night or two, to teach you a lesson." Robin grinned sheepishly.
"You could not forgo a tumble in bed yourself, for more than one night let alone two, you passionate hussy, so do not make empty threats". He leaned forward planting a firm kiss on her red cheek.
"I was only trying to see that all was going well with the two of them, you know how awkward it can be at the beginning".
"You leave well alone, your interference might do more harm than good," said Jane, waggling her spoon threateningly.
"They seem to me to be very well in love, and will find the way of it without your assistance." Robin returned to his duties and was pleased when about an hour later; the young couple could be seen returning, walking, and skipping down the slope towards the inn. Robin indicated a table and chairs that he had arranged outside under the dappled shade afforded by the large oak, which grew in the yard of the inn.
" Take a rest from your excursions, my lovelies," he said with a large, knowing, grin on his face." Then seeing Jane coming out from the kitchen, he held off from any further teasing.
"Now, Mary my dear" said Jane. "I have something to seek your advice about, in the back parlour. Let's leave these two reprobates to talk about their old father Thames, which in spite of its liquid theme, I find a very dry subject."

The women walked back into the building arm in arm, chatting and giggling like old friends. The men watched them go, then filling their pipes from the tobacco jar, which Robin had put out for the purpose, they leaned back contentedly and began to discuss the latest happenings on the river, for which Robin was eager to gain more up-to-date knowledge.
"Tell me Edwin how goes it with your father?" Edwin drew a long slow pull on his pipe.
"He is well indeed, and about to build a new wherry, I am to have the Anna, I will purchase her plank by plank. He is also trying to have me join him as a 'fireman' for the Sun Insurance, but such things take time." Robin eyes

showed that he was pleased to hear such comforting news.
"So! you young Turk, life is shining her face in your direction at this time to be sure, and what of Mary, are you to make her an honest woman?"
"Robin, I am bursting to tell someone, and pleased that you are the first to hear of my good fortune. Mary has this very day agreed to wed me. I am altogether delighted. I now know what it means to say 'my cup runneth over', mine is gushing its contents to be sure." Robin beamed with delight.
"Steady at the helm young man; keep your cup steady, you don't want to spill all you have achieved by a foolish move. You have much to take on board, so lower yourself down from that cloud, get your feet on the ground, and plan carefully. You are a lucky dog indeed, with good people about you; a happy life awaits you, if you plan carefully." Edwin looked pensive.
"Tell me Robin, what know you of the Egyptians? We passed some on the road coming here, and stopped to have our future told by an old woman from the camp, they seemed friendly enough." Robin considered the question.
"They are an undeniably strange people; I always think they have the look of pirates about them, with their coloured headbands. The old villagers from here about are very wary of them. It is said that they steal children when their own women are barren. They are also said to have strange gifts, like witches, they claim to be able cure all manner of ailments, and also to be able to see into the future, but it wonders me that if a man can predict the best course to navigate, why is he kept so poor?", they both laughed at the thought.
"The old woman was indeed strange," continued Edwin.
"She told things to Mary, some good, but some bad, she then told me that Mary would only hear the good, and after, when I questioned Mary, it was as the old woman had said, Mary did not remember any of the bad things she had been told".
"Odd indeed" commented Robin.
"She also told me something strange that I can make no sense of. She said I would be remembered long after my death, but my name would not be known, what do you make of that?" Robin shook his head, I have no understanding of those people. It is my belief that if they say enough, some of what they say is sure to come true." They both laughed again at Robin's down to earth view of the world.
" Take my advice Edwin, don't break your mind trying to understand the ravings of an old woman, keep a sharp look out for yourself. With all matters going so well in your favour, you must be extra careful not to take risks, I would not like to see you fall foul of that Chambers family, your father and you are always at war with, and find yourself in a fight, or have a accident, or 'God forbid it' be taken by the press before you are protected by the Sun Insurance. It is my experience that when things are going well, they often can suddenly take a sheer in the opposite direction." Edwin looked closely at his friend.
"You had your time at sea Robin; tell me what it was really like. It seems to have cost you an eye, but in return provided you with adventure and this fine inn. not that I have a wish to follow your example you understand", he

said laughing.

"Well Edwin, let me tell you this, in my opinion it is something to be avoided. It was a fearful time to be sure, I sometimes thought I would not come through; there are many pitfalls in the Navy, apart from the excitement of battle. I know of more men taken for service, who died of disease and misfortune, than were ever killed in the fighting battles. I was plainly lucky, first and foremost, my ship was well managed, and we had the good fortune to win a valuable prize, but most are not so fortunate. No lad, keep to your river, and to close handling, let others have their adventures navigating the wide open seas." Edwin drew on his pipe. "Tell me of your sea battle and how you lost your eye," he asked persuasively. Robin settled back, pleased to relate the story.

"It was in the seas off the coast of the land of Africa, near a place the sailors call 'White man's demise". It was a place where men of our colour skin can not survive. Such diseases were to be found ashore in that place, that it put the fear of God into us all. Even to fetch clean water was a dangerous mission. We had been on our commission for nearly two years, our tour was almost at its end, the ship's hull was covered with barnacles and weed, the ropes, and yards were rotting through, and the ship was alive with rats and vermin. We dare not put her ashore to careen her for a scrape down, for fear of the natives and or disease."

"It was as we were about to set sail for home, when we sighted a Spanie, she was large, much bigger than our frigate, with more guns and bigger shot to boot. Although she out-gunned us, we were the more manoeuvrable and faster through the water as it turned out, we also had the better captain. We had sighted her during the morning watch and gave chase, but it was late in the day before we came near enough to bring her to fight us. This was strange, for we expected that with her size and power, she would have come at us immediately. What we did not know was that she had important passengers aboard. When we came within range of her guns, our captain put our bow straight at her, showing only a narrow profile for her gunners to aim at, he had chosen his approach well, running with the wind astern, not needing to tack or alter course in any way. This type of advance is unnerving for any gun crew, and the Spanies had the worst of it. Their captain, thinking that it was more important to keep the sun at his back, had allowed our captain to take the advantage. They were side on to us, firing their cannons as quickly as they could reload them; we had balls falling to both port and starboard of our ship as we came on. They only got three shots on us, one was on deck, which took away the anchor chain hatch, the other two hit the hull, but being on the bow were bounced off by the angle of out stem planks, causing hardly a scratch.

The nearer we got, the more erratic the aim of the Spanie gunners. When at last she was in range with our own guns, the captain put us hard over, slipping the wind from our rags, so that we were side on to the Spanie's foreword quarter. We only put a dozen or so shots into her, when she suddenly struck her colours. But they are a bad lot those Spanies, for as we came alongside, thinking she had surrendered, they came at us with a vengeance. Lances, knives, swords and pistols. We had our cutlasses, and the officers had their pistol-shot to fight them off, but it was our carpenter and cook, with the help of the sail maker who won the day for us. While we were chasing her and during the hand to hand fighting , when I was busy losing an eye, they had prepared a mixture of black powder, tar and wax, in the galley, which they rolled into small sailcloth bags. These little bombs when lighted and thrown onto the enemy ship, they caused havoc, allowing the rest of us to win the day".

"When it was over, we found that we had lost only six men, with another twenty wounded. The Spanies had lost over thirty, with near fifty disabled. We locked the survivors away below, and took the officers with the passengers on board our ship. Our captain put a prize crew over to sail the Spanie back to home, and we set off in convoy for old England. It was then that we discovered that the passengers were very important. We had captured the French ambassador to Spain and his entire family.

When we arrived home, the value of the bounty for freeing them, plus the prize for the vessel, and all the valuables she was carrying on board, was worth a small fortune. Even after the usual vultures had taken their toll on our rights, and the Admiralty had dipped their grimy fingers in our pie, the share left for the crew was most worthwhile. My share was enough to buy this place. The good luck of losing an eye also meant that the press would not want me again. I was for sure one of the lucky ones, but Edwin beware, remember most seamen are not so fortunate".
"I have no wish to see the world," said Edwin with feeling.
"My sails are now set for nearer to home, my course lies with Mary close alongside, and hopefully a few smaller tenders in tow as time passes, if God be willing."

Mary and Jane emerged from the Inn, Mary was carrying a large basket with a snow white cloth tied across the top.
"Look Edwin, our first betrothal gift of bed linen" Mary's face was shining with joy, she had obviously told Jane of their plans.
"No going back now you lucky dog" smiled Robin and they all laughed together.
"When you name the day, let us know, and we will dance at your wedding"
"You will be the first to know it. Father will be very pleased to see you again," promised Edwin.
"Robin, the hour is late and we must be on our way, even if our hearts would like us to tarry," commented Edwin, truly reluctant to leave his friend and his merry wife. Then with much hugging and slapping of backs, the young couple left the peaceful inn and their cheerful friends, setting their course for the smoky city and home.

The journey back seemed to be quicker that the one coming out. They walked along taking turns to carry the heavy basket, chatting and making plans for their future. When they came near to the camp of the Egyptians, they could see ahead of them a large, noisy, crowd of people; some were shouting and waving sticks, others were banging tins together and throwing dirt.

" What is afoot here?" asked Edwin of an old man who was standing back from the main crowd.

"The Egyptians are being run off with 'rough music', they have been stealing again." Edwin pushed his way through to be nearer the front. He could see that the camp was being taking down hurriedly, and packed into the caravans by the women. Some of the men of the camp were standing guard, lunging with long poles and waving their long knives at the mob, while others were backing the horses into the shafts of the caravans. "What have they done?" asked Edwin of the people near by. One village woman, who was holding her apron up to her mouth in anxiety, replied. "They have blighted the crops for miles about here, we have never seen such bad conditions, our hay is ruined by the heavy rains, and our swine are thin from lack of fodder. The next thing will be the disappearance of our children; one boy is already missing since this morning."

"Could he not be just playing and has forgotten the hour? This is the first fine day for a long spell" suggested Edwin, knowing that he had himself run off to play many times when a child, causing his mother great anguish. "No! No! They are wicked," replied the woman.

"Let them move off to plague others, they are not wanted here, with their bad spells and evil enchantments". Edwin could see that he could say or do nothing to help; he was a stranger himself, if he argued too much, and the crowd might turn their attention on him and Mary. Reluctantly he returned to her and they skirted the crowd to continue on their way.

Mary and Edwin walked on, now quietened by the event they had just witnessed, pondering on the outcome for the Egyptians, sad that they had been unable to help. Where would they go? Who would accept them? Would their life always be so? Were they condemned forever to be hounded from place to place? Country people were very suspicious, distrustful of anyone who was not from their own corner of the land. The countryside for all its beauty, harboured many dark secrets, the villagers were known to be very close-mouthed about what went on, they were even mistrustful of each other.

Edwin, like all people from the City, had heard many stories of the 'country folk' how they would decry one of their own community to the visiting 'witch finder general' and would watch as some poor old lady was half drowned in the ducking stool, then tortured to a point when she would rather accept death, than protest her innocence any more, she would be forced to admit her witchcraft, and be burned alive at the stake before her accusers. They sometimes exchanged children like cattle, so that one family with too many, would sell or give a child to another family with too few. In some remote parts, it was said that human sacrifices were still held at harvest time. A young boy identified from his birth as 'the special one' of the village and called by the magic name of fertility, would on the shortest day of the year be built into a giant figure of straw and branches, to become the 'Green Man', then to be burnt alive in the fields, as an offering to the forces of nature, to persuade the Gods of renewal, to turn the heavens, making the days grow longer, and the cycle of growth to begin again.

Mary and Edwin reached home when the sun was down, the candles were twinkling dimly in the windows of the houses. One house however was brightly lit; it was the house of Bridget.
"She is about her business of making soap," whispered Edwin as they passed the old women's door, and could smell the odour.
"She will be caught one day for sure; all that light and smell will attract the attention of the Mayor's men. It concerns me that my mother is one of her customers".
"My mother to" said Mary.
"Most people here about take her soap, they could not otherwise afford to buy soap with the high tax placed upon it. I think half the neighbourhood would be put into the Clink if the Mayor were to stop her boiling of bones".
"That is a thought," laughed Edwin, I would suggest the list, with that old hag at the top of it.

It took a long time to say 'good night', the couple did not want to part. Edwin was pleased that the sombreness of passing the camp of the Egyptians had now lifted, that they were back again in the happy mood, which had made this such a special day. Suddenly, Mary drew him to her and hugged him with all her strength, then quickly releasing him she ran inside, blowing a kiss over her shoulder into the air as she went.

Edwin walked home as if on a cloud of contentment, He would have liked to talk to someone and tell of his good fortune, but he only passed a gang of 'found levellers' cleaning out the contents of a cess-pit into their filthy carts, and making a great stink about it. Edwin hurried on, then reaching the door of his house and letting himself in, he looked about; all were abed. He had far to much to think over to go to bed himself, so raking up the embers of the dying hearth, he lit one of his father's pipes, and settling back in the fireside chair, he began to go over in his mind the wonders of the best day of his life.

CHAPTER ELEVEN
Trapped at the Tavern

It was early in the morning watch on the first day of the week. Mr. David Lawrence Master Gunner of Her Majesty's Ship-of-the-line Gloryana stood looking over the side of the ship towards the shore. He was a thinly built man of medium height, his gaunt face, long thin nose; the closely set eyes matched the cruel curl his mouth. His appearance gave fair warning of his harsh, merciless, temperament. Mr. Lawrence stood musing over the orders he had just been given by the First Mate. His gaze was fixed on the shore, on the road that led to London. The vessel was lying afloat at Greenwich; she was now clean and equipped after a long three-month refit at the Deptford Yard. Repairs to hull-damage caused by ball and shot had been completed, a new mast and rudder had been fitted, a new set of sails, with new rope yardage, and six new cannon had all come aboard. The ship had been rid of her rats and vermin by drowning her in the dry dock and she was now up again, free from pests, and lying at anchor waiting to furnish her crew numbers, ready for her next commission.

David Lawrence, Master Gunner of the vessel, had once again been detailed off to form an impressment gang. It was a job he did not much relish, but never-the-less would complete the task with his usual ruthlessness. He ordered his usual gang of men to accompany him, each chosen for their strong build and hard nature. When they had assembled the kit , which they knew from past experience they would need for their trip to the City, they would head off towards London in search of their prey. The ship needed at least six more able-bodied men as seamen for the crew, and David Lawrence knew where to get them.

David had once worked the London River himself as a Lightening man. He had progressed well at driving the great open barges, using the long sweep oars to row the barges up and down the river, back and forth with the tides. These large open vessels that were used to lighten the big merchant ships of part of their cargo, to enable them to berth at the shallower wharves of Wapping and the Upper Pool. It was because of his knowledge of the working men of the river, that he was always successful with impressment duty; he knew the ways of the rivermen, and where to find them. Watermen were the best type to press into service, they knew their way about most vessels, and how to use the ship's equipment and ropes, they were also very good in close harbour work, handling the ship when in sheltered water. These men would be at the top of his list to fill the vacancies needed aboard Her Majesty's Ship Gloryana.

Having chosen his usual gang of five strong seamen, David ordered them to load up the ship's cutter and take the gear ashore. Once there, they unloaded the equiptment into a small hand-cart. When all was ready and strapped down securely, David took them into the local tavern and purchased them each a large rum from the 'impressment purse' he had been given. The men downed the fiery drink with great gusto. David then ordered them all outside to man the cart, and they set off for the City with the warm glow of confidence in their bellies. He knew the men would serve him well in this endeavour; he had had reason to punish each of them at some time during the last commission, and he knew them to be afraid of him. He believed in looking for a reason to lay on punishment for men he wished to control, and to make it severe. Most men so treated would gain respect for him, and would in future react quickly to any order he gave them without question, this was a vital requirement for a Master Gunner when at sea in a storm or if in a battle. The men soon got used to his hard ways and even admired him, they joked about how long a new crew member would last, before he was to receive a harsh punishment from Mr Lawrence.

The press gang struggled along with the two-wheeled cart, which for all its inconvenience, they had found on past expeditions was very useful; it was much easier to bind a man and take him back to the ship on the cart, than to drag him along, or carry him if he was unconscious. It was also important to hold a man secure, for if he escaped before he was signed onto the ship as part of the crew, the Navy Board would have no recourse over the man, and could not prosecute him for escaping, even if they captured him again. The old cart with its iron shod wheels slowed them down somewhat, but at last they arrived at Southwark without incident. Once there, they stowed the cart at the back of the usual tavern they used on these trips, and entered the smoke filled interior.

The tavern stood on the southern approach to the bridge, built back from the roadway. It was ideally situated for David's purpose, close enough to the City to gain quick information, yet not too close to frighten away his prey. David ordered his men a meal of salt pork and bread, washed down with cool clean ale. David looked around the room, he could see that there were eyes watching him and his men, eyes that would wag the owner's tongue through the taverns and Inns before the day was out. He knew that the word would quickly spread that a press gang was active in the area. He must not delay in his mission or he would net only the dregs of the Port, a poor catch that would need much chastisement to make them of even small use aboard the ship. The First Lieutenant's words rang in his ears. "I want no idle mouths to feed, victuals cost good coin, their three square meals must be earned, bring me only healthy rogues who will work for the Queen's shilling".

The alert of the Port to his arrival might well suit David, for he had another plan and he needed the word to reach certain people, contacts within the Watermen's community, who for a few coins would inform him of what was happening among the river journeymen, the inns and taverns they were using and of the most likely places to pick up the unwary. He sat leaning back on the bench, watching the entrance of the tavern, allowing his men to sink a few more pots of ale. He did not need to wait long before the door slowly opened and man in a dark cloak and tall hat slipped inside. It was one of the Beadles from Watermen's Hall from over the bridge. The Beadle skirted the room surreptitiously, then entering a curtained alcove at the back. David slowly got to his feet, and making as if he was leaving the room to relieve himself, he quickly and quietly slipped into the alcove. The Beadle was sitting at a small table; he was a man David had done business with many times before. David opened the curtain slightly, beckoning to a tavern maid who came over immediately, he ordered rum for them both. The two men sat in a curtained alcove supping the fiery liquor, talking quietly for a good hour. Eventually a purse changed hands and the Beadle left, slipping out through the tavern's back door into the evening's gathering gloom. David returned to his men and instructed them on their part in his plans.

<========>

Edwin had arisen bright and early that Monday morning, he felt wonderful, at peace with the world about him, nothing was beyond him now that he and Mary had united as only man and a maid in love could. He felt as if he could conquer the dragon of St. George single-handed. He came down to the kitchen whistling a gay tune. His sister Agnes beckoned him over to her side, there was a message for him, left with her to pass on, she whispered it to him out of earshot of their mother who was busy at the hearth. The message was from his friend George, saying that the group of mates were all going to Great Bess's that night, and that if he could come he would treat him to a pot of ale. Edwin's mind leapt at the thought of the chance to tell his mates of his good fortune and of his intended marriage with Mary.

Nell gave him a good breakfast of hot porridge followed by some slices of cold beef left over from the previous night's meal. She was busy preparing a red kerchief printed with large white spots, placing a chunk of bread, some hard cheese and a paper twist of pork dripping in the middle. She carefully tied the four ends of the kerchief together to form a carrying handle. This would be his midday meal, or a later snack if he was able to buy some victuals during the day. Edwin's father had left early that morning to meet old Johnson the shipwright, to truck with him about building the new wherry. He had left a message with Nell for Edwin to meet him by Church Stairs causeway at midday.

Edwin sat at the kitchen table, he was so excited with the news he was holding inside, that he felt he would burst if he did not tell the girls. He decide that he could not contain his joy any longer and calling his mother and sister to him, he told them of his agreement with Mary, and the plans they had made to settle down. The women were overjoyed at the good news, "All is going so well for you, you lucky great oaf" cried Agnes, hugging him about the neck. His mother had her apron up to her mouth, in her usual pose when not sure of what she was expected to say. For her this news meant losing her only son from the house, but at the same time, she was delighted for his happiness, and that Mary would become another daughter to her. The girls flooded him with questions; they wanted to know when the great day would be and where would they live? Edwin was at a loss to get a word in between the rush of enquiries.

"Come about the two of you, we have not decided all these things. Mary must first tell her parents and I have not yet told father".

"Your father will be delighted altogether, and so will Mary's folk to be sure," cried his mother in exasperation, as if these were incidentals not even to be considered.

"Now off you go to your work and leave us to make plans for the both of you, we must start the arrangements, come Agnes make yourself ready we must off to Mary's house and talk about this news with her mother, there will be lots to do, yes lots to do". Edwin could see that no words from him would stop his mother from interfering, so he resigned himself to the fact of it.

At last he said his goodbyes, warning that he could tarry no longer, being already late and must rush for fear of losing his work at the pipe-boring yard, then with a promise to tell them the full story of his day out with Mary, and how he had bewitched her into accepting him, when he returned home later that evening, he smacked his sister on the rump and giving his mother a special hug, he left the house, then as if an after thought he called out at he passed through the door, that he might be a little late home that night, as he was seeing a friend abut some regular work. Agnes cast her eyes to the ceiling, tossing her head at this blatant lie, but she kept her counsel as a dutiful sister.

Edwin had to run to arrive at the yard in time, then throwing off his coat he grabbed two of the long handled metal hooks from the rack on the wall, and quickly joined the other apprentice as they began unloading a wagon load of freshly cut tree trunks. When the cart was empty, they helped the driver to load the wagon with sacks of wood chips from a pile in the corner of the yard. These shards of timber, cut from the inner part of the trunks by the action of the boring rods, were a valuable resource for the driver. When dried, they were ideal for starting a fire in the hearths of homes, and sold very well in the villages as he passed through on his way back to Mr. Pett's Wood, where he would pick up his next load of trunks.

The rest of the morning was spent in lifting the trunks one by one onto the boring frames for the master borers to work their magic. It fascinated Edwin to watch these men at work. When the boring was finished and a wide hole cut through the trunk, they would ream out the thick end with a special tool, which looked like half of a large spoke-shaver, while at the narrow end, another man would trim it into a blunt point using an adze. The tree trunk had now been transformed into a section of water-pipe to be laid under the streets of London. When trimmed and finished, the new section of pipe was lifted by Edwin and another boy, to be stood on end

against a wall where the weather would harden the timber over the next weeks, before it could be used for its watery function.
As the sun climbed to its zenith in the hazy sky, Edwin looked up at the bright orb, reckoning the time to be approaching midday. The Master Borer saw Edwin looking at the sky.
"Time to go lad" he confirmed.
"Your rowing work calls to you I can see, so be off until tomorrow when we will wrestle with a few more trees." He took his leave of the men, doffing his bonnet to the Master Borer who paid him his dues for the morning's labour, then bidding them all farewell, he made his way from the yard along the towpath to the river, turning left along towards Church Stairs, where he was to meet his father with the Anna.

On arrival, he found Alfred in deep conversation with another wherryman whose boat was also moored alongside the landing. Seeing Edwin arrive, Alfred broke off the conversation saying.
"I must away William, my son is here to relieve me, and I must be about my fire duties, I will pass on the word of what you have told me." Edwin nodded a greeting to his father's friend and climbed aboard the Anna.
"Drop me down to Platform Stairs, son" instructed Alfred, a little distracted by what he had heard from William.
"I want to call in at the Angel Inn, William has just told me that the Press gangs are about, they have been spotted over at Southwark. We must be on guard for ourselves, and for others. Keep a sharp look out yourself Edwin. You cannot be too careful, although I wager they will aim to complete their dirty business later on, during the dark hours."
Edwin wanted to tell his father the news of his impending marriage, but the time seemed not fortuitous. Alfred was preoccupied, and Edwin could not bring himself to give him the news, reasoning that his mother would soon make his plans known to her man, and that he could answer the inevitable questions later, he certainly did not want his father to know that he was going out that evening to celebrate, he felt sure he would try to dissuade him. Edwin rowed the Anna up to Platform Stairs where he saw his father ashore.

"I will see you at home early this evening; it will be the safest place to be."
Edwin felt trapped by these words, he did not want to lie to his father, but he felt he had no choice.
"Yes father, of course." The lie left a bitter taste, and Edwin wanted just to get away from this awkward moment. So bidding his father a curt farewell, he pulled away quickly from the causeway. He decided to seek a fare further up river in the Pool, thinking that he might try over near to the Tower, where he often had luck at this time of tide. It was a short pull across the water, giving Edwin a chance to stretch his joints at the oars. This was different work for them after the heavy lifting at the yard and Edwin was much better suited to it. As he came alongside Custom House Stairs, he heard a strident call for 'Oars'. Always a sound to please a watermen's ears, he turned his head towards the source of the shout. An

elderly man came hurrying down the stairs, and clambered immediately into the boat to sit heavily on the passenger thwart.
"Where to! Your Honour" asked Edwin with a friendly grin.
"Take me to Pimlico and quickly", said the man. Then with a sudden thought.
"What will you charge me?" Edwin sucked in a sharp breath and looked the man up and down carefully.
"Quickly you say Sir, well I can just about shoot the bridge on this flood, and with a strong effort, I could get you there within the hour, but it will be a hard pull to be sure, and I will be fit for no other work after it is done. What say you to nine pence?"
"I say that is treble the normal fare, I will pay six pence for the same effort". Edwin sucked his teeth again, putting on his crestfallen look.
"You truck with me like a hard man of business, and me but a poor waterman inexperienced in the ways of finance, and must therefore give in to my superiors. You shall have the trip you want, with all my effort on your conscience for just six pennies then." He backed the Anna away from the stairs and turning the boat up-stream he pulled away for Pimlico, nimbly using his foot to ensnare a piece of the man's fine coat on the pins under the seat. Edwin was pleased with himself, he had negotiated a good fare, he would put on an act of being worn out when they got to Pimlico, but in truth it was not a difficult row.

By the time they reached Garden Stairs, and the passenger had paid his coin and disembarked, to attend what seemed to be urgent business, judging by his anxious state, the misty sun was much lower in the afternoon sky. Edwin decided, that as no other wherries was plying from here, he would wait and see if any business was to be had, hopefully going back towards the City. He spent the time paring his fingernails, sharpening his blade, and tidying the boat's cleaning gear, but after an hour or so, with no sign of trade, he decided to paddle back empty, holding hard along the north bank, and listening out for a call to work. He was down to Westminster before he heard a shout. This was Chambers territory, Edwin looked around to see if any of his old enemy were about. The coast seemed to be clear, so he rowed into Whitehall Stairs where a well dressed man with an elegant lady close alongside was waiting for a wherry.
"God's blessing to you Sir" beamed Edwin, putting on his 'Jolly Boatman' act.
"Where are you bound this fine day" The man seemed amused by Edwin's good nature and smiled back.
"Take us to Old Swan, with your cleanest stroke and no splashing if you please."
"I never splash my passengers Sir. Unless they are Roaring Boys and upset my oars with their rocking about. I will have you there before you know that you are aboard and as dry as a swan's crest". Then offering his hand to the fine looking lady, who took it very delicately, looking him straight in the face while she stepped aboard. He handed her into the after seat, where she gave him a beautiful smile as she sat down. Edwin felt honoured to have

such a beauty aboard, he knew immediately by her smiles and gestures that this was a courtesan, and a very expensive one to boot no doubt. He let go the line and sat down to his work, he considered catching the man's fine coat on his secret pins, but decided against it on this occasion. He liked the look of this lady even if she was a high-class harlot. He would play no tricks with a working woman.

He backed the Anna away from the landing, turning the boat's head down stream for Old Swan.

"Hoy there! You black hearted son of Bridewell bawds, you dare show your ugly face upon my stairs, stealing my living, you nitty radish-monger". Edwin turned to find one of the Chambers coming up fast on him, rowing hard.

"It is you then, you filthy gong leveller, you offspring of a dunghill". Retorted Edwin.

"Take your pox ridden face away from my good passengers lest you frighten them, as you do the horses of the City." Edwin knew that this young Chamber had suffered a bout of the pox a few years back, and had the scars to prove it, although they were not visible unless close up, he knew that the lad was embarrassed by the pockmarks. Chambers stopped rowing holding his distance, as Edwin had guessed he would.

"You pimp to your mother and stallion to your sister, you think to cheat us again with your stinking boat, but you reckon badly with the Chambers this day, you black dog.shit." Edwin was not surprised by this tirade, it was a normal exchange between rivals on the river, he noticed an uneasy look on the lady's face and concern on the man's.

"All noise like a pot with no filling, he will not approach any nearer Sir, he is afraid that you may take his number" assured Edwin, trying to reassure his passengers. They both looked out of the boat as if they were not concerned by the episode, but no doubt the story would be told at the dinner-table later that evening. Edwin rowed on his way, leaving the irate Chamber in his wake.

On approaching Old Swan stairs, Edwin could see that there were three wherries ahead of him. He brought his boat alongside the causeway with a gentle crunch as Anna slid into the chalk on the riverbed. The man paid him the fare he asked, and added a good coin for drink-geld, then as they left the boat and made their way up to the lane above, the eyes of the other watermen followed the alluring sway of the lady's every move. Edwin made fast his boat and went over to Jonathan's wherry. He had been pleased to see his friend at the landing and wanted to have a chat with him.

"Ho! Edwin, carrying a pretty cargo today I see," greeted his friend.

"To be sure, to be sure, and a compliant filling inside that fine sack, I will gamble. How goes it with you Jonathan?"

"I am as well as the chicken coop's cockerel, and looking forward to tonight's get-together. Bess has a new serving wench for us to admire. A good-looking maid I'm told. What time will you be there Edwin?".

"I will be early, I have no wish to go home to find I have some duty imposed on me by father that will prevent me from going. I will grab us a good table where we can admire this new damsel,".

The young men chatted away happily for some time, until Jonathan's turn came and took him away with a fare to Lambeth. Edwin waited hoping that a fishmonger might take him and his boat down river in the direction he preferred to go. The tide was now well past half ebb, and the bridge was usable again. Sure enough, people started to appear, looking over the wall and calling for oars. There were now several wherries plying from the stairs. Edwin was lucky he got what he wanted, two well-dressed men wanting to go to Deptford. Edwin embarked his passengers and pulled for the nearest bridge arch. Shooting the bridge with ease, he soon pulled down to Lower Watergate Stairs where the men disembarked. It was now beginning to get dark, so Edwin pulled Anna back up to Church Tier and moored the boat safely inside the roads for the night. He waited only a short time before a passing empty cutter, maned by friends, gave him passage over to Wapping, from where he made his way along to Bess's tavern 'The Four Master'.

On entering the tavern, Edwin found the place busy, he was surprised to find it so at this early time. Apart from the hardened drinkers, most men found their way to the taverns later in the evening. He looked around to see what choice of table he had for his mates. Near the middle of the room was a good sized one with only one bench. That will do nicely he thought and proceeded to pull another bench into position.

"I am sorry young Sir, that table is reserved" it was the voice of one of the serving maids and she was addressing him with a pleasant smile and approaching with her hips swinging.

"Tonight we are having a story telling and that table will be used by the tellers." Edwin considered the girl. She was pretty and trim of figure, she stood with hands on hips and swaying provocatively, gazing straight into his face.

"I have friends coming and will need a table capable of seating eight or so." She smiled at him, head on one side, as if judging his stock".

" I see you are a man of the river, Bess has instructed us to give your trade the best seats in the house. Look I have a good table over here that will take you and your friends' altogether."

Edwin could see that the maid was flirting with him and he liked it. This must be the new serving wench he had been told about, the lads would be most impressed if he had broken the ice with her for them. He looked about the room.

"Tell me where is Fanny this evening?" The girl answered immediately, surprising Edwin by her knowledge.

"She is not working this night; Bess said she is not required. I think she is about the town with her own rivermen." Somehow, Edwin did not much care for this maid, she seemed too knowledgeable for a newcomer, and how did she know so much of his friend Kenneth's affairs? But then she was good looking, the other lads would like that, so he let the thought drop from his mind.

"I would have a platter of your best victuals and a pot of ale, while I wait for my friends, I would like you to meet them when they arrive".
"I would be honoured indeed, I have a liking for watermen," she winked and floated off to bring his order.
"Not my flavour of meat," thought Edwin.
"I have a better bird already in my nest," his mind turning to his Mary.

Edwin noticed that Bess was sitting at a corner table with a man who was still wearing his cloak. The man wore a soft floppy hat pulled down on his head, but Edwin could see that he was thin of face with a long sharp nose. He watched them, trying to guess what new deal Bess was trucking, probably persuading the man to sign away all his rights from his next voyage for a loan here and now. Or was he one of the evening's storytellers negotiating his fee?
"Here kind Sir, your victuals are arrived and hot for the eating, with a pot of our best for your thirst. I have put a little something else in to warm up your spirits." Edwin tasted the ale; a draft of rum had been added, it laced the drink in a most agreeable way.

Edwin tucked into his food. It was a hot pudding with plenty of mutton and kidney stowed inside the suet duff, the white mound floating on a sea of piping hot gravy. It was unusual for Bess to serve hot food; her tavern was not noted for its food, but more for the entertainments. He finished his meal, then sitting back on the bench he glanced across the room towards Bess, but the corner table was now empty.
"Another poor soul taken for his all" speculated Edwin.
"Hoy mate, spark up your torch I am coming aboard." It was George full of life as always and grinning from ear to ear.
"You looked to be far off with all your lights out. What are you drinking to make you dream so? I would have some of that mixture"
"Ale laced with rum, if you smile kindly at the maid, which will not be difficult, the rum is free. Try the pudding, I can recommend it to be sure".
George ordered his wants and soon others had joined the table, all chatting, and trying to charm the pretty serving maid, who seems to be in her element with the attention of these rivermen.

As the evening wore on, the serving maid approached the lad's table carrying a large tray of pots of rum, which Edwin had quietly ordered.
"What's this?", cried George as the girl served a pot to each of them.
"Have you won a wager or robed a passenger? Edwin raised his cup.
"Good friends I am to set sail on the sea of matrimony. I want you all to toast my future with Mary".
"Well done you rogue, it be time you settled down, you are not built for the free life the rest of us enjoy, it is best you leave your share for us". Edwin leaned across the table aiming a mock blow at his friend.

A sharp rap on a table made them all look up. It was Bess standing on the table which had been reserved as a little stage.

"Tonight my merry men I have a treat indeed for you all, we are to hear tales of adventure and the unusual, not the nonsense you lie about among yourselves, but true stories, told by men who know how to tell an adventure. It has cost me a pretty penny to get them here for you to enjoy this evening, so be attentive, pay attention, I will have no haranguing, or shouting till the telling is over." Loud applause erupted within the room, for these men liked nothing better that a good rousing tale to brighten up their lives. A good story teller was worth more than a ballad singer or a play actor.

"My first guest is a traveller of the world, and he has a story to tell about our fair City and later, of his adventures in the land of Russia'". She paused for effect.

"I give you Mr. Ebenezer Froth."

A tall man shuffled forward from a nearby table and was helped up onto the table and into a chair placed there by the serving maids. He was a man in his fifties with snow white hair above a strong jawed face, his eyes were small and set close together, darting about, penetrating every corner of the room.

"My name is Froth and my family was of this City," he said in a strange accent.

"A City, which used my family ill. I come from a long line of men of this river, but I myself did not follow the trade, for I was taken away to another land, and I will tell you why." Edwin and the other young watermen looked the man over intently. Froth had the ring of a river name, but none of them new of any Froths still alive.

"My family suffered many indignities and much misfortune at the hands of the City Fathers of London, but found our place with a man, who was great by name and great by nature. That man was 'Peter the Great'. King of Russia. A good and kindly giant, who took many watermen from the Thames with him when he returned home, rivermen who had been badly used by their own monarch. He took them back to the land where he was King. They helped him build the greatest City ever seen. But that story is for later. I will first to tell you of a misfortune to my family, from their involvement in an incident, which is still mentioned every day by you and yours without knowing the injustice which lies behind it".

"Friends, you see before you the only survivor of that family, who laid claim to an ancestor who was destroyed in the infamous confrontation between two of the great Company Guilds of this City. Forgive me my bitterness in this matter. Even after over two hundred years this story is guaranteed to cause old Ebenezer irritation." So saying he took a long draft from his jug of ale.

"My claim is that my ancestor was used, without recognition of his part in this famous tale. It is now left to me in my pursuit for the truth, to discover if our suspicions and correct. This is a story that has produced an idiom, which has entered into the very fabric of the English language, but never a mention of the Froth's part in it all. My ancestor was a riverman and rowed for a Guild, as a crewman in their ceremonial barge. In 1484, that year of the notorious river battle, he was positioned in the crew on the port side of the barge, rowing at the number five bench. Now listen to the event unfold and judge my family's claim for yourself".

<========>

The argument between the Guilds of the Taylors and the Skinners, had raged for as long as anyone could remember, a long time indeed, as both Companies were able to date their origins back to the thirteenth century. Over the years since their formation, many of the guilds of the City had vied with each other to attain their position within the hierarchy of the City, particularly those of the 'Great Twelve', who considered themselves the elite among the trades of the Liveried Companies. From the early times, the merchants and traders of the City protected their interests by forming themselves into Guilds, an idea they had imported from the continent. At first there was no official order of precedence, but as the City and its Guilds grew in importance, it became seemingly vital, to secure the highest placed number possible in the hierarchy.

It was in the fifteenth century that the precedent within the great twelve, the oldest and most powerful of the Livery Guilds, finally settled into an agreed list. The growth and power of the Mercers, Grocers, Drapers, Fishmongers, Goldsmiths, etc. all secured their positions at the top of the list, from this time on. However, the Skinners and the Taylors had continued to argue as to which one of them should hold the number six position, this honourable number seemed worth fighting for, particularly on the side of the Skinners, who had on many occasions in previous centuries, held the coveted position. During the years leading up to the dispute on water, many confrontations, and even street fights between supporters of the two Guilds took place, with violent arguments flaring up over the matter of their respective claims to the favoured number six place.

It was in the year 1484 that the argument grew in crescendo during the year when Mr. Billing became Lord Mayor; it was then that things finally came to a head. As was the custom, Mayor Billing was determined to have a great show of himself on the river. To celebrate his inauguration, he spent a great deal of time, effort and coin in organizing the grand and prestigious water pageant. It was expected that the Lord Mayor's annual river procession would be the grandest spectacle of his year in office, an event which enabled him to display himself as their Mayor, to the citizens of London. On the appointed day in April of that year, the great Livery Company's Barges assembled on the river, at the boundary line between the Cities of London and Westminster. Slowly and gently the vessels manoeuvred, their liverymen and freemen lifting their bonnets in respect, as the great vessels glided past each other, arranging themselves into their jealously guarded numbered positions behind the Lord Mayor's barge. By luck or perhaps by judgement, both the Skinners' and the Taylors' barges found themselves at equal distance from the coveted number six station, the position immediately astern of the Goldsmith's barge.

As was usual, it had started with customary great deference being paid to each other, by the members of the City's Guilds. There was much bowing, doffing of bonnets and raising of tankards in toasts, to the Liverymen aboard the other barges, as they ceremoniously moved past each other on their progress to their ordained positions. Banners were dipped in salute, a courtesy shown to each barge's Master by the other. The Liverymen of the City were on display to the citizens of London and were on best behaviour. All were dressed in their finest clothes, their great barges beautifully decorated in full glory. Some had been specially painted for the event, their elaborate carvings newly gilded for the occasion. Some were decked-out, with expensive carpets draped over their deck-houses for all to admire, thus showing the extravagance and wealth of their Guild.

This was a great day for the new Lord Mayor of the City of London, and the Liveries were supporting him in his annual showing at his special River Pageant. London was ruled by the merchants, it was from this class that the Mayor the sheriffs and the Court of Aldermen were drawn. It had been thus since the time of King Edward 11. However, this was also an arrogant class of clever businessmen, some of whom had started from very poor beginnings. It was a great honour to have achieved freedom of the City, with membership of their trade Guild. It added to their sense of self-importance and gave them high regard, something that they would defend to the very end. The scene was therefore set for the belligerent event that followed.

There had been some delay in the arrival of the Lord Mayor's Barge. While waiting, many of the Liverymen had taken substantial liquid refreshment, which led to light-hearted joking and some ribald remarks between the members of some of the different Guilds, with a little egging-on of their barge's crews, wishing to show off their vessel's manoeuvrability, the ceremonial decorations, and the prowess of their oarsmen.

That year's Master of the Taylors, Company had spent a great deal of coin on lavish ornamentation of his company's barge, as had the Master of the Skinners' Company. The air was redolent with unwarranted pride and self-importance. Members on both sides considered that their barge and their company was the superior and deserved the more prominent number six position. The two barges in question were eventually moved forward by their Bargemasters. Both were heading towards the stern of the Goldsmiths barge, which was already in its number five position behind the Fishmonger's barge. The Skinners were coming from port, the north side of the river, and the Taylors approaching from starboard, the direction of the south bank. As the great, eighteen oared, vessels, with their eighty or so passengers neared the disputed place, each Bargemaster, unknown to the other, had been instructed by the Master of his Guild, to gain the coveted number six position at all costs.

The Bargemaster sent the order forward from his steering position at the raised stern of the barge, to the senior waterman rower, 'the stroke-giver', who was the man in close charge of the oarsmen. This complicated system of passing on orders to control the barge's movements, was not a problem during the normal slow ceremonial progress of a Livery barge. However, under the circumstances of that moment, full of emotion, passion, and pride, with the need for quick responses by bargemasters and oarsmen alike, it proved to be disastrous; it was too slow a method for sending the instructions, or orders to the oarsmen.

A race was now on, the finish being the number six position behind the Goldsmiths. It would now be impossible to stop quickly, but worst of all, it was being acted out in full view of the citizens of the City, and the hierarchy of the City's Guilds. It was an open secret for all to see that a race was taking place. The oarsmen were being encouraged by their respective passengers to pull harder, bribes were offered, and promise of coin was made. At the crucial moment when one or the other of the barges should have given way, no order could be passed quickly enough, to back oars, and slow the vessels down.

The great Livery barges crashed together, side into side, like two great monsters in a sea fight. There was the sound of splintering oars, and the nerve jangling noise of tearing timbers, both craft were locked in an embrace of each other's torn planks. The now enraged freemen of both vessels hurled abuse at each other, wine bottles were flung, blades were drawn and night-pots were thrown. As tempers rose in response to the accusations being hurled and at the insults being shouted, the Liverymen from both craft, felt committed to redress the imagined loss of face. A great brawl broke out between the passengers and crews of the two vessels. The Liverymen watching from the other Guild barges, stood transfixed aboard their vessels, astonished at the scene before them, only able to watch in amazement as the battle ensued.

The Lord Mayor had a full view of the fracas from his City Barge, as did the population of the City, who were standing along the banks of the river. Mayor Billing hung his head in disbelief and shame; he could not believe what he was witnessing. His embarrassment was complete, when the citizens lining the shore realizing what was happening joined the cacophony of sound with peals of laughter.
"A true show, a true show, do it again next year," the shout went up.
When at last sense prevailed and the vessels were parted, it was discovered that one man was dead and several others injured. One liveryman had been run through the arm with a rapier, others had been hit by flying bottles and pewter pots, yet others contaminated by the contents of night pots.

The story-teller stared at his audance.
"My faimaly claim that the unfortunate dead man was the man rowing at

number six in the Merchant Taylor's Barge. He had been cut through the neck with the splintered end of a broken sweep oar. "Have I not the right to make complaint that no honour has ever been paid to our man, that the identity of his death is kept very close, and that no recognition for his part in the making of history was made?". He looked around with accusing eyes.
"As always the City keeps its hatch closed as to the truth of it." He spread his hands wide, bending over at the waist, daring them to disagree. "So my friends, what does this City owe to my family? Was it not better for my family, when given the opportunity, to follow 'Peter of Russia' and be appreciated for their skills? Would you not also be improved to seek you fortune and adventure away from the vested power of this London of yours? He sat back in his seat, to continue his story.

"After the collision of barges in the 'Lord Mayor's Show', the Masters of the offending Guilds were summoned before the new Mayor at the Guild Hall, to give an explanation of their Company's conduct on that infamous day. All that could be said of the cause of the confrontation, reverted to the same old argument, as to the respective claims of their companies to the number six position within the Livery hierarchy. This being unacceptable to the Mayor, he furnished a most sensible judgement, in fact, 'A judgement of Solomon'. His verdict was to the effect, that the companies would in future alternate their claim to the coveted position, by the year. This year one company would be number six and the other number seven, the following year they would reverse. The Masters, full of shame, accepted the adjudication on behalf of their companies, that each year forever more, they would be reversed from six to seven. For Londoners the event became an ongoing jest, it even entered into every day parlance, in that when confusion existed which could not be agreed by sensible compromise, the parties are said to be. All at sixes and sevens".

The silence of the room was broken by applause as the audience realised the origin of this well used phrase.
Another rap on the table, and they looked up to see that Mr Froth had dismounted from the table and Bess had taken his place.
"There you have it my brave men," she cried.
"A family driven from their trade by the indifference of others. Often it is necessary to take a risk and seek a new destiny, you are fortunate to have the means so near at hand with all the ships of this port waiting to offer you adventure. Now we can hear from another man who took his chance and sailed away to adventure".
There followed two more tales of adventure, told by individuals who had found adventure. They told of storms and seas the size of houses, of rocks and dangers. They told of lands of hot sun and others of cold ice which never thawed, of animals and men of other races so different, that it was hard to believe without the witness of a man's own eyes. The audience was thrilled with the stories; many were flushed with excitement and banged the table with enthusiasm at the thought of seeing such things. The stories

told of battles both on sea and on land, of boldness and bravery which won the day. Each storyteller made it obvious that they looked down on those that stayed at home.

Music suddenly started up in the form of a drum beating to a rhythmic chant. It was Bess, she was back on the table beating time with her arms, to an aluring chant, then stepping down with the help of the girls, began to circle the room, encouraging her audience to follow her in this rhythmic song.

"Come listen to me and I'll tell you a tale,
of green rolling seas and of billowing sail.

Of men and of danger, of deeds of the strong,
of fighting and sailing and the righting of wrong

Of Frenchies and Spanies, of gold and of gain.
Adventure and fortune on the great Spanish Main.

The papist old Spanies do pillage the lands,
of Inca and Indie, the American man.

Those Spanie's great Galleons do plunder and steal,
But we'll teach them a lesson with good English steel.

We'll take all their silver, their gold and their wealth,
We'll share it among us, and toast their bad health.

Come stand on the deck with the wind at your back,
With topsails a straining and yards fit to crack.

Fight the bad Spaniard, attack on the run,
We'll rip them asunder, with sword, knife and gun.

We'll take all their booty, their silver and gold,
And tuck it away with the rest in our hold.

Then away to the lands of honest sunshine,
With hot blooded maidens, good vitals and wine.

Well fish in the water and play on the sand,
Till our hearts feel the pull of our own green land

Then home to old England, we'll pick up the Trades,
That good wind will bring us back safe to our maids.

Well share out the treasure, we'll pay off our debts,
We'll drink a few toasts and we'll place a few bets.

*We'll then use the rest to set up ashore.
Become a rich Burger and venture no more.*

*Then settle with Wife, at home in good heart,
To live on our memories, and tell all of our part.*

*Come live like a man, not a mouse, or in stealth.
Take the Queen's shilling for adventure and wealth.*

*So join the queen's Navy for adventure and gold.
Not dwell in your corner, just getting old".*

As always, Bess's overpowering personality took over, and the whole room stamped their feet to the rhythm of her chant. She grabbed some of the young men as she passed, forcing them by her vibrant persona to fall in behind her. All heady with the stories, the free rum and this beguiling chant, they willingly joined in, including Edwin and two of his mates. Just like the 'Pied Piper' of Hamlin, she led the men in and out between the tables. Then as the euphoria reached a crescendo, she steered her dancers out through a side door into the backyard.

Outside in the yard, pandemonium broke out, as the men realised that the press was lying in wait for them. It was Mr. Lawrence and his gang. The dancers panicked and ran off in all directions. Edwin was unfortunate, being near to the back of the line, he found himself trapped as the door slammed behind him, locked shut by Bess's new serving maid. His reactions were slowed down by the effects of the rum, but he was ready to fight his way out from this unforeseen danger.

Edwin's body was shaking at the realisation of his predicament, his way back was closed off by the locked door and by a man lurking near to the wall, the way forward was blocked by another of the gang. Edwin now had his blade out ready to defend himself against the thin faced man who stood before him. The man had a rope's end dangling from his hand. Seemingly unimpressed by Edwin's blade, he stood with knees slightly bent waiting for Edwin's lunge. Edwin steadied himself; the effects of the mixture of rum and ale were slowly dropping away, he was ready to make a play for freedom. He drew back his arm, about to make a feint, then to slash out, and make a run for it. He was not confident however. He was like a wounded animal in a trap with no obvious route of escape. A knot of despair was growing in stomach, he felt an impending catastrophe surrounding him, all his future plans were melting away into disaster in his muddled mind. Suddenly a blinding pain erupted on the back of his head, a great cloud of blackness descended slowly over him, he had the curious view of the night sky rotating and falling, then the cobbles of the yard came rushing up to meet his face.

CHAPTER TWELVE

Shipped to adventure

Edwin awoke suddenly to a loud shout. A thunderous, angry voice filled his bemused head with vibrating sound, then before he could muster his thoughts, a searing pain exploded in his left ankle. Startled and confused by the noise, the pain, and dark that was all about him, he sat up quickly to grab at his agonizing foot, only to thump his head violently against a hard wooden beam just a few inches above him. This new pain now competed with the agony in his ankle. Disoriented by the confusion of pains, he lurched to his left and felt his body swing alarmingly towards open space, he found himself swinging frighteningly in mid air, terrifyingly unbalanced. Briefly he recognised the feel of a hammock swinging under him, desperately clutching at the air to find something firm to grab for support, his fingers scraped over hard wooden surfaces, but finding nothing to grip onto, he pushed hard against the timber in an effort to right himself. His body now swung violently back in the opposite direction, then with a sickening feeling of falling, he tipped out of the canvas cot into an abyss. He was now hurtling face down, his mind in a sheer panic. His forehead hit something soft, but firm, which jerked his head back painfully as his chest hit more of the rough wood which seemed to surround him. He rolled over, and slipping off this latest obstacle he came to rest on his back, spread-eagled over what proved to be a long timber bench.

His body hurt everywhere, his mind was reeling, a confusion of thoughts strained his senses. Why was he fully dressed and fallen from a hammock in this strange, dank smelling, wooden place? Where was he? Slowly his senses began to return to his throbbing head. The loud voice had moved away, but could still be heard in the distance, echoing off the hard walls. "Up and at 'em yeh scurvy bunch, away from those whores, show a leg, show a leg, out of ye pits I tell yeh, I say lively, before you feel the end of me rope".
Edwin's memory returned progressively and he remembered what he did not want to remember. It was a total disaster. He was aboard a dreaded naval ship. The greatest fear of his life had occurred, the Press-gang had captured him, and taken him aboard a man-of-war. He was now impressed for service in Her Majesty's Royal Navy.
"No! No, it could not be, this was worse than death itself, a living nightmare. Great feelings of self pity welled up inside him, flowing through his body like a raging tide; an uncontrollable misery swamped his mind. For a moment the pains of his body were forgotten, he felt sick and frightened, totally lost. Hot tears welled up into his eyes, and a growing blockage was choking his throat.
"Welcome aboard me hearty" said a deep, oak-rum voice from nearby. "That's one quick way to disembark ye'r pit." Edwin looked up and in the dim lantern light made out the shape of a small, thickset man, sitting across

the table from where he lay collapsed across the bench. Edwin did not answer; he had other more important thing to deal with at that moment. He rolled over painfully onto his side, and with an agonizing effort sat up on the bench, burying his sore head deep into his hands. "You'll soon learn not to put your foot out of ye'r pit" said the gruff voice. "Boatswain Tyson has broken many an ankle with that Turk's-head knot in his rope's end".
"What happened?" croaked Edwin, now massaging his painful ankle. "Ye'r had ye'r foot over the side of ye'r hammock lad" said the voice, "Tyson hit it with his rope's end. He'll do it every time if you invite it". Edwin was loosening his boot and rubbing the painful, blue and yellow swelling. The pain gradually subsided into a dull ache. He then felt his back with both hands, exploring the bones for damage; this part of him at least seemed to be recovering. He looked across at the voice.
"Me name is Patrick Murphy" said the man. Edwin looked at the weather-beaten face, with its smooth, black, shiny hair. As his eyes became adjusted to the dim lighting, Edwin could see that Patrick was a broad shouldered, somewhat squat man, with a square face built onto a short, stout, neck. The face held a smirked expression, which Edwin later found to be a permanent feature, from a sabre slash that had deformed the corner of the man's mouth. The man's hair was heavily tarred and smeared back into a hard twist at the back of his head, giving the impression that it was painted onto his head.
"My name is Edwin, I'm a Thames waterman and I've been ......".
"I know lad, I know, interrupted Patrick.
"It happened to most aboard this ship," he said with some feeling. "Come alongside the vitctualing board here, and have some of this food. Be quick, you don't want to be late on deck on ye'r fist watch now do ye'r?". Edwin looked at the food set out on the plank before him, for a plank was what the table proved to be, a wide timber board slung between the cannon, fixed at one end to the ship's side, by a simple leather hinge and hung from the deckhead at the inboard end by a double rope. The food was arranged on a square piece of wood with a hollowed out section in its centre. Suddenly Edwin realized that he was hungry, he took the offered victuals, and started to eat, but in spite of his hunger, he had trouble in getting any of the food past the lump in his throat, tears welled up again inside his eyes, he dropped his head, not wishing for Patrick to see this show of emotion.
"Now lad", said Patrick smiling his twisted grin.
"You're here for the duration of our commission, and you had better soon come to terms with the fact of it". He looked kindly at the boy remembering his own first hours after capture.
"It is not as bad as you probably think it to be. The victuals are usually good, and if you watch your step and control your tongue, you may well come through right enough to the end". He smiled his scarred smile again and pointed across the deck.
"Now take a dip of water from the tub over there, and I'll take you up to meet the rest of your shipmates".

The shock of the morning light, as they emerged from the gloom of below decks into the brightness of day was startling. Edwin screwed up his eyes against the glare of the bright sun. The sounds around him were familiar, they were ship's sounds, ropes creaking and water splashing and above it all men's voices. These voices however were not the normal melee of curses, the joking and banter of the ship's crews he knew in London's port. Each voice was controlled, either giving an order, or answering. They were clear, crisp, commands that were answered in the same urgent tone.

Edwin's eyes were now becoming accustomed to the brightness of the day. The pains in his body were receding, his mind was again taking control of his senses, but he was still frightened, alone and fearful of what would become of him. He suddenly remembered his father's words, about controlling fears.
"When you are fearful lad, as comes to all of us at some time, remember this. A man afraid dies a thousand deaths, but a brave man dies but once". Pushing the thought of his home and family to the back of his mind, Edwin looked around him. Men were everywhere, climbing rigging, coiling rope into tidy mounds; some were scrubbing a section of the bleach-white deck, using wooden buckets filled with river water, into which they dipped the heavy Holy-Stones, before attacking the planking with vigour. All were busy at some work of other; they were getting the ship ready to leave port. Patrick took him by the arm and almost running, propelled him aft to the poop deck. They stood at the bottom of the steps leading up to this raised part of the ship, waiting it seemed for some sort of command.

"Bring him up seaman Murphy" said a well-spoken voice.
"Ay. Ay sir" replied Patrick, and with these words he pushed Edwin up the steps to stand before a tall, fair haired, good looking man in full naval officer's uniform. His hand was resting nonchalantly on the hilt of the long sword hanging at a comfortable angle from his belt. Edwin had never been so near to an officer of the Queen's navy before; he was impressed by the splendid dark blue and gold apparel. On the Thames, these men mostly travelled in the naval cutters, or in the Commissioner's barge, which was always crewed by seamen, or by specially chosen watermen.
"New man Murphy?" said Lieutenant Frobisher. It was more a statement than a question.
"Ay Sir, came aboard last night, Mr Frobisher " replied Patrick.
"Ah Yes, pressed I believe" said the officer. Then with the snapping voice of someone who was used to giving orders.
"Your name young man" Edwin still felt sick and bewildered, but through the clouds of his desolation, he knew that he must not show his true feelings. He stood upright, and looked the officer straight in the face and said.
"Edwin Crossback your Honour" The officer smiled at the gratuitous promotion.
"Sir, will be sufficient when you address an officer", he commented. Then turning to Patrick he said.

" Murphy I think perhaps, you had better show Mr. Crossback the ropes over the ship, and give him a few pointers for his survival". "Ay, Ay, Sir" said Murphy with a wry smile on his weather beaten face. "We'll have him and the other new men mustered in the forward Mess-Deck at next change of watch". He turned again to Edwin and said with a good-humoured smile.
"Make the most of what life has dealt you lad, you might even find that you enjoy it, don't you know".

Patrick took Edwin back to the main deck and showed him over the open areas, explaining each rope and what it did as part of the ship's rigging, while keeping out of the way of the crew preparing to lower and set the sails.
"You know a lot of this from your work on the river, but bear in mind lad, the Navy has its own ways of doing things. One important thing to remember above all is to always stay below deck, unless you are on your watch or otherwise ordered, and remember also, that on deck we do everything at the run. Never walk about your duties, even if your legs are shot away from under you", he said with a grin.
Edwin's mind was now a mixture of emotions. One minute his interest was aroused by his new circumstances, the next, his emotions verged back to the black panic, his life seemed to be over with. His family. His Mary. His mother. What would his father say? What would he do when he found that his son had been taken? Hot tears whelmed up again behind Edwin's eyes, he fought them down again, his pride coming to the rescue. The worst feeling was the great lump that had formed in his throat, a growth that was still making it difficult to talk, to swallow, or even to breathe properly.
Patrick could read the signs of despair in his young prodigy. He knew only too well the feelings, which were raging inside the young lad, but he also knew that he must not, under any circumstances show too much sympathy. The boy's only chance was to quickly accept his new life, and come to terms with the fact of it for the next few years. He must make the most of what life had dealt him, and concentrate on getting something out of the experience. It was of course too early to tell Edwin any of this, but Patrick had a feeling about this young man, he felt certain that he would come to terms and would settle into his new life aboard Her Majesty's Ship Gloryana.

Patrick took Edwin back down to the Mess Deck, which would be his home for the foreseeable future, the cramped place that he was to share with 200 other men. He showed him where his hammock must be stowed, explaining the way that hammocks were used in a battle to block up holes in the ship's side, and how they would be stowed in nets around the decks to give protection to the sailors from shot, while they were fighting or repelling boarders. Patrick explained that after he had signed the 'Ships articles', he would take him to the Quarter Master to be issued with his kit.
Patrick looked at Edwin with the concerned look of a friend. "Lad, there is something you have to know before you go before the Officers, it is very important to you, it could affect your very life while you

are aboard this ship". Edwin looked at the older man from under the cloud of black gloom which engulfed him.

"I know it is difficult to think straight at this time, but you must, because this is very important" said Patrick.

"What is it" said Edwin, his interest now raised to a point of fresh alarm. He knew he must keep his wits about him, for he was in strange waters indeed.

"They will ask you to make your mark to the ship's articles".

"What does that mean", asked Edwin still bemused. Patrick looked into the young man's eyes.

"If you sign, it means that you are a volunteer. If you refuse to sign, it means you are an impressed man".

"But I am already caught by the Press Gang" said Edwin somewhat bewildered.

"You have this one chance to change that" said Patrick.

"You mean I can get home?" said Edwin his eyes suddenly bright with hope.

"No! No! lad, there is no way out of serving this ship's commission. You have got to give up any idea of home for some years to come, but if you sign on you will be considered, and treated, as a volunteer, not as a 'Pressed' man" explained Patrick calmly. Edwin could not see the point of this conversation and showed it in his face. Seeing this disinterest, Patrick said more forcefully.

"Look lad, a volunteer is entitled to a share of bounty, but a pressed man isn't, do you understand me?". Edwin looked back at him still not seeing the point.

"A share of what bounty?"

"Prize money!" emphasized Patrick.

"The chance that you might make your fortune". Edwin had been told many times of the slim chance of gaining a share of prizes, and also about the dangers involved in the sea battles. He had long ago decided he could find a better way to make his fortune than by such an off-chance way of becoming rich. Volunteering for the Her Majesty's Navy was not for him. Patrick could see he was not getting through to the lad; Edwin was so homesick he could not think straight, or appreciate the advice being given, but he must somehow get him to understand. It would be a big mistake if the lad did not sign on with the crew.

"Now look at me lad" he said earnestly".

"I have been in this man's Navy for many years, it is true that I have not made a great fortune, but I have had some small prizes, I have good savings held ashore, and I still have the chance of the big one, now pull yourself together and listen to what I am about to tell you".

At first Edwin argued that he would never sign as a volunteer, it would be like agreeing with this wickedly unfair system that was the plague of Thames watermen. However, as he listened to Patrick calmly explaining what he might lose if he did not put his mark to the ship's log, that he would anyway be exposed to the same dangers whether he signed or not, or that his commission would not be any the longer for signing. He began to see that volunteering might be the best he could make of a bad set of choices.

Then suddenly he had a thought, it was a leap of hope, his heart jumped at the possibility. He remembered being told, that until a man had made his mark, or was entered in the log as impressed, he was still a free man being held under duress. If he could escape before the meeting, the Navy could not even punish him, as he was not yet one of their own.

He was back in the world, suddenly he felt full of determination, his despondency was gone, he now had hope. Patrick noticed the lad's eyes narrow and his face brighten. He knew immediately what the lad was thinking, it was always the same. They always thought to escape. "Come about lad, hold steady if you think to jump ship, for you will not get the chance, that is why Mr. Lawrence and the rest of the press gang are stationed ashore, they get extra for recapturing runaways, and then you will not even be offered the chance to be marked in the log as a volunteer." Edwin's hopes were dashed, he could see the futility of his plan, and his shoulders dropped in disappointment.
"Take it from me lad, there is no way back, the ship is getting under-way as we speak," said Patrick kindly.
"Come to terms with this new adventure in your life, it will make a man of you and might even make you rich into the bargain." Edwin looked into Patrick's weathered face. He could tell that the man meant him well and that his advice was based on much experience. He now realized that he must bow to his fate.

That evening in the crowded mess-deck, Patrick introduced Edwin to his new shipmates, the men who he would spend the next years with, and whom he would become to know better even than his own family, or so Patrick assured him. They seemed the normal mixture of characters, some were friendly straight off, others were quiet, biding their time until they could weigh up the new man. Yet others were morose, withdrawn, begrudgingly nodding a greeting at him before scuttling away into their favourite corner.

As he considered his new acquaintances, a pipe call went up announcing that the victuals were ready, everyone made for the table planks sitting tightly together on the benches on either side. The square wooden platters were passed along to the end to where the duty cooks filled them to the corners with a steaming mixture of pork and greens. The plates were then passed back along the plank to each man. Edwin was about to take a proffered plate, highly laden with food, when a frighteningly misshapen hand suddenly grabbed his wrist. It was like a warm, damp, toad, fastened tight to his arm. Edwin immediately let go of the plate, which fell onto the table spilling its contents. He wrenched his hand free and looked up into the eyes of the owner sitting opposite. Edwin's face must have had a look of repugnant disgust upon it, for the owner of the crippled hand pulled it quickly away, to hide the offending appendage in the dark underside of the table plank, and grabbing at another plate of food being passed along with his good hand. However, the look he gave Edwin held obvious hatred, the loathing in his dark deep-set eyes made any use of words unnecessary. They were eyes that reminded Edwin of a madman he had once seen close up at the Bedlam prison in London.

<========>

Mary stood at the wooden table in the small kitchen, her hands and arms covered to the elbows in white flour. Her mouth hung open and her eyes were wide in astonishment and dread at what Agnes was telling her. She could not believe what she was hearing. She felt the room spin about her and grabbed at the table for support.
"But we were together only this Sabbath, we were making plans to wed, how can this have happened?" Agnes came around the table and held the other girl by the shoulders to steady her.
"Come Mary sit down, It has been a shock to us all, but don't give up hope, father is this very moment on his way to the ship, he will plead Edwin's case to the Captain, we may yet get him back."
"It cannot be true, it cannot be so," cried Mary through her tears of anguish. "He will be killed to be sure. I will never see him again," then burying her face in her apron, she ran from the room, wishing only to be alone with her grief.

The house door swung open and the sturdy figure of Nell entered. "Where is she, how has she taken it?" Agnes looked at her mother, her own face streaked with anguish. Then she too burst into tears, as a fresh flood of emotion hit her.
"Come now child it is bad news, indeed it is, but he is not dead and with good luck and Mr Crossback's eloquence, or the coin he has taken with him, may still save the day. We will have Edwin home yet."
Agnes looked at her mother through tearful eyes, reassured to see the strength of resolve in the older woman. For all Nell's pretence of perpetual bewilderment, she had an inner strength which always came to the fore when needed, and this was such a time. She knew she had to hold her small family together in this crisis.
"Mary is in the yard, she needs to be alone to gather her strength," said Agnes wiping away the tears from her swollen eyes.
"Where is father now? Will he manage a release?" Agnes's eyes were bright with hope as she searched her mother's face for reassurance. Before Nell could answer, the door swept open again and Mary's mother rushed in.
"Nell, Agnes, my dears, I have just heard the dreadful news, what shock, what disaster, what is to be done".
"We are doing all that can be done." Said Nell, putting her arms about the woman and navigating her to a chair, where she eased her considerable frame down and began waving a hand across her face to cool her flushed cheeks.
"Mr. Crossback is on his way to the ship to try for a release. Go to Mary, she is in the yard and needs her mother's comfort in this misery, she has much need of you to reassure, and give her strength." Nell's voice was

encouraging, it gave the other woman something positive on which to concentrate, and was just what was needed.

<=======>

Alfred had taken all the coin that he had, hidden away in various places about the house, but he had not gone straight to the dockyard as he had first intended, after thoughtful consideration, he went instead to the home of the Fire-chief of the Sun Insurance. The man recognized Alfred as one of his fire fighting crew and knew him to be a good and sober worker. "I am sorry to bother you Chief, but I am here on urgent business" Alfred's face was white with concern. The Chief could see that the matter was important.
"Come inside" offered the Fire-Chief, indicating with a sweep of his hand a small room just inside the doorway. Alfred entered, the Chief indicated a chair, and they both sat at a small table.
"I have had some bad intelligence concerning my son Edwin, and I come to seek your help in the matter," explained Alfred. The Chief did not answer, but sat back and waited to hear what the man had to say. After hearing the story which Alfred outlined in brief detail, he was truly saddened to hear the misfortune of the man's son.
"How can I assist the lad?" he asked wanting to help if he could.
"Well Chief, you know that I have had Edwin's name on the list to become a Fireman for the Sun Insurance for some time, I am hoping that he is near enough to the top of that list, for you to give me a letter saying that he is about to be made as fire crew. I feel such a letter may help me when I plead his circumstance to his captain for a release."
"Yes, I will gladly do it, In truth he is still a little young I believe, but I can make an exception in this case, I have no love of the press myself. Come with me, we will form the letter together." They went through to a small back room and sat at a tiny writing bench, much used for the purpose, to judge by the ink stains, which covered its surface. As soon as the letter was finished, Alfred made his farewells, thanking the Chief profoundly for his understanding and help.
"I wish you good luck in your endeavour Crossback, it is a difficult task you have ahead of you." Alfred tipped his hat in answer, then half running, he made his way up to the road that would lead him to the old bridge.

Once there, he crossed over to the City side and climbed down the steps which led to St. Botolph's landing stairs. Three watermen were waiting at the causeway and Alfred was pleased to see that one of them was Frederic, a good friend of his. Calling the man over to where they could not be overheard, he told his comrade of the disastrous happenings, how Edwin had been taken by the crew of a Naval ship, and was now at Deptford or Greenwich aboard a man-of war. Alfred explained that he hoped to reach the ship before the lad was signed on and that he would plead a case with the captain for his release. Frederick acted quickly; he called another waterman over and told him he needed him to row two-up with him, to help take Alfred as fast as possible to Greenwich to rescue Edwin from the navy. The three men boarded Frederic's wherry and were soon pulling hard at the oars with the assistance of a strong ebb tide under their keel.

Alfred was pleased that they had the tide with them, but he knew that an ebb tide might also mean that the naval ship could already be underway, taking the ebb flow down river and out to sea. He sat with clenched teeth watching the two men pulling hard at their work, wishing to take an oar himself, but knowing that he must not be exhausted when they arrived. He would need all his wits about him for what he was about to attempt. They were good oarsmen and were making the boat race through the water. He tried to relax his mind from its turmoil, planning what he would say in his supplication to the ship's captain. He felt in his coat pocket, reassured by contact with the money and the paper on which he pinned his hopes.

At last they rounded Cuckold's Point, Alfred got a first glimpse of Greenwich in the distance. There were no ships afloat at the Deptford yards, but he could see four ships at anchor in Greenwich reach. All of these had their rags reefed tight to the yards, but the one that concerned him the most was a fifth ship. This one was getting under-way, her anchor was aweigh and her sails were dropping into position. As he watched, she pulled her anchor up into the cats and was already moving through the water, slowly turning her head down-stream towards the sea. Hoping against hope that the vessel he had seen leaving was not the one with his son aboard, Alfred concentrated on the other vessels. Two were obviously newly arrived; one even had her paying-off pennant still flying, showing that she was just back from a long commission. Of the other two one had her masts undressed, and was obviously just off from the yard. Men were over the side painting and making good the ornamentation of her Poop Deck. The other ship was being prepared to go ashore, probably to be drowned in the dock, to rid her of her rats and vermin. Alfred decided that the most likely ship to have his son aboard was the one being finished off.

The wherry came gently alongside the ship's gangway, and Alfred called up to the watch.
"Permission to come aboard Sir" Alfred looked up for a response from the deck.
"What business have you with the Queen's Navy?" said a harsh voice, issuing from the mouth of a head poking over the ship's side.
"I have a document for the Captain," called Alfred, knowing that the mention of a manuscript always sounded important.
"Come to the top of the gangway, and wait while I fetch the Officer of the watch," said the voice, obviously impressed by the word document. Alfred climbed the gangway and stood on the deck as ordered.
"What is your message?" said the cultured voice of an officer as he advanced across the deck still buttoning his coat, and not at all pleased at being disturbed from his meal.
"It concerns the false arrest of an important young man taken by mistake

for impressment," answered Alfred trying to make the matter one of importance, and therefore of unease to the officer.

"We have taken no impressments as yet, we are only just afloat after refit. Are you sure you have the correct ship?"

"Indeed not Sir, we only know he is aboard a vessel moored at Greenwich, your ship seemed the most likely." The officer eyed Alfred up and down. The man seemed somewhat educated, albeit roughly, but was poorly dressed in the manner of a wherryman. He wondered if he should send him packing for wasting his time, but something cautioned him to be careful, he decided to deal with the man as a messenger, and to furnish any information which might be relevant.

"The only ship taking on fresh crew was the Gloryana and she has left with this tide. I fear you are probably too late, if he is aboard, your man is bound for a long voyage to be sure. The Gloryana is bound for a two-year commission. Give me the document and I will see that our Captain receives it on his return, he will no doubt lodge it with the Admiralty." Alfred's heart dropped at these words.

"Thank you Sir, but I think I should report back to my superior, he can lodge the paper himself with a Justice. Thank you for your time and for the information". The words caught in Alfred's throat, as he realized that he had lost the race, and that his son was already bound for a new life, a life that he could no longer help him with. He looked down stream in the direction of the great salt sea.

"God be with you Edwin, I only hope that I taught you well enough for the trials ahead of you," he said the words quietly to himself.

<========>

It was astonishing, how quickly Edwin had come to terms with his new situation; he seemed to have fully recovered from his ordeal. Like a dog fallen into the river, he had shaken himself off mentally, and had largely regained his spirits. It was but six weeks since the ship had sailed from Greenwich, and he had been so busy learning the different way of life aboard a Navy ship, that he had almost forgotten the pain and grief of his capture. The ship had sailed almost immediately after he was taken on board, leaving him no opportunity to send a message to his family to tell them of his plight. He knew however, that his father would soon find out what had occurred, and would discover what had happened to him. In the mean time, he set his mind to fitting in with his new shipmates.

They seemed a bizarre bunch, coming from many walks of life. Some were watermen, mostly from Gravesend, a few 'uppers' from the upper reaches of the river. Edwin found himself the only one from London. One man was a farmer who had never even seen the sea before, he was fascinated by the immensity of the open water. With not one speck of land to be seen for weeks on end, he kept referring to the green acres of water which surrounded them. For Edwin to it was also a shock to encounter the vastness of the ocean. Like most watermen, he had small respect for saltwater sailors, when seeing them trying to manoeuvre their vessels in the close waters of the Thames, usually having to call for local knowledge to help them. Now however, that he was in their environment, he could appreciate that the skills they cultivated were in navigating the great oceans of the world, where they had room to choreograph the ships movements with great sweeping changes of tack, in good time to reset sails and rigging. He now admired them for overcoming the natural fear of having nothing from which to take a bearing, other than the stars when they were on view, and how they had a blind trust in their instruments. These were brave men with adventure in their very souls. Edwin was in fact coming to like and even enjoy the way of life of seamen. The food on-board was good and plentiful, three square meals each day, as the sailors insisted that their wooden plates were filled to the very corners with victuals.

Patrick had befriended Edwin and had proved to be a good mentor. His hard won experience and sound advice, gained over the many years he had served at sea, had more than once saved Edwin from making a mistake. The Irishman liked the lad; he liked his vigilant ways, his canniness, and his willingness to learn. Patrick had also gained from the friendship, the lad had a sound attitude towards life and a natural awareness, even cleverness, a sensible way of avoiding trouble, which Patrick sometimes lacked. A little more control of his temper, was something the Irishman could certainly benefit from.

Life aboard the Navy ship ran to tight rules, but to his surprise Edwin found that he liked this way of life. He gradually learnt where he should be, and at what time of the watch, how long each duty should take him and the most efficient way of doing it. Some of the men were always straining to catch up with their work, but Edwin was usually ahead of himself and seemed to have ample time for all he did. He even helped others, and gained himself friends by his helpfulness. Only one of the crew was against him, it was Matthew Gerth, the man with the crippled hand. He had taken a dislike of Edwin from the first moment, which seemed to border on hatred. At every opportunity he would spread a bad word about the lad, even to the point of lying. Fortunately he usually went too far, and it became obvious that it was his vengefulness that lay behind the words. Patrick had served with Matthew before and knew him to be a bad lot.
"He always needs to have a whipping boy to focus his evil tongue on, most think him mad, and mostly harmless. However, take no chances Edwin, I have seen him in many fights, he is a mad devil indeed with a blade in his hand, I saw him once chop a Spaniard's head clean off his body with one stroke of his cutlass. It was when we were repelling boarders once in the Mediterranean Sea. He certainly looked like a madman on that day, covered in the man's blood from head to toe.

One person in particular had noticed the new young seaman Crossback going about his work, and was impressed with what he saw. Lieutenant Frobisher had kept a surreptitious eye on Edwin since he came aboard. He had earmarked him for a few of the famous 'Frobisher tests'. These he planned in such a way that the lad would not know that he was being tested. It was a little game the Lieutenant played while at sea, a game that not only passed the time, but often produce useful and sometimes surprising results by sorting out the potentially useful men, from the cannon fodder.

One day the Lieutenant called Boatswain Tyson to the poop deck to give him new instructions concerning the securing of the ship's boats, which were stowed on crutches above the gratings of the ship's hold. "I want you to give thought to the way these boats are secured," he instructed.
"Although they are well tied off naval fashion and stoutly fastened, I am not satisfied that they could be released quickly enough in an emergency. Perhaps we should have some fresh thinking on the matter." Frobisher looked at the confusion in the man's face.
"Boatswain, I am not criticising your work, the fastenings are according to the book, I have checked. However, I seek to find a quicker method of releasing them if the need should arise. Take some of the new men and set them the problem, you never know, they are not yet set in their ways and may have an idea or two, especially the young Thames watermen, don't you think?" The boatswain was a little concerned, he liked things to be done by the book and was suspicious of any form of change, but the officer wanted a fresh look, so he would obey.
"Ay! Ay! Sir I will see about it immediately."

Patrick and Edwin were busy splicing a heavy rope as a spare for the lower crosstree of the main mast, when the boatswain found them; he already had two others in tow, and ordered the four seamen to follow him to the main hatch. Once there, he explained that he wanted the cutter and the jollyboat tied down in a way that was just as secure, but that could be more quickly released.
"Now give some thought to it, and when I return I will see if you have come up with the same ideas that I have on the matter, this is a test of your seamanship." So saying, he left them and went about other business, hoping that what he was doing was correct, and that he had understood Mr Frobisher's meaning. The men started to examine the ropes that held the boats. It was the general opinion that only by eliminating some of the lines could they concur with Tyson's wishes.
"But that would mean they are not as strongly secured," said Edwin. "They will have less rope holding them. He will not like that".
"What say you then?" asked Patrick, knowing that the lad probably had some idea of his own.
"The trick lies not in the lines, or the lead of the fastenings, but in the knots themselves. To undo these knots in a storm is impractical, if wet or in cold weather it will be impossible".
"Ay lad, we would cut the rope free with our knives, as we always have," contributed one of the other men. The conversation was now getting very involved, none of them noticed the slim figure of Lieutenant Frobisher

standing behind the nearby mast, listening to their discussion. "What's your answer to that Edwin," asked Patrick grinning. "We were told to make it quicker to free the boats from the fastening lines, I don't think we are meant to use our knives to do it, only as a last resort. On the river, we tie off and let go lines many times a day and could not afford such a loss of cordage. We use many knots which are quick release, mainly for lashing down tarred sheets to protect the goods in the lighters, we could try some of those".

"I know those fiddly things, they are for calm water use" said one of the seaman.

"They are for thin lashings and not suitable to be used on this thicker cordage, in a rough sea".

"Well we have to show Tyson something, come on lets try a few versions to see if they would work". Edwin's enthusiasm was catching; the other man shrugged his shoulders, but helped with undoing the tight knots that held the boats. Edwin showed the others two or three versions of quick-release knots and they all agreed that one might be good enough to show Tyson.

The boatswain arrived back just as they were tying off the last turn. "What have you come up with?" he said tugging at the lines and looking at the new type knots. The others stood back behind Edwin, making it clear that this was his responsibility, and that he would have to explain the system to the doubting Tyson.

"We have kept the same amount of rope boatswain, to maintain the holding down strength, and the same leads for the lines, which have been proved over many years, but we have changed the knots to quick-release, If you pull on this part of the line, it will release itself even if wet or cold". Tyson took hold of the line and gave a quick jerk, to his surprise the knot unravelled itself immediately. He tried the other knots and in a few seconds the lines that had held the jollyboat were lying on the hatches.

"Not bad, not bad, but they could be accidentally pulled" said Tyson quietly impressed with the result, but not willing to admit his total satisfaction. "It is similar to what I had in mind and worth a try. Redo the knots and we will see if they stay easy to release after a good wetting. Then off you go back to your duties."

Lieutenant Frobisher smiled to himself, He was impressed that not only had the young seaman Crossback come up with a good solution to the problem set him, but that he had been willing to stand up to the boatswain to explain the matter, while the other men had moved behind him. A sign of natural leadership? Perhaps, perhaps. We shall see in the fullness of time.

The months rolled past and the ship passed from the cold waters of the Atlantic across the great ocean into the warmth of the Caribbean. The first landfall was a small island off the Bahamas where they took on fresh water and victuals, fresh food which included a whole deck-load of the most delicious fruit, most of which Edwin had never before tasted. The round of the watches and ship's routine became second nature, he found that his internal clock became attuned with the cycle of ship's life. However, for some unknown reason Edwin's duties were changed, he did not know why this should be, however, he liked his new watch with its fresh duties.

Edwin was now stationed on the poop deck, his job being to relay messages from the deck-officer to the helmsman. Sometimes on night watch when it was quiet and he judged that the deck officer was in a good mood, he would ask questions about navigation, and about the stars. He was fascinated by the heavens, on a clear night it was as if he could reach up and touch the bright lights above him. He loved the way that they came out one at a time, as if turned on by God. It was the seventh star that was his favourite; it had a beautiful blue tinge and reminded him of Mary's eyes. Lieutenant Frobisher was his favourite deck-officer. When he was on watch he would often explain to Edwin about navigation in a simple and understandable way. Most of the other officers would surround the subject in mystery and talk as if it were a great magical gift, but to the Lieutenant it was a science and could be learnt by anyone with half a brain.

One day they sailed into a bay at the end of the island of Samana, at the far side of the bay was a small town called Kings Town. The Gloryana dropped anchor and the longboat was put over the side to take the captain and some of the officers ashore. Edwin found himself at an oar of the small vessel. He was delighted at this chance of seeing the local people of this place up-close. He was seated near enough to overhear the captain talking to his officers. "Frobisher, I am uncomfortable that none have noticed us arrive, or have come out to greet us, it is unusual indeed, the place looks deserted. Take four of the men and look the place over, while we wait in the boat. Be sure that there is nothing amiss." The boat fetched alongside the stone built wall of the harbour and was made fast.
"Jones, Randal, Cob, Crossback, pick up a cutlass each and come with me", ordered the Lieutenant. The men named responded quickly, wondering as were all the others, what was amiss with this place. They climbed the stone steps up to the cobble quay above, and looked around. Not a person was to be seen.
"Jones, Randal, make your way to the right and I will take the rest of you to the left, to investigate, but keep in sight at all times with a pipe call every minute". The men did as bidden and fanned out along the harbour front.
"Over here Sir" called Cob, who was looking through the window of a house. "I can see someone lying on the deck inside, and they are moving." Lieutenant Frobisher ran over and taking one look, decided to force the door of the house, he went inside telling Edwin to follow him. Lying on the floor in front of them was a man of older years, who looked as if he was at death's door itself. Edwin bent to help the man, but was instantly restrained by the Lieutenant's sword.
"Do not touch him Crossback, I fear we have encountered the reason for this place's desertion. The plague is here, see the black boil on his neck? That, if I am not mistaken is a pustule of the Black-death, Recall the others we must return to the boat and send in the ship's surgeon."

They reached the edge of the harbour once more and the Lieutenant looked over to the boat below.
"Captain Sir! I think that there is plague here in the town. We have found one man who is dying and showing all the signals of the disease. With your permission we had better stay here and put ourselves into isolation while Mr Blake comes ashore to take a look." The Captain looked perturbed. "I thought it too damned quiet. You are right Frobisher, we will return to the ship and send Blake over. You and your lads find a clean place to lay-up while we consider the options." The remaining sailors fell to their oars, glad to be leaving this place and pleased that they had not been chosen for the now quarantined shore party.

As the boat began its long pull back to the ship, the Lieutenant ordered the four men remaining to follow him. He led the small party along the quay until they found the beach. This beautiful stretch of bright yellow sand led up to a thick stand of coconut palms.
"We will make camp up there," he said pointing to the trees. "But first we will wash ourselves and our clothes in the sea." Soon they were all stripped off and began dunking their garments in the health giving salted water.
"Now for a camp" shouted the Lieutenant, signalling the men out of the water and pointing to the tree line. The men soon had a good fire going and began drying their clothes. They then set about building a serviceable camp, using their knives to cut down palm fronds to build a good roof cover.

"Crossback, come with me, you others finish the camp and start another fire to get plenty of water on the boil, I think I heard a running stream over yonder, but drink nothing until it has been well cooked". Edwin followed the officer as he led the way back to the town. They entered the deserted streets, but not a living soul was to be seen.
"Do not touch a thing with your hands, only use the tip of your blade which we will put into the fire when we get back." Edwin was pleased that the Lieutenant seemed to know what he was doing, it gave him reassurance, and he followed on with confidence. They made their way to the house of the dying man, but on arrival found that the poor soul had passed on to a hopefully better world.
"You take the other side of this street and look into any windows or doors that are open. See if any others are alive, but do not enter or try to force you way in".
"Ay! Ay! Sir. whispered Edwin, wondering why with none to hear them, they were talking in such low tones.

They were about half way along the street when the Lieutenant stopped outside an open alleyway.
"Come here lad" he called softly to Edwin. As Edwin approached, he could see a body lying in the alleyway and then as they looked closer, they could see another slumped over a small cart further into the passageway.
"My fears are well founded," commented the Lieutenant almost to himself.

"Many have died here from the pest, and the remainder fled away for fear of their lives I'll be bound". Just then, they both heard a faint moaning sound. It was like an echoing voice on the wind calling from far away. Following the sound, they eventually came to the tall wall of a building on the outskirts of the town. The sound was emanating from somewhere within the walls. Someone was calling out in anguish but in a tongue Edwin had never heard before.
"Slaves or prisoners no doubt" said the Lieutenant.
"The poor devils had been left locked in their chains while their captors have run away." Edwin shivered at the thought of such a fate.

By walking around the wall they came across a great double door, into which was set two small, barred, openings. Looking through these apertures into the dirt courtyard within, the sight before them took their breath away. Lying on the ground were several bodies, some of which were devoid of their heads and limbs, Dark stains of dried blood were all over the packed soil. Edwin could make out two heads, which had been rolled up against the wall of the low level building; it was from this building that the sound was coming.
"There is a poor devil still alive in a cell," observed the Lieutenant.
"Shall we force the gates Sir?" asked Edwin.
"No! to be sure, we must wait for Mr Blake the surgeon to test for pestilence before we enter. But we will give hope to those still alive, by calling out our intent." The lieutenant looked at the lad.
"Crossback, climb to the top of the wall and call out to those inside, tell them who we are, and what are our intentions. Come I will help you mount the wall". Edwin half scrambling, and half pushed by the Lieutenant, gained the top of the barricade. He now had a better view of the carnage inside, but now his nostrils were now violently attacked by the smell of death. Gagging from the overpowering stench, he put his kerchief to his lips and braced himself to call out to the deserted chambers of the cell block.
"Ahoy there, you below, can you hear me? Can you understand my language?" Immediately the moaning stopped, but no reply came.
"We are from Her Majesty's Ship Gloryana. We are come to help. What is your situation?" A deathly hush now descended on the place, still no reply came from the building.
"There is no response Sir" called Edwin back down to the Lieutenant.
" I fear that they are too near to death, or are afeared of us".
"Come back down Crossback, at least they know we are here". Edwin prepared to descend, when he heard a feeble voice call out in a frail but passable English.
"God has answered me, I am not forsaken." Edwin squinted his eyes at the low building, trying to peer into the blackness of the small hole which acted as a window.
"Who are you? How many of you still live?" There was a faint reply but too soft to understand.
"We will be back soon with water and food and our ship's surgeon". Then as

an after thought.
"Keep your faith, we will not be long."

As they made their way back to the camp, they met Mr. Blake advancing toward them with two marines who were his helpers and carrying his box of equipment. The Lieutenant quickly reported to the surgeon, explaining what they had found and what precautions he had taken to keep his men from the disease, which he feared was the pestilence.
"You have taken the correct action Mr. Frobisher. Now give me your man to guide me to the prison and continue on to prepare your camp. I will join you later".
"Crossback !" called the Lieutenant. Edwin's heart sank, he did not want to have to go back to that evil place, but he had no choice. He looked over to the Lieutenant for instructions.
"Go with Mr. Blake to show what we have found".
"Ay, Ay Sir" said Edwin, then taking an extra cutlass offered by the officer, he turned and started back towards the town prison.

On arrival at the gates to the compound, Mr. Blake ordered the obstruction broken in. It took several minutes to achieve the removal of one of the gates, but at last they were inside.
"Bring my box and follow me," said the surgeon to his helpers. "You Crossback come with me." Edwin reluctantly followed as ordered. They cautiously approached the first body lying against the wall. The surgeon turned the man's head with his stout cane. A low groan emitted from the poor wretch.
"He will be dead within the hour" declared Mr Blake. They found two more still just alive, but unable to talk or move.
"All here seem dead or to be dying, are you sure you spoke to someone alive in this hell-hole?" he looked at Edwin.
"Yes Sir to be sure, but the voice came from over yonder." He pointed to the middle of the building. Mr. Blake made his way along the line of holes, which acted as windows, looking inside each one as he passed. Then they all heard it. It was the unmistakable voice of a man praying. They approached the window-hole from where the sounds were coming, and Mr. Blake looked inside.
"Quickly, give me the water cask" called out the surgeon, and leaning through the window pushed the small barrel inside. Edwin was alarmed to see their only medical man seemingly taking such chances with what was after all only a prisoner or a slave.
"Let's have this cage open. This seems to be the only way in, so we will enlarge it into a suitable opening". He said, pointed at a small timber hatch set low in the wall next to the window. The men worked at the cavity using their cutlass, and soon had a large enough gap for them to see inside. Mr. Blake entered with the light of day flooding into the cell with him, they could see four bodies lying on the dirt floor, all were in irons both at the wrists and at the feet. Three were not moving and to judge by the awful smell had been dead some time. Astonishingly one man was sitting up, his

back against the wall staring at them, as if trying to decide if this was a dream or truly the end of his nightmare.

Mr. Blake pushed the water cask towards the man using the end of his cane. At first the prisoner just looked at the water, as if not believing his eyes. "Go ahead man, drink, you may keep the cask with you", said the surgeon. The man, who they could now see was a large black man, slowly reached for the cask and pulling the bung with great effort, gradually raised it to his lips. His eyes closed and they could all see the ecstasy in his body as the liquid cascaded down his throat.
"Not too much at once, take a little and often", insisted the surgeon. "Put the cask next to you and tell us what has happened here." The man obviously understood English, for he did as he was told and looked closely at his rescuers.
"There is the 'Black Death' here Sir, many have died, and the others have run away into the hills".
"We guessed as much, but how have you survived".
"It is God's will that I live Sir. He wants me to testify to the horrors of this place, and to the corruption of the town's leaders who caused this misery. I am an innocent man imprisoned for telling the truth, which God knows to be a fact".
"Do you know the whereabouts of the ones who ran away?" asked the surgeon.
"No Sir, not for sure, but I know the places in the hills where to look". Mr Blake looked into the man's face.
"You know that I cannot allow my men to touch you, for fear of contamination?" The man nodded his head.
"Nevertheless, we will release you from your chains and find you better accommodation, if you promise to cooperate with us and keep your distance until I am content that you are free of the pest." The man nodded again confirming his agreement, sitting back against the wall to enjoy the first piece of mind he had encountered during the long nightmare.

"I need a volunteer to free this man and stay to guard him. It will mean that you will also have to stand off from the rest of the shore-party until this plague has run its course." He looked expectantly at the reluctant sailors. Edwin considered his thoughts, which were racing within his mind. On one side, he felt compassion for the man before them, but on the other, he did not want to be alone in such a dangerous situation. The man might be a murderer apart from a carrier of an awful death. None spoke up to volunteer. Mr Blake prepared himself to order one of them for the duty.
"I will stay to guard the man Sir" Edwin heard himself saying.
"Well done lad, I will give you food, some medicine, and tell you how to administer it, should the need arise. Now the rest of you make your way back to the camp, I will follow shortly" Mr Blake gave Edwin detailed instruction and then left to join the others at the camp.

Edwin carefully searched the buildings nearby as he had been instructed and at last found a small office tucked away at the end of a narrow alley. There were no bodies in either the alley or the office so Edwin entered and looked around in the dim light. On the wall was a line of hooks on which hung keys. Using his cutlass, he unhooked some of the keys which seemed to be of a size to fit the leg-irons and carrying them before him on the outstretched blade he returned to the prisoner.

"If we are to be together for some time, I should know your name." He asked the negro with an enquiring look.

"Yes Sir, my name is Josef Abrathat. I am, or I was, the bookkeeper for Mr Nicholas Doxlay, the inn-keeper of this hateful town".

"You do not need to call me Sir, my name is Edwin, but I would prefer it if you called me Crossback. Take these keys Mr. Abrathat, and try to free yourself from those irons. I have found an empty cell for you, where I have left food. Bring the water cask with you, and we will make you as comfortable as this dreadful place will allow. But be warned I am willing to run you through with my cutlass if you make any move contrary to my orders, you understand that you are my prisoner?" Again, the man nodded weakly, and taking the keys, he painfully removed the leg and wrist irons. It took several attempts for the negro to get to his feet, but at last he was upright, swaying from side to side. He was a very tall man, and had once been powerfully built, now his skin hung about him like a baggy coat. Several times Edwin was tempted to help the man, but he remembered the Mr. Blake's warnings, and left him to stagger and scrape along the walls. "He might be telling the truth Crossback, but take no chances, keep him at cutlass length", the surgeon had said.

They finally reached the comparative comfort of the empty cell, and Josef collapsed onto the clean straw Edwin had found, and had arranged in one corner, then slowly he began to eat the food set out for him. Edwin sat himself in the opposite corner, and considered what he must do, how he was to sleep with this man in the same room. The door was broken, perhaps he could make a repair and lock the man inside. He looked again at the pitiful sight before him and pondered.

"Mr Crossback, if it gives you peace of mind, I will put the irons back on. We will both need to sleep this night and although I am willing to give you my word that I will not try to escape, I would not blame you for mistrusting the word of a stranger." Edwin looked closely at the man, he seemed honest enough, but how could he be sure. He remembered his father telling him once that if you listened carefully to a man's story you could gain much information about his character from the way he told it, and even more from what he avoided saying.

"Tell me your story, and I will then judge what is best to do with you." Josef's eyes brightened as if reading Edwin's thoughts.

"I was once a slave taken from a village in Africa as a small boy. I am much travelled, not always in the best of comfort, but I always made the most of my situation. I found that I could learn quickly the ways of white men, and although I soon learned to read and write in the English language, my greatest aptitude was for numbers, a skill that I have found many seek to avoid for lack of persistence. I therefore made my way up life's ladder as a keeper of record-books, which I believe to be the surest way to business success. I arrived here some three years ago in the company of Mr. Doxlay the inn-keeper, to set up in business with a view to becoming his partner if the enterprise prospered". Josef stopped and took a long drink from the water cask, and a bite out of a ship's biscuit. He followed this by a second deep draft of water, before continuing.

"At first, all seemed well enough, but then strange amounts of expenditure began to appear in my reckoning, there were also amounts missing from the profits. On questioning Mr Doxlay on the matter, I finally discovered that he was under threat from some of the town leaders, and was ordered to pay them money, on menace of harm to his family." Edwin listened intently to the story. After another pause for more biscuits and water, Josef continued. "Having no family of my own to put into danger, I decided to try to stop this evil dealing, which at that time I thought only involved one or two of the officials. My intention was to report the matter by letter to the authorities in England. In that belief I could not have been more wrong, for when I confided my intentions to the leader of the town's superiors, a man in whom I thought I could trust, I was arrested for my trouble on a charge of sedition, and thrown into this hell hole." He paused and looked at Edwin to judge if his words were believed, then reassured, he continued. "Before you is the result of my efforts at honesty. After three months of imprisonment, rumours began to circulate. Even in here, we heard more and more of the terrible happenings going on about the town, and of the horrors of the Black Death as it struck the citizens, then one morning we found that even our jailers had run away, leaving us locked in, to die in our chains. Those that broke loose fought among themselves like madmen, settling old scores. We could hear the carnage going on in the yard. How many have survived with me Mr Crossback?"
"You are the only one we have found in here with life enough to survive, and none in the town," said Edwin, now believing the truth of the man's story. Edwin decided that he could trust this man.

"Mr. Abrathat. I am going to put you on your honour to keep your distance from me and not to try to escape. In return, I will put your story to Lieutenant Frobisher when he returns as a true and honest account. He is a good man, and I will plead your case for freedom."
The night was now closing in, the negro made himself comfortable on the straw and was soon sleeping the sleep of the exhausted. Edwin settled down with his back against the wall and like the true waterman that he was, wandered off in his mind to consider the events of the day.

The next day Edwin was about early, he left the negro to his much needed sleep and went to check on the bodies in the yard. It seemed that the end had come during the night to all those suffering, he prodded each body with a stick, but detected no response. He searched the office once again, and finding a trap door under the floor covering, he raised the wooden plate and discovered a store of ropes and tools. Taking out a suitable looking grappling hook and some stout line, he made up a means of moving the bodies without the need to touch them. Back in the yard he pulled each corpse to the far corner, and soon had a pile of over twenty. The smell was almost overwhelming in spite of the kerchief tied over his mouth. Then using some of the bags of lime, which he had found stacked in a small space at the back of the office, he covered the bodies with a thick layer of the sharp smelling powder. The light wind, which seemed to favour the island, at last began to dispel the stench of the lime did its work.

Returning to the cell, Edwin found Mr. Abrathat stirring from his sleep.
"How fair you this morning?" he asked.
"I am well, and pleased to be alive. I thank you most sincerely Mr. Crossback.
"Let us eat more of the victuals," said Edwin pushing some of the food across the floor. They ate in silence, each to his own thoughts. When they had finished, the Negro looked up at Edwin and asked.
"May I have your permission to try to stand and perhaps take a step or two Mr Crossback?" Edwin gestured his acquiescence, and the big man slowly got to his feet. His limbs were obviously stiff, but by supporting himself against the wall, he took a few painful steps.
"Well done my man" said a voice from the door. It was Lieutenant Frobisher, who neither of them had heard approaching.
" I am pleased to see that you are improving. Mr. Blake has told me of your recovery, I will hear your full story in due course. Crossback has this man caused you any trouble?
"No Sir, to the contrary. He has told me his story, and it seems he might be able to help us to discover what happened in this place".
"Indeed, you say. Give me the gist of it." Edwin reported what Josef had told him of the corrupt town's leaders, and how they had run away and left the people to fend for themselves. Frobisher nodded.
"We will deal with those rogues later, but first we must clean the town and bury the bodies; we have brought lime with us, but I see you have also found a supply. It will all be needed I am sure".

It took three days to dig the mass graves and pull the corpses in, to be covered with the quick-lime. Some buildings seemed so contaminated that Mr. Blake's ordered them to be burn down. At last, the smell of death was gone from the Town and the air sweet again, Mr Abrathat had mostly recovered and assured Mr. Blake that he was able, and keen to direct the shore-party up into the hills to discover the whereabouts of the runaways. After taking stock of the situation, the Lieutenant decided it was time to track down the miscreants.

Early on the morning of the next day, Mr Frobisher assembled a well armed search-party and after a briefing on the plan of attack, they moved off in the direction of the heavily wooded hills, which dominated the high parts of the island. He directed Edwin and Abrathat to go ahead, keeping them a safe distance from the main party, ordering them to leave clear signs for the others to follow. Edwin was amazed at the fortitude of his new friend. Josef was obviously still weak, but his determination to right the wrong done to him, kept him going. As each day passed he seemed to gain in strength. Edwin now carried a musket and Josef had been given a cutlass; the seamen in the main party were also well armed.

After four days of searching, they at last found signs that their prey was near. Edwin left Josef to watch, while he returned to report to the Lieutenant. On receiving the news, Mr Frobisher decided to wait until nightfall, so that the attack might have the advantage of darkness and surprise. The wait for darkness seemed long, each man determined not to give away their presence. At last it was dark, and with the sounds of the forest creatures singing in their ears, they quietly approached the rebels' camp. Then with loud blood-thirsty shouts, as if storming a ship grappled alongside, the attack began.

The battle was a feeble affair; the group were completely unaware that a Naval ship had arrived or that their wrongdoing had been discovered. It had been their intention to wait out a few months, then return and bury the evidence of their crimes, after which, they would rebuild the community based on their same corrupt system, and those who had evidence against them would be deceased. They had not thought it possible that a man would survive in that prison hell-hole, to be able to bear witness and charge them with their offences. Some of the town officials, realising that retribution was at hand, had resisted the attack with half-hearted musket fire, but as two of them were quickly shot through by musket ball, the remainder capitulated, throwing themselves on the mercy of Her Majesty's Navy. The captives, who numbered about eighty, were taken back to the town, and at the suggestion of Josef, were ensconced in the old prison, bestowing on them a taste of the terror they had inflicted on others.

CHAPTER THIRTEEN
The Queen is dead Long live the King

Mr Doggett was beside himself with joy. The old Queen was no more and the new King was to be the Hanoverian George of the Protestant faith. He would be the first King named George to sit upon the English throne. However, the thing that delighted Thomas Doggett the most, was that the King was very supportive of the Whig Party. A superb turn of events indeed for the fortunes of his chosen brand of politics. There would of course be difficulties with this new King, Doggett knew that he spoke very little English, and was said to be "unimaginative", but perhaps that could be put to good use, by those in power of the Whig party, they could perchance more easily manipulate and steer the Ship-of State on a course of their own liking.

The old Queen had been a great disappointment to the Whigs, the dullest Monarch ever, thought many of her subjects. From Doggett's point of view her caution and slowness to react, held back the aspirations of his party, Thomas and his friends now saw this changeover to the new regime as a breath of new life into their ambitions. No more would they have to endure that overweight drudge, who had ruled more like a housewife than a Queen. A woman whose life was made bitter from the loss of so many children, who suffered from dropsy, gout and over eating. It was even rumoured that in her final years this amazingly fat, pathetic figure, swathed in bandages, had to be carried about in a chair, and even lowered through trapdoors from the upstairs apartments of her palace in Kensington. It was also well known that the Queen consoled herself in her misery, with quantities of brandy, which she drank from a teacup. She had acquired many nicknames during her reign, but the one Doggett liked the best was "Queen Log", for in his mind this epithet summed up the sad, miserable, mournful, old lady.

As the first year of the new King's reign wore on, it became obvious that George 1st was very Prussian in his attitude. Although descended from James 1st he was of a very different character, certainly unimaginative and stolid to a fault, making no effort to learn the language of his people. The King preferred to surround himself with German speakers, who talked with him continuously about his beloved Hanover; the matters of British government were left to be dealt with by his advisers, who were dominated by the Whigs. Doggett thought this was the most perfect situation for his party, and as the first anniversary of the King's accession approached, he racked his brain to think of a suitable manifestation of his support. Others with better means at their disposal were planning elaborate celebrations, far beyond anything Doggett could afford. Anyway, he did not want to be just one of a following group of sycophants, he wanted to do something for himself alone, something that would bring him repute, perhaps even to the notice of The King himself, or better still the attention of the ruling Whigs behind the throne.

One evening as he walked down to the water stairs at Bankside, to find the wherry he had hired to take him home after his exhausting evening on the boards. He suddenly remembered the young waterman who had given him the advice on how to arrange oars from Southwark after dark. That good advice had been to send word to Watermen's Hall early in the day to order a wherry, and have the boat waiting for him when he finished at the playhouse. The small extra payment had proved well worth the cost, avoiding the inconvenience and danger of crossing the old bridge late at night. He shivered as he thought of the experience he had once endured on that stormy night, when he was nearly murdered by a foot-pad up on the bridge, perhaps to be thrown into the river, never to be found by his loved ones. It was following that incident that Thomas had met the young man, taking his wherry for the homeward journey to Chelsea. Thomas had not encountered that lad again, even though he was prone to use the wherries frequently. If he had, he would have liked to have thanked him for his help, and given him a good coin for his useful advice.

The boat was waiting as arranged at the landing. Other people wanting to take boat gave Doggett a sour look as he passed them to descend the steps to the water, leaving them to wait in hope of a passing wherry. One or two were somewhat drunk and making fools of themselves. Thomas now knew that because of the boisterous behaviour of these few, the landing would be avoided by the watermen. He carefully stepped down the stairs and was handed into the small vessel by the boatman. He recognised this wherryman he was often the one waiting for him when he ordered oars.
"Good evening my man, we have the tide with us tonight I see"
"The tide and I are at your commandment, your honour, we should make Chelsea well within the hour, God willing." Handing Doggett into the passenger seat, he offered him a canvas pull-on to keep his legs warm. The man then sat at his rowing bench and backed the boat away from the landing, sliding her out gently to meet the tide on its upriver run.
"A fine night to be sure" said Doggett half to himself. The wherryman nodded in agreement.
"I remember a night when this journey was not so pleasant; I was rowed by a young newly freed waterman, a young man who took me home in great style, against both the tide and wind. He pulled a powerful oar I seem to remember"
"Do you know his name or number? I might know of his whereabouts," inquired the wherryman.
"No I fear not, but I wish I had asked, for he did me a service that night"
"Was he a wager-man?" asked the boatman, only half interested in what his

passenger was saying.
"I think not," said Doggett. "I believe he was too young to have acquired backers."

Doggett suddenly sat up bolt-upright in his seat, he had just had a wonderful idea, it answered his dilemma, the way he was seeking to demonstrate his importance as a Whig, but best of all without any contribution from others. He would use London's natural stage, and the men of the river would be his players in a wondrous drama, free for all Londoners to see and enjoy. The wherryman looked up expecting an answer to his question, but seeing that the old actor was busy with some thought he had just had, he decided to leave the man to his contemplations.

The plan was forming itself slowly in Doggett's mind, it was so simple, he would devise a wager, rowed between waterman, a race for which he would give a grand prize, grand enough to be of interest to these secretive souls. It must be something that they would want to compete for, something special, but not necessarily expensive. Doggett could see in his mind's eye hundreds of men fighting at their oars to win his prize, the river would be full of wherries racing each other. "No! No! That would not do", he thought to himself. If he depleted the boatmen's service on the river by such a show, he would be hated by the citizens for the inconvenience, if not imprisoned by the Lord Mayor. Anyway what a nightmare it would be to organise. A few men only competing would be much better. Any event that was restricted was always more attractive to competitors than one open to all. A memory suddenly flashed through his mind, he remembered that there had been six men at Swan Stairs on that night of the storm.
"Yes!" he thought, that was a good number, no more than six shall race for my prize, and the start shall be from the Old Swan tavern near to those stairs where I took boat.
"It shall start above the bridge, to avoid any complication with shooting the arches, but will still be in the heart of the City." Thomas's mind was racing, he wriggled on his seat with excitement, he could not wait to put all this to paper.
"Yes! Yes! Of course, the finish shall be at Chelsea where I lodge at the Swan Inn. From Swan to Swan, what fun this is indeed. It is all coming together wonderfully." Doggett did not realise that he was speaking his thoughts out loud, until he saw the boatman look up questioningly.
"How many miles is this pull from the old bridge to Chelsea," asked Doggett. The man considered for a moment.
"About five or just under your Honour" replied the man wondering if this was a trick question concerning the fare he would charge, but he had taken this man before and had encountered no problem with payment.

Thomas sank back into his thoughts once again and continued his planning. He had the course of the wager now set, he had the number of competitors, but he needed somehow to make this wager special. He remembered that the young man who had taken him home that night, had been recently freed from his master in that year. Thomas decided that he would limit the entrants to young watermen in their first year of freedom from their apprenticeship. That way he would always get young blood into his wager and also avoid the problem of the same person winning each time it was raced. Too often pulling wagers on the Thames were dominated by one or two well supported powerful oarsmen, who with their backers were out to win the purse at all costs. This was always to the detriment of the others less fortunate. There were many such wagers each year but the winner was always one of the favoured few.

"That's it!" he thought, it would be an annual race, rowed to commemorate the King's accession, by young wherrymen in their first year, and competed for on the anniversary, that way no man could win it more than once. Doggett smiled, it was all coming together splendidly.

He now had the stage, the players, the time, the place, and the rules. He only needed the prize and the curtain could rise on a performance free to all, performed annually, forever. His name would be remembered by the citizens for this generosity. But what prize should he offer, a gloriously painted 'Backboard'? No that was common place, there were more backboards given as prizes, than you could shake a stick at. A new wherry for the winner perhaps? No! Far too expensive, such a valuable prize would cause trouble for the organiser of the event. Such a prize would attract the devious and the ruthless.

He thought again about the young waterman of that night, and what he had told him of his trade and of the river people. He remembered the pride the lad had displayed when talking about his peers, the Queen's watermen and their magnificent uniforms. The Bargemasters of the rich families, and the men chosen to row the great Livery barges of the City Guilds. Doggett knew that some of the Livery Companies provided ornate badges for their crews and especially for their Bargemasters.

"A badge depicting something special about the King would be a good prize," he thought to himself. He remembered being told once of The King's pride in his place of birth, and of the symbol of his city 'The White Horse of Hanover', which represented 'Liberty'. That was a good word to be placed upon a Thames watermen. A prancing horse on a badge of silver depicting the word 'Liberty', that would be most suitable thought Doggett. His mind turned again to the young wherryman who had worn a coat with many patches and repairs. Perhaps a new coat for the badge to be displayed upon would add to the attraction, but made up in what colour cloth? He thought for a moment.

"Yes, of course, the orange-red of the Royal Household. Now that would be a prize well worth rowing for."

At last they reached Chelsea. Doggett could not wait to get to his room and put his ideas down on paper. He quickly paid the wherryman, almost running up the causeway and along to the Swan Inn. As usual the door was locked against night intruders. Mrs Bridges was a cautious woman. Thomas knocked loudly knowing that his landlady was a little hard of hearing. He hopped from foot to foot while he waited anxiously for her to let him in. At last he could hear her drawing the bolts, as soon as she had the door half open, Doggett pushed his way in.

"Quickly Mrs Bridges be a good woman and bring paper and quills, I must write something down while it is fresh in my mind".

"Your supper is set out in your room, it is a cold collation. You can not expect me to cook so late at night." Doggett winced; the silly old woman always said the same thing even after all these years, she still complained about his late hours.

"It is my profession Mrs Bridges, as I have explained these many times, performers and the managers of playhouses must work late. It is our lot in life to be about when most people are abed. Now paper and ink if you will."

The old lady shuffled off mumbling under her breath. Doggett went up to his room, moved the cold supper from the table, and prepared to write down his thoughts.

The next morning found Doggett about early in his rooms at Chelsea, he had not slept well, his mind too full of his plans. He must tell his friends of his great idea. He would ask Mr Downes to look through his writing, he had a good hand, and as a script writer, would knock the wording into better shape. Ciber and Wilks must also be told, and Tony Aston of course, if he could be found, but that would be all for now. The plan must be kept a secret, lest others might take it for their own.

Later in the day, Doggett took a wherry from Chelsea stairs to the City. He wanted to visit the Hall of the Watermen's Company, to find out what governances there were on the setting up of wagers. He must find out the cost of every thing, he therefore had made a list of the items of the probable outlay.

The cost of the cloth
The charge for making it up.
The silver buttons, perhaps also buckles if he could afford it.
The price of silver for a good size badge.
The engraving and the design.
The cost of pamphlets announcing the wager.
Any charges to be made by the Watermen's Company.
The cost of help with the organisation, and supervision of the race.

Doggett looked at the list, he could see that this idea was beginning to look expensive.

<========>

After the adventures on the island, a temporary Governor was installed to run the town, in the form of one of the ship's officers. Whose duty would be to stay behind with a party of sailors to help him keep order. He would do this with the assistance of Mr Josef Abrathat, who was keen to show what could be done to make the island profitable for the Crown. They would wait until a ship could be sent out from England with a permanent Governor, and a contingent of soldiers to relieve the sailors.

The crew of the Gloryana finally said their farewells and sailed off to show the British flag at other islands along this untamed and dangerous coast. The days were long and hot, the drills were becoming monotonous. And as the wind did not vary by even a degree, it meant that to keep the men busy the captain ordered unnecessary reefing and un-reefing of the rags, with a full sail change twice each week. This hard and difficult work, did as was intended. It kept the crew hard at work; they were only too pleased to get to their hammocks each night, with no time or energy for arguing or troublemaking. For Edwin however, this was a frustrating time, he did not take well to doing unnecessary things. He hated the monotonous work of bending on and off the great canvas sails, just for the sake of doing something.
"Why are we doing it yet again?" he groaned to Patrick one day. "I am fed up with this unnecessary labour" Patrick took the lad to one side out of the earshot of the others, they pretended to be remaking the line on a belaying-pin while he explained.
"These are dangerous conditions Edwin, more so even than a bad storm. Men with idle hands are apt to turn to mischief, unlike you who would always find employment for himself. Some would begin to create discontent, and to influence others to follow them into trouble. You know that many have quantities of drink hidden away. Well that liquor mixed with idleness, is a bad brew indeed, and the Captain knows it well. That is why he keeps us so busy and tired. Go with it lad, it is to be sure, for the best.

The one sided hostilities Edwin was having with Matthew continued. The man seemed obsessed with his dislike of the lad. It had now reached a point where Edwin had to ensure where the man was at all times and to constantly check if any of his kit had been tampered with. He once found a sharp spike fastened upright in the filling of his hammock, only just avoiding being spiked, as he swung up into his pit one night after returning from watch. Matthew seemed annoyed when Edwin did not challenge him about the matter. Everyone on the mess-deck knew who had planted the spike. It was as if Matthew was looking for an excuse for a confrontation, but Edwin did not rise to the bait. Another night he found his hammock lines almost cut through. If he had swung up and in as was usual among sailors, he would have spilled out onto his head. He talked the matter over constantly with Patrick, who urged him to steer clear of a fight with the madman.

One early morning aboard the Gloryana, the crew were roused by the duty watch with the urgent call to gun stations. Edwin tumbled out of his hammock, pulling on his clothes as he ran to his cannon station on the main deck. He was part of Mr Caudridge's gun-crew. Edwin was pleased with this position, as this man was among the best at organising his men.

Each man in the team had a main function, from which he would not vary unless one of the team was put out of action. This meant that each man had to know the duties of all of the other members of the gun crew, as well as his own, in case of loss. The next crew along the deck was Mr Knox's crew. They too were a good crew, except for the fact that Matthew Garth was part of that team. Edwin had often caught the man looking at him, as if wishing to do him some harm. This day was no exception, the madman's obsession seemed as strong as ever, it showed in his dark black evil eyes.
"We have sighted a privateer and she has turned to attack" shouted Mr Cauldridge above the grinding of the gun-carriage wheels on the deck, as the crew slewed the weapon into its place pointing it out through the firing port. "She don't know what she's in for the fool, if she thinks to mix it with us."
"Take up slack and pull me darling's mouth through the port" he called to the men, and the cannon's tip passed out through the side of the ship. His enthusiasm fired up his men, who worked as one to aim the gun and make ready to shoot.
"Lift ye head for father, me darling, and bark at those fools, spit in their rigging and bring down them yards me lovely." Mr. Cauldridge was almost lying along the barrel to line up the shot. Edwin's duty was to put the next charge into the barrel after a discharge, and the cannon's recoil inboard. Patrick who was in the same team as Edwin, had to ram the charge down the barrel with a long handled ram-rod, then when the ball was rolled in, with the wadding, he would ram the lot tight down into the barrel, making a good fit ready for the next shot. The cannon was then returned through the port by the pulley ropes, which pulled the gun forward. This meant that for some time Edwin was standing holding a charge of gunpowder in his arms, waiting for the cannon to recoil ready for reloading. Unbeknown to Edwin, black eyes were watching, and had noticed this fact. Mad Matthew's duty was to place the small firing charge of powder into the flash pan of his cannon, he did this from a small barrel of powder that he held in his arms.

The first shot came from the privateer, not even reaching the Gloryana. This however, was the signal that had been waited for. The order was given to open fire and Edwin's cannon roared, rearing backward from the force. He jumped forward, waiting keenly for the water mop to be withdrawn from the barrel. He then slid his charge into the end and backed up to his standby position while his charge was followed by the ball and the wadding. A great crescendo of sound erupted as other guns opened up, which made it impossible to hear any orders, everyone relied on their training and on doing their part of the firing sequence. A ball from the privateer hit the ship further along from Edwin's position. He could hear men screaming even above the cacophony of sound of the cannon fire, but his blood was up and he was not alarmed.

Black eyes were still upon Edwin, Mad Matthew was watching his every movement, The madman had devised a plan. At every opportunity, he was scattering a handful of black powder over towards Edwin's feet, slowly building a trail of the powder toward his perceived enemy. He did this each time he filled the firing pan of his own cannon, and while his crew were concentrating on their own actions. In the confusion nobody noticed what evil he was up to. In the excitement Edwin did not notice the build up of powder on the deck between him and his enemy. Mathew was grinning with glee, as he poured another handful of gunpowder from the keg, his hand now black from the fine powder. His plan was building nicely; when enough powder was built up, he would use the touch bran from the sand bucket and ignite the trail. The resulting burn would maim his rival for sure, and perhaps even rid him of the man whose self-important presence he detested.

Matthew's opportunity came during the height of the battle, all the gun crews were working hard at firing and reloading, men were sweating with exertion, and deaf from the noise of combat. He had built up a good amount of powder towards Edwin's feet, and now watched for his chance. Matthew's gun fired and all hands were working to reload, he stepped forward to grab a glowing brand from the sand bucket, but at the same time, one of the crew, steeping back from swabbing the gun barrel, knocked against him, and instead of grasping the brand at its bottom end, Matthew's fingers gripped the smouldering taper near to its glowing top. The powder covering his hand was the first to catch, then in a flash the dust that had settled on his jacket was also consumed, the flame shooting across to the keg he was holding under his left arm. The explosion which followed obliterated Matthew and half of his gun crew. Fortunately, Edwin had just stepped forward as the blast ran across the deck, but it ripped the clothes from Edwin's body propelling him into the path of his own cannon, which at that moment was recoiling from a shot. The wheel of the heavy gun carriage ground across his right foot, leaving an unrecognisable bloody mess hanging from the end of his leg. He felt no pain. His eyes were wide open as he looked at the gory disarray which had once been his foot, the shock of the sight slowly taking over his mind, he passed away into a place of unconsciousness.

When Edwin came to, he was in the galley, laid out on a side table. He could see that he was surrounded by many other men all bearing horrific wounds and in various states of distress. He could hear nothing, although the mouths of the men were moving and their eyes showed the torment of their pain. He tried to sit up, but a throbbing erupted down his right side of his body, he looked as best he could to see the cause. He was naked all over, and his skin along that side was blistered into pink and red eruptions. Then suddenly remembering, he looked down to his foot. No! It had not been a dream. There to prove the fact, hung a bloody bag of crushed bone in its place. A hand touched his shoulder, he looked up into the sweating face of Mr Blake the surgeon. His lips were moving but he was making no sound, then he pointed to his ears and then to Edwin, slowly mouthing the word "deaf from cannon". Edwin understood, he pointed to the remains of his foot. Mr Blake nodded and grasping Edwin's shoulder made a sign with his other hand, it was a thumbs up. He then moved away to more urgent patients. Edwin watched as the surgeon with his helpers removed legs and arms, and sewed up the most dreadful wounds. Then came Edwin's turn. He was carried over to the centre bench of the galley, and a leather strap pushed between his teeth for him to bite on. A cloth was placed over his face and two men grabbed him on either side, holding him down expertly, in such a way that he could not roll or move in any direction. He felt his leg being turned to the left, then a grinding pain as the surgeon's saw bit into the bone above his ankle. A wave of pain washed over him and he slipped gratefully away into unconsciousness.

Edwin awoke to the faint sounds of the sea, his hearing had returned a little, but before he could rejoice at this fact a burning pain leaped up from his damaged foot, he tried to grab at the offending place but more pain from his right side prevented any further movement.
"So Crossback, your luck holds. I thought we had lost you." It was the faint voice of Lieutenant Frobisher standing alongside Edwin's cot.
"I had you put up here on deck to benefit from some good sea air. It has been four days since the battle and you have been in and out of consciousness many times. I know your hearing is limited, but I think you would wish to know the outcome of the engagement, and something of what happened to you. But if your pain is too much I will return later." Edwin realised that he was grimacing with the pain emanating from his foot, but he tried to speak.
"It is my missing foot and my side sir. Did they seal my leg with pitch?" Mr Frobisher nodded.
"Yes Crossback, no more dancing for you my boy, but Mr Blake assures me that you will walk again, first with crutches, and perhaps later with a short peg. Now would you like me to tell of the battle?"
"Yes sir, and I would know if my friend Murphy is survived."
"I am afraid Murphy was lost to the same explosion that took your foot, as were six other men. I understand that a fool of the charge-filler in the next gun crew to yours, caught himself on fire and exploded the keg of powder he was holding. I am looking into the matter more deeply however, there seems to be some inconsistencies in the story, which I will get to the bottom of in due course".
"The battle sir, how did we fare against the privateer ?"
"Alas we lost her, we did her some damage, as she did to us, we were gaining the upper hand however and had the winning of her I feel sure, but the explosion at your's and the next cannon occurred and put us in disarray, and she made off into the smoke and mist, she would have been a good prize to be sure, but there's the rub of it, she got away". The lieutenant made as if to wander off.
"Sir, may I enquire if Matthew Garth was lost to the explosion?"
"Yes he was, in fact the whole matter seems to have been his mistake, that fool lost us a valuable prize."

It was several weeks before Edwin was fully up and about, and able to return to light duties. In that time two more men had died of their wounds, and were put over into the deep with the usual ship's ceremony. The blisters on Edwin's starboard side had reduced to a wrinkled, parchment like substance, which he thought resembled a ship's chart, complete with the contours of the hills and valleys well displayed, with the rivers shown in red zigzagging lines. His leg had healed into a stump just above the ankle. This part still caused him the most pain. The ship's carpenter had fashioned a short peg out of a piece of timber, with a padded hollow in the top, into which Edwin could insert his stump. It had straps at either side which attached to a leather garter fastened around his leg below the knee. Edwin persevered with this wooden stump, using it for longer and longer periods, first with, and then without the use of crutches. He was growing more proficient as the weeks passed, managing to walk a few paces wearing the peg. He developed a curious gait with a swinging skip, which seemed to be quite usable. He was determined to present himself to Mary on two legs, walking unaided when that happy day came.

It was almost June when the ship reached Gibraltar, the gateway to the Mediterranean sea, they put into the harbour for provisions and fresh orders. Some of the crew were allowed to go ashore and returned full of gossip. The big news was that the old Queen was dead, and that a new German King 'George' now ruled the Kingdom. It seemed that the politics had also changed, the King favoured the Whigs, which meant the Tories were on the decline. The Captain called for a muster of the ship's company on deck and confirmed the rumours by announcing.
"The Queen is dead, long live the King". A double tot of rum was passed out, and the rest of the day given over to 'make and mend'. Edwin's watch was confined to stay onboard for this short visit, but he was eager to know if there was any correspondence for the Gloryana. He questioned each boatload as they came back from ashore, but alas, there was no word from his family. After only a three day stay in Gibraltar, the Gloryana set sail, her orders were to proceed to 'The Thames London'. The crew were overjoyed at the new orders. For some of them this meant home, for the others it still meant an end to the Gloryana's commission and travelling on to see their families. The atmosphere on board was merry. Everyone from the captain down seemed happy, and passed many a pleasantry when meeting each other on deck.

One evening as the crew sat in the mess-deck telling yarns, while the ship lazily rolled and slopped along on her homeward journey, the conversation turned to the change of monarch, and the royal way of life, but none was knowledgeable, and much exaggeration was expressed.
"This King is more tolerant of the religion of others," said one.
"But will he pay his sailors more, or treat them better?" said another.
"He will be like all the others, living from the fat of the land without a care for others," said a third.
"I would not wish to be a King" said John the first speaker.

"They may eat and live well, but the intrigue they must endure will take its toll of their mind and drive them mad. I am all for the simple life". Then one of the seamen called out.
"Come Crossback tell us what we might see when we reach London. Yes!" went up a chorus of voices.
"tell us of your Royal River Thames, did you ever see the Queen? Can she really cure illness by touching?" Edwin moved to the table.
"I know nothing of the Queen, but I did see her barge once when she was aboard. I was but a small boy. I was out helping my father in his wherry.

The story which Edwin now told, had happened many years earlier. Edwin explained that on that day he had first heard the Queen's Whiffler. This man dressed in red livery, was stationed in the bow of the Royal Barge and was calling out as the vessel approached.
"Make way for the Queen's barge. Make way there." His father had quickly pulled the wherry over to the side of the main stream to let the Royal Shallop have its right of way. Then bowing and doffing their bonnets in unison with the passengers, they watched in fascination as the vessel sped past. It had eight men at the oars, all dressed in the bright red and gold of the Royal household. They were pulling powerfully with at a high rate of work, in well-practised unison. There were two whifflers on board, one at the bow and one in the stern, it was the bowman whose duty it was to clear the way by calling ahead, but when the vessel reached its destination both whifflers had the duty of holding the barge safely alongside the landing while their Royal passenger disembarked. Edwin's father had pointed out The Queen's Bargemaster standing in the stern of the barge, leaning forward and staring intently ahead. He was steering the vessel using its long ornately carved tiller. The Bargemaster was dressed in Court livery of a crimson tailed-coat, with matching knee breeches; his stockings were white, above black, gold-buckled shoes and like all persons of the Royal Household, he wore the black, domed, cap.

Edwin had not been able to see inside the tilt of the barge, but his father told him that with eight Royal Watermen at the oars it must be the Queen herself. Other members of the Royal family would only have warranted six oarsmen, some were allowed only four to propel their barge. Perhaps" said his father.
"The Queen is on her way to Greenwich Palace on important business of State." The shallop barge had been travelling with the tide flow, and was making very fast progress.
"At that speed they could be at Greenwich well within the hour," he added, watching the oarsmen's actions with a knowledgeable eye. Two other six oared Shallops were accompanying the barge, but these were having trouble keeping up with the larger, better-manned vessel. Alfred knew that at this pace there would be some very tired men at the oars when they reached their destination.

"I have also met some of the Royal watermen in their quarters at Somerset

House," Edwin was now telling the crew in the mess deck, who seemed fascinated by his account.

"Tell us more lad," said an old sailor who normally had little to say for himself. Edwin enjoyed being the centre of attraction, it was something he would not have dared to be if Matthew Garth had still been alive. He started to relive the story.

<========>

One day his father Alfred had came home flushed with good news; he had been hired to deliver some barrels of soft soap and liquid tar to a very special place. He was to pick up this small cargo from the Navy yard at Deptford and take it to the Royal Bargehouse at Somerset House. Glowing with pride at this unexpected honour, he had decided to take his young son Edwin with him for the experience, and perhaps if the chance presented itself, to see inside the old Palace, parts of which dated back to the time of the religion changer, the old King Henry. Alfred knew that he had only been hired for this job because it was a messy business handling leaky barrels of the grubby muck called 'liquid tar', and that of the slippery 'soft soap', which was not much better to deal with. Soap however, was a very valuable commodity due to the high tax levied on it, and Alfred was proud that he had been trusted with the delivery. The Royal Bargemaster no doubt wanting to avoid the risk of any spillage in one of the Royal Household vessels, had therefore ordered the hire of a wherry to do the dirty work.

Alfred and Edwin were up, and about early, on the day of the trip. They took the Anna from her moorings, then with Alfred at the oars, pulled her down to the Victualling yards at Deptford. On the way they passed hundreds of tall ships at anchor, all waiting for a berth to come free further up river in the port itself. The ships looked almost deserted; most of the crews having been put off pay on reaching port, leaving only a skeleton crew to look after the vessel. Even these men were only paid a subsistence allowance. Edwin looked up into the forest of tall masts wondering at their height.

"Son, you can now see why these ships can be caught by wind in a great storm", pointed out Alfred, noticing the engrossed interest of his son. "They can take down the sails, but those tall masts and yards still hold a deal of blow, especially when a ship is at anchor. Only three years ago in that great spring storm we had, many ships from here were blown away, dragging their anchors and heaping themselves up like broken sticks on the far shore. With so few men aboard little could be done to stop the damage. Edwin listened attentively.

"After that storm had passed," continued Alfred. "A great whale, which measured some five and fifty feet, came up river to here. I saw it son, it was over there, a great grey beast." Edwin tried to imagine a fish as big as that, it would be bigger than their house including the rooms altogether. "Look over yonder", said Alfred, indicating with a nod of his head a grand building on the south shore, partly hidden behind the ship's masts.

"That is where the King of Russia, called Czar Peter resided a few years back. I saw him many times sailing the yard's yacht, or rowing on the river. He was here to learn the art of ship-building and boat handling." Then with great pride, he added
"We English are the best in the world at it, you remember that lad." Edwin puffed out his little chest with reflected self-importance.
"They named his favourite tavern after him when he left," continued Alfred. "When you are older, you and I will visit the 'Czar of Muscovy's Head' and we will drink to the health of a good man." He smiled at the boy's excitement at the thought of drinking with his father.
"The Czar Peter liked the Thames people you know," continued Alfred. "When he returned home to Russia, he took five hundred watermen into his service, to help him build a great new city. He was a giant of a man almost seven feet tall. He was one of the few good men," said Alfred with feeling. "One of the very few".

At the yard they collected the four smelly barrels of tar, and two of soft soap, loading them on board the Anna. They placed them on a piece of old sailcloth to keep the contents from staining the burden boards of the wherry. Then, tying them securely together with a stout turn around the passenger thwart to steady them, they cast off from the yard's jetty, and started the long pull up river. Alfred was seated at the sculling oars, while Edwin sat in the bow, helping by rowing in the bow, randan style. He was using an undersized oar, that his father had altered especially for his small frame. It was a long pull even with the flood tide in their favour, and they had to stop several times during the row to steady the barrels, whenever they passed through choppy water. They passed scores of ships, many of them putting cargo over the side into lighteners and flatboats. Some ships were moored at wharves, their cargo flying through the air on the ropes of derricks into the small window hatches of the warehouses. Men in leather jerkins and skull-caps were using large, metal, hand-held hooks to move the barrels, boxes and bags. They were clambering all over the ships, which were either being emptied of their freight, or loaded with new cargo.

As they approached the upper Pool, the river seemed more and more alive with activity and noise. The smell of spice, pine wood, rope and tar pervaded the air, getting ever stronger as they drew near to the old bridge. Alfred had judged it well; the tide was flowing strongly, but not enough to make it dangerous to shoot the bridge arch. We will take 'Roger Lock' he called over his shoulder, indicating with his head which of the nineteen arches he had chosen to shoot the Anna through. As they passed under the stone curve, gliding smoothly with the gentle push of water. Edwin could see men working on the bridge's cofferdams. They were repairing the heavy timbers of one of the dams, which was filled with stone pieces, earth and rocks; Edwin had never been so near before, this was the first time his father had taken him through the bridge in his boat. It was a great thrill, he knew it was a dangerous place, especially so on the Ebb tide, when the water could not easily get through the many narrow arches, and cascaded down into the Pool of London like so many waterfalls.

Once through the bridge, which they managed without incident, it was as if they had entered another river, suddenly all seemed peaceful and quiet by comparison with the activity in the Pool on the lower side of the bridge. The sounds were also different; Edwin could hear more easily the calls of the lightermen and watermen. A shallop was leaving the landing in front of Fishmongers Hall. Her Bargemaster called out to Alfred to make way for his much faster vessel. He could also hear someone calling for oars, and looking over at Old Swan Stairs, could see a well-dressed man in a red cloak standing on the causeway, signalling at them. Seeing no passengers aboard he must have thought that the wherry was for hire.
"Oars! Oars I say, over here wherryman," called the man, waving his kerchief animatedly.
"I am taken your highness," called out Alfred in reply to the man. "I am carrying goods, not bodies, this trip." The man stamped his foot in frustration at the sarcasm, and at the lack of a Wherry.

Further along, Alfred pointed to some activity over on the south side of the river.
"Look lad, they are launching the Goldsmith's barge today. She has been out of water for many weeks at Falcon Drawdock. See?" he said pointing his finger at the beautiful livery barge.
"Hard by Paris Garden Stairs, she is now finished and ready to be launched. We can pull over and take a closer look." They neared the sloping Drawdock, and gained a good view of the great barge. The vessel was held up high on a grid of stout timbers, waiting for the tide to lift her, and float her clear of the shore. Her gilding work shining in the sunlight, and the timber of her great cabin glowing with bright new paint.
"She is over three and seventy feet in length, and with eighteen men at the sweeps, she can carry sixty of the Goldsmith's Liverymen with music and victuals altogether," remarked Alfred. Edwin looked up at the great vessel in wonder.
"It was once here that the Royal Barges were once built and kept, but that was long ago," reflected Alfred. Then leaving the draw-dock behind, they pulled Anna back across the river to the river bank on the City's side, to complete the last leg of their trip.
"Ship your oar now lad, and make ready the lines, we are not far off" instructed Alfred. Edwin pulled his small oar aboard, remembering to keep the wet spoon off the seats as he had been taught, and started to coil the head line into his hand ready to throw. Alfred was now pulling strongly and they soon arrived at their destination.

The Royal Watermen were known as a haughty lot, they kept themselves very much to themselves, spending much of their time in the various Palaces where they occupied 'Grace and favour' accommodation, or at Somerset House where the Bargehouse was sited under the great building.

On reaching Somerset House, Alfred rounded the wherry into the slight flow of the flood tide, and hailed the building for instructions. A Royal Waterman, his coat unbuttoned, and without a hat, appeared on the terrace above the stone arch. He seemed to be expecting the delivery, and signalled them to come in through the great opening. Edwin's heart leapt with expectation. Alfred navigated the wherry through the entrance, manoeuvring her inside into the dark interior of the Bargehouse. As his eyes became accustomed to the sudden gloom, Edwin could see two beautiful Shallop barges moored together, alongside a set of stone landing stairs, which were cut deep into the inner wall of the building. To the left, there was a sloping beach of finely chopped chalk and fine gravel. It was here that the vessels could be grounded on a falling tide, to make repairs. Overhead were great beams with lifting gear and pulleys, there were huge amounts of rope and line stacked all about. On the landing next to the barges, stood a long rack into which were placed upright, in precise order and precision, at least two dozen sweeps, the blades showing forward, with their spoons glowing with the colours of the Royal Crest painted on them in full painstaking detail.

As Edwin and his father looked about them in wonderment, a voice called for them to come over to a smaller landing under the sterns of the Royal Barges. With a few deft strokes of his oars, Alfred brought Anna into the place indicated. As they fetched gently alongside the timber landing, another Royal Watermen, this time without any coat at all, wearing a white linen shirt with large sleeves caught in at the wrists, jumped into the wherry. Without a word he began to examine the barrels, tapping them with the butt of his knife, making sure that they were full, he paid special attention to the valuable barrels of soft soap. Seemingly satisfied he turned to Alfred and with a smile said.
"Do not take it amiss wherryman, it is my responsibility to check and test all deliveries, I must do it to all who enter here, from the highest in the land to the lowliest". He was a man in his thirties, well built and with a healthy glow to his friendly face, then looking at Edwin he said.
"Who do we have here? A young wherryman indeed". The man had a kind manner about him and Edwin liked him immediately, he smiled back. "How old are you lad," asked the man. Edwin answered saying that he was eight years, almost forgetting to add 'Sir'. Alfred explained that he had brought the boy with him, for the experience, and the opportunity of seeing inside the great barge house, he hoped he had not broken any rule by doing so. The man said it was good to see the next generation of watermen coming along, and that it was a good day to visit because the house was almost empty.
"The Royal Family have gone to Hampton Court for a month, and most of the superiors have followed them," said the man cheerfully "Even the Bargemaster is away with them. We that are left are having a well earned rest, just doing some small repairs and cleaning the barges." He looked down kindly at Alfred and then at Edwin.
"How would the two of you like to have a look around inside the palace?"

Alfred and Edwin were overjoyed at such a chance, stumbling over their words in thanking the man.

"Leave your boat here then. I will have a footman unload those barrels. Come with me." Mooring the wherry to the stout wall rings provided. Alfred and Edwin climbed out from the boat onto the landing stage. "Follow me" said their new friend and led the way through large double wooden doors, which led onto a stone staircase, this they climbed to the next floor, the man then led them along a long corridor to a door marked with the Royal Watermen's Plastron crest. As they entered the room, the man called out with mock authority.

"Stand by men, we have important visitors from the river."

There were five other men in the room, all dressed casually with their coats off and some even without their shoes. In one corner a good fire was roaring away, giving a warm glow to what otherwise would have been a cold damp space. Two men were sitting at a long wooden table; one of them leaned back in his chair.

"What is this come to visit us then? Old Father Thames and his apprentice?" he sneered. Edwin could feel his father stiffen at these unkind words. Then he heard him say in very measured tones, using a most respectful voice.

"Good morrow Sirs, thank you for allowing us this visit. I have told my son Edwin here, of the great honour that Her Majesty's Watermen enjoy, of their prowess as oarsmen and rivermen, and their known respect and help for those in the trade less fortunate than themselves." The man looked embarrassed, but Alfred went on.

"I have told him of the gifts you make to our Guild, that bring relief to the old and decayed of our fraternity. I would therefore take this rare opportunity to thank you all, on behalf of the many less privileged in our trade." The Royal Watermen in the room all stopped what they were doing and looked at Alfred in astonishment, they had not expected to hear such cultured words from a simple journeyman of the river. The man at the table looked a little sheepish, but thanked Alfred for his kind words saying. "Yes, well said. Thank you for your kindly words. We like to help the old and poor of our trade when we can."

The Waterman whom they had met with first, whose name he now told them was Job Pennel, took them to a side bench where a good display of food was laid out. There were the remains of a haunch of cold mutton and half a platter of pickled fish, to one side was a mound of crumbs and some broken slices of buckwheat bread. He bade them take their fill and sit themselves at the table; he then brought them each a pottery jug filled with ale, and sat with them at the table watching with a wide grin as they enjoyed the food.

Some of the others in the room joined them at the table, asking questions about Alfred's work and the Crossback family. Job said he had noticed that the wherry's backboard displayed some successful wagers that had been won. Edwin, proud as ever of his father's achievements, started to tell of Alfred's races. Putting a restraining hand on his son's shoulder, Alfred calmed his son's enthusiasm and changed the subject, asking the assembled their opinion of the new Royal Barge built the previous year for the Prince of Denmark.

"All that have rowed in her agree that she is a straight and true vessel, and that she runs well through the water," said Job.

"But the sweeps are still new and need to be rowed-in before we can judge her true speed", observed one of the other men.

"Mr. Hill the Royal Bargemaster likes the boat, and if he is happy, then we are all well pleased, for if he is miserable he can make life very difficult for us altogether.

The conversation then turned to the recent petition, which had been presented to the Court of Lord Mayor and Council, on behalf of their trade, particularly to an entreaty regarding the limit on the number of apprentices made in the bye-laws. Many of the men in the room did not know the detail of the document, but to their surprise Alfred produced a copy of the paper from his coat pocket, Edwin knew that his father had many unexpected friends, in semi important positions, and guessed that he had acquired the copy from one of them. Again to their astonishment, in a clear precise voice Alfred began to read the document out to them.

"By virtue of an Act of Parliament.

The Lightermen and Watermen were incorporated, and a power put in their hands to make bye laws for the good and benefit of the Company, and amongst others under-mentioned, but some are offending to our trade. This is the offending Bye Laws here written.

No waterman shall take an apprentice until he is free seven years, and then to have but one at a time, on penalty of twenty pounds.

No Lighterman to have an apprentice, until he is an owner of two lighteners or flatboats, nor but one at a time either in his own name or in the name of any other, at the penalty of twenty pounds.

None to bind an apprentice under eighteen years of age, except the son of a Waterman or Lighterman, and they to be sixteen years old, under penalty of twenty pounds.

The above bye laws tend much to hinder the increase of Watermen and Lightermen and by consequence in a few years will so decrease the number of them, that there will be but few, nor any young men to supply Her Majesty's navy on occasion, and carry on the service of the river for the benefit of the City.

For though the laws are of short date, it hath so decreased the number of Lightermen that there is not sufficient number of able men to carry on the trade, and at this time eighteen shillings per week is given for the whole year, to a journeyman that in the last war served for thirteen shillings per week.

Many more will be the mischiefs and inconveniences that will attend the government and the City, if those bye-laws are not set aside. But we will mention no more at present, least we should be too tedious".

End of petition.*
*(Extracted from The history and progress of the Watermen's Company by John Humpherus)

Alfred confirmed that the original document had been signed with the names of seven rivermen of good standing in the fraternity. A heated conversation followed, all agreeing with the petition, saying that if the bye-law was not changed it would be the ruin of the river trade. With such restriction on bringing in new young men, and the press taking them so early, only chaos would result. One man said he had heard tell of an apprentice who was taken by the press on the very day of being newly bound to his master. All agreed that an apprentice should be allowed to serve his master at least one whole year, before he could be taken for the Queen's Navy. Edwin listened to all this with a little fear in his heart, he hoped that the wars would all be over when his turn came to be apprenticed.

On discovering that Alfred could not only read but could also write a fair hand, something that none of them could do with any proficiency, the men asked if he would finish the wording of a petition they were putting together, which they intended to present to the Lord Chamberlain. It was a petition asking for an increase in the cloth allowance for Royal Watermen's uniforms. It explained that their work took a heavy toll on their livery, and that the present issue of new cloth that they were given was not enough. Alfred was happy to oblige and put his hand to writing the document.

Edwin was keen to know more about the Royal Watermen. Job, who could see that the boy was bored with the conversation, took the lad to one side and showed him the uniforms and their ornate decoration. Edwin was surprised to see that up close, the cloth of the livery was in a bad state of repair, there was much patching and mending, most of it hidden under the gilded plastrons, which the men wore to the front and back of their coats, but on the arms it was very visible when seen close to. Edwin thought that some of the damage looked as if cut by sword thrusts.
"Is it dangerous to row the Queen?" he asked. Job laughed heartily.
"It certainly was in the past," he said.
"We had a man shot while serving Elizabeth in 1581. It was said to be an accident, but that did not help the wounded waterman. Another was shot in

1586, again said to be an accident with no recourse." Edwin was intrigued by this history.

"When did the Royal Watermen first start?" asked the boy. Job pondered and then replied.

"Well nobody seems to rightly know when we were started."
"It seems that King John was taken to Runnymede by barge in 1215 to sign the Magna Carter, and that the Barons were also there in their barges". He thought for a moment then said.

"We know of Walter Fesalock who was given the appointment of keeper of London Bridge. He was the King's Bargemaster in 1385, and of John Calecote was Bargemaster to King Henry VI, and of Robert Savage who served King Henry VII, so it all goes back a long way lad." Edwin was impressed.

"Were there more accidents Mr. Pennel?" asked Edwin excitedly.
"Well yes there were" smiled Job.

"We nearly lost a Queen in 1264." Edwin's eyes opened in astonishment.
"How was that, please tell?" said the boy excited by the prospect of another story.

"Well", mused the man, "King Henry was in argument with the City fathers for not providing the money the King needed for the provisions of war", Job explained, lighting his pipe.

"He retreated to Kent and arranged to send a number of ships from the Cinque Ports to block the Thames, to prevent the City from receiving provisions. His Queen, Eleanor of Aquitaine, being resident in the Tower of London, was terrified by the neighbourhood, and of the very dangerous commotions against the King. Although defended by the Tower, she resolved to go by water to her Castle at Windsor. She called for her barge and boarded safely. However, as she approached the bridge in her gilded vessel, accompanied by her ladies-in-waiting, the populace had heard of her plan, and assembled against her. There was a general cry of 'drown the Witch' and besides abusing her with the most opprobrious language, and pelting her with rotten eggs and dirt, they had prepared large stones to sink the barge when the royal party should attempt to shoot under the bridge. At this time, the Mayor interposed for the Queen's protection, and conveyed her in safety to St, Paul's. But the barge was overturned and a Lady of the bed-chamber was drowned, also the Royal watermen say that one of their own in that crew was lost to the river."

The boy could have stayed for hours listening to the stories of these special men and their duties, but his father said that they must take their leave to catch the tide back. And so they left these privileged men in their beautiful, damp, old house. Then climbing once again aboard the Anna, they pulled out into the river and turned the boat's head down-stream. Edwin's mind still full of the sights and stories he had to tell his mother that evening. The visit had been a great success and during the pull back to Rotherhithe, Alfred had said that Edwin should keep in contact with these men. "They seemed to like you lad, and could be helpful to you in the future".

Alfred wondered who would sit on England's throne when the boy's chance of an appointment came. Some said that the Queen would soon die and that having no heir, the Kingdom would be at the mercy of the many who wanted to take control of the Throne. From what he knew of the times of the Civil War and the rule of the Dictator Cromwell, Alfred hoped that a good accession would follow Miss Carriage's demise. He hoped it would be a King. It seemed fitting for a man to be the next to reign; he would like his son to serve under a King as one of the Royal waterman, but he knew that their family was too small and probably without enough influence for Edwin to be considered. However, this day's visit might help.

Edwin finished telling the story of his visit to the Queen's barge-house. All seemed to enjoy the story, and pressed him to tell them more about life on his river, but before he could respond, a clattering of feet descending the mess-deck ladder announced the arrival of boatswain Tyson. "Pipes out! Lights out!" he cried. "Up and into your pits before yeh feel the end of me rope." There was a scramble to rig hammocks, and climb into them. The lantern was turned down to a dim glow, and the mess deck settled down for the night. Edwin lay in his hammock, his mind now back to his old life. He ached to be home again, and to see his family. Most of all he needed to talk to his father, to apologise to him for disobeying his advice, and for causing so much trouble for them all.

CHAPTER FOURTEEN

THE RACE

It was the month of February in the year 1715. Most of the Thames wherrymen had pulled their boats ashore, high out of the water, in readiness for the usual winter freeze. Alfred Crossback however, still had work with his boat. He was on hire with the Anna to a shipping company, who often employed him to deliver papers and instructions to ships moored in the river, and to take their agents off to visit the ships. The late afternoon found him wearily pulling his way towards King Stairs, to disembark his passenger. The man sitting in the boat's stern was the merchant's messenger, who had already boarded three ships in the pool to deliver documents and now wished to be put ashore. It had been a long hard day of rowing for Alfred, and the inclement weather had not helped to moderate his exhaustion. He had noticed of late that the bad weather, drained him more quickly than in earlier years. He now tired very rapidly, the least effort seem to take his last strength.

At last they reached 'King's stairs', and his passenger made ready to disembark. Alfred sat huddled against the cold wind, holding the wherry alongside the causeway with one hand on the frosty mooring post. "Do you not want paying for your efforts boatman?" inquired the passenger, Alfred had not asked for his fare, but sat at his rowing bench with shoulders hunched. The agent looked at the bent old man with some pity, the man reminded him of his own father, who had been a Lumper in the pool of London, and who, in his final year, had looked just like this frail specimen before him.
"You have earned your coin this trip, tell me, how much do I owe you?"
"Three pence, if you please sir" replied Alfred sheepishly, now realizing that he had forgotten to ask for the fare. The man paid the sum asked, and seeing that the boatman was having trouble getting to his feet, he said. "Stay seated my man; I can disembark myself without slipping." He looked again with sympathy at the wherryman.
"I think you should also finish your work this day, and go to your bed. The weather is closing in, and it is starting to snow. Enough for today is my advice, I bid you a good evening." He stepped nimbly out of the wherry, and made his way carefully along the slippery causeway to the roadway at the top.

Alfred knew that he should be pleased to have finished his work so near to his place of mooring, and should take the agent's advice and go home. However, he was feeling tired and decided to dwell a little and take a rest before putting the Anna onto her mooring. He moved himself across onto the passenger thwart with great effort, pulling another pull-on over his shoulders for extra warmth. Then settling down with his back arched over his knees, he relaxed his body into this comfortable, familiar position, and

began to think.
As always his thoughts were about his son Edwin. Where was the lad now he wondered, it had been over two years since his capture, without any word of the boy or of the ship he was aboard. Alfred had gained small pieces of information from the Admiralty Office, intelligence which indicated that the ship had been to the Caribbean Sea, that she had been in a confrontation, and was now on the homeward leg of her commission, Edwin's name was not listed as being among the dead, but the information was not confirmed and could well be false. The loss of his only son from among his small family had been a great blow to Alfred. It had affected his health, something that he had always taken for granted.
Now everything was such a great effort. He had been forced to give up his work as a fireman for the Sun insurance, and was earning less and less income as a wherryman. It was his daughter Agnes who kept a watchful eye on him. She was now happily married to her cooper, and had produced their first child, a little son Robert; this was Alfred's first and only grandson, and a rare ray of true pleasure in his morose life. It was also Agnes, who in spite of the work of her own family, kept an eye on the Anna, making sure that her repairs were kept up.

The great strength of the family had as always been Nell. She was determined that all would come well in the end, and chided her husband for his depression and lake of faith.
"Edwin will come back to us, I am sure of it. Come Alfred, where is your famed determination, we must all keep together at this time, and be ready for his return", but Alfred knew more of what happened in those ships of the Royal Navy than did his good wife. However, he kept this information all to himself, not wanting to worry his wife or daughter with his fears for Edwin's safety.

Alfred suddenly noticed that he and the boat were covered by a good inch of snow, where had the time gone? Had he slept? He thought not, but anyway he must now make his way home. He tried to move, but found that his cold body would not respond, he was fixed in this sitting position. Somehow he did not care, he had no pain, in fact it was rather pleasant to just sit here, with the soft sounds of the snow all about him.
"Father! Father, are you there?" it was the voice of Agnes, coming it seemed to Alfred, from a long way off. Another pleasant thought flitted across his mind as he began to think about his daughter, and his little grandson.
"Father is it you? I thought the boat was empty and abandoned." She was wrapped against the weather in a warm woollen cloak, and was peering down at him from the causeway through the thickening snow. "I could not see properly through this flurry." The girl stepped warily aboard, then peeling the woollen scarf away from her father's face, she peered down at him.
"Father it is time to go home, mother has hot soup ready, a full pipe for you, and a pot of hot rum, with your chair set out next to a roaring hearth. Come now, let me help you." She removed the pull-ons from his back, and half

supporting, and half lifting the heavy man, she managed to get him out of the wherry onto the causeway.

It needed all of Agnes's strength to get her father to the house, but once within hailing distance, she called out for her mother to help, Nell came out quickly, anxious to assist. Curiously she did not ask what had happened. It was as if she was half expecting such an incident. They manhandled Alfred inside, and sat him down in his fireside chair, where after a large bowl of piping hot soup, Alfred began to thaw out. The women fussed about him, with a long pipe, and a pot of his favourite rum. At last his chin began to unfreeze, and he was able to speak without his voice trembling. "Agnes! My thanks for what you did for me. I fear that I was so cold; I lost all feeling and any use of my legs. Tell me daughter, what happened to the Anna?"
"She is pulled out of the water, and is now covered over for the rest of this winter," explained Agnes.
"I sent word to Kenneth to put her safely away. He will do the work properly for you. Sit back and enjoy the evening with us all together." Alfred sat back in his chair stretching his legs out to enjoy the warmth of the fire. He had noticed of late that he could not seem to get warm, however much he wore, or how scorching the fire might be.
"There will be no more river work for you Mr. Crossback, until the spring is well in attendance, I will see to that altogether." It was the voice of Nell coming from the stove, and both Agnes and Alfred knew by her tone, that she meant every word of what she said.

<========>

Mr. Doggett was hard at work with the plans for his wager. He had just returned from the printer with an armful of pamphlets. These declared that. A wager race was to be organized by Mr. Thomas Doggett Esq. It would be held on the Thames in honour of His Majesty's first anniversary. The prize for the race would be an orange-red coat and a badge of silver. It would be rowed on the first day of August of this year of our Lord 1715, the anniversary of The King's ascension, to celebrate a most successful year as King of this great land, and would be held in perpituity thereafter. The course would be from the Old Swan stairs near London Bridge, to the Swan Inn stairs at Chelsea. A pull of four miles and five furlongs. The wager would be open only to young watermen, who have become free of their masters within the year. The race would be prepared and judged by Mr. Doggett himself, and all the rules and constitutions as set out would be strictly observed.

Thomas had organized everything. He had arranged to hire a four oared shallop, from which he would judge the race, plus two four oared cutters, which would be used to carry his special guests. It was early in the year, and Doggett sincerely hoped that he might have time to get a Royal personage to attend his wager. If so, he would rearrange matters so that the shallop, with the comfort of its tilt, would be given over to the royal party and he would administer the race from one of the cutters. On making enquires in certain quarters however, he had been told that the King was not a lover of the water, and was indeed averse to using small boats, also that his majesty would probably be out of the country for the remainder of the year. Even so, Thomas still hoped that perhaps he might be able to attract someone from the Royal household. He intended to broadcast the event over the next months, and hoped that with his playhouse contacts, and knowledge of the theatrical, he would be able produce a good turnout on the day.

The watermen's guild had shown a little interest in the event, but as it was only to be held between young men in the first year of their freedom, the feeling of the rulers was that there would be limited gaming on such an affair, and therefore small reward for the company's involvement. Some of the overseers voiced the opinion that the wager would fizzle out within a year or two, as the contestants would always be virtually unknown to the gaming fraternity. Others however, thought it a good idea to hold a wager for untried oarsmen. All the best Thames wagers were dominated by a few men who devoted their time to winning purses, leaving the ordinary watermen with little chance of gaining a prize. It was eventually decided that the company would give tentative support, and see if the event would stand the test of time. The race was after all, only being held to honour the present King, therefore, what would happen when a new monarch came to the throne. They all smiled at Doggett's insistence that the wager would always be held on 1st August, and would continue forever.

Doggett was unperturbed by the misgivings of others. He now had the bit between his teeth, and was not a man to give up easily. He had already spent more than had been his intention on this wager, but somehow all the pieces of the event seemed to fit so well together, it made him feel as if a greater hand were assisting him. He was determined to show those doubting Thomas's that his wager would be a success, and that it would survive.

Word had been sent out about the race, to all the plying stairs along both banks of the river, and Doggett had visited many of the stairs himself, explaining the rules and reason for them. The remarks that came back indicated that the idea was well liked by the journeymen, although there were some criticisms. Some said it was too long a race for young men, others said that so many would qualify, that it would take weeks to whittle the number of competitors down to only six. Doggett checked with the clerk to the watermen's guild, who confirmed that some 500 men completed their apprenticeship each year. After more thought on this aspect of the wager, Doggett decided that he would not falter in his commitment to his initial rules. The course would stay between the two Swans. He argued that the long distance might deter some of the 500 men who could qualify. However, regarding the problem of finding only six competitors from among so many, he decided to leave the matter to chance. He would hold a draw one month before the date of the race, which would determine the six young men who would compete.

The silver badge, weighing twelve ounces had been designed, to depict 'Liberty', the white horse of Hanover. The work of making it up was with a good silversmith. The cost of the completed badge would be five pounds. The cloth for the coat had been chosen, and had cost eighteen shilling, it was now with the tailor in readiness. With the buttons and appurtenances, the making would cost one guinea. The attending boats had been promised, Mr. Burt of the Admiralty Office had promised to help with the management of the race. Tony Aston could not be found, he was probably abroad, or in the clink for debt, thought Doggett, smiling to himself at the memory of his rascally friend. However, Mr. Wilks and Mr. Cibber, late joint managers with Doggett of Drury Lane, were assisting with the promotion of the occasion, so all the arrangements were in place. Doggett was still hoping to persuade a Royal presence to grace the event. He also hoped for the attendance of as many of the highest in the Whig party as could to attend. In all Mr. Thomas Doggett was pleased with himself. Even if the thought of the cost of it all made him flinch.

<========>

The month was now March. This year it was as windy, and as cold as ever it had been. Alfred had taken to sleeping in his chair by the fire each night, in an attempt to keep himself warm. He had not stirred from the house since that night when Agnes had brought him home. His good wife Nell worried over him incessantly, spending most of her time trying various remedies and preparations to make him well again, but she could see that in spite of her best efforts, her man was declining little by little, day by day. Agnes was equally worried about her father, and spent much of her time at her parents house. By day she would bring the baby Robert, which cheered up Alfred. He would hold the baby on his knee, telling him tales of the river, and of the watermen's history, none of which the one year old could comprehend, but he cooed and smiled as if enjoying the stories, his bright little eyes and chubby limbs enchanting Alfred.

One evening Agnes had come on her own, leaving the baby with her husband. After the evening meal, which Alfred had eaten while sitting by the hearth, from a plate on his lap. The women began to clear away the dishes and tidy the room. Quietly, Alfred called to them from his chair. "Mrs. Crossback, Agnes, I want you to come and sit by me, I have something I would say to you both". Nell continued to fiddle with the clearing of her table, fumbling the knives and platters away into their places, as if in avoidance of an unwanted conversation with her husband, but at last, she settled down in the chair on the opposite side of the hearth to her spouse, and Agnes sat on a small bench between her parents.

"I have recently looked into the face of death" said Alfred somewhat dramatically," and I would talk with you both about your future without me." Both women started to say something, but Alfred held up a hand to stop them.

"I know that it is an uncomfortable subject, but I fear it is necessary." He paused as if listening to a voice inside his head, and then continued. "I always hoped that Edwin would take over the helm of the Crossback's family from me, but of that we can not now be sure", He leaned forward and took his wife's hand in his.

"Good wife Mrs. Crossback, you have been my main mast, and my strongest sail, since we first met on that fortuitous day, and married together for our life's voyage. I want you to know that I could not have had a more compassionate or happier support to my doleful life, than your cheerfulness and inner strength. Between us, we have no need to say the words. My deepest feelings are known to you, just as yours are known to me. I will leave you provided for Nell, I have coin put away as you know. You must use it as you see fit, I know I can rely on your prudence." Nell started to say something, but Alfred again held up his hand to stop the words. The woman closed her mouth tight, letting her tears run unchecked down her checks. Alfred turned to his daughter.

"Agnes, you have wed yourself to a good man, who though is not of the watermen's trade, can as a Cooper support you well, a trade with perhaps sounder expectations than ours of the river. I see a happy future for you both. The happiness I have enjoyed in having known my little grandson is beyond my use of words. Thank you my dear for all you have done for me." He smiled at his daughter; she smiled back at him through her tears. Alfred continued.

"I have concentrated much effort on Edwin in my teachings and guidance, but I have seen that you are the most like me in your ways. It pleases me to think that my vigilance, and caution of life's traps, will be handed on through you, to yours." Agnes lifted her apron up to her face to wipe away her tears. Alfred noticed the show of emotion, but continued without comment.

"It is my hope that Edwin will one day return. He and I parted on unhappy terms, which saddens me in my thoughts every day. I now know that I will not live to see him, or that I will be acquainted with his children. I now realize that my punishment for my carelessness is never to see him again. It is the burden I will take with me to the grave. If he returns, I would ask you to tell him of my love and forgiveness, and say that I felt sure that I have his pardon for not protecting him well enough. That will be my solace." Alfred stopped, as if thinking his next words through carefully.

"It is my concern, that if Edwin returns, he will need much help. I wish therefore for him to have the Anna, and through her, to make a good life for himself with Mary." He looked tenderly at the tear stained faces of his small family.

"If however he does not return, then sell Anna, and divide up the profit between you." Again he paused. Then attempting to lift their spirits a little, he continued on a new tack.

"There has been much more in my years that I have enjoyed, than I have had to endure, and that is the most any man can expect from life. Like all men, I can not escape the consequences of existing in this harsh world, and as my time draws to a close, it pleases me that I have this chance to tell you of my love, and of the pleasure you have both given me, in spite of my sometimes sombre nature". Alfred's eyes seemed to brighten as if thinking of pleasant times.
"I am of late reminded much of my father. I remember that he once explained the sequence of a man's existence to me," Alfred mused over the words in his head, wrinkling his brow as if struggling to remember them.
"He told it thus, through a waterman's understanding of London's river and the tides."
"A riverman is intimately in tune with his watery trade. Each day as the time of the tide slips a little later on the hour, so a watermen's internal time compensates. They can feel the river's being in their very blood. For them the tide is like the cycle of life itself.

When the flood tide's life begins to swell along the riverbanks, it is the birth of a newborn tide; it is the feeling of life beginning.
They watch the first movements of the anxious little wavelets running along the water's edge, they likened it to a small happy infant, playing ahead of the main body of water. This is the healthy young child of the tide's life. They say. 'the tide is making'.
There follows a stronger push of water, investigating more deeply in and out of all the nooks and crannies of the river's banks, the many creeks, streams, as it courses along on its inquiring way. This is likened to the behaviour of an inquisitive juvenile. They call this 'The young flood'
Then comes the full bore of water, it comes with power, energetic, inevitable and unstoppable. It has all the thrusting arrogance of a strong young man. 'The full flood'.
When this exuberance is spent, and the river is full, there comes that time of confidence and abundance, of a man in his prime. Full, proud, arrogantly contented with himself. High and wide. 'The top of the tide'
After this will be a short, composed, period, just as a man will experience in his contemplative, prime years of life. The knowing that he has reached his zenith, and that a change is coming, that a turn of circumstance is due. Now begins the ebb, slow at first, but also inevitable. It is relentless. It will gain in speed, as undeniable as the ageing process itself, but unlike the flood tide, as it gains in pace it has an air of loss mixed with it, an inevitable diminishing of assurance. A decline of confidence, like that which bedevils a man after his prime, when little by little, his influence drains away. Just as the river is now laden with the detritus of the City, the middle aged man is also burdened down, carrying his worries and responsibilities as the river does its debris.
As the tide now runs out, like an ageing man, old-man Thames slowly slips away, revealing an unattractive body, the unconcealed mud, clutter and dross of the shoreline. Like life itself, the tide finally comes to a feeble halt, as in the ignominious death of an wizened old fellow, inevitably beaten

down by powers and subtle forces of which the young are not even aware. At low water the river is small and thin, a pale shadow of its former self. Its tributaries, creeks and feeder streams all now on show, uncovered, like the exposed, picked and scattered bones of a dead body.
But unlike man, the river will be regenerated by the pull of an unearthly body. The Moon, the Night Goddess, brings vitality back again with a new tide, her life giving force revitalizing the water of the river.
So continues the rhythm of the eternal renewal of the Thames, to revive the City and its population". Alfred's voice was trailing off.
"But I think my father mistaken. A man is also renewed, he is reborn through his children, and through the children of his children, and that is a happier thought indeed."
Alfred's head dropped onto his chest, he was suddenly asleep. Nell got up and rested his head back more comfortably onto a soft pillow; she pulled the blanket over him, tucking it under his cold legs. His breathing seemed regular, if a little shallow, so the women decided to let him sleep. Agnes stoked up the fire, and they left the room to the sleeping man, and to the quiet crackle of the hearth.

<========>

The ship had a favourable wind in her sails as she headed towards the Thames estuary. Edwin was at the helm, he was very proud to be in control of the ship as they sped towards the land, and was enjoying himself holding her onto the given course. Since he had lost his foot and was excused normal duties, it seemed to Edwin that Lieutenant Frobisher had given him much notice. The Lieutenant had taken him in hand, and had gone out of his way to help the lad. instructing him in navigation and ship handling. After some time spent observing the young Thamesman, the Lieutenant had started asking him questions, these were of a general knowledge nature, and it seemed to Edwin, had nothing to do with the sea or ships of the line. However they served a purpose for Mr. Frobisher. In fact, the Lieutenant had closely observed Edwin even before the accident, there was something about the young man that intrigued him. There was the way he had of doing things that showed he could use his brain, the lad always seemed to work out the most efficient way of going about a particular task, even in his everyday duties.

On one occasion the boatswain had ordered him to lash-down the great fresh water barrel, which was positioned in a timber cradle just clear of the ship's centre hold. He noticed that Edwin had not just replaced the lines that held the barrel, and which were prone to work loose, or could wear through from the movement, but that he had walked around the barrel, looking closely to find the reason why the lines had come away. He watched as Edwin had closely examined the lead of the lines, and looked carefully at the direction a sea might come on board to strike the keg, making it move it on its cradle, and causing the lines to work loose. He then set about redoing the whole job. Frobisher guessed that he was considering the problem from a small boatman's point of view, The seamen had used leads which although strong, were difficult to adjust, and had to be completely undone before they could be made tighter. Edwin had eventually used a piece of boarding net, stretched over the barrel, with an arrangement of lines to keep it in place. This arrangement held just as well, but the lines were quick and easy to adjust. He rearranged the net and the lead of the lines so that they would take the strain from any direction that the sea might come aboard to strike the keg.

"These rivermen do things in a more subtle way that my seamen", thought the Lieutenant.

"They seem a little less ruthless in their work than the naval crew. Most likely because of the way they learn to moor their boats for both the ebb, and flood tides of the Thames." He had noticed when in the port of London, that the wherrymen moored up their boats with gentle springs and bridles, which nursed their fragile vessels while at rest, keeping them out of harms way.

The finished tie-down of the keg, was a much-improved system, and made the barrel more secure in its cradle. If a green acre from the sea was to hit from any direction now, the net with its new line arrangement would brace against the force. Edwin had called the boatswain over to check that he was satisfied with the new arrangements. After a little tugging and pushing, Tyson pronounced that they would give the new lashings a full trial in the next storm, and that Edwin would be responsible if the ship's water barrel was lost overboard.

After the mishap with the cannon, which the Lieutenant conceded was not the fault of Edwin's gun crew, he had decided that even without a foot, the lad still had potential, and thought to try him out at the ship's helm. Edwin had taken to this new job like a duck to water. For him the ship was like a larger version of his Anna. He could feel the ship's movements through his body in the same way as with his wherry.

He had rowed with his father many times down river to where the water rolled into longer troughs and stands, and had felt how the boat had behaved differently to the way it responded to the shorter chop of the upriver water. Steering this great ship through different wave formations was similar. For Edwin, coaxing the ship along was like handling a large friendly animal, he had no fear of the vessel and gave no thought to her great size, Many helmsmen were fearful, and wrestled with the ship that they were steering. It was often a hate relationship, they were determined to dominate the huge beast, trying to force her to their will, Edwin's way was different, he nursed the ship, predicting her every move, and making his countering adjustments early, almost before she moved off from her course. Even with only one good foot, he felt the ship's movements alive through his legs, as she strained to the pressure of the wind, as if trying to the push the sea away. Each list or yaw fed fresh information through Edwin's body and into his brain, to which he responded seemingly without thought. Now after three months of his new responsibility he was one of the best steersman aboard.

Lieutenant Frobisher could see that the lad was a natural at handling the ship. He noticed that Edwin seemed to correct the ship's run with the smallest movement of the helm, without even realizing that he was doing it. As she moved a little off course, he admired the way the lad would handle the helm just enough to keep her on the correct heading. It was a rare gift, and he had seen it in only a few people. This was the sort of helmsman he would like to have at the wheel in a sea battle. He decided that he must find a way of keeping this lad in the navy; he would be most useful, even with a missing foot.

Edwin's throat was tight with excitement. His river, the Thames, was ahead of him. Memories and emotions came rushing back, with the familiarity of feeling for the old river. His mind ran over his past working life, he knew that although he had changed in so many ways, and that he now quite liked the life at sea, he was still a riverman at heart. To him the water of the Thames was alive, it was a living being.

He liked the ancient idea of the old religion, that revered the river as a god, the great worm dragon that was all important to the area, not only to the watermen who earned their living on its fickle surface, but also to the inhabitants of its fertile valley, and to the people of the London City, for whom it brought trade and prosperity. The city itself owed its very existence to the beneficent water-monster which flowed through its centre. The breathing movement of the beast's tides in and out of London gave a beat to the very life of the area, especially to the City and its population. The citizens of London were very aware of their river.

The watermen used the power of the tides in their everyday business. It was less effort for them to travel with the flow than to row against it. The most obvious service to do this was the "Long Ferry" from London to Gravesend. This downriver ferry service had started back in the mists of time, each vessel would take it in turn to go in a strict rotation, on the turn of the tide, when the flow changed from flood to ebb. It was said that the Long Ferries, which had for centuries rowed from the old City down to Gravesend, and always left at high water after the tide turn, had produced the common usage of the word "turn" as used in "your turn to do something". It was claimed to have come from the boatmen's idiom, and the river's tide turns. The Master of the long ferry would call out for passengers, telling them that the next turn of the tide would be his. My 'turn' to leave the City for Gravesend. At first glance it was easy to be sceptical about this claim, but when considered carefully, it is difficult to think of a better explanation for this curious usage of the word. Certainly the sailors and seamen who knew many strange languages, none of which had a similar expression, did not dispute the claim.

The Long Ferrymen of Gravesend were a strange, close-knit group, with an extensive river history of independence and rivalry. They kept themselves to themselves, always away from the London watermen, who they considered to be against them. When in London, they only used certain inns, taverns and alehouses, which were frequented by their own kind. They were descendants of the old tribes of Kent, based among the chalk cliffs of the south side of the lower Thames, this bank of the river differing so dramatically, from its rival on the north shore. The two sides of the river were like opposing countries, the south side being dry and warm, with rolling hills, farms and grazing sheep, while the north side, seeming cold and windswept, with wide, open, flat, marshlands. The London watermen did not normally go near the Long-ferrymen unless forced to do so for business reasons. They called the Gravesend men 'Chalkies', a nickname used in the same way as 'Uppers' and 'Lowermen', the names given to men working upriver, or downriver, of London.

It was quite alarming to observe the way the Chalkies would ferociously protect their traditional rights. When necessary, they could work out to the last part of a farthing, the division of the fares between themselves, and the crew of a subservient London tilt-boat, which if there was trade enough, would travel with the Long Ferry to Gravesend, transporting the 'Superiors', the higher fare paying passengers. These six oared Shallops, although faster and offering some protection to their passengers from bad weather by a tilt, were the more expensive option to take, than the open Long Ferry boat with its huddled passengers, its partial cargo, and sometimes even the companionship of the odd sheep. However, the Long Ferry owned the 'turn' by historical precedent, and had the right of passage. A Tilt boat must therefore pay over a percentage of its takings, to the Long Ferry's crew, this being only necessary however, if the ferry was not completely full. It was truly a mystery to the London waterman, as to the way all this worked out, or how and when it had started. Like so many things to do with London and its river, the long ferry's origins were lost in the long past history of the old City and its waterway.

Edwin sniffed the air, he could now smell the land, it was the scent of England. He had seen many places in the last years, but none as fair as his homeland. His heart was leaping with the joy of it. He was at last on his way home, and would soon be with his Mary, ready to take up again with her the plans they were making for their life together, before he was so ruthlessly taken away from his love. He was not as complete a man as he had been, but more or less intact. Now that he was maimed, and without a foot, he would never again be taken for impressment, yet he could still row for his living. He trusted against all hope, that all was well at home, and that the Anna would still be his to use when he returned. Edwin had not been able to send any word of the misfortune he had suffered in losing a foot, he wondered what they would think of it. Would Mary still want him? He somehow felt sure of her love and support, and that of his family. He was surely lucky to have such good people always at his side.

The ship came into the estuary of the Thames, running before a good wind, as if in a hurry herself to get her young helmsman home as soon as was possible. They soon reached the fork in the waters where the river Medway split off from the Thames on the port hand. The officer of the watch had decided to turn a blind eye to the crowded decks of the ship, and so everyone who could find the slightest reason to be on deck was there, eager to see the land approaching them. The entire crew was manning both sides of the ship as they entered the Thames proper, particularly the watermen. The 'uppers' from the upriver towns of the river, and the 'lowermen' from places like Greenwich and Woolwich, but it was the chalkies who were predominant, straining to get the first glimpse of their home town of Gravesend.

The ship worked her way up the narrowing river, passing places and villages, which to Edwin and many others on board, were as well known as their own family. Edwin wondered what feelings would be passing through the Chalkies as they looked over at the passing land. They would have to stand and watch as they passed their homes at Cliff and Gravesend. The temptation to jump over the side and swim ashore must be unbearable. A sweep of excitement ran through the men looking over the port side. They could see the spires of Gravesend. Edwin remembered the old Teutonic name for the town, Graefin Sand, (Barons' Beach). It was here, on the only suitable sandy shoreline in the area, that throughout history, invading armies led by foreign noblemen, would beach their ships, to prepare themselves and make ready to attack London. Perhaps thought Edwin, that is why even to this day, there is such hostility between the London watermen and the chalkies, who were said to have always helped these attackers, in their desire to devastate the city.

The ship sped on; they next came in sight of the town of Erith. It was here that Edwin was relieved at the wheel by the Captain's favourite helmsman, a seaman by the name of Pennyford. Edwin had struck up a friendship with this coxswain, and had learnt much of his life story. The man had been born on a farm, in a small village, in the county of Devon. He had started his working life at the age of seven years, helping as a farm-hand, but at fifteen he was taken for impressment by a marauding naval gang. He had found that he had a liking for the life of a seaman, and had risen through the ranks to become a top helmsman, acquiring a high standing as the best coxswain on every ship on which he served.

As the new man took over, Lieutenant Frobisher noticed immediately the different hand on the helm, and looked around to see what had caused the change. The ship was now much more restrained in her movements, more strictly controlled, pulled back very firmly, allowing her only a little of each run that she tried to make, she would be heaved back onto her course by a strong, unforgiving hand, but thought the Lieutenant, a hand without sensitivity.

Finally they approached their anchorage at Woolwich, and with a neat piece of seamanship Pennyford turned the ship into the wind, and brought her to a stop facing into the flood tide, ready to drop anchor in Galleons Reach. To a man, the ship's crew were overjoyed to be ending their long commission. It showed in their ready smiles, and in their eagerness to finish their tasks. All were no doubt thinking of someone ashore with whom they would soon be reunited. The ship's cutter was quickly put over the side, for the Captain to go ashore to receive the ship's orders. Edwin was down below in the mess deck, making up his hammock and packing his sea-bag. His watch was to be given first leave, and he wanted to be aboard the very first boat to go ashore. The captain returned within the hour, and Edwin's watch was called to muster on the main deck. Each man was duly signed off, and the captain bad them all a gracious farewell, saying that he had found them a sound crew, and that he was sorry not to be giving them notice of prize money. He finished by saying that he hoped to see them again, perhaps aboard his next ship. Then piling into the ship's boats, laughing and joking like little boys let out to play, they were pulled across to the shore and climbed up the stone steps, cut deeply into the river wall, there for the first time in months, to set foot at last on solid land,.

Edwin had to be supported and helped up the steps to the roadway above. His legs felt very strange without the ship's movements under them, and what with his wooden peg adding to his unsteadiness, it was a good ten minutes before he felt confident enough to walk without holding on to the wall. His limp seemed much worse on land than it had been aboard ship. He tried a new version of his swinging gait, endeavouring to make a more natural look to his walk. It would not do to arrive home with an exaggerated limp.

"Crossback! Over here." It was Hobbs, one of the upper Thamesmen, standing next to a large wheeled wagon across the road from the quay, now surrounded by some of his other shipmates.

"We are offered a ride to London in this cart, for thrupence each. It will pass through Rotherhithe and we can drop you there on our way." Edwin hobbled over to the cart, and was pulled aboard by willing hands to sit on the soft sacks of wool that the cart was carrying. As the wagon rolled off, the men began to sing a cheery sea shanty, picking up the rhythm of the cart's wheels, as it bumped and rolled its way along the road towards the City.

<========>

It was now the end of July, and Thomas Doggett was even more busy that usual. It seemed to him that each day was more filled with things to do than the one before. Why was it that even when by the end of a day, all matters were seemingly settled and put in place, by the very next morning he was faced with a fresh array of problems, and now time had run out. The day of his race was almost upon him.

"Could nobody do anything for themselves? Why did he have to look into every little thing?" If he were to be honest with himself, he of course knew the answer. The truth of it was that he did not trust anyone to organize his wager, insisting on his personal involvement in every little detail. Only one thing had not been achieved, and it saddened him somewhat. He was now resigned to the fact that nobody of high importance was to attend, but no matter, he would say to himself. It was their loss. The race was like a mission to him, for some reason he felt driven to make a success of the event, nothing would detract him, he would check into every detail. The six competitors had been chosen by ballot. The coat was with the tailor for final fitting. The silver badge was magnificent, only needing the winner's name to be inscribed by the silversmith. The oarsmen would provide their own wherries, but Doggett had inspected each one, to be sure that they were all matched. His shallop and the other vessels following were ordered and standing by. The publicity had produced a sound response, and many hundreds were expected to witness the race. Only one more day to go, and Mr. Doggett's Coat and Badge wager would take place. A race that would be continued forever. He felt sure of it.

<========>

The wagon reached Rotherhithe and Edwin bad an emotional farewell to his shipmates. He remembered Patrick's words, it was true that he had got to know these men so well, that they were like brothers to him, and parting, probably never to see them again, made the moment poignant as he stood and waved the wagon out of sight. He decided to go to Mary's house first, as that was on his way to his home. However, on knocking at the door he was surprised for it to be opened by a strange woman. On inquiring about Mary's family, he was told that the candle maker had moved away, and that he had gone to live in Canterbury. The woman said however, that the daughter Mary had stayed on, and now lived with Nell Crossback. He thanked her for the information and hurried on to his family home. At last he came to the house, whistling his recognition pipe as he approached, and shouting a greeting before reaching the door. Nell suddenly appeared on the doorstep wiping her hands on her ever present apron. "Edwin! Edwin! Is it you? Can I believe my old eyes? Are you home at last? But you are limping, what have they done to your foot?" Before he could make any reply, she engulfed him in an enormous hug. No words were needed. Edwin knew that at last he was home.

"Come inside Edwin we have much to tell each other. Mary is living here with me now. She will be home soon from her work. You will be proud of her achievements she is a fine seamstress." Edwin noticed his mother's face darken with a sad contemplation, he looked at her quizzically. Guessing what he was about to ask her, she ushered him inside, and sat him down at the kitchen table, seating herself on the opposite side. She looked intensely into his eyes.
"Edwin, I have dreadful news, which must be told immediately, although I fear it will mar the joy of your homecoming." He looked into his mother's cheerless face, dreading what she might tell him next, then guessing at the worst news possible that she might acquaint him with, he held his breath. "My son, your father has passed away, he died some months ago, and we had no way of telling you, other than sending a communication through the

admiralty office, which, although we did so, we were informed it would not reach you within a full year."

Edwin felt the room spin, his senses were hit by a great cloud of loss. All the joy of his homecoming melted away. He slumped his head heavily on to the table.
"I wanted to tell him so much, we parted on a discord, which has concerned me ever since. How was it with him mother?" he asked.
"He died of exposure. The worry of losing you to the press, played on his mind, and he did not take proper care of himself when out in the boat. Agnes found him one day frozen stiff, just sitting in the Anna. She brought him home, and we nursed him, but the cold had entered his bones, he could never get himself warm again after that. He died in his sleep, here in his chair during the night. I found him the next morning. He had a smile on his face, and looked in death, ten years younger; I do not think he suffered." She took up Edwin's hand.
"Your father wanted you to know, that he too was miserable at the way you parted, but laid no blame on you for that. His only hope was that you would come home to us, and take up your life again. He has made arrangements for you to take over from him with the Anna." Edwin asked if he might go to his room, and be alone with his thoughts for a while.
"Yes, of course my dear, I have kept your room for you, the same as always. Go and clean up and gather your thoughts. Mary will be home shortly from her sewing work. What fun it will be when she sees you! Go and make ready." Edwin climbed up to his attic room with a mixture of feelings, a deep sadness at the loss of his father and mentor, and joy at the prospect of seeing his Mary again.

"Edwin! Edwin! Come quick, she is coming, I can see her at the end of the road". It was his mother calling from the doorway of the house, where she had bee watching out for Mary's return. Edwin came clattering down the stairs, and out into the roadway, then seeing Mary he began a hop-step-and jump run, stumbling to meet her, forgetting all his intentions to hide his infirmaty as much as possible and to present himself upright on two feet,. He lurched and staggered, striving along the road at the best speed he could manage, to his love.

"Edwin! Is it really you? God be praised you are safe and home again". They fell into each other's arms, Edwin relying heavily on her for support. She had of course noticed his strange stuttering hobble.
"What have they done to you my love?" Then before he could answer. "Never mind for now, all that matters is that you are home, you can tell of your adventures later. Come, let us go inside, before the neighbours come out, and keep you from me even longer with their questions." Then with more cuddles and kisses, they went inside the house to join the smiling Nell, who had now arranged large pots of hot-spiced wine, which were waiting for them on the table. Nell had sent word to Agnes with the news of Edwin's return, and soon his sister arrived with her husband and the baby,

who was soon bouncing on Edwin's knee as if they had always known each other.

That evening as they were about to sit down for a splendid meal, prepared by Nell and Agnes, there came an urgent knocking at the door. Nell opened up and was almost pushed over by Kenneth's great frame bounding through.
"Is it true?" He exclaimed as he burst into the room. Then setting his eyes on his friend sitting at the table.
"You rogue! You scoundrel! You are indeed back from the dead, and I am the better for seeing you again." Edwin got to his feet and the two men embraced, slapping each other on the back.
"Well! And what have we all been worrying about? You look as fit as a butcher's dog". Then noticing Edwin's strange stance.
"Or do I speak too soon? I detect a list to port. Are you damaged during your absence? But before Edwin could start to explain Nell interrupted the men.
"Come Kenneth, sit and join us, we have plenty of food to share, and we are all anxious to hear of Edwin's adventures". And so with the wonderful meal of roast capon, buttered carrots and parsnips, accompanied by several jugs of good clean beer, Edwin sat contentedly with the people closest to him in the whole world, and slowly unwound his story, explaining how he was lucky to have lost only a foot and not his life altogether. He had to repeat several times the parts about the battle, and the island with the plague, at the insistence of Kenneth, his friend being entirely impressed and fascinated by Edwin's adventures.
"Tell me Edwin, were there many other Thames watermen on the ship" asked Kenneth.
"Did they catch only me on that night at Bess's tavern?
"No to be sure, they caught five, but all except you had papers excusing them impressment. The officer in charge was not pleased that the ruse he had arranged with Bess, had caught only one fish. Be assured Edwin, the lads and I, with some help from the tavern maids, have made Bess pay dearly for her deceit in this business. She will be relieved to see you safe, and will be pleased to make amends, in the hope of us stopping our persecution." Kenneth was keen to hear more of Edwin's narrative, but the women were less enthralled with all the dangers he had endured, they were only pleased that at last he was home, and therefore changed the subject to home matters and future plans. The celebration of his homecoming went on long into the night.

The next morning Edwin rose late, he came down to the kitchen to find that Mary had already been to her employer to explain her good news, and had been given the day off to be with him. Nell gave Edwin a leather purse, saying.
"Your father left this money for you to celebrate with a home coming meal. Now be off with you both from under my feet and spend it together, I have the feeling that Alfred will be watching over you. Edwin surveyed the two

women before him.

"Mother, Mary, I can not tell you how I have dreamed of being home again, of seeing my river once more. I had hoped to be working with father in the Anna. I now know that I will never again hear his special whistle, and can not work with him any more, but Mother, I too have the feeling that he is watching over me."

The couple decided to spend the day visiting the City. Edwin was keen to see the river, the pool, and the old bridge.
"Come then," said Mary. "Let us go to the smoky city and see the sights." They left the house and were lucky to find Mr. Knight preparing his cart with a load of dry goods, for delivery to Westminster.
"I would be pleased to drop you off at the bridge on my way," he said observing Edwin's limp, but making no comment. They climbed onto the cart and were soon bumping along on their way. Edwin had the feeling that his bones were jiggering about inside the skin of his body. They laughed as they tried to speak, their words staggering out of their mouths in a jumble of speech.
"Travel by river is still a more comfortable ride, so business should be good for wherrymen," he whispered as best he could into Mary's ear, making her smile.

They arrived at the south side of the bridge and asked Mr. Knight to let them off.
"I will be passing this way later in the afternoon." He promised. "I will look out for you, to take you home to your good mother Nell." They thanked him, and as he drove off towards the west, Mary whispered.
"I think Mr. Knight is willing if Nell would be. He often asks about Nell's welfare whenever he meets me in the village." Edwin snorted his disapproval at the very thought of his mother remarrying.

Standing on the approach to the bridge, they looked about them with growing exhilaration. It seemed that there were people everywhere.
"There must be something special on today," said Mary. "The last time I was here, a foreign King's ship was visiting the Pool, and the Royal Barge rowed down to attend him. Perhaps it is another such visit." She suggested. Edwin was in no hurry to cross the bridge yet, he wanted to savour this moment of his first sight of London for nearly three years.
"We will take a look at the Pool later, but first I would see if there are any changes here at Southwark." Then remembering something he said.
"Father once told me that when the old Romans built the first bridge here long, long, ago, they stationed a small garrison of solders on this side, to protect the southern approach to their city of Londinium. That garrison was called the 'South Works' and over the centuries, the name has slowly changed to Southwark. Around that garrison grew up a village community to provide for the needs of the soldiers, and so the entertainments and amusements that we still see today, and now call 'the stews', all started back

then. Mary, it is as old here at Southwark as the City itself." He gazed about himself enjoying the sights, sounds, and smells that he had so much missed.

"Mary, let us to the Rose Garden Inn. I was taken there by father after my freedom was granted by the Watermen's Company. It will be a fitting place to spend his coin on the meal he wanted for us. Let's see if they still serve the food the old fashioned way on Trenton loaf bottoms." They walked the short distance along Tolly Street, and entered the inn. Memories of his father flooded back immediately, he could feel his father's presence in this place, it was a most pleasant feeling. They sat in a window seat overlooking the river and watched the busy chaos below them that was the port of London. A young tavern maid came to the table to ask their wishes. Edwin ordered them a meal of roast beef, with hot soused greens and roast parsnips. Do you know how they make Trenton bread?" he asked Mary. The girl shook her head, a little shy and subdued by being in such a public place. "The baker bakes a special loaf on the hot floor of his oven, he then cuts off the 'upper crust' which goes to the wealthy houses and rich people as soft bread. The bottom flat dish of the loaf, is then used as a plate for holding food, it soaks up the gravy and is most delicious to eat."

The meal arrived and they set about it with relish. When the first course was finished, he ordered large helpings of suet pudding covered with thick sweet honey. Then after the meal, to finish with, Edwin called for a long pipe of tobacco, and a hot chocolate drink for Mary. They sat talking for a good hour making plans for the future. Finally Edwin paid the bill, adding an extra coin from his father's money, saying to the smiling tavern maid. "This is in memory of my father, who was a good man."

They left the inn in a happy mood, deciding to walk over the bridge, by using the pathway on the down river side, from where they would gain a good view of the river from between the houses as they passed. Finding an opening large enough to walk into, they looked down at the array of ships, dumb-boats and lighters below, all busy loading or discharging cargo. "No sign of a royal ship, or the King's Barge here," said Edwin, a little disappointed.
"Perhaps something is happening on the upriver side of the bridge," suggested Mary. They returned to the roadway and picked their way between the carts and carriages crossing over the bridge to the pathway on the up riverside, and there came to the opening between the Chapel and the bridge's lifting section. A crowd of people were milling about, looking over the side at the water below. The couple pushed their way forward to the edge, and looked down. The river was full of small boats carrying an assortment of people. In the centre of this melee, six young men in their shirtsleeves were pulling their wherries into a line, abreast of the Fishmongers' Hall. In the front of this building were even more people watching the event, which was obviously the start of a wager race. Edwin turned to the man standing next to him, who seemed to be getting quite

excited by this occasion.
"My pardon Sir, but what is this race, is it for a special reason?
"Yes indeed, it is for the King's first year, they will race from here to Chelsea village, for a red coat and silver badge." Edwin looked down again at the men lining up for the start; they all seemed very young and fresh for such a long race.

A man in a red cloak was standing in the bow of a shallop, calling to the oarsmen through a brass loud hailer. The man seemed to be the organizer, and look somehow familiar. He was calling the men forward, and insisting on a straight line up. Two cutters were ahead of the rowers, waiting to go off in the lead of the race, obviously intending to keep that position to the finish. The racing oarsmen were each anxious to gain an advantage from the start, but the man in the red cloak was being very strict, and would allow no benefit. Being satisfied at last, he held his kerchief high in the air, and in a loud theatrical voice, that even those on the bridge could hear clearly, he called the off, dropping his kerchief down in an exaggerated gesture at the same time. The race was away, with the young men pulling strongly into the run of the ebb tide. An assortment of other boats, four and six oared, pulled out to follow behind the racing men. Each vessel hoping to keep the wager in sight, for their passengers to enjoy.

"It is a long pull to Chelsea", commented Edwin, remembering the times he had rowed that course.
"There will be some tired arms, and more than a few blisters this night, I am sure of that" They watched as the race slowly disappeared into the distance, then as the crowd began to break up, Edwin and Mary started to amble off the bridge towards the City.
"You know Mary," said Edwin, suddenly remembering something. "Father once predicted that one day there will be boats that can row themselves, and that they will carry many times the number of passengers we do today, without the need for any oarsmen. He said it would be the end of our trade." Mary looked thoughtful, contemplating this strange notion.
"How will that be then?" she asked.
"What will become of the wagers and races, without watermen?" Edwin pondered her question.
"Perhaps the future of rowing will be only for sporting wagers, and for gaming men, without wherrymen taking a part." Mary turned to him with a twinkle in her eye.
"Perhaps when that day comes, maidens will also pull in the races, and perchance will beat the men."
They laughed together as, with Mary supporting Edwin's unsteady gait, they meandered, arm in arm, from the bridge towards the old City.

THE END

VERSES FROM THE PAST

Let your oars like lightning flog it
Up the Thames as swiftly jog it,
And you'd win the prize of Doggett
The glory of the River!

Bending, blowing straining, rowing.
Perhaps the wind in fury blowing.
Or the tide against you flowing.
The Coat and Badge for ever.

"Probably from an eighteenth century Ballard-opera,
sung at the Hay-market by Tom Tug.
Written by an unknown poet of the Thames"

<=======>

I was the pride of the Thames.
My names is Natty Jerry,
The best and smart and flashy dames
I've carried in my wherry.

For them no mortal soul like me,
So merrily did I jog it,
I loved my wife, my friend you see,
And won the prize of Doggett.

In coat and badge so neat and spruce,
I rowed all blithe and merry,
And every waterman did used
To call me happy Jerry.

"A waterman's song, preserved by the Fishmongers' Company. 18th century.
Writer unknown"

<=======>

Over 1400 patriotic songs were written by Charles Diblin, many of which were give-away war songs, commissioned by the government for the purpose of influencing watermen to join the Navy, for which Diblin received a pension of £200 per annum. He died in 1804.

GLOSSARY WORD INDEX

Almshouse: Home for the support of the old, poor and the decayed
Adze: A flat axe with a long arched handle
Licence Plate: Waterman's License number, worn on the upper left arm
Bargemaster: Captain in charge of a rowing barge
Beadle: Guild Inspector: Early form of policeman
Breast Rope: Mooring to the side of a boat or ship
Bridle-rope: A mooring to hold a vessel fast alongside
Capstan: A hand powered lifting device
Careen: To purposely list a ship over to allow work on her hull
City Fathers: Lord Major and City Council
Cooper: A man who makes barrels
Disembark: To leave a vessel.
Draw Dock: A tidal repair beach
Embark: To come on board a vessel
Ebb: The tide draining out to the sea
Farthing: A forth part of a penny
Flood: The tide running in from the sea
Footpad: A street robber
Frost Fair: When the river froze over, the ice area was used for merry-making
Gunwale: Top edge of the side planking of a boat or ship
Guinea: A coin worth one pound and a shilling
Holy-Stone: A sandstone brick for cleaning the deck
Knave: A person with a bad or naughty reputation
The Livery: The Trading Guilds of the City of London.
Journeyman: A trades-man who travels to his work
Lash-down: An arrangement of rope fastenings
Landing Stairs: A place where Wherries would be waiting for passengers
Livery Hall: Grand building for the business of the Trading Guild
Liverybarge: Large vessel for entertaining the Guild members
Lifting beam: Wooden lifting device, early crane
Lumper: A port-worker. A cargo handler
Mercers: Livery Guild, number one in order of precedence.
Mooring Post: Upright Post for tying a boat's catch-line to
Overseers: Ruling body of the Watermen's Company.
Old London Bridge: Bridge with 19 arches. Acted as a weir/dam particularly on the ebb tide
Oars!:   A call for summoning a Wherry (Water Taxi)
Playhouse: An early theatre

Press Gang: Naval personnel, taking men from the streets for service aboard fighting ships
Port and Starboard: Larboard and Starboard, the left and right hand side of a vessel
Penny: A 12th part of a Shilling. (Twenty shillings to one pound)
Poor's Fund: A charity for the destitute
Poop Deck: High part at the after end of a ship
Queen's Navy: The fighting force for the sea
Raddan style: When a Wherry is rowed by two men, one with two oars (sculling) the other with one oar (rowing)
Royal Waterman: Chosen men to row the Royal Barge
Royal Barge: The Monarch's fast Shallop, river transport
Rulers: Overall government of the Watermen
Rowing Wager: A professional rowing race between Watermen
Samson post: The main mooring bollard sited at the bow of a vessel
Shallop: Fast oared vessel for river transport
Sham-lock: To pretend to lock up
Stand Off: Keep away
Stem-band: The iron strip at the bow of a vessel
Spar: Cross beam on a ship's mast
Spritsail Barge: A shallow drafted sailing barge, with over 2000 square feet of sail, used for coastal work
Spring mooring: A rope or line leading forward or aft to keep a vessel in position
Swan Upping: The annual catching of the Queen's birds for marking
Tickling: An illegal practice of shaving away timber to make a vessel lighter for racing
Tilt: A small cabin or enclosed area for the protection of passengers
Tow rag: An outcast of the City, employed to pull the Western Barges upstream
Trenton Loaf: The flat bottom portion of a bread loaf
Victuals: Food and sustenance
Watergate: A river entrance to a grand house
Wherry: Small one man operated oared vessel for carrying fare paying passengers
Wherryman: Licensed Waterman in charge of a Wherry
Waterman: Person, trained and licensed via the apprenticeship system of the Watermen's Co.
Whiffler: Lookout stationed at the bow of a Royal Barge
Water pageant: River parade
Westminster Ford: Shallow crossing of the river at Westminster

ISBN 1-41205528-8